FINANCING PUBLIC LIBRARY BUILDINGS

Richard B. Hall

Neal-Schuman Publishers, Inc.
New York   London

Published by Neal-Schuman Publishers, Inc.
100 Varick Street
New York, NY 10013

Printed and bound in the United States of America

Library of Congress Cataloging-in-Publication Data

Hall, Richard B.
    Financing public library buildings / by Richard B. Hall.
       p.   cm.
    Includes bibliographical references and index.
    ISBN 1-55570-165-5
    1. Library buildings--United States. 2. Public libraries--United
States--Finance.   I. Title.
Z679.2.U54H35 1933
022' .3' 0973--dc20
                                             93-39647
                                              CIP

This book is dedicated
to my loving wife Sybil and son, Kyle,
and to all those who have had
and will have the vision and courage
to undertake the financing and construction
of a public library building.

Contents

Photo and Illustration Acknowledgments

Fig. 2-10, p. 63
"Interior view of library furnishings, Wesley Chapel Branch, Dekalb County Public Library, Decatur, Georgia." Provided courtesy of DeKalb County Public Library. Permission to publish granted by DeKalb County Public Library.

Fig. 2-11, p. 66
"Interior view of library furnishings, Chula Vista Library, Chula Vista, CA." Provided courtesy of Marshall Brown—Interior Designer, Inc. Permission to publish granted by Marshall Brown, Marshall Brown—Interior Designer, Inc.

Fig. 2-12, p. 68
"Alameda, California, Public Library VDT terminals." Provided courtesy of KT McGowan. Permission to publish granted by Alameda Free Library (City).

Fig. 6-2, p. 191
"View of the the new Phoenix Central Library." Provided courtesy of Bruder/DWL Architects. Permission to publish granted by Phoenix Public Library.

Fig. 6-4, p. 199
"Peninsula Center Library, Palos Verdes Library District, California." Provided courtesy of Zimmer Gunsul Frasca Partnership. Permission to publish granted by Debra Joan Barbour, Associate Partner, Zimmer Gunsul Frasca Partnership.

Fig. 6-5, p. 201
"Rancho Penasquitos Branch, San Diego, CA." Provided courtesy of San Diego Public Library, City of San Diego. Permission to publish granted by William W. Sannwald.

Fig. 6-7, p. 209
"Sacramento Public Library Central Building." Provided courtesy of Esto Photographics. ©Jeff Goldberg/Esto.

Fig. 6-8, p. 214
"South Chula Vista Library, Chula Vista, CA." Provided courtesy of LPA, INC. Permission to publish granted by Chula Vista Public Library.

Fig. 6-9, p. 220
"Tucson-Pima Public Library, Tucson, Arizona." Provided courtesy of Steven Meckler. Permission to publish granted by Tucson-Pima Library.

Fig. 6-10, p. 225
"Rendering of the Los Angeles Central Public Library Building." Provided courtesy Hardy Holtzman Pfeiff Associates. Permission to publish granted by Los Angeles Public Library.

Fig. 6-11, p. 229
"Kern County Library, Bakersfield, CA." Provided courtesy of Kern County Library. Permission to publish granted by Diane R. Duquette, Director of Libraries, Kern County Library.

Fig. 6-12, p. 231
"Sara Hightower Regional Library, Rome, Georgia." Provided courtesy of James W. Buckley & Associates, Inc., Swainsboro—Albany—Rome. Permission to publish granted by Sara Hightower Regional Library.

Fig. 6-13, p. 233
"Oxnard Central Library, Oxnard, CA." Provided courtesy of Whisler-Patri, Architects; Paul Bielenberg, photographs; copyright 1992. Permission to publish granted by Gail P. Warner, Library Director, Oxnard Public Library.

Fig. 7-3, p. 243
"Rendering of San Francisco Main Library." Provided courtesy of Christopher Doyle. Permission to publish granted by Ken Dowlin, City Librarian, San Francisco Public Library.

Fig. 7-5, p. 270
"Huntington Beach Public Library Donor Opportunities." Provided courtesy of Ronald L. Hayden. Permission to publish granted by Huntington Beach Public Library.

Fig. 7-6, p. 271
"Newport Beach Donor Wall Mock-Up." Provided courtesy of Elizabeth Stahr. Permission to publish granted by Newport Beach Public Library Foundation.

Fig. 7-7, p. 273
"Pledge Card/Contribution Envelope." Provided courtesy of Elizabeth Stahr. Permission to publish granted by Newport Beach Public Library Foundation.

Preface

More library facility projects come to grief on the shoals of financial difficulty than on any other hazard. In this volume, *Financing Public Libraries*, Richard Hall provides the practical compass and charts needed to avoid such a catastrophe. While others have written bits and pieces about library facility finance, this is the first and by far the most comprehensive treatise on the subject. Hall navigates through the treacherous financial reefs that all-too-often threaten library building projects.

For nearly two decades, Richard Hall has been charged with overseeing state-funded public library building projects, first for the State of Georgia and now for California. He now brings to bear a wealth of personal knowledge gained from this experience as well as the accumulated wisdom of others in this field. In addition, he has utilized the information gleaned from several years of association with the compilation and analysis of statistical data for the annual December 1 issue of Library Journal devoted to *Library Architecture*.

The scope of the volume is daunting in itself and reflects the true complexity of library facility finance. Whether the reader is the librarian, library board member, finance officer, city or county official, or a lay person involved with library facilities, the text speaks with authority and thoroughness.

Richard Hall deals with the nitty-gritty of both the process and the realities of finding adequate financial support. Step-by-step he shows how planning for financing must parallel planning for the project as a whole. Both in broad outline and then in minute detail, the author acquaints the reader with every aspect of project financing. Beginning with the very first chapter, he proves the necessity for thorough preparation and warns against the use of common short-cuts which so often prove to be the jagged reefs that doom library building projects.

The second chapter deals with the all-important methodology for developing an accurate initial project cost estimate and then refining the proposed budget as planning proceeds. Every line item contributing to the cost of the project is covered, including some that are often overlooked, misunderstood or underestimated. Especially helpful are the discussions concerning furniture and equipment, perhaps the element most frequently underestimated with dire consequences for all too many projects.

Subsequent chapters trace the historic as well as the current roles of Federal, State, Local and Private funding sources and provide helpful data on how these might be utilized. These carefully documented chapters will also prove invaluable to all who labor to promote, refine or create new legislation for library building financing.

Richard is logical in his approach and meticulous in examining every aspect of library facility financing. The array of facts he has mustered to support his conclusions and recommendations are convincing. Step-by-step procedures complete with sample forms mark the course the reader is encouraged to take. Brief case histories taken from his own wealth of experience have been used to great advantage as a means of illustrating significant points. An abundance of tables and charts add further understanding.

Financing Public Libraries is a most welcome addition to the literature on library buildings. As the basic reference text on this subject, it should receive wide recognition and acceptance by all those who must grapple with the problems of financing library building projects, whether large or small.

Raymond M. Holt
Library Consultant

Acknowledgements

As with most books, there have been many people who have made significant contributions to the author's efforts. First, I would like to thank one of my mentors, Dr. Herbert Goldhor, who helped me publish my first journal article and planted the seed of this book many years ago when I was a graduate student. I want to thank Pat Schuman for her willingness to take a chance on the book and for her willingness to stick with me even when the manuscript took longer to complete than originally intended.

I am particularly indebted to Ray and Sarah Holt for all of their encouragement over the years and their willingness to read the final draft and provide me with comments. Thanks are also extended to other "readers" such as Kathryn Stephanoff for her willingness to comment on the "Private Sources" chapter, Donald Fork for his review of the "Federal Sources" chapter, Joe Natale for his review of the "State Sources" chapter, and Cy Silver for his review of the "Local Sources" chapter.

Special thanks are in order to interior designers Karen Wheat, Marshall Brown as well as David and Andrea Michaels who provided information about library furnishings and equipment costs. The author also wishes to thank Elizabeth Gay for the information provided about the Los Angeles Central Library project. Appreciation is extended to the editors of *Library Trends* since some information included in this book is based on the article "Trends in Financing Public Library Buildings" which was first published in *Library Trends* (Vol. 36, Fall 1987, pp. 423-453).

Library Journal has also been mostly generous in allowing me to reprint text and data from the June 15 issues (1988 to 1992) concerning articles on public library referenda as well as their construction statistics in the December Architectural issue (1967 to 1991). All such information is copyrighted by Reed Publishing.

Thanks are also extended to the many people who provided information, encouragement as well as illustrations for the book, not the least of which are the following colleagues in State Libraries which provided significant contributions for their state's in the "State Sources" chapter:

Fred D. Neighbors, Assistant Director, Alabama State Library

George V. Smith, Acting Director, Alaska State Library

Mary Louise Jensen, Building Consultant, Connecticut State Library

Jane Gafvert, Administrative Librarian, Delaware State Library

Lorraine D. Summers, Assistant State Librarian, Florida State Library

Thomas A. Ploeg, Library Programs Coordinator, Georgia State Library

Joe Natale, Library Construction, Illinois State Library

Jim Nelson, State Librarian, Kentucky State Library

Sharron McFarland, Staff Specialist, Maryland State Library

Patience Jackson, Library Building Consultant, Massachusetts State Library

Kathryn Merkle, Special Services Director, Mississippi State Library

Bonnie J. Buckley, Head of Planning, Nevada State Library

Vianne Connor, Public Library Construction Program Manager, New Jersey State Library

James L. Farrell, Jr., Library Development Specialist, New York State Library

John Welch, Assistant State Librarian, North Carolina State Library

Barbara Weaver, State Librarian, Rhode Island State Library

James F. Beasley, LSCA Title II Coordinator, Tennessee State Library

Robert R. Walsh, Building Consultant, Virginia State Library

David Childers, Fiscal Officer, West Virginia State Library

Jerry Krois, Deputy State Librarian, Wyoming State Library

Last, but by no means least, I must also acknowledge the very significant contribution of my wife, Sybil, and son, Kyle, for their patience with me during many long hours when I was unavailable during the manuscript's preparation. This document has truly been both a professional and personal "family" effort.

Introduction

This book was written to provide library managers, trustees, library friends, and government officials with the necessary information to plan and finance a public library construction project. It is intended to take the mystery out of at least one aspect of the process—the budgeting and capital financing. There are many mythologies as well as very real pitfalls associated with the process of building or remodeling a public library facility. This book aims to shed some light on this process and to allow library supporters to sleep better at night during their efforts to finance the project.

The building process is not easy: it requires a high degree of commitment and unending work and involvement. But the process can be exhilarating, and, when completed, it provides the backers of the project with the tremendous satisfaction of a job well done which will benefit the community for many years. Each project is different, and local planners must take the information presented in this book and apply it prudently to their own local situation. Further, it is acknowledged that this book outlines the best possible way to go about the process, and it is unlikely any community will be able to completely meet all of the recommendations presented here. However, the book can serve as a road map to provide the reader with the best and least dangerous route.

As well as a planning document, this book is designed as a resource for locating the needed funding from various sources which are available to local officials. It is organized to allow easy access to the four major categories or sources of funding: federal, state, local, and private. Regardless of how a dollar finds its way into a library project, it can be traced back to one of these four sources. The first three are based upon some form of taxation of individual citizens; the last source comes solely from the generosity of those citizens. But even these four categories are somewhat artificial since the source of all funding is ultimately "We the People." There are many philosophies on where funds should come from for public services such as libraries, but it should always be remembered that there is really only one source. While it may be helpful to categorize funds into four sources, this book does not express a preference for one source over another. It is up to the reader to determine which source of funding and which financing method best meets the requirements of the local project and the community.

The first chapter, "Planning the Library Construction Project," covers the process of assembling the planning team; producing a needs assessment, a facility master plan, and a building program; and developing architectural plans. Chapter 2, "The Project Cost Estimate," explains in detail the steps necessary to develop a preliminary budget for the library project. This chapter also includes planning forms and an example of a project budget for "Anytown, USA." Chapter 3, "Potential Funding Sources," assesses possible funding sources, provides some historical background, and demonstrates recent trends in finding sources for public library construction. Chapter 4, "Federal Funding Sources," provides an overview of federal programs that have provided funds for public library facilities, including an in-depth look at the Library Services and Construction Act (LSCA) Title II program.

Chapter 5, "State Funding Sources," provides an overview of state funding and discusses the major state grant programs providing funds for public library construction. This chapter also provides a comparative analysis of the state programs, and discusses how to start a state-based program as well as the advantages of state grant programs for public library construction. Chapter 6, "Local Funding Sources," outlines local funding sources including referenda campaigns for general obligation bonds along with numerous alternative "creative financing" methods. Chapter 7, "Private Funding Sources," provides an overview of private fund-raising for public library buildings and discusses the private fund raising capital campaign.

Planning the Library Construction Project

1

The first step in any endeavor is always the hardest one to take. However, as with most activities, the first steps in the process of building a new library or improving an existing one are often the most crucial because they chart the course of the entire process. The preliminary planning for any public library construction project consists of strategically assessing the needs of the local jurisdiction for public library service, creating a facilities master plan for the delivery of that service, and then developing specific building program statements for any anticipated capital improvement projects. If any of these steps is overlooked or performed poorly, subsequent efforts may suffer significantly and result in a less-than-desirable public library building. A high-quality planning process and top-notch planning documents require great care in the early stages, but they help to avoid potentially disastrous results. Figure 1-1 demonstrates the interrelationships of the major steps in the planning process.

In most library building projects, the library director takes the initiative to start planning the new facility, but occasionally this responsibility falls on library trustees. Local governmental officials may begin the process if there currently is no library service offered in the jurisdiction. Whoever assumes the leadership role must make certain of one thing: it is essential to assemble a talented and well-balanced planning team. A dedicated and carefully selected team of library planners will make all the difference in obtaining the quality planning needed to develop any capital project.

ASSEMBLING THE PLANNING TEAM

Frequently, there is a temptation to choose members of the planning team only from the library board. While some mem-

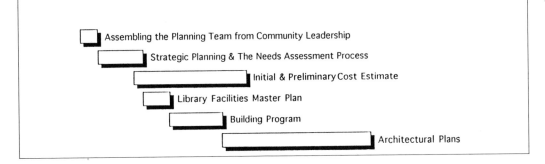

Fig. 1-1. The Library Facility Planning Process

bers of the team will come from the board or the friends group, it is important to look beyond these individuals to find members. Public library capital improvement projects will ultimately require raising substantial sums of money, and whether this is done with a referendum or through private fundraising, it is greatly enhanced if representative members of the larger community are members of the original planning team. These individuals, having been with the project since the beginning, will not only understand all that has gone into its planning and development, but will have developed a vested interest in the project. They will do a better job of selling the project to the community than anyone, and may even become key steering committee members in a future political campaign or fundraising effort.

Many times the planning team seems to fall into place without a lot of effort, but this is not always the case, nor is it always desirable. It is best if the team members can be carefully hand-picked for compatibility and expertise. There is no room for mere space fillers on the planning team. It must be made clear to prospective members from the outset that the team is expected to produce results. The members must be able and willing to work together with the emphasis on work *and* together. The ideal team member is committed, willing, and able to become involved in a long-term project.

The library planning team is likely to expand or shrink at various points over the course of the project, but there should always be a core group of members who see it through from start to finish. This task can last for several years. The planning team members need to have qualities which will assist in the effective and smooth operation of the planning process. They should be highly motivated individuals who are respected in their own areas of expertise. Receptive to the ideas of others and able to compromise, they must be leaders who are able to work together.

The actual size of the planning team is not important, but it must not be too large to operate effectively. It should have an odd number of members in case controversial issues must be resolved with a vote. It may be helpful to establish committees within the planning team so that each member has specific responsibility in an area. This approach will expedite the planning process and ensure that there is assigned leadership for each aspect of the project. The following are suggested sample committees for planning public library building projects: Needs Assessment Committee, Facilities Master Plan Committee, Building Program Committee, Financial Committee, Site Selection Committee, and Architectural Selection and Plans Review Committee. Some of these activities may be combined if the project is relatively small and continuity of membership and leadership is important. However, it is helpful to spread the responsibilities so that no one becomes overloaded with planning duties and "burns out" at an early stage.

As mentioned, the planning team can be expanded as needed. At various stages it may be helpful to bring on new members who have expertise in particular areas. Individuals with experience in real estate, banking and finance, insurance, public contracting, engineering, and the construction industry may be needed at some point during the project. Professionals will have to be hired as well, including attorneys, library consultants, architects, interior designers, and others. All of them will contribute to the project at one time or another, but the core group of library supporters will be responsible for seeing the project through to the end.

THE NEEDS ASSESSMENT

Once the planning team has been established, the next step is to define the need for a new or improved facility. This step is critical. Therefore, unless the library management already has considerable experience with such activity, most communities retain a library consultant to help develop a needs assessment. It is also very important at this early phase of the project to actively involve the community, particularly the political "movers and shakers," in the process of determining the need.

At this time, it may be helpful for the planning team to form a needs assessment committee composed of one or more of the core planning team members and several community members who represent the library's service area. It is important to obtain input from all segments of the community. These individuals become part of the campaign strategy and may be asked to deliver their support, financial contributions, and/or votes for the project when the time comes.

The needs assessment is one of the most important steps in the planning process for a public library building. It is to a large extent the basis for the library building program. A well-done needs assessment provides a foundation for the library's plan of service, the building program statement, the architectural plans, and the project budget, as well as the capital improvements financing campaign. Determining the need for a new or improved public library facility requires the collection, analysis, and effective display of the information created.

In most cases, the impetus for performing needs assessment is a perception by the library management and governing body of the existing library facility's inadequacy or inability to provide adequate services to the community. This perception must be supported by facts and translated into an effective, persuasive plan of action. The needs assessment has several steps which should be performed in sequence for best results:

- Determining the library service area
- Analyzing the community

- Analyzing the community's need for library service
- Developing a library plan of service
- Determining the existing library's service inadequacy
- Determining the existing library's physical inadequacy
- Assessing the projected space needs
- Evaluating the alternatives
- Developing a facilities master plan

Determining the Library Service Area

The first step in the needs assessment process is to determine as precisely as possible the geographic boundaries of the library project's service area, which is comparable to a retailer's market area. Most local planning departments can assist in defining the exact geographical boundaries of the service area. It may be advantageous to align the library service area with local planning units to help collect demographic data. There may be natural or artificial geographic barriers that should be considered as well. Once the service area's precise physical boundaries have been defined, its nature and characteristics can then be studied.

Analyzing the Community

The second step is the analysis of the "community" as defined by the service area. It is necessary to determine the current size and projected growth of the population to be served. This is important in order to plan the size and scope of the project as well as the library services to be provided. Information regarding the characteristics of the target population will be very useful when fundraising activities begin, whether funds come from a private fundraising drive or a public referendum.

In addition to the population growth projection, knowing the specific demographic characteristics of the community is critical for developing a plan of service for a public library. This information is particularly important if the demographic characteristics are changing rapidly as they are in many high-growth communities. Library planners should start with any existing data available and attempt to collect more from additional sources. Again, the local planning department is the best place to start the search for demographic information. This agency should be well acquainted with the recent and projected demographic trends in the area. Demographic data are available from other regional, state, federal, and private sources, some of which can be accessed through online database searches available in many libraries.

Demographic information such as age, race/ethnicity, occupation, education, economic status, and even voting patterns are all important factors to be considered. Because these factors affect how the library will be used, they are essential in the development of a plan of service. It is helpful to look at the demographic patterns of the specific library service area in comparison with those of larger populations in nearby cities, the county, state, and nation. This analysis often provides a focus on the features of the service population that are unique and therefore demand special attention.

Analyzing the Community's Need for Library Service

In determining the community's need for library service, it is useful to gather information on the patron's current and historical library use patterns. This information provides a baseline for the next step of determining what future library usage and delivery patterns will be based upon changes in the demographics of the community. One way to obtain this information is to perform a community survey. There are many methods for performing such a survey, as well as various levels of sophistication. A written survey mailed to

the community on a random-sample basis is one possibility. This approach may elicit responses from nonusers of the public library as well as users, which can provide very important information. Telephone or face-to-face interviews can also be utilized to gather more in-depth information regarding user attitudes and opinions about desired services as well as delivery techniques. Holding community forums and focus group meetings is another effective method of gathering information.

It is generally advisable to involve all possible segments of the public during the needs assessment process in order to establish trust, credibility, and consensus and begin the process of building coalitions. The needs assessment is an opportunity to start the process of developing political consensus in the community and establishing grassroots support for the project. Any activity that involves a large group of community leaders or neighborhood representatives will have a stronger impact than a plan that has been developed by library staff and other "insiders." Further, the needs assessment will generally be clearer and more comprehensive if a larger group of individuals is involved.

This will most likely mean bringing into the needs assessment committee some community leaders such as school officials, clergy, members of community service organizations, members of the business community such as the Chamber of Commerce, and government officials. It is usually helpful to define the membership of the needs assessment committee through some form of official proclamation by the board of trustees or other governing agency.

All needs assessment activities are directed toward better understanding the community's need for library service and are an important precursor to developing of the library's plan of service. In addition to this community input, it is important to assess regional, state, and national trends and changing concepts in public library service. At this step, all possible methods of providing service should be considered in light of what is known about the library's service area.

Developing a Library Plan of Service

The process of analyzing needs for public library service usually uncovers new or alternative ways of providing service to the community. It is a challenge to the library's professional staff, library consultant, and needs assessment committee to explore the best combination of traditional and innovative approaches to serving the people within the proposed library project's service area.

This step culminates in the development of an effective plan of service based on all the preceding data and considerations. The service plan is best executed by library professionals, with the assistance of library consultants. However, the needs assessment committee should be available to respond to drafts with specific points of interest or concern. The plan of service should be well documented and ultimately form the basis of the library building program statement.

The plan of service should be founded in a written mission statement and should identify appropriate service roles[1] along with a detailed description of the services that will be offered. The plan of service should project the changes in the library organization and identify any special requirements necessary to implement the plan. As support justification, the plan of service should provide and summarize any service standards or guidelines utilized which come from local, state, or national levels. Finally, the plan of service will include projections in the growth of collections, user seating, staff workstations, special equipment, and meeting-room space.

Determining the Existing Library's Service Inadequacy

Once a plan of service is in place, it is possible to determine the service inadequacies of the existing library facility. It is important to document these inadequacies in order to justify the need for the new or improved facility. This process is best accomplished by spelling out the facility's shortcomings in housing the needed collections, seating, staff workstations, special equipment, and meeting-room space as already defined in the plan of service.

Determining the Existing Library's Physical Inadequacy

In addition to describing the existing facility's service limitations, it is important to describe the limitations of the physical plant of the existing facility. The age and condition of the existing facility are important considerations in determining the need for a new or improved facility. Determine the condition of the building's structural system, electrical power and data distribution system, lighting system, mechanical (HVAC) system, etc. In many cases, it is not only the lack of space that impedes the plan of service, but also the various building systems. For example, an inadequate electrical power or data distribution system can inhibit the introduction of electronic information delivery systems.

Assessing the Projected Space Needs

Once the library plan of service has been completed and the existing library facility's limitations have been documented, it is time to assess the projected space needs for the new or improved facility by transforming the service plan into a preliminary statement of space needs. Rough space allocations should be made using the basic components of a public library: collections, readers' seating, staff workstations, special equipment, meeting-room and nonassignable space (See the *Wisconsin Library Building Project Handbook*[2] for a detailed analysis of this approach). The compilation of these space requirements will provide an estimate of the gross square footage needed for the project.

The projected space need can be compared with the space available in the existing library building. The difference between the two figures is the amount of additional space needed to adequately serve the community. Comparing the existing space with the projected space needs is an effective way to demonstrate the need for a new or improved library facility. There may in fact be several ways to meet the projected space need. The problem is to determine the best and most cost-effective way of doing so.

Evaluating the Alternatives

In evaluating the alternatives, there are usually several options, including:

1. Building a new facility;
2. Expanding and remodeling the existing facility;
3. Converting an existing building into a library by purchasing a building and then remodeling it; or
4. Remodeling the existing library building without any expansion.

In many cases, it is not obvious without a great deal of study which approach is best to meet the long-term space needs for the community. It is important to find a way to compare the advantages and disadvantages of each potential method for meeting the space need.

When several alternatives are available, it is helpful to develop a matrix which compares each potential project solution against a common set of pertinent criteria.[3] This comparative approach usually clarifies the issues and focuses the arguments for or against each possible option, revealing the best solution. The process of comparing alternative solutions provides

the planning team members with an in-depth understanding of the pros and cons of each approach. Further, it solidifies their understanding of the space needs and the plan of service along with generating their committment to the best possible solution. This is important once the job of selling the project to the community begins. It must always be kept in mind that well-informed and committed advocates will be needed to convince funding agencies of the worthiness of the proposed project.

If it is possible to reach consensus within the needs assessment committee regarding the best solution, each of the members will feel a commitment to the project. This becomes particularly important when the going gets rough and opposition groups attack the proposed solution for whatever reason. Using a group approach as well as the matrix will usually mean that all possible alternatives have been considered and either supported or rejected for specific reasons. This is helpful since it is important not to become publicly embarrassed when an opposition group attacks the "best" solution by proposing another (and inevitably less expensive) solution which the planning team has not considered. If the supporters of the project can respond immediately and effectively with specific reasons for rejecting the opposition's proposed alternative, their influence can often be effectively eliminated.

Summary

A comprehensive needs assessment should result in documentation detailing the drawbacks of the existing library facility and defining the community's need in terms of the plan of service and projected space requirements. The needs assessment should also evaluate the alternatives and recommend a solution. The final document should communicate the facts in a straightforward and unbiased manner. It is usually helpful to develop a summary document that graphically displays the

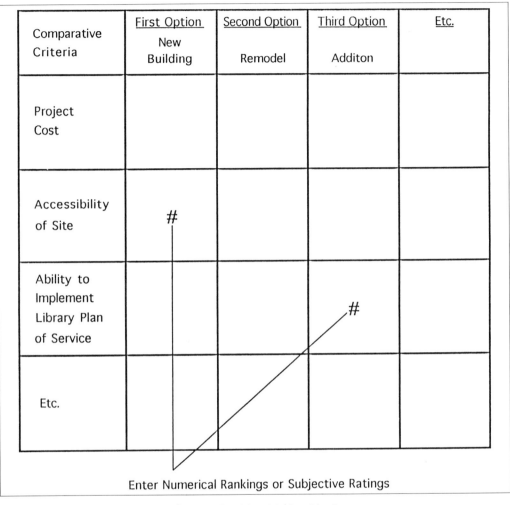

Comparative Criteria	First Option New Building	Second Option Remodel	Third Option Additon	Etc.
Project Cost				
Accessibility of Site	#			
Ability to Implement Library Plan of Service			#	
Etc.				

Enter Numerical Rankings or Subjective Ratings

Fig. 1-2. Decision Making Matrix

critical information and conclusions. This is the document the planning team and needs assessment committee can use to help promote the issue to the community and local public officials. It should provide irrefutable evidence of the need for a new or improved library facility or multiple facilities.

The needs assessment will also be useful during the pursuit of funding, regardless of the source. It can be used with the public and with major donors to justify the expenditure of public or private funds for the project. The needs assessment will provide, in part, the basis for the "case state-

ment" for private fundraising drives. It will also provide the basis for much of the strategic planning for a referendum campaign. Out of the need will grow campaign themes as well as the main message that the voters of the community will hear before they go to the polls.

DEVELOPING OF A LIBRARY FACILITIES MASTER PLAN

The needs assessment process may result in a plan to build or remodel a single library building, but in other cases several building projects may be required. When this occurs, it is important for the planning team to come up with a facilities master plan which addresses all the long-term needs, based upon the service areas, community needs, plan of service, and condition of existing facilities.

Usually library consultants are called upon to write a facilities master plan based on the needs assessment. This plan will identify clearly defined service areas and recommend space allocations for branch public library facilities to serve each of these districts along with a recommendation for the central headquarters library. The facilities master plan is the precursor to the building program. It will briefly outline the potential library services to be offered at each location and the approximate number of collections, readers' seats, and staff workstations, along with a rough determination of the amount of space necessary for each facility. It will discuss the scope of each building project (new construction, remodeling, expansion, etc.) and may attempt to estimate project costs. The facilities master plan may also present a priority ranking for each project so that library planners and local funding agency officials can set priorities. Once the facilities master plan is finished, it will be necessary to develop detailed building programs for each proposed facility as needed.

THE BUILDING PROGRAM

After the needs assessment and facilities master plan, are completed, the next step in the planning process is creating a building program. This affects the preparation of the project budget because it defines the library project's scope and size as well as detailing the necessary furnishings and equipment. The building program is an in-depth statement of what is needed in the new or improved library building. Raymond Holt states that its "primary objec-

tive . . . is to describe the purpose, functions, relationships, and operations of a particular library in terms of its space needs, functional relationships, environmental requirements, and all other characteristics."[4] The building program should provide an overview of the scope of the project as well as summarize the pertinent community and demographic information from the needs assessment. The proposed library's plan of service will be discussed in detail along with any specific roles, goals, or objectives. The plan for service will be interpreted, in part, through projections for collections, readers' seats, staff workstations, meeting-room requirements, and any special equipment. However, the building program is more than a simple listing of this information.

Through a facility space analysis, the building program defines the major administrative areas or divisions of the library such as:

Circulation Services
Reference Services
Periodical Services
Browsing Services
Children's Services
Young Adult Services
Public Meeting Services
Book Collections
Audiovisual Services
Special Collections
Staff Services
Extension Services
Administrative Services
Technical Services

These major areas of the library are further broken down into specific "spaces" that can be described in detail. For example, the spaces for the circulation division might be:

Public entrance and lobby
Interior book drop room
Circulation desk
Materials sorting area
Circulation workroom
Circulation supervisor's office

DIV:	SPACE					SF:

OCCUPANCY	HIGH	AVE	SEATS	COLLECTIONS:
PUBLIC				
STAFF				

FUNCTIONAL ACTIVITY DESCRIPTION:

SPATIAL RELATIONSHIPS:

SECURITY & SUPERVISION:

COMMUNICATIONS & ELECTRICAL:

ILLUMINATION & FENESTRATION:

ACOUSTICS & HVAC:

SPACE FINISHES & FLEXIBILITY:

✱	FURNISHINGS & EQUIPMENT	✱	FURNISHING & EQUIPMENT

Fig. 1-3. Space Data Sheet

Each space should be given a name and allocated a square footage based on the activity to be carried out within it as well as the furnishings and equipment needed to support that activity. Many factors need to be addressed, including the potential occupancy of the space; the number of collections to be housed; the physical relationship of this space to other spaces; security and supervision concerns; communications, electrical, illumination, and fenestration needs; acoustical, heating, ventilating, and air conditioning (HVAC) requirements; and the necessary furnishings and equipment. The "space data sheet"[5] in Figure 1-3 is an example of a format that can be used to display this information in the building program.

This approach is helpful because "programming is analysis, and design is synthesis."[6] To solve a problem, one must first break it down into its parts before trying to reassemble (synthesize) them in the best way possible. Programming is the science and art of defining the problem by collecting and analyzing the data that determine the need for a new facility. Subsequently, the space analysis part of the program describes the essential physical and functional requirements that must be considered in designing a new facility.

The library building program is a communication tool. Along with defining what is necessary to implement the library project, the building program provides the architect with a guide for the library's design. To do this, the building program must also describe to the architect the spatial relationships between the various divisions and areas of the library. This can be done in either matrix or diagram form. The building program is a working document that should be reviewed by the planning team at various draft stages and updated throughout the course of the project if necessary. The architect should carefully analyze the building program and follow it as closely as possible in developing architectural plans.

ARCHITECTURAL PLANS

Once the building program is completed, an architect will be hired to develop architectural plans for the building. Some architects begin with a predesign process that confirms the building program with the library planning team. This process involves a review and possibly further definition of the building program to make certain both the architect and the library planners clearly understand what is desired. Once this is accomplished, the architectural firm will develop a conceptual plan, which is an early version of what the library building will look like. It will be presented to library planners and supporters for review and feedback. The library design is very preliminary at this stage, and changes can be easily made to reflect input.

The plans development process will next go through the steps of schematic plans, design development plans (preliminaries), and contract documents (working drawings and specifications). At each phase, the plans will become further developed. They will become increasingly difficult to change without resistance from the architect and potential cost to the owner. At each of these steps the architect should furnish cost estimates. Most library projects are presented to local funding agencies based on project cost estimates performed at the schematic plans stage. However, prior to this time, much project cost estimating will already have been performed by the library planners. The relationship of this preliminary cost estimating and the provision of professional architectural services will be discussed in the next chapter. There is more to estimating to be sure, architectural services are extremely helpful and often necessary during the process. Chapter 2 describes in detail what library planners must consider when estimating the cost of a new or improved public library construction project.

REFERENCES

1. Charles R. McClure et al. *Planning and Role Setting for Pubic Libraries: A Manual of Options and Procedures* (Chicago: American Library Association, 1987).
2. Raymond M. Holt, (2nd Rev. ed. Anders C. Dahlgren) *Wisconsin Library Building Project Handbook.* (Madison, Wisc.: Wisconsin Department of Public Instruction, 1990).
3. Raymond M. Holt, *Planning Library Buildings and Facilities: From Concept to Completion* (Metuchen, N.J.: Scarecrow Press, 1989), pp. 215–17.
4. Ibid., p. 43.
5. Richard B. Hall, "Communicating with Graphics in the Library Building Program," *Illinois Libraries* 67, (November 1985), p. 781.
6. William Pena and William Caudil, *Problem Seeking: An Architectural Programming Primer* (Washington: American Institute of Architects Press, 1987).

The Project Cost Estimate 2

OVERVIEW OF THE PROJECT BUDGETING PROCESS

Before library planners can start looking for funds for facility improvements, they must have a reasonably accurate projection of the total project costs. Once the planning team has performed the needs assessment and defined the project scope with at least a draft of the building program, it is necessary to start developing a project budget. Unfortunately, there is often a temptation to provide local funding agency officials with early cost estimates based upon inadequately researched cost figures. It is the author's experience that premature decisions regarding the amount of funds needed for the project often create significant difficulties and result in a lack of funds necessary to properly execute the project. Far too often library planners get trapped by rudimentary cost estimates released before they are tested and refined. It should be understood that such early estimates can be off by as much as 100 percent from the final cost of a project.

The premature release of cost estimates occurs relatively frequently, often because pressure is exerted on library planners to provide them too early in the planning process. It may also occur because of a general lack of understanding about the costs of library buildings or how to prepare an adequate budget. The temptation to release preliminary cost figures must be resisted. Be forewarned that once a cost estimate has been provided and reported in the local media, it takes on a life of its own and will forever be associated with the project. This is why it is wise not to discuss project costs with anyone outside of the library planning team until the project scope has been clearly defined and the cost estimate is as accurate as possible. Since library planning meetings in most states are required to be public meetings, it may be difficult or even impossible to keep early financial information out of the press. In such a case, it must be stressed that the figures discussed are *rough estimates* subject to change as the project develops and are not officially endorsed. This is particularly true if the architectural plans and detailed construction costs based on the plans are not available.

Unfortunately, individuals and occasionally government officials may attempt to impose their will upon library planners and insist that arbitrarily determined construction cost figures be used in conjunction with the project. For example, a community may obtain a $1 million windfall and officials decide to give the money to the library for a new building but stipulate that there will be no additional funding. What appears on the surface to be a positive step in financing the library may not be if the library building project actually requires $2 million according to the needs assessment and planning. The planning team must resist the temptation to accept the money if the construction project is to have a reasonable chance of success. It is compromise from the start, if the planning team accepts a given amount of funding and then plans the project to fit those available funds rather than the real need. The absolutely worst way to prepare a budget for a library building is to have a specific amount of funds arbitrarily established by a funding agency. When library planners are told that no more funds are available and they must plan the project within these parameters, the possibility of building a public library that will truly meet the needs of the community is greatly diminished.

The planning team should control both the planning process and the project's budget and should also provide a realistic budget that is as complete and well documented as possible. This is particularly important when the cost figures are challenged, which they undoubtedly will be at some point. Project cost figures should be released only when library planners have progressed far enough through the budgetary planning process to have confidence in them. In order to be accurate and usable, cost estimates must be based "in the real world" and reflect the type and quality of facility that is appropriate for the community.

In order for library planners to arrive at a project cost estimate that they can have confidence in, they must understand that developing a budget for a library project is an ongoing process that will continue until the end of the project when the decisions are made about how to spend the final remaining funds. There is no one point at which the planning team can say "This is it, this is the cost and it will not change." Not until all expenditures have been made and there is a final accounting will the actual costs be known. Capital project budgets simply can not be accurately fixed at the beginning of the planning process and remain static. The process of developing a capital budget is extremely complex and fraught with uncertainties as

well as subjective assessments involving quality and quantity issues.

The Initial Budget Estimate

The budget development process starts with a very rough "initial" cost estimate for the project in the early planning stages, it progresses to a more precise "preliminary" estimate as the planning develops into schematic plans. This preliminary estimate will become "final" when it is presented to the funding agency with a request for funds, but it is not final even at this stage. This estimate will become more detailed and accurate as the project proceeds through the various architectural plans submissions. When the project is bid and contracts are let, fairly firm costs will be known. Even then, however, unexpected conditions may arise, resulting in change orders that increase costs.

The initial estimate of project costs will give library planners a rough outline, or a budgetary range. Even though imprecise, this step is critical to the overall success of the project and must be treated with respect. Without responsible financial planning, the project will undoubtedly be doomed—either to failure, to embarrassment for those involved in planning the project, or to a library building which is mediocre at best. Initial estimates usually start out utilizing rough cost-per-square-foot figures for construction, furnishings, and equipment gathered from various sources. Planners begin to build a preliminary budget by obtaining various comparative figures from nearby towns, similar projects within their own community, national averages and ranges, and the experience of other library planners. It is useful for planners to look at the project cost estimate from as many different angles as possible at this stage. Often percentages of costs are applied, for instance, ten percent of the total project cost for furnishings and equipment. Clearly, this initial

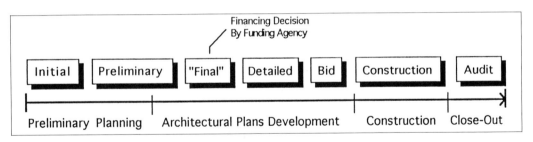

Fig. 2-1. The Budget Estimating Continuum

phase produces very general cost estimates that need much work to make them specific enough to be useful to a final cost estimate.

However, this approach will begin to provide library planners with cost range such as "the project should cost between $3 and $4 million." Once library planners begin to define the specific parts or line items of the project in more detail, then the initial cost estimate becomes a preliminary budget estimate. This preliminary budget will undergo many transformations as it evolves into a final estimate that can be used with funding agencies. However, even after the final cost estimate is made public, it will continue to be revised. Revisions in estimated costs for furnishings and equipment, for instance may need to be revised as new technologies reach the marketplace or as last-minute programmatic changes force the adoption of new methods of providing service. As Figure 2-1 shows, the project estimating process is a continuum. More detailed revisions occur during final plans development, during bidding, and during the construction of the building right up to the final audit.

Once the initial cost range has been determined, the next phase is to refine the figures by detailing each of the individual line items that make up the initial estimate. This preliminary project budget estimate will still only be a ballpark figure and probably require professional assistance from library building consultants, interior designers, architects, engineers, and even professional cost estimators. Under

no circumstances can a reasonable cost estimate for a library building project be determined until the library building program has been at least roughed out or, better still, completed. Without this document, there is no way to tell what the final square footage of the building will be. Further, the building program defines the necessary furnishings and equipment for the project, which is information the interior designer or architect will require in order to produce a reasonable cost estimate for the furnishings and equipment contract.

Preliminary Cost Estimate

Once these professionals are brought on board, the final stages of the preliminary cost estimate can be accomplished. Along with the development of conceptual and schematic plans, often soil engineering studies will need to be performed to refine the costs for construction as well as site development. Location-specific, costs will to become apparent at this point. For example, if labor or materials costs are particularly high in the area, then "average" cost-per-square-foot figures will need to be increased.

Once the architect and engineers define the shape and structure of the building along with the materials to be used, then professional cost estimators can perform a unit cost estimate and provide library planners with a new degree of confidence. Interior designers can also provide unit cost estimates for the furnishings and equipment contract. The costs for professional services and other project needs become clearer at this point and library planners should begin to see a relatively realistic picture of what the final cost of the project will be.

To get to this point, library planners will have to spend some money. Professional services usually do not come free, and few are willing to work on a contingency basis. Therefore, library supporters will need to raise funds from private or other sources to support preliminary planning. This is money well spent because it will help avert project cost overruns by providing library planners with as realistic and accurate a project budget as possible. As mentioned, project budgets are typically placed before local funding agencies once schematic plans and the resulting final cost estimate are completed. This is an acceptable procedure, but if library planners want an even more accurate estimate, it may be desirable to hold off until design development plans are completed. The advantage of waiting is that the estimates provided by professional cost estimators will be based on significantly more information.

Library planners must understand that even the detailed estimates provided at the design development stage will change as the project progresses. Regardless of the estimates at design development and final working drawings stages, the project budget will most likely need to be revised when the building is bid. Typically, the project will come in somewhat over or under the estimates. In some cases this adjustment will be significant, but in others it can be handled by the contingency fund. Sometimes library planners will have to negotiate a bid price in order to get the construction contract down to within the budgeted amount. This can sometimes be extremely difficult and costly. If the bidding climate is such that it looks as though the project may not come in within the budget, or that it will be very close, it may be prudent to select some items that are expendable and bid them as "alternates." This

forces contractors to give prices that can either be accepted or not based on the base bid for the project and the available funds.

The project budget will be in flux right through bidding for the building and the furnishings and equipment contract. Once construction starts, the contract may need to be modified to meet unexpected existing conditions such as soil problems or the introduction of owner-initiated change orders. To limit costly change orders, library planners should try to make sure the project's final working drawings include everything the building will need. Change orders are especially expensive if they require substantial redesign or, worse, on-the-job demolition and reconstruction of work already performed. The abuse of change orders by owners and contractors is one of the prime reasons many construction projects come in over budget. This can be controlled not only by good planning and prudence on the part of the library planners, but also by a comprehensive and well designed set of working drawings and specifications as well as competent construction management.

In most construction projects unknown conditions or problems of some kind will arise that will affect the budget. This is why every public construction project should have a reasonable contingency fund factored into the total project cost estimate. It should also be understood that not all architects, engineers, or, for that matter, professional cost estimators are equally good at providing accurate cost estimates. For this reason, library planners should include research on the track record of firms in this area in the criteria of selection as they interview architectural firms. Many firms have a habit of completing projects on or under budget; others do not. The ability to provide good cost estimates has nothing to do with the ability to provide attractive and well-designed buildings, but it is difficult to deliver the latter without the former.

At best, budgeting a construction project is a constant balancing act between numerous line items that need some additional funding. If the furnishings and equipment bids come in high, for example, there may be an urge to "raid" the contingency fund at that time. Doing this too early may place the building contract in jeopardy. However, once the building is substantially completed and the risk of costly problems reduced, project officials can look at expending contingency funds for extra items of furnishings and equipment, upgrading finishes for the building, or purchasing books for an opening-day collection. At this time the contingency fund may be expended for "extras", or the funds can simply be saved and returned to the funding agency to be used to retire debt if bonds were sold for the project.

Final Audit

These final adjustments in the budget signal that the project is coming to a close. Funds will need to be left for such activities such as the move into the new facility and a final audit, but most of the budget's line items will be close to final at this point. Only when the audit is completed will the library planners know the total cost of the project. It is helpful to obtain final audit cost figures from other jurisdictions that have recently completed library building projects, particularly those that closely match the size and quality of the building desired. These figures cut through vague remembrances and rose-colored lenses and provide the clarity of actual costs. Library planners, of course, need to review these figures with the understanding that they are now out of date and represent what other communities did, not necessarily what is needed for their own project. Regardless, these figures will shed light on the expenditures that need to be estimated realistically from the outset.

THE INITIAL PROJECT COST ESTIMATE

One way to develop an initial project cost estimate is to look at public library construction costs across the country over the years. This approach provides local library planners with some perspective from which to view their project. However caution must be exercised since these figures are national averages, and there is no "average" project anywhere, only many variations on a theme. A good source for library construction information is *Library Journal's* December architectural issue,[1] which reports library construction statistics annually. The *Library Journal* statistics, which have been collected since 1968, represent all kinds of public library buildings (branches, central libraries, system headquarters, etc.) ranging in size from a few thousand square feet to several hundred thousand square feet. These statistics are a reasonable starting point for library planners who have never planned a building before.

A rough initial budget estimate for a new public library building can be constructed utilizing the four basic cost categories used in the *Library Journal* construction statistics. These categories are construction cost, equipment cost, site cost, and other costs. Table 2-1 shows the 24-year average percentages of costs in these categories as well as the most recent five years of data:

TABLE 2-1. Average Cost Percentage of Total by Category* (for new library buildings)

	Construction	Equipment	Site	Other
All years (1968-1991)	75.1%	9.9%	6.4%	8.6%
Rounded Off	75	10	6.5	8.5
Last five years** (1987-1991)	73.1%	11.4%	6.7%	8.8%
Rounded Off	73	11	7	9

*Complied and calculated from various six-year cost summaries of *Library Journal,* December issues from 1968 to 1991. ©Reed Publishing
**Proportionately adjusted from data to equal 100% total.

Over the 24-year period for which *Library Journal* has collected construction statistics, the average cost for construction of a new library building has been approximately 75 percent of the total project cost. The average cost for equipment (including furnishings) has been approximately 10 percent; the average cost for the site has been about 6.5 percent; and the average cost for all other expenses associated with the project has been about 8.5 percent. In the last five years, there has been a slight shift in the percentages with construction dropping to 73 percent of the total cost, and equipment increasing to just over 11 percent. The percentages for site and other costs have increased somewhat, but not significantly.

The range in individual years over the 24-year period for construction has been between 70 and 80 percent, while the range for equipment has been between 8 and 14 percent. The range for site costs has been between 2 and 12 percent and the range for all other costs has been between 7 and 11 percent. While the percentages for each category have over the years remained relatively consistent and stable, there have been substantial shifts from year to year indicating that there are probably substantial variations in individual projects. The author once again urges caution with the use of project averages such as these. It is not uncommon for library planners to see significant variations in the percentages for their projects when compared to these national averages.

One of the difficulties of discussing project costs is that they all vary dramatically. One project may have a site that is already owned by the local jurisdiction and therefore no cost is reported. For another project, located in a prime commercial area, the site cost could be a significant portion (20 to 30 percent or more) of the total project cost. Construction costs also vary tremendously because of the different quality levels as well as variable materials and labor costs from one part of the nation to another. Likewise furnishings, equipment, and "other" costs such as architectural and engineering fees vary significantly from project to project.

Still, one has to start somewhere in establishing an initial cost estimate, and national averages at least provide a framework. It must be understood, however, that the final budget estimate will probably not be very close to the original cost estimate. With this disclaimer in mind, the author offers Table 2-2 which shows the total costs per square foot for new public library construction based on the last 24 years of *Library Journal* data. Figure 2-2 provides the same information as Table 2-2 in graph form. The reader is reminded that these figures (as all other square footage figures offered in this publication) are based on the total *gross* square footage for the library building. This is quite different from the *net* square footage which is the space needed for the library activities and excludes the *nonassignable* square footage that is necessary for walls, stairways, elevators, corridors, lobbies, rest rooms, mechanical rooms etc. If library buildings are planned on the net square footage instead of the gross square footage that includes the nonassignable space, library planners will discover a shortfall of approximately 20 to 30 percent of the funds necessary for constructing the building!

Total Project Cost Projections

It is obvious from these data that there has been an erratic but continuing escalation in total project costs for public library buildings over the last 24 years. Inflationary pressures have obviously had a major role in these increases. Regardless of occasional recessionary periods, in all likelihood inflation will continue to increase total costs of library construction projects well into the next century. Based on an ex-

TABLE 2-2. Average Total Project Costs per Square Foot for Public Libraries* (For New Buildings)

Fiscal Year	Total Project Cost Per Square Foot for New Buildings
1991	$115.86
1990	110.92
1989	120.24
1988	99.51
1987	99.93
1986	85.79
1985	82.76
1984	98.52
1983	76.56
1982	68.93
1981	75.81
1980	61.70
1979	41.87
1978	54.73
1977	54.55
1976	48.27
1975	43.14
1974	41.74
1973	37.36
1972	38.27
1971	32.10
1970	31.78
1969	29.76
1968	N/A

*Based on the total gross square footage of the projects.
©Reed Publishing

TABLE 2-3. Projected *Library Journal* Total Projects Costs Per Square Foot (New Public Library Construction)

Fiscal Year	Total Project Costs Per Square Foot		
	High Avg.	Medium Avg.	Low Avg.
1994	$153	$138	$125
1995	160	144	130
1996	167	150	134
1997	173	155	138
1998	180	160	143
1999	187	165	147
2000	193	171	152

trapolation of the data, which reflects the continued inflationary growth of the past 24 years, Table 2-3 shows projected national averages of the total project costs per square foot for new public libraries in a range of what should be reported in *Library Journal* in upcoming years.

Keep in mind that these figures are averages, and that costs for individual projects may be significantly higher or lower. It should also be noted that projects which are documented in the most recent issue of *Library Journal* have an approximate three-year lag in their figures. These projects were bid on average about two years prior to their completion; further, the time between completion and being reported in *Library Journal* is on average one year. Because of this time lag, it is important to understand that annual inflationary cost increases must be factored into any use of the *Library Journal* construction statistics. In addition, when planning a project, it is important to estimate the cost of construction when the project is to be bid, not the day it is planned. So if the anticipated bid date is a year in the future, an additional annual inflationary projection must be factored into the estimate.

Table 2-4 adjusts Table 2-3 for the three-year lag and provides total cost averages that can be used by library planners to determine "average" total project costs. This type of projection is risky at best since it assumes a consistent increase in all project costs—an assumption that may prove false if inflation picks up dramatically or a severe recessionary period intervenes. At any rate, the projections are at least reasonable based upon past experience and can be used as a preliminary point of reference in the cost estimating process.

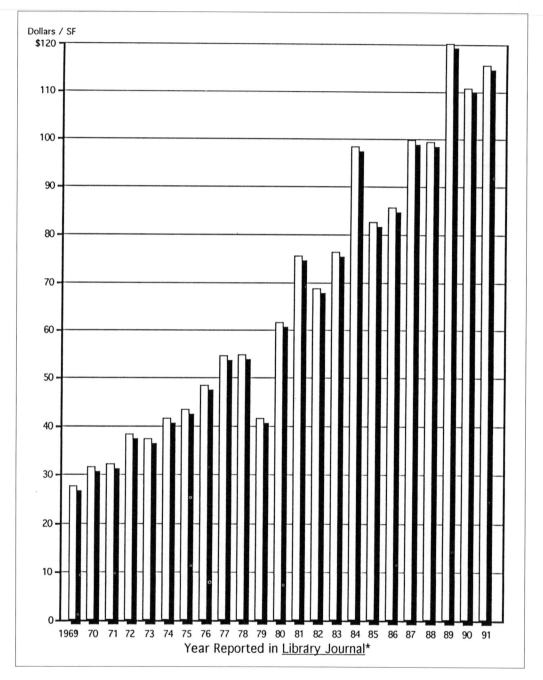

Fig. 2-2. Average Total Project Costs per Square Foot for Public Libraries

Table 2-4. Total Project Costs Per Square Foot Projections (new public library construction)

Year	Total Project Costs Per Square Foot		
	High Avg.	Medium Avg.	Low Avg.
1994	$173	$155	$138
1995	180	160	143
1996	187	165	147
1997	193	171	152
1998	200	177	156
1999	207	182	161
2000	213	188	165

Sample Initial Project Budget

In order to utilize Table 2-4 for planning purposes, select the year in which the construction project will be bid and read to the right to the appropriate column to determine the high, medium, and low average total cost per square foot figures. For example, if a project will be bid in 1994 and it is felt that the project will fall close to the medium range for all public library projects, a figure of $155 per square foot would be utilized for the total cost per square foot estimate. Based on this figure of $155 per square foot, one can begin to develop an initial cost estimate for a project that will be bid in 1994. In order to come up with the categorical cost estimates for equipment, site, etc., the average rounded off percentages for the most recent five-year period will be used in the following example. Based on the $155 per square foot, the construction cost for the project would be approximately $113 per square foot (73% of $155); the equipment cost would be $17 per square foot (11% of $155); the site cost would be about $11 per square foot (7% of $155); and the other costs would be $14 per square foot (9% of $155). The project cost estimate based on a 10,000-square-foot building estimate would look like Table 2-5:

Table 2-5. Initial Budget for a 10,000-Square-Foot Library Building

Construction:	$113/SF × 10,000 SF	=	$1,130,000
Equipment:	$ 17/SF × 10,000 SF	=	170,000
Site:	$ 11/SF × 10,000 SF	=	110,000
Other:	$ 14/SF × 10,000 SF	=	140,000
TOTAL:	$155/SF × 10,000 SF	=	$1,550,000

The next step is to refine the estimate so that it becomes more realistic and specific to the project at hand. For example, the first thing that might come to mind is that the cost per square foot for construction is too high (or low). It may appear that a library building can be built for less in the community because several libraries have been built in nearby communities for considerably less. Fine, start making the adjustment. Perhaps the site cost is irrelevant because the site will be given by a local donor, or that it is much too low for the piece of property that has already been selected. The furnishings and equipment costs may be reasonably accurate for basic shelving, tables, and chairs, but not when audiovisual, electronic, and other miscellaneous equipment is added to the budget. If the site is being donated, the community may want to do "a little something extra" with the quality of the interior furnishings and finishes. Other costs may be trimmed because the city attorney will provide the legal work, and the architect can be hired at a relatively low percentage because they are all hungry for work right now.

Project Cost Variations

The average total project costs will vary widely from state to state and project to project. A few examples will demonstrate how wide this range is. In the last five years of *Library Journal* data, the range of total cost per square foot was from just a few dollars to a high of $676! The range of costs can be significant even within a given individual state. On the whole, the average total cost for all projects that were granted state bond funds in 1991 in California was $250 per square foot. This is well above the national average, but even among these projects there was a great deal of variation. The total cost per square foot ranged from a low of $125 for a project in a rural region to $375 for a project in the Los Angeles area market.

The King County Library System in Seattle is currently in the middle of a facilities expansion program that will result in 18 public libraries ranging in size from 5,000 to 80,000 square feet. At the time of this writing, some of these projects had already been bid, and some were still in the planning stages. The total cost per square foot for the projects ranged from a low of $180 to a high of $395 with an average of $327. Part of the reason these costs are so high and range so widely is that the King County Library System is required to pay for significant off-site costs such as road improvements, sewers, etc., like any other "developer" in the construction business. While the actual cost figures may not be as high in other states, the range from top to bottom will likely be as significant. This information should demonstrate that an accurate project budget cannot be determined until considerably more detailed work has been performed than reviewing national averages.

However, the initial budget estimate is important to help the planning team get a handle on the relative scope of the project and the amount of money required to fund it. It is the first of many steps toward the "final" budget that will be used with funding agencies. Knowing the initial budget in the early stages of the project can assist planners in the preliminary determination of possible funding sources. If the project cost estimate is relatively low, perhaps all the funds can be raised from the private sector or from the general fund of the city

or county. If the cost estimate is high, a referendum and/or state or federal grant may be necessary to fund the project. Preliminary planning can begin at this point, but cannot proceed very far until the planning team has a more detailed estimate.

PREPARING A PRELIMINARY PROJECT BUDGET ESTIMATE

The following discussion provides various options from which the library planners may choose to develop a preliminary project budget. The worksheets at end of this chapter may be utilized to develop a project budget for any public library construction project.

Land Acquisition

In most new library projects and many expansion projects, it is necessary to obtain property for the new facility. If land must be acquired, the cost of the land for the project is usually determined through a process of negotiation. The owner states an asking price, if the library planning team is interested in the property, they will make an offer. This is frequently done through a real estate agent, but if the owner has not listed the property with an agent, the potential buyer negotiates directly with the owner. Regardless, the process proceeds through a series of offers and counter-offers until the seller and buyer agree upon a price and terms which result in a sales contract or purchase agreement.

Sometimes, acquisition of land entails condemnation proceedings by a government agency. In such a case, the cost of the land will be set by the courts in most states under the provisions of eminent domain. It must be kept in mind that the public agency that is condemning the land will also have to pay appraisal fees, court costs, and legal fees. In some cases, these costs can become significant if the condemnation proceedings are lengthy and/or the determination of the land's market value is complicated. These costs vary, but an estimate can usually be provided by legal counsel.

Because local real estate costs and conditions vary so much around the country, it is impossible to provide much guidance regarding the cost of land for an individual project. Even within a municipality there will be significant variations in land value depending on numerous factors. The site selection process cannot be casual or superficial. Determining a good site is critical for the long-term health and effectiveness of the public library building. Land costs for public libraries are, extremely site specific. However, some national statistics may be of help.

As previously mentioned, in areas where land costs are high, a good site can often run as high as 20 to 30 percent of the total project cost. As far back as 1958, the well-known library building consultant Dr. Joseph Wheeler felt that 50 percent of the project cost was not too much to pay for a good site if it was especially well located.[2] This would be particularly true for an urban site in a major metropolitan area or in any area where land costs are high. Good sites for public libraries usually require a substantial amount of money. Recently, library sites in Charlotte, North Carolina, and Sioux City, Iowa, cost approximately 50 percent of the total project. Library sites in high-cost urban areas may run in the multimillion-dollar range, and good sites in rural areas are likely to cost several hundred thousand dollars unless the area is economically depressed or the project very small.

One way to justify the high cost of a good site is to spread the cost of the site over the entire life of the building. Assume a total project cost of $6 million for an "okay" site and $7 million for an excellent site. The preferred site costs $1 million more than the adequate site in the same community, but the building will probably serve the community for 20 years or longer. Excluding financing charges, this $1 million will cost about $50,000 more per year to acquire which means that the $7 million project will cost $350,000 per year and the $6 million project will cost $300,000 per year. If the better location attracts more people and gives the library significantly higher use, the site may well be a bargain. The community will be getting "more bang for the buck" by receiving more from the library with a relatively smaller additional annual cost. A library site should be regarded as a long-term investment for the community. The additional $50,000 a year is a 17 percent increase over the $300,000 per-year cost. However, if the better location brings in 25 or even 50 percent more people and the use of the library increases proportionately, the investment of an additional $50,000 per year will have been extremely wise.

As shown earlier, the site costs for the most recent five years of *Library Journal* data for new building projects is approximately 7 (6.7) percent of the total project costs, but variation in the percentage for site cost for individual projects included ranged from 0 to approximately 50 percent. This can be demonstrated in the projects funded in 1991 with state bond funds in California. The percentage of the total project spent on site costs ranged from a low of 3 percent to a high of 30 percent with the average being 13.5 percent for all projects. The range reflects significant differences in land value between urban and rural areas. The average is high because of the high cost of land in the urban areas of California, which accounted for the majority of projects funded. While the range for California is very wide, this kind of variation can also be seen in other states and regions of the nation.

Another way of looking at site costs is

to calculate the site cost per square foot. Table 2-6 shows the average cost per square foot of the public library building (not the site) which is attributable to land cost:

Table 2-6. Average Site Cost Per Square Foot of Building

1987	1988	1989	1990	1991	5 Year Average
$3.68	$7.18	$8.06	$8.26	$9.54	$7.34

©Reed Publishing

The average cost for a site for projects reported from 1987 to 1991 amounts to approximately $100,000 per project. If the current rate of increase for the last few years holds, sites for new public libraries could be reported at around $13 per square foot of library building space or more for the 1993 *Library Journal* statistics. However, 1994 site costs should be estimated (considering the three year reporting lag) for about $18 per square foot of library space or more if the national average is applicable. Based on the *Library Journal* national average, the site for a new 10,000-square-foot library building should cost about $180,000. Again, bear in mind the great variation in site costs from state to state and even within a state. For example, in the California projects, the site cost per square foot of building space ranged from a low of $5 to a high of $100 with an average of $34, reflecting the high cost of land in California, and demonstrating how difficult it is to rely only on national averages. In order to determine a reasonable estimate for land costs, library planners must learn what commercial-grade property is going for in their community. This information can usually be obtained from the tax assessor's office, from appraisers, or from local real estate agents. One of the best ways to determine land costs in a community is to look at the sales price of comparable parcels of land that have sold in recent months. Only through investigating

the local real estate market can a reasonable cost estimate be determined. The preliminary estimate will usually be based on a rough calculation of dollars per square foot of land. Again, this figure varies widely within a state and even within a local community. For projects recently funded with state bonds in California, the range of the cost per square foot of land was from a low of 18 cents in one rural community to about $50 in a metropolitan area; the average for all projects was about $5.75. Once the approximate range of the cost per square foot in a community is known, library planners can then start to look with a value-conscious eye at various parcels of property.

An example may show how to determine the cost of a site. Assuming that retail property with good visibility and accessibility ranges between $20 and $30 per square foot, it would be reasonable to use an average of $25 per square foot. This figure would be multiplied by the amount of square footage needed for the site. If the project needs approximately one acre (43,560 square feet) of land, the cost for the site would be just over $1 million. This may seem like a lot of money for a library site, but remember, it will serve the community well for 20 to 30 years or more. Don't be dissuaded from investing for the long term in a site for the library.

Determining the Size of the Site

Along with being knowledgeable about the cost of land in a community, the planning team must have an idea of how much land is needed for the project. This determination in itself can entail fairly complex decision-making. First, the planning team must know the square footage of the building. This will not be known precisely until the building program has been completed (and in some cases until the architectural plans are drawn), but it may need to be estimated by the end of the needs assessment process.

Second, a decision must be made about whether the building will be built on one level or on multiple levels, and if so how many. Most library building consultants recommend that, in order to conserve staff and lower the library's operating budget, public library buildings of 30,000 to 35,000 square feet or less be kept on one level. If this is not possible, or if the building is larger, the library will probably need to be planned as a multistory structure. In this case, the planning team must estimate the building's "footprint," or how many square feet of the site's surface area the building structure will occupy. If the structure is to be 60,000 gross square feet, it might be determined that the building should be built on two floors. If the floors were of equal size (30,000 square feet each), the building's footprint would be 30,000 square feet.

Next, the amount of land needed for a future expansion of the library building should be estimated. This may be difficult, but based upon growth projections as well as the facility master plan, the library planning team should be able to make an intelligent guess as to how many more square feet of the site should be set aside for future additions. Again, this figure must be translated into a "footprint" square footage figure since the addition could also be multistory. To leave this step out is to ignore the fact that a public library building grows as its community grows. It is always best to leave some land available for future expansion or the building could become "landlocked" with no apparent way to enlarge the facility when the time comes.

The next consideration is parking for the library. As Hoyt Galvin discovered in his nationwide survey of public library directors, the amount of parking required for a public library building ranges from one to two square feet of parking space for every square foot of library building, resulting in a rule of thumb of 1.5 square feet of parking space for every square foot of public library building.[3] The amount of parking

required will also vary from community to community. In suburban or rural areas where everyone drives to the library, a higher proportion of parking space may be needed. In urban areas with mass transit and significant pedestrian access, less parking may suffice. In a suburban setting, a public library that is part of a shopping development may be able to get by with less earmarked parking since patrons can utilize the shopping center's lot. In addition to the currently planned project, an adequate number of parking spaces to support a future library expansion should also be anticipated and planned for.

Finally, the necessary setbacks on the site should be calculated. Most communities have local zoning laws that require buildings to be set back from the street or property lines by a specific number of feet. There may also be regulations mandating that a specific percentage of the site go into landscaped space. The architect may wish to enhance the project and community with "aesthetic" setbacks beyond those required by code. If these setbacks are overlooked, it may result in a site that is too small and either unsatisfactory or even potentially unusable.

All these factors must be considered when determining the size of the site. As a rule-of-thumb, a rough ratio of three to four square feet of site to one square foot of library building is often used for single-story library buildings. When all factors have been considered and the needed size of the site is known, the planning team can begin looking for an adequate site. This process must be undertaken with diligence and thoroughness. However, once a desirable site has been selected, there remains the negotiation to obtain it for the best possible price and terms. Library planners should keep in mind that there are many options available to them during this process.

For example, if the property is being purchased from a wealthy individual or developer, it may be possible to agree on a price that is below market value if the seller needs a tax write-off. Or, in some cases, the developer may provide some site development services such as grading to "sweeten the deal." If services that are readily available to the developer can be negotiated into the purchase agreement, the savings could reduce the overall project budget. However, be certain these services are precisely specified in the sales agreement. Defining the property lines and describing the characteristics of a site are also extremely important in any land transaction. Occasionally, an outright purchase of land isn't necessary, because a site lease for a specified number of years can be arranged. Long-term leases for 50 years, or, even better, for 99 years, can be a good way of getting the initial project costs down as long as the annual lease payments aren't prohibitive. Remember, the library will be making those payments for a long time, and if there is no buy-out provision at the end of the lease term, the property—and frequently the improvements on it—revert to the lessor.

Land Surveys

For projects for which it is necessary to acquire land, or even for addition/remodeling projects where the land is already owned, it is necessary to hire a professional land surveyor and commission a boundary survey. It is essential to know the precise boundaries of the site so that library planners know exactly what they are acquiring and there are no boundary disputes at the end of the project.

Beyond a simple boundary survey, which is usually all that is necessary for a preliminary title report and deed recordation, it is often wise to commission what is termed a locational survey. This will specify the location of any major characteristics of the site, including but not limited to: water lines, sanitary and storm sewer lines, gas lines, overhead and underground power and telephone lines, any streets, drives, railroad, or other right-of-ways, billboards or signs, trees, fire hydrants, fences, structures, or encroachments of any kind. Frequently, when this type of survey is performed, some very interesting aspects of the site may be uncovered. For example, perhaps there was once a gas station on the site and an underground gas tank is leaking toxic chemicals into the ground. Knowledge of this during sales negotiations is critical since this problem would be very expensive to clean up.

At some point it will also be necessary to obtain a topographical survey. Required

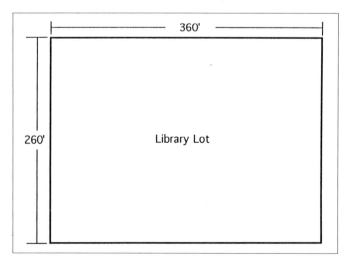

Fig. 2-3. Boundary Survey

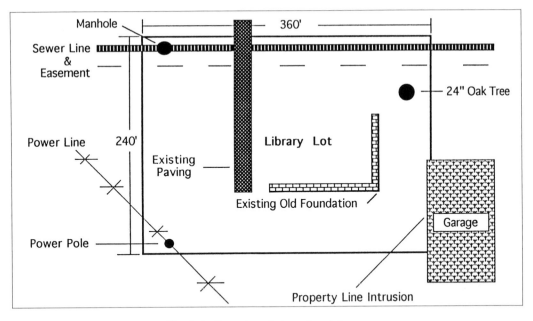

Fig. 2-4. Boundary & Locational Survey

by the project architect, this survey shows the precise elevation of the land and is necessary to establish the grading requirements for the project as well as to specify the ground floor and foundations of the building. A topographical survey can usually be done after the land has been acquired. However, it will often be less expensive overall to have the surveyor perform all three types of surveys (boundary, locational and topographical) at one time. The cost for these surveys varies from locale to locale and depends to some extent on the size of the parcel and how busy the surveyors are. Simple boundary surveys in rural areas can cost as little as a few hundred dollars.

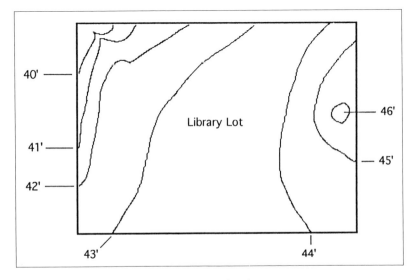

Fig. 2-5. Topographical Survey

In major metropolitan areas, however, all three surveys may run several thousand dollars.

Appraisal

Once a site has been tentatively chosen, it is wise to have an appraisal performed by a real estate appraiser. While this will cost money, it will take a lot of the guesswork out of determining the site's value. There are many levels of appraisals available, and library planners will have to determine what is needed based on the size of the project, the local real estate market, and the level of detail necessary to arrive at a reasonable fair market value. Real estate agents often have a good working knowledge of the value of land, but they generally do not have the professional credentials necessary to provide an appraisal for commercial-grade property.

There are varying degrees of qualifications in the real estate appraisal field. Library planners should be sure to hire someone who has the training, expertise, and experience to accurately appraise the property under consideration. Municipal and county governments may have individuals on staff who have adequate credentials and can provide appraisals, but this is relatively uncommon. If an appraisal must be purchased, the best quality appraisal for the money should be sought. Since library sites frequently fall into the category of "commercial property," it is usually best to find an appraiser qualified to appraise commercial property. The MAI (Member Appraisal Institute) and the SREA (Society of Real Estate Appraisers) are two associations to which competent appraisers belong. If the property is of considerable value and/or the determination of the value is controversial or difficult, it will generally be best to obtain the services of an appraiser with these or similar affiliations. Again, the cost of a competent, professionally prepared appraisal varies depending upon a number of factors, but expect to pay a minimum of $2,000 to $3,000 (maybe less in rural areas) and up to $20,000 or more for property in a high-density urban market.

Legal Fees, Title Report, and Title Insurance

In addition to an appraisal, there are other costs associated with acquiring a site, including legal fees and the cost of title work. In many states, it is important to have an attorney knowledgeable in real estate transactions represent library planners during the acquisition process. The attorney and/or title company reviews the property's title and ensures that there are no unacceptable exceptions to its future marketability. Standard utility and right-of-way exceptions are usually not a problem unless they greatly reduce the buildability of the site, e.g., a sewer main running through the middle of the property. However, other kinds of restrictions and encumbrances can be a major impediment to holding title in fee simple. These include "reverter" clauses that require the title of the property to revert to heirs if the property is no longer used for "educational purposes."

Frequently, library planners will be asked to accept a "gift" site for the project which allows the property to be used only for "library purposes," with the stipulation that if the property ceases to be used for such purposes it (and the improvements upon it) will revert to the grantor or grantor's heirs. Library planners should look long and hard at this kind of arrangement since it severely limits how the property may be used in the future. There are numerous types of encumbrances, restrictions, easements, covenants, reservations, or limitations which an attorney should check for during a title search. Any number of items may be uncovered that could be unacceptable to library officials. Remember, the library site will be around for a long time, and it is usually best to hold title free and clear of any restrictions.

If library planners decide to acquire the property, it is prudent in most states to acquire title insurance for the property to protect the new owners from claims by previous title holders. Without this kind of insurance, previous title holders could come forth and win interest in the property through court action. This kind of action can tie up property for years. It could also result in the loss of capital on the part of local jurisdiction, slow the library project down, or halt it completely.

Again, the cost of legal fees, title work, and insurance varies significantly. An estimate can usually be obtained from a municipal or county attorney's office or from private firms if necessary. Library planners should budget at least a thousand dollars and often more for the legal and title work associated with acquiring a commercial-grade site unless the legal work is performed pro bono. It is occasionally possible to obtain free legal services from a community-minded attorney's firm, and there is nothing wrong with asking for private-sector in-kind support for a public library project. However, it is not advisable to depend on it when planning the project budget.

Option to Purchase

As part of the sales agreement, the attorney may be able to help those acquiring the site with an option-to-purchase agreement. An option is used when the party purchasing the property pays the seller a specified fee for the right to purchase the property at a specified price at a future date assuming certain aspects of the transaction are acceptable to the purchaser. In short, an option buys time. It holds the property for the buyer and allows the buyer time to make certain that the purchase makes sense and the land is being acquired at a reasonable cost. While options may cost as little as $1, they may also run into the thousands of dollars if the property is in demand and ex-

pensive. An option may be desirable if the library planners don't actually want to acquire the property until they know the funding for the project will be available. An option may be used to reserve a site until a local referendum is passed, or until a state or federal grant application process is complete. Further, an option may be wise if library planners need time to perform surveys, environmental assessments, or soil engineering studies, which are necessary to determine if the site is viable.

Demolition and Toxic Waste Removal

In addition to the purchase price, the actual cost of acquiring a site may include the cost of demolishing and/or removing existing buildings, structures, foundations, paving, trees, or even underground storage tanks or toxic materials. Estimating these costs can be difficult and extremely risky without professional assistance. Rough estimates for the removal of buildings can usually be obtained from general contractors or, if the job is large, a contracting firm that specializes in demolition. However, the cost of demolition work varies among contractors, so it's a good idea to obtain a minimum of three estimates. Even better, obtain assistance from professional architects, engineers, and cost estimators if possible.

If the demolition is complex such as removal of a large structure or toxic materials, an engineering specialist will be needed to provide a preliminary estimate. The removal of toxic materials including asbestos is governed by restrictive state and federal regulations which must be adhered to carefully for health and safety reasons. Unfortunately, these requirements are costly because of the manner in which the hazardous materials must be handled and disposed of. Soil and ground water contamination and the removal of asbestos from an existing building are problems that can quickly run into the hundreds of thousands of dollars. In addition, they must be contracted separately and supervised carefully by qualified professionals. This will require a separate bid document, a separate contract, and construction administration separate from that of the general contract. Cost estimating is extremely tricky for this kind of work, and the true costs are frequently not known with any precision until the work is done.

Normal demolition work is frequently performed as part of the general contract unless it is highly specialized or substantial in scope, in which case it may be done under a separate contract by a firm specializing in demolition. This separate contract may be negotiated, but is usually bid like a general contract since the work usually falls under public contract laws. Sometimes the demolition contract may involve demolition within a building that is being remodeled, such as the existing library building or a building that has been purchased for renovation and transformation into a library building. The same approach applies in this case, but estimating is more difficult because it is necessary to define exactly what will be demolished and what will remain. It will be necessary to retain an architect as well as engineers and begin plans development before a reasonable estimate can be obtained.

Site Development

In addition to demolition, the cost of acquiring a site includes the cost of developing the site. Again, this cost is frequently bid as part of the general contract, but it may also be bid separately. The kinds of costs usually associated with site development include, but are not limited to, the following:

- Removal of unsuitable soil from the site or changing the grade level to improve the buildability of the site;
- Removal of rock, stumps, or other obstructions;

- Addition and compacting of structural fill dirt to compensate for the removal of unsuitable soil and/or to raise the grade level for such purpose as raising the site out of a flood plain;
- Specialized foundation support such as driving pilings;
- Parking structures, paving, curbs, gutters, and sidewalks;
- Patios, pergolas, outdoor seating, or sculpture;
- Retaining walls;
- Landscaping, signs, and site utilities such as lighting;
- Connection fees for water, sewer, etc.;
- Drainage control, storm retention ponds, control of water courses and flood plain management;
- Mitigation of negative environmental impact of the building such as provision for wetlands, etc.; and
- Off-site costs such as street widening, signalization, utilities improvements, etc.

Typically, the construction-cost-per-square-foot estimate of the building will include normal site development costs such as minimal clearing, grading, parking lots, and landscaping. However, if the situation is unusual, it will be important to estimate these atypical site costs separately. Site development costs can vary significantly.

When a site is being considered, or even after it has been selected, it is often tempting to ask a contractor what the development cost would be for the site. This approach is not recommended. It is difficult to obtain estimates from contractors for site development work if the work has not yet been specified by an architect or engineer, because it is impossible for anyone to provide a cost estimate if the scope, quantity, and quality of work are unknown. Unless the site work is very straightforward, it will probably be necessary to employ either an architect or an engineer to get even a ballpark estimate. These individuals can sometimes visit a site and provide rough estimates for preliminary planning purposes. However, it is difficult for them to provide accurate estimates without further study, if the site development work is at all complex. This means that with projects that will entail significant site development work, there will not be a firm cost estimate until architectural plans have reached the design development stage. Occasionally, the costs will not be known until working drawings are available or even until the day of the bid. It should come as no surprise that projects frequently run into trouble with overruns in site development costs.

The question becomes, How does the planning team avoid falling into a "bottomless pit" of site development costs? One way is to consider potential site development costs during the site selection process. Library boards are often offered a "free" site as a gift, but subsequently find that the cost of developing the site is well beyond what the purchase price of another, better-located site might have been. When evaluating a site, it is important to take a hard look at its condition and try to understand what will need to be done to place a library building and parking there. If the site has a significant slope, there is likely to be a substantial cost for cut and fill of soil even with plans that optimize the slope. This process can be extremely expensive since it frequently means removing soil by digging out a hillside, hauling it off with dump trucks, and then bringing in new structural fill soil that can be compacted to carry the load of the new building's foundations. Unfortunately, the amount of this kind of cut-and-fill work cannot be accurately estimated until the architect has designed the layout of the building and parking lot, but ballpark estimates may be possible from an experienced architect.

Sometimes cut-and-fill work is needed even when the site is level. The soil's characteristics may make it unable to support the foundations of the building. This may be the case if, for example, it is alluvial soil with a high level of organic material, making it soft and mucky. This kind of soil must be removed completely and structural fill (soil that can be compacted to support a building) must be purchased and transported to the site. There are many other conditions that may require removing the soil or dealing with in some manner. Soil can be expansive, be previous fill with trash or old stumps in it, be contaminated with toxic materials, have a high water table, or have rock obstructions that prevent construction. The problem is that it may not be possible to discover these problems just by looking at the surface. A sub-surface soil engineering study is necessary to determine the subterranean characteristics.

Soil Engineering Study

This study goes by many names and may be referred to as a geotechnical report, foundation study, or soil boring report. It attempts to determine what is under the site and any special geologic conditions including, but not limited to, caves, tunnels, mine shafts, unstable slopes, active seismic zones, and areas prone to liquefaction (soil that becomes "soupy" and will not support the structure). In order to examine this subsurface, generally it is necessary to either dig holes with a backhoe, or more typically, perform soil borings. The results of these tests determine what the foundations for the building will have to be and whether or not specialized systems will need to be utilized to adequately support the structure.

Library planners should be aware there are engineering firms that specialize in this line of work. These companies can be found through an architect or even in the yellow pages under "Engineers—Foundation, Geotechnical, or Soil." The cost of this service varies tremendously based on the scope of the job and the locale. For a small job where only one or two borings are needed, and in a low-cost market, the cost may be as low as $1,000 to $2,000. More typically, for medium-size jobs, the cost will range from $5,000 to $50,000 depending upon what needs to be done over the course of the project. Soil testing starts at the beginning of a project, and usually continues throughout the initial phase of construction as the site is prepared for the foundations of the building. For large projects in urban areas, the soil engineering costs can become substantial. However, these costs should be viewed as an insurance policy. The initial cost, although significant, is minor compared to the disastrous results that can occur if the reports are not done properly.

As with all construction work, it is usually best to obtain proposals or bids for the preliminary soil investigation from three licensed engineering firms. The question of the placement of the borings will need to be clarified early on. It is best, if multiple borings are to be performed, to have this work done under the guidance of the project architect. This is important since the architect will likely direct the engineering firm to perform the borings on the site under the proposed foundation lines (and frequently on the four corners) of the building. If a project architect has not yet been selected, then the preliminary exploratory borings should simply be performed in the central part of the site or in the areas that appear to be of greatest concern.

The soil study prepared by the engineering firm subsequent to the borings will provide conclusions about the soil conditions. It may be necessary to obtain the assistance of an architect to interpret the results, but often the engineering company will explain the results in lay terms. If the report recommends that the top 20 feet of soil on the entire site be removed and replaced with structural fill, it doesn't take a Ph.D. to figure out that the site development cost will be significant. However, the exact cost is impossible to determine with-

out additional professional assistance. Further, if the borings are stopped by rock two feet below the surface, or encounter substantial ground water in the form of a spring, or uncover the foundations of an old building, there may be reason for concern and ultimately added costs for the project.

The key is for library planners to understand the study and discover what the resulting site development costs are likely to be for the project. This information can then be utilized in the site selection process and/or in the development of the project cost estimate. However, it must be understood that these costs will not be precisely known until fairly late in the project. While it is possible that no significant site problems will be encountered once the project is under construction, serious soil problems may be discovered only after excavation for the foundations has begun. If the contractor discovers unacceptable soil conditions which were not uncovered by the soil engineering study, the contract will likely have to be amended. For this reason it is wise to have a reasonable project contingency fund that takes potential site problems into account.

Environmental Assessment

In states where there are strong environmental statutes, local jurisdictions may have to perform some type of environmental assessment study to determine if the library building project will have a negative effect on the environment. The requirements of these statutes vary significantly and must be ascertained by consulting the local planning or public works department as well as state environmental monitoring or regulatory agencies. As the requirements vary, so do the costs of performing the studies. Further, even within a state various levels of environmental analysis may be required depending upon the site. In some cases, it can be determined from an initial study that there is very little impact, but in other cases a full-blown environmental impact study may be necessary with public hearings and considerable engineering and even legal work.

In California, for example, the California Environmental Quality Act (CEQA) requires local jurisdictions either to claim an exemption for the project, file a negative declaration based on an initial study, or perform an environmental impact study. The exemption takes the least amount of time and effort if the case can be made that the project by its nature will not negatively effect the environment. The negative declaration, which is the next level, takes more time (usually several months) and effort because an initial study must be performed. A full environmental impact study may take six months or more and result in significant planning costs. Depending upon the outcome, the jurisdiction may or may not be able to build the library project on the site under consideration. It is difficult to project the costs of these kinds of studies since they are so site specific. However, they will typically range from a few thousand dollars if little needs to be done to $10,000 to $20,000 or more if a major study must be performed.

Relocation Costs

Another cost of acquiring a site may be the cost of relocating businesses or individuals residing on the site. In order to buy a site, it may be necessary to entice a seller with the promise to relocate a business by paying for moving expenses. If families or businesses are displaced by the library project and federal funds are involved, relocation expenses must be paid.[4] Unless the land is vacant, relocation costs are a practical part of the site acquisition process. If a business currently owns the site that is being acquired, obviously the cost of relocating will be considered by the seller as part of the purchase price or else

additional monetary assistance will be necessary.

Purchasing a Building

Along with the acquisition of a site, it occasionally makes sense to purchase an existing building and convert it into a public library. This approach is taken if a suitable building can be found. Because there are usually trade-offs with this kind of project, this option is not advised unless the building is in a good location and well-suited for conversion to a library. The preliminary decision to convert an existing building is usually made during the needs assessment process when the planning team is evaluating alternative solutions.

There are many factors to be weighed when considering this kind of project, not the least of which is the purchase price of the land and building. As already discussed, it is usually essential in this case to get at least an appraisal to determine the property's fair market value. It is also extremely important to involve an architect and engineers early on in this type of project. To a large extent the value of the property, and therefore the purchase price, depends on the condition of the building and, most importantly, the cost to convert it. In other words, the cost of developing the property is directly related to its present condition.

One consideration is the condition of the building's superstructure. Can the floors hold 150 pounds per square foot carrying load to support library bookstacks? Are there structural problems caused by stress or lack of maintenance? Does the building meet current seismic codes? Are the roof and exterior walls in satisfactory condition? Is the column spacing acceptable for an economical layout of library bookstacks and other furnishings and equipment? Is the building divided by structural interior walls that will make staff supervision difficult or costly?

There are many other factors to consider. What will it take to make the building operate in an energy-efficient manner? What level of insulation does the building have? What is the condition and efficiency of the heating, ventilating, and air conditioning (HVAC) system? Are the exterior windows energy efficient? Is the present lighting system energy efficient or even appropriate for public library purposes? What about the presence of toxic materials such as asbestos? Does the configuration of the building allow an efficient public library to be housed in it? Can the building be easily modified to meet requirements for disabled access?

In order to answer these questions, it will be necessary to engage professionals to study the building extensively. Exactly what is needed and the costs will be discussed in the sections on professional services and remodeling since this type of project is essentially a remodeling project. Whether the project involves conversion and remodeling, expansion and remodeling, or new construction alone, the cost of the construction contract for these types of activities is of major interest.

Construction Contract

In most cases, the amount spent on the construction contract for the facility will be the single largest expenditure in the project budget. Therefore, considerable time and effort should go into determinating this figure. However, in many situations, this determination is left to chance or the whims of individuals who are relatively uninformed about construction costs or the costs for public library buildings. This approach must be avoided if at all possible; it can only be characterized as flirtation with disaster. The most critical factor in the project budget is the cost of the construction contract for the building, whether for new construction or remodeling. Estimating the costs of remodeling

work is particularly difficult, but even determining the cost of new construction is not easy since it depends on so many variables. The following discussion will provide assistance for library planners in estimating the cost of the construction contract.

New Construction

In order to determine a preliminary cost-per-square-foot-figure for new construction, the planning team should look at as many sources of comparative cost figures as possible, and decide which approach or combination of approaches makes the most sense for the project at hand. Along with library trade publications which provide some information on public library construction costs, there are several cost-estimating publications which can be of assistance. State libraries or professional library consultants knowledgeable about construction projects can frequently provide recent facility cost figures as well.

As reported earlier, the construction costs cited in *Library Journal* averaged 75 percent of the total project cost for the last 24 years. This figure has dropped slightly to 73 percent for projects constructed in the last five years. The range for any given year has been between 69 percent and almost 82 percent. This range is even greater when individual projects are examined. For projects that have no site costs (because the land is already owned or donated) and low furnishings and equipment costs (because the existing furniture is used in the new building), the construction cost can amount to over 90 percent of the total cost. On the other hand, projects that have very high site costs (50 percent of the project), and high furnishings and equipment costs as well as other costs, can have a construction cost that amounts to less than 40 percent of the total. There is obviously a lot of variation in the percentage for construction, but then there is also a significant variation in the actual cost per square foot for construction as well.

The December 1991 *Library Journal* statistics indicate that the cost per square foot for new public library buildings completed between July 1, 1990, and June 30, 1991 was approximately $80 per square foot. However, this figure must be viewed in comparison with previous years. The average cost per square foot of new public library buildings has steadily increased since the late 1960s. The available figures from *Library Journal* begin at just under $20 per square foot in 1968 and rise gradually, although erratically, through the 1989 figure of over $90 per square foot, before dipping down again slightly. Table 2-7 shows the average construction cost per

Table 2-7. Average Construction Costs Per Square Foot for Public Libraries*

Fiscal Year	Construction Contract Cost Per Square Foot for New Buildings
1991	$80.18
1990	80.49
1989	91.40
1988	69.67
1987	73.71
1986	64.01
1985	61.91
1984	80.44
1983	58.38
1982	52.49
1981	56.98
1980	48.11
1979	33.12
1978	40.22
1977	40.95
1976	36.52
1975	32.45
1974	31.17
1973	28.67
1972	27.59
1971	23.87
1970	23.39
1969	21.95
1968	19.62

*Compiled and calculated from various six-year cost summaries of *Library Journal*.
©Reed Publishing

square foot for all public libraries reported in *Library Journal* and Figure 2-6 shows the same data displayed in the graph form.

From this information, it can be seen that during the first ten-year period of data collection, the average cost per square foot increased fairly steadily. In 1979, there was a decided drop in the average cost per square foot. This may have been caused by the recession of the late seventies along with the flood of federal funding for public works. It may also have been the change in the data collection method utilized by *Library Journal*. Whatever the reason, the cost figures significantly increased throughout the 1980s, although the increase became more erratic from year to year. The increases in the early eighties are understandable because those years were highly inflationary, but the trend continued to the end of the decade, with significant "spikes" in 1984 and 1989. While the data appears to correct itself from these deviations each following year, the overall trend is definitely on the increase.

This increase reflects a strongly inflationary period, with the average annual increase a little over 5 percent per year. This trend obviously demonstrates the increasing construction costs in general over the last two decades in the United States, but it also reflects to some extent an increased demand for quality in public construction projects. Based on the *Library Journal* data, Table 2-8 attempts to project what will be reported in *Library Journal* as the national average costs per square foot of new public library construction in the years to come.

Again, it should be kept in mind that the projects displayed in the most recent issue of *Library Journal* reflect a three-year lag between the date the projects are bid and when they are reported. Because of this time lag, annual inflationary cost increases must be factored into any use of the *Library Journal* construction figures. In addition, when planning a project it is impor-

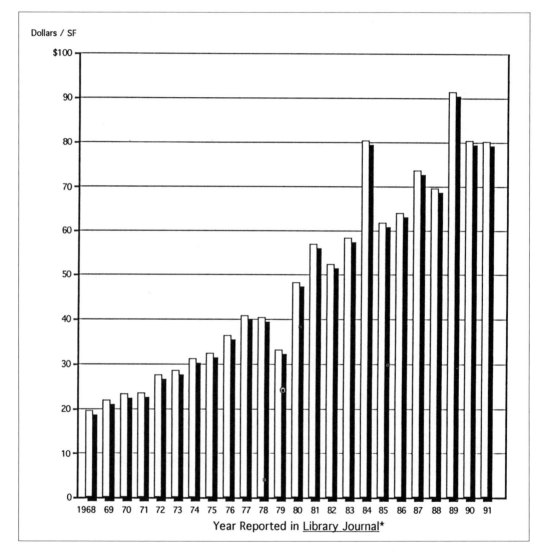

Fig. 2-6. Average Construction costs per Square Foot for Public Libraries

©Reed Publishing

Table 2-8. Projected *Library Journal* Construction Costs Per Square Foot

Fiscal Year	Projected Construction Cost PSF for New Buildings		
	High Avg.	Medium Avg.	Low* Avg.
1994	$108	$95	$82
1995	112	98	85
1996	115	101	88
1997	118	104	90
1998	122	107	93
1999	126	110	95
2000	130	113	98

*The average range is based on a high, medium and low projection of the growth rate.

tant to estimate the cost of construction when the project is to be bid, not the day it is planned. So if the anticipated bid date is one year into the future, an additional inflationary projection must be factored into the estimate.

Based on the *Library Journal* projections and including the lag time for reporting and publication, it is possible to project national average costs per square foot for each year for the next few years. Table 2-9 can be utilized by library planners to determine approximate square-foot costs for new con-

Table 2-9. Projected Construction Costs Per Square Foot (new public library construction)

Year	Projected Construction Cost Per Square Foot for New Buildings		
	High Avg.	Medium Avg.	Low* Avg.
1994	$118	$104	$ 90
1995	122	107	93
1996	126	110	95
1997	130	113	98
1998	133	116	100
1999	137	119	102
2000	140	122	105

*The average range is based on a high, medium and low projection of the growth rate.

struction based on national averages. Find the year that the project is anticipated to be bid and then read to the right to determine the high, medium, and low average cost per square foot estimates.

Again, this type of projection is risky since it assumes a steady increase in construction costs which may prove incorrect; construction costs are notoriously sensitive to inflationary spirals and recessionary drops. At any rate, the projections are based on in actual project costs and can be used with some degree of confidence as long as they are adjusted to local conditions. However, keep in mind that these figures are national averages, and that the construction costs for individual projects will vary above and below this range.

The projected figures based on the *Library Journal* statistics provide a starting point in determining the cost of new construction. However, there are numerous other factors to consider, such as the season when the building is being bid, the general economic climate, the quality of the construction desired, and the typical cost of construction for the locale. While national average figures are helpful, it must be understood that they include a combined total of all public libraries built in the country, which range from the very spartan projects to grand monuments.

Regional Variations: The cost of construction varies significantly from one part of the country to another as well as from one part of a state to another. As a refinement to the average cost data, it is possible to look at the construction cost figures for libraries built within the state or the region of a proposed library project. The first step in this process would be to look at recently reported projects in the same state as the proposed project. Further, projects in the state which are located in comparable communities should be studied in detail. It would be prudent to contact the library administration for these projects and request detailed budgetary information and even time to sit down and discuss the costs of their project.

Visits to Comparable Communities: Visiting a recently completed library construction project in a comparable community can be extremely enlightening. It not only gives library planners the opportunity to see the finished product, but it also allows communication with individuals who have just been through the process. These people are usually more than willing to discuss their "war stories" which may be of help in planning the new building. It is usually wise to visit several projects to get different opinions and to see the different ways successful libraries can be designed.

Along with discovering the interesting and positive aspects of these projects, planners may also learn about a few things they will be eager to avoid. In general, these visits usually create a good deal of enthusiasm and excitement about the project. They also tend to bring out a sense of civic pride when planners see the contrast between a nearby community's library and the inadequate facility at home. This personalizes the project and creates a vested interest in a successful outcome for the project.

Comparable Public Construction Projects: It can be helpful to learn about local construction costs for other public projects such as museums, community college libraries, courthouses, city halls, auditoriums, post offices, and some private-sector buildings such as banks. As the planning team collects this kind of data and compares construction costs for different kinds of facilities, members become more knowledgeable about the potential costs of their own project. The more informed the planning team becomes about this subject, the more accurate their budget estimates will likely become — and the more educated the planners will be when dealing with architects and engineers regarding the project's costs.

Private Sector Estimating Tools: Another important approach in assessing the construction costs for any project is to inspect currently available construction cost indexes such as those published by Marshall and Swift[5] and R. S. Means.[6] These indexes collect construction cost data for various building types, including public libraries, and can be very helpful in assessing the construction costs for any project. Generally, one uses these indexes by first identifying the most recent cost-per-square-foot figure for public libraries and then multiplying that figure by a "locality adjustment factor" provided in a set of tables. As an example, assume that the national average cost per square foot is listed as $100. The next step is to look up the municipality or county where the project is to be built (or one nearby if the one sought is not listed) and find the adjustment or "multiplier" factor. This factor, usually expressed as a decimal, should then be multiplied by the average cost-per-square-foot figure to arrive at the average cost for construction in the desired locality. For example, if the adjustment is 1.30, the construction cost would be $130 per square foot. In some of these indexes, there are additional calculations to perform based on the size of the facility, the linear footage of the exterior of the building, the type of construction, etc.

One of the problems in using these indexes is that they don't always agree with one another. This is due in part to different methods of data collection, but also to the reality that construction cost estimating is not a perfect science. One may wish to choose one service over the others or average different figures provided by the various indexes. In California, the Marshall & Swift index was used recently with the state bond program because Marshall & Swift is a West Coast firm and it was felt that they had a better handle on western construction costs. It should be understood that these commercial indexes, usually don't include costs for site development, demolition, or any built-in furnishing and equipment. It should also be understood that the *Library Journal* construction cost figures do include site development and demolition costs and frequently also include built-in furnishings and equipments costs when these items are bid as part of the construction contract. Regardless of the discrepancy, these two approaches provide an additional perspective and baseline information on the potential cost of construction. With this information, and the costs of comparable nearby projects, library planners should be able to estimate a range of possible costs for the construction contract.

Level of Quality: The final step in assessing the project's construction cost is to determine the level of quality appropriate for the community and any site-specific considerations such as the quality of surrounding buildings and planned developments. However, ascertaining the desired quality level for a community can be difficult. There are many aspects to quality of construction, but the most obvious is the quality of materials and design. Obviously, marble columns will cost more than wooden ones, or a copper roof more than asphalt shingles, etc. But the comparisons don't stop here. The question of quality applies to the entire building, from the structure to the power and lighting plans to the finish schedules, and will definitely have an impact on the cost of construction.

Certain design requirements may be present because of the location and the quality level of development surrounding the site. Sometimes specific types of design are dictated by code or convention. If the building is to be located within a civic center where existing buildings exhibit a particular architectural style, the architect will be hard-pressed to justify departing significantly from that style. It is important to be aware of these limitations and the costs involved before determining even the preliminary estimate. It would not normally be appropriate, for example, to plan a $75-per-square-foot library in a community center where buildings were recently built at a cost of over $140 per square foot.

Obviously, a library built in an area where expectations are high with respect to public architecture will be costlier than libraries in most other areas. Likewise, projects built in small, rural communities with easy access to inexpensive materials and labor may cost substantially less than the national averages. As with the total project costs, the variation in construction costs can be significant. Again, as an example, the projects funded in 1991 with state bond funds in California varied tremendously. The planned cost of construction ranged from $75 per square foot to a high of $150 per square foot and averaged $115. Site development and demolition costs are not included in these figures, and it is interesting to note that when these costs are factored in, the resulting average cost per square foot increases to $145.

Another example of construction cost variations is the Dekalb County Public Library, in Decatur, Georgia just outside of Atlanta. In the late eighties and early nineties, this library built 12 branches and expanded a central library facility. The projects ranged in size from 4,000 square feet up to 53,000 square feet. The average cost per square foot for the buildings alone was $74 with a low of $55 and a high of $82. When site development costs are added, the average cost per square foot for these facilities increased to $93 and ranged between $71 and $115. Construction cost, excluding site development, in the King County Library System in Seattle, for the 18 projects in progress is averaging $149 per square foot with a low of $87 and a high of $210. This information demonstrates that regardless of where in the nation a library is built, a fairly substantial variation in construction costs can be expected within a state, region or even a locale.

One only has to look in the *Library Journal* statistics for the last five years to see the variation in the construction costs per square foot for libraries. For example, while the national average cost per square foot ranged between $65 and $90, the states of California, Connecticut, Florida, Georgia, Illinois, Maryland, Massachusetts, Michigan, Minnesota, Nevada, New Jersey, New York, North Carolina, Ohio, Virginia, and Washington had projects that cost over $120 per square foot. The states of Alabama, Arizona, Arkansas, California, Colorado, Delaware, Florida, Georgia, Illinois, Indiana, Iowa, Kansas, Kentucky, Louisiana, Maryland, Michigan, Minnesota, Mississippi, Missouri, Montana, Nebraska, Nevada, New York, North Carolina, Oklahoma, Oregon, Pennsylvania, South Carolina, Tennessee, Texas, Virginia, Washington and Wisconsin all reported projects that cost less than $50 per square foot over the same five year period. Some of this variation can be accounted for by differences in the economies of different states, but not all of it can, because some of the states (California, Florida, Georgia, Illinois, Maryland, Michigan, Minnesota, Nevada, New York, North Carolina, and Washington) appear on both lists.

There is obviously substantial variation in construction costs because library buildings are built at varying levels of quality. Only local library planners can ascertain the appropriate quality level for their facility. This should be decided carefully and with reasonable input from the community. In many cases, it is obvious what the community wants, but often it is not, or worse, there is a great deal of argument over the subject. Funding agencies will often want to be involved in this decision; this is appropriate since they are likely to foot the bill to a large extent. It is often

important for library planners to try to provide a range of costs (for example, between $90 and $100 per square foot) to help keep the discussion within reasonable boundaries.

For example, if it appears that a reasonable cost for "average" construction in the area would be approximately $80 per square foot, the planning team may wish to use this figure as a starting point. The argument goes like this:

> You would agree that our community is at least "average," would you not? Well then, we could build the library building for $80 per square foot, or we could try to build a slightly better facility that will help create some civic pride in the community. You know that community "A" built a library recently for $100 per square foot and we're certainly better off, aren't we? Of course we are. The location we've picked is a good one, but it's right next to that new development with all that really nice architecture. We wouldn't want the new library to look shabby in comparison, would we? Did you know that those buildings cost about $110 per square foot? Yes, that's right, and they were built just last year for that cost, but you know construction continues to go up every day. How would you feel if we tried to build the library for at least $115 or maybe even $120 per square foot and really made it something to be proud? Yes, I agree buildings cost a lot these days, but you usually get what you pay for.

Armed with the information regarding variable costs and a general idea of the desired level of quality for the facility, the library planning team should be closer to a cost estimate that is reasonable and defensible as well as customized to the project's specific locale. Once all historical cost information has been gathered and analyzed, it is time to come up with a number. There is, however, one last consideration to make in order to arrive at the preliminary construction cost estimate.

Inflation: It is not appropriate to plan projects based solely on the cost of previous projects, since those costs are dated. As can be seen from the previous example, some cost escalation should be planned into the project, particularly in highly inflationary times. A reasonable inflation factor must be added or else a shortfall is very likely at the time of bidding the construction contract. This is particularly true if the building will not be bid for at least another two or three years. The question is, What is a reasonable rate of inflation to use? Again, this varies from one region to another and changes from year to year. As discussed earlier, historically, public library construction has gone up approximately five percent per year over the last 24 years. This is a reasonable figure to use unless better information is available.

It is wise to verify this figure with those working in the construction industry, if possible. Construction cost estimators probably have the best handle on the rate of inflation in the industry, but architects and contractors will also have some idea. Sometimes momentary downturns or "spurts" in the industry can provide library planners with either a windfall or a shortfall. There is not much to be done to plan for these variations in the economic climate except to have a reasonable project contingency fund available for shortfalls and be ready to upgrade finishes or furnishings and equipment in the event of a windfall. Be aware that these kinds of variations can be as much as 10 to 15 percent or more during significant shifts in the economy.

While information from individuals in the construction industry is often useful, care must be exercised in what one asks for. One mistake library planners often make is to ask local contractors about the cost of constructing a library. While it is a contractor's business to quote construction costs, this is normally done based on a set of completed working drawings and specifications. Without these detailed documents, a general contractor cannot accurately estimate the costs of a public

library or any other building. Due partly to the electronic age, library buildings are much more complex and therefore more expensive structures than many contractors may realize. Further, it has been the author's experience that the quality level envisioned by general contractors and library planners are often widely disparate. Only after the architectural drawings have been developed is it reasonable to request assistance from a contractor regarding the possible cost of a building. As a matter of fact, as will be discussed later, it can be helpful to have the plans reviewed by trusted local contractors during the design phase providing they will not be bidding on the job.

Another tempting approach is to ask local architects what they think the cost of the library building will be. First, this is simply not appropriate to ask of architects who are not employed by the library planners. Ethically, the practice is questionable and it may not even be helpful. It makes sense only for an architect interested in a potential job to attempt to understand what the potential wants to hear and then provide it. At this stage an architect "off the street," like a contractor, lacks any real basis for more than an educated guess since no plans or specifications exist. Generally, most architectural firms are very professional and interested in arriving at a realistic cost for all projects they work on. However, because of the inherent lack of objectivity created by their desire to be hired for a job, some architects may not always be as straightforward and accurate as one might wish in providing estimates at this early stage. They may be persuaded that the best way to get a job is to provide the client with cost figures that are low. This only creates a lose/lose situation for both the architect and the library planners. Or the architectural firm may indulge itself and set the cost figure above what is necessary to increase the fee (since most fees are based on a percentage of the construction cost), or provide a "monument" which can be later used as a marketing tool for future jobs. While most architects would not exercise either of these options, it is not appropriate or advantageous to place the temptation before an architect who may end up working on the project.

The appropriate time to ask an architect the cost of a construction project is during the design of the project after the firm has been hired. In fact, an architect should be required to provide budget estimates at all three stages of plans development, schematic, design development, and final contract documents. Further, library planners may be well advised to obtain a "second opinion" from an independent professional cost estimating firm as the plans evolve. Ultimately, the cost of the building will not be known for certain until a contractor bids on the project, but at these successive stages an architect skilled in cost estimating should be able to provide increasingly accurate estimates.

In reality, the planning team will not know the actual cost of construction until the building has been bid and built and all change orders and liens have been settled. However, this is a little late to determine the budget. So, based upon the information presented in this book as well as other sources, the library planning team must come up with a construction cost figure. It is never easy, but as long as the team is sincere and diligent at arriving at a number, the chances of "getting in the ballpark" are greatly improved. Care should be taken to document the decision since undoubtedly the preliminary cost figure will be questioned by someone during the process of finding funds for the project. If the process is well justified and can be easily and quickly explained, the chances are the planning team's figure will gain credibility with the community and funding agencies.

Permits, Utility Connection, and Development Fees: Many communities require construction permits as well as utility connection and development fees that are charged to projects. Frequently, these permits and fees are waived by a local jurisdiction for its own public construction projects, but not always. It is important to look into this matter early. If the library project will be charged for building permits, water and sewer tap fees, or standard "developer" fees such as signalization, road improvements, etc., it is important to know these costs as soon as possible. In some communities these fees can run into the thousands of dollars. Sometimes certain permits and fees can be assessed whether the project is for new construction or remodeling.

Remodeling

The term "construction contract" often includes more than just the constructing of new square footage. It also means the remodeling, retrofit, or rehabilitation of existing buildings. Remodeling may take several forms for a public library project. The first and most obvious is simply a remodeling of the existing library facility. This may result in a minor rehabilitation of certain aspects of the facility such as a retrofit for disabled access, energy conservation, or a facelift of various finishes. Remodeling may also include more extensive structural changes that completely reorganize the building. This can be an extremely challenging project that is often difficult to budget because internal demolition and reconstruction sometimes involve costly unknown conditions that must be remedied. Whether the remodeling is a minimal "cosmetic" change or a more extensive rehabilitation of the structure involving tearing out walls, ceilings, and even floors, cost estimating for remodeling is difficult and must be performed for the most part by professional architects, engineers, and cost estimators. A substantial contingency fund is almost always prudent.

Addition/Remodeling Project: Another kind of remodeling project combines an addition with remodeling. In this case, new square footage is added to an existing library at the same time the building is being remodeled. It is almost impossible to build an addition on an existing library building without some remodeling. In fact, there is usually a greater need for remodeling than is generally acknowledged at the beginning of the project. Usually, it is discovered during either design or construction that the scope of the job has been underestimated. Perhaps there is some unforseen code requirement that must be met, or the condition of the existing facility is not what it was thought to be. The latter often occurs with buildings that were not built according to their original plans and specifications. In situations where the original plans and specifications no longer exist, it is possible that hidden conditions such as the presence of asbestos may be discovered during remodeling. Whatever the problem, these situations must be corrected and this is one of the reasons that such projects often involve cost overruns. In short, there is no precise way to estimate the costs of a remodeling project with absolute certainty even with the help of professionals. It is prudent to have an even more generous contingency fund available for remodeling projects than for new construction.

Conversion Project: The third type of remodeling project is the conversion of an existing building into a public library. There are many examples of buildings that have been converted into library facilities, from fire stations to furniture stores. Library planners must recognize that this type of project usually involves a certain number of compromises and trade-offs with respect to both the exterior design of the building and the interior layout. The following discussion regarding the conversion of an existing building actually applies to any type of remodeling project. During all remodel-ing projects, but most frequently during a conversion project, the library planners are constantly involved in evaluating the cost/benefit ratio of many suggested approaches to the work.

For example, public libraries generally work best in the long run if there is a good deal of flexible open space that can be easily supervised and rearranged later. This may mean that internal structural walls need to be removed, which can be extremely expensive. There are many such considerations when a building is being acquired for the purpose of conversion. The cost of acquiring a building, as with a site, includes both the purchase price of the property and the cost of development. While the cost of new construction is admittedly high, it allows considerably more freedom of design in terms of both functionality and aesthetics. Library planners must determine if the cost savings of buying an existing building are significant enough to accept some design trade-offs. For some projects, this option can cost as much as new construction or even more. This is usually not acceptable unless the existing building has historical significance.

Feasibility Analysis: Before deciding to embark on a conversion project, it is essential to conduct a feasibility analysis. This study should evaluate the condition of the building under consideration as well as its suitability to house the planned public library. The first step in any feasibility analysis is to make certain that the existing structure is large enough to accommodate the library's spatial needs, or that there is land available to expand the facility if necessary. After this, other aspects must be considered including a structural analysis, inspections for hazardous materials, an energy analysis including mechanical and electrical systems, and general building code compliance, as well as an overall architectural and engineering cost estimate review.

These steps can take considerable time and be extensive in scope as well as costly if the building is sizable and the analysis complex. Individual aspects of a feasibility analysis for an existing building are described below.

Structural Engineering Study: After determining that the building is large enough to house the library, one of the first considerations should be the building's structural capabilities. This requires an engineer to perform a structural engineering analysis. The general condition of the building should be surveyed including the foundations, walls, columns, floors, and roof systems. It is particularly important at this point to understand that the minimum load requirements for open bookstacks is 150 pounds per square foot. All areas of the building except for planned office space should have this floor load capability to allow for future rearrangement of bookstacks.

There are varying levels of structural engineering studies and library planners should be careful to obtain only what is necessary, but not less that what is appropriate. If the building is very old, out of date from a code compliance standpoint, and in poor condition, the engineering study should be in-depth. If the building is relatively new, meets current codes, and has been well maintained, the engineering study may be almost cursory. Because of this variation in the level of study needed as well as the varying size and complexity of existing buildings, the cost of a structural study ranges significantly. The only way to budget for this expenditure is to get quotes from an architect or engineering firm.

Asbestos Study: Another important investigation is a building survey for the presence of asbestos. Asbestos is commonly found in older buildings but is considered a health hazard. It is important to determine if asbestos is present and, if so, in what quantity and form. The next determination is if the asbestos will have to be removed or encapsulated and how much this will cost. Since asbestos is considered toxic and must be handled with care and disposed of in a specific manner, its removal can be expensive especially if it is pervasive or difficult to reach.

Again, the cost of the studies will vary as will the cost of asbestos removal. State OSHA offices can frequently provide a list of "certified" asbestos consulting firms capable of providing asbestos surveys. Based on the results of these surveys, these firms can occasionally provide estimates on the cost of removal, but frequently this cannot be done until an architect has developed a demolition plan and a cost estimator has provided a cost estimate for the work. Asbestos can quickly turn what appears to be a relatively inexpensive building into an extremely expensive one.

Energy Audit, Mechanical, and Electrical Inspections: Most buildings built before the mid-seventies are significantly less energy efficient than those built after the energy crisis of 1973. Regardless of when the building was built, an energy audit of its various systems should be performed to determine how it can be made more energy efficient and brought up to modern standards. As part of the energy audit, a mechanical engineer should inspect and report on the heating, ventilating, and air conditioning (HVAC) system. Further, the quality and quantity of building insulation in the walls and ceiling should be reviewed along with any other physical systems such as windows and doorways. In addition, it is wise to have an electrical engineer inspect and report on the building's electrical and data communications systems. In each case, the engineers should provide a report indicating what is necessary to bring the existing facility up to current state and local building codes.

Once again, the cost of these inspections depends on the degree of study needed, which depends in turn on the scope of the project and the size and condition of the existing structure. Architects can often assist with this process, but actual cost estimates for the studies will usually have to be quoted with the assistance of engineering firms. It is always best to obtain several price quotes, to contact references, and to see copies of previous reports. If a sloppy preliminary study greatly increased the cost of a previous project, it would be helpful to find this out in advance.

Architectural Review and Cost Estimator: Once all these studies have been completed, it is necessary to have them reviewed by an architect and cost estimator. These professionals can assimilate this information and provide library planners with a preliminary conceptual plan and estimate of what it will cost to remodel the building and bring it up to current building codes. *It is extremely difficult, if not impossible, for lay people to estimate the cost of remodeling.* These costs are extremely difficult to estimate accurately even for professionals in the construction industry. There simply is no way to provide an accurate cost per square foot figure for remodeling projects because these costs are far too project-specific and technical in nature. Cost estimates for remodeling can only be developed as the plans are developed and on the basis of professional analysis.

At the same time, however, it is occasionally useful to try to come up with a very rough estimate for remodeling work without the use of professionals just to get a ballpark cost. While this process is not generally recommended other than at a very early stage of estimating a remodeling project, it is possible to use the following formula for estimating remodeling based on the costs for new construction in an area:

Costs for remodeling existing structures typically can be estimated based on a proportion of the cost of new construction. A project involving an area of minimal remodeling can apply an estimate of 25 percent of the cost per square foot for new construction to the area of the building being remodeled. A moderate remodeling project can estimate remodeling costs at 50 percent of the cost per square foot for new construction. And a major remodeling effort would require 75 percent of the cost of new construction. In some cases, such as full restoration to a historic period, the costs for remodeling a building or a part of a building can approach or even exceed the cost for new construction.[7]

Again, caution must be urged, since part of the difficulty of using this approach is that the determination of what is "minimal," "moderate," and "major" is not only subjective, but subject to errors in judgment when made by lay people with little experience in estimating construction costs.

While some architects and engineers with a lot of experience in remodeling can take a cursory look at a building and provide a ballpark figure, these estimates are extremely soft and should not be utilized by library planners. Experience frequently shows that such estimates are low. Most professionals will advise caution and indicate that their estimates are contingent upon further study. Final decisions regarding the feasibility of the project should not be made until the detailed studies are performed. This is one of the reasons that remodeling projects of any kind are costly. It is possible to spend a significant amount of money on simply studying an existing building only to find out that the cost of remodeling it is prohibitive. Even if the cost appears reasonable at this early stage, costs will change, sometimes dramatically, as tests and other work progress. Even though the project cost estimates should become more and more realistic as plans are developed, there may still be a surprise when the bids come in, since contractors frequently give themselves some degree of "cushion" when bidding on remodeling projects.

Architectural and Engineering (A&E) Services

In addition to the specialized engineering studies required for remodeling projects, it is necessary to budget for routine design services to be performed by professional architects and engineers for any construction project. These services are necessary either for remodeling or new construction. Architectural and engineering fees are necessary for developing plans and specifications for constructing the building. On small projects there is sometimes the temptation to skip this step and go straight to a contractor to have the building constructed, but, this approach will almost always end in disaster. Library planners will need to contract for several phases of design services in order to have a successful project.

Conceptual Plans

Conceptual plans provide library planners with an early design or "concept" of the project. For a new building this will usually be a preliminary site plan, a basic floor plan that identifies the major programmed areas of the library, and some rough elevations, or "massing studies" of how the building will look. This first step is important for library planners and the community to get an idea of what the library will look like and how the basic spaces will be arranged. It also enables the architect to get the owner's input into the design at an early stage. This input is essential throughout the process in order for the architect to provide the client with a satisfactory design. If the client is unhappy with the architect's concept, it is not difficult at this point for the architect to rethink the project and present a new concept without losing much time or money.

In addition to looking at the proposed building elevations, the planning team should carefully review the site plan.

Library planners should also review the floor plan with an eye towards the functionality of the building. What must be worked out with the architect at this point is the allocation of the major programmed areas of the library. In order to ensure that this is done adequately, it is usually helpful to call in a library consultant at this stage. Library consultants usually have considerable experience in further interpreting the library program to the architect and explaining why certain designs that look good on paper may not work in reality. The goal at this stage is to develop a plan in which the basic spatial requirements of the major programmed areas have been met. The planning team should not proceed past this phase until this has been accomplished or there will be considerable difficulty later on.

Schematic Plans

Schematic plans are developed once conceptual plans have been approved by the owner. The schematic plans should, at minimum, include a site plan showing the library building, parking lot, access roads, and any anticipated future expansion. They should provide elevations of all four sides of the building, one or two sections through the building, outline specifications describing the type of construction, and a floor plan showing a complete furnishings and equipment layout to scale.

It is particularly important at this stage to obtain a well-thought-out furnishings and equipment plan for the library. While some architectural firms may resist it, library planners must realize that this may be the single most important factor in creating a building that will work well as a library. If the furnishings and equipment called for in the building program cannot adequately be laid out on the floor plan, the building will probably never function efficiently as a library. *Library planners should not approve schematic plans until they are certain the plans will meet the functional requirements of the building program.* Again, it is important at this time to work with an experienced library consultant who understands the problems associated with a quality functional layout for a public library building.

It is easy to get caught up with the exterior look of the building and whether or not it matches nearby buildings and to forget to look carefully at how the interior of the building will function. If this happens, the library staff and patrons will suffer for years with a library that is difficult to use and expensive to operate. Considering the long-term consequences, it is prudent to spend a little extra time and money to engage experts to work with the architect and interior designer to produce the most functional library possible.

Design Development (Preliminary) Plans

Once schematic plans have been accepted by library planners, the architect should be instructed to complete "preliminary" or design development plans. These are similar to schematic plans but provide more detail. A site plan, elevations, and building sections show a great deal more detail than at the schematic stage. Along with draft specifications, there should be a preliminary finish schedule indicating the types of materials to be used on floors, ceilings, and walls for all interior spaces. Architectural floor plans showing the "final" furnishings and equipment layout with all major and critical dimensions and all columns and walls are shown along with room designations.

This last set of plans is critical. It is the basis of two other plans that will be provided by the electrical engineers and/or lighting consultants. A lighting system plan and an electrical power and signal plan should also be prepared at the time of design development for review by library planners. These plans should be carefully compared to the furnishing and equipment layout to make certain that adequate lighting, pow-

er, and data distribution are provided where needed. One of the best ways to do this is to have the two sets of plans created so that the lighting plan and the power and signal plan can be overlaid or printed on the furnishings and equipment plan. This allows library planners to see how the two plans line up and precisely determine if the placement of light fixtures and power and data outlets is satisfactory. Other plans, such as preliminary mechanical and plumbing plans, may also be produced at this stage as well as a preliminary signage plan.

Library planners must carefully review all aspects of the design development submittal since this is the last chance to make significant changes before the architect moves into working drawings. Significant changes after this point will be expensive and time-consuming. It is particularly important for library planners to study the electrical and lighting overlays. These two plans show the relationship of the library's furnishings and equipment layout to the building's lighting, electrical, and data distribution systems. If the lighting or placement of outlets are not correct at this point, they are not likely to adequately meet the library's needs once the building is completed. Again, it is vitally important to obtain the assistance of a professional library consultant, together with the library's professional staff to review these plans to avoid any mistakes that could affect the building for many years.

Working Drawings and Specifications (Contract Documents)

After the design development plans have been accepted, the architect will begin work on the final contract documents, more commonly called working drawings and specifications. These documents will form the legal basis on which contractors will prepare bids for the library building. A complete set of construction documents, including all drawings, specifications, and

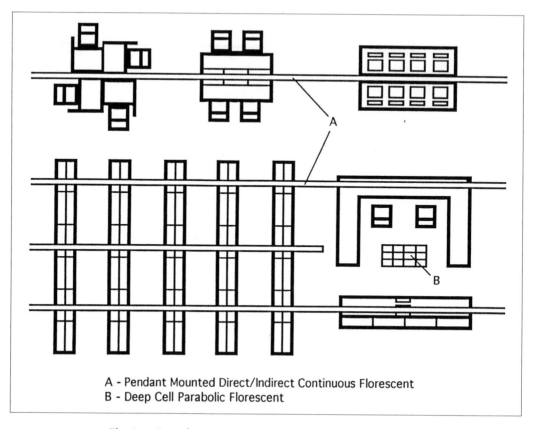

A - Pendant Mounted Direct/Indirect Continuous Florescent
B - Deep Cell Parabolic Florescent

Fig. 2-7. Furnishing & Equipment Plan with Lighting Overlay

contract language along with all other documentation required as part of the bid package, will be submitted to the library planners for approval before the project is bid. All building systems should be descriptively diagrammed to fully illustrate their proposed scope and function.

If the library planners do not have the technical expertise to adequately review these plans themselves (which is usually the case), it will be necessary once again obtain expert assistance. While it is helpful to have a library consultant review the plans at this stage, it is even more important to have them reviewed by someone with experience in the building industry. If library planners have access to a local codes official or a public works department that employs such individuals, the work-

ing drawings as well as each phase of plans development should be reviewed by them. If local public works officials are not available, library planners may wish to employ a private construction management firm to review and double check the plans. If this is not possible, it would be helpful, at a minimum, to have the plans reviewed by someone like a retired contractor, architect, or engineer, who can usually be retained for a nominal fee.

Architectural and Enginering Fees

The fees for architectural and engineering design (A&E fees) are usually quoted together, in most cases, as a percentage of the construction contract, although occasionally a lump-sum fee can be negotiated. The cost of architectural and engineering ser-

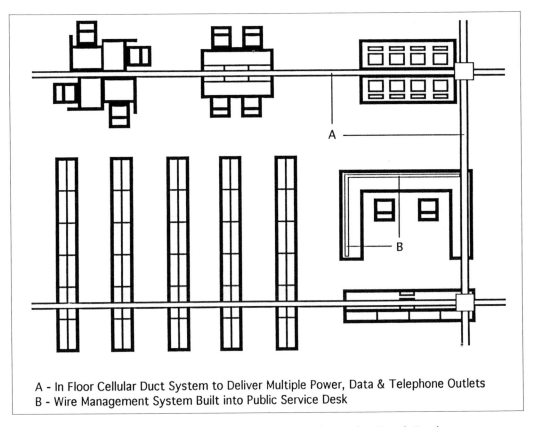

A - In Floor Cellular Duct System to Deliver Multiple Power, Data & Telephone Outlets
B - Wire Management System Built into Public Service Desk

Fig. 2-8. Furnishing & Equipment Plan with Electrical & Signal Overlay

varies tremendously depending upon a number of factors. The first is the size of the project. Smaller projects usually require a higher percentage in order to make the job cost effective for the architectural firm. The second factor is the type and complexity of the project. A highly complex project such as a remodeling job may command a higher percentage than straightforward new construction. The depth and quality of design services desired also affects the fee. If the client wants only basic services, the price is lower than for services which include in-depth feasibility studies, models, computer-aided design, or community presentations with audiovisuals.

Architects and engineers, like other professionals are in business to make a profit. If they are in high demand, their fees tend to rise. Nationally or internationally known architects and engineers usually get a higher percentage than local firms. The distance the architect or engineer must travel to the job site will also increase the cost of services since reimbursable expenses such as mileage and meals may be added to the fee. Fees also vary from one part of the country to another and between rural and urban areas. Economic downturns can result in lower negotiated A&E fees if firms are "hungry" for work. Occasionally, other factors will affect fees. Sometimes a community-spirited firm is willing to provide some work at a reduced rate. This is not a common practice, however.

The range of A&E fees that library planners may see quoted for architectural and engineering design services is usually between 6 and 12 percent (although fees of 15 and even 20 percent are possible). These fees include the architect's fee plus standard engineering fees such as mechanical, structural, electrical, plumbing etc. These are often referred to as "basic services" and do not include fees for specialized consultants such as acoustical and traffic engineers or telecommunications or signage consultants. These costs will need to be negotiated individually if the services are needed. A&E fees at 6 percent are truly basic services; don't expect any fancy models or renderings. This level of fee is usually seen only in rural areas for straightforward and simple new construction projects. Fees at 12 percent should give the client a good deal more than basic services unless the job is particularly difficult. The rates library planners will most often see quoted for library projects are between 7 and 9 percent (8 percent average) with regional variations. Remember, the A&E fee is calculated as a percentage of the construction contract, which will usually include any site development and demolition and may well include some built-in furnishings and equipment. Further, architectural firms will frequently ask that reimbursables expenses such as the costs of reproducing plans and specifications be paid by the owner in addition to the percentage fee, although this can often be negotiated.

In addition to actually drawing plans and writing specifications, most architectural firms offer construction administration — monitoring the construction for compliance with the contract documents. This service is optional and may not be necessary if library planners have access to a public works department that is qualified to perform this activity. Further, there has been over the past decade or two a trend toward separating the design and construction administration activities, which provides for a somewhat improved checks and balances system in the construction industry.

Construction Management

Local Public Works Department

For communities that have a local public works department, this agency may be heavily involved in the management of the project, including design approval, code compliance, and construction administration. Public works departments frequently are funded in part by internal charges for these activities on a project-by-project basis. Many communities have a standard percentage of the construction cost for administration services which is funneled to the public works department.

Some very large public works departments have architects and engineers on staff who not only will review the design documents, but also may do the design work on a relatively small job and avoid contracting with an outside architect altogether. This approach has advantages and disadvantages, and library planners should study it carefully. Most public works departments will perform code compliance plans reviews and many will perform contract administration. It is frequently to the advantage of library planners to have public works department staff (asssuming they are available and competent) handle the day-to-day administration of the construction contract by reviewing change orders and payment requests from the contractors as well as monitoring construction.

Construction Management Firm

If no local public works staff is available, a common alternative is to hire a construction management firm to review the architectural plans and assist with scheduling, cost estimating, bidding, and general management of the construction contract. This includes construction administration activities such as on-site inspections, reviewing payment requests and change orders, etc. Some construction management firms also offer a service known as "value engineering," which is essentially reviewing the design documents and cost estimates from a cost-benefit standpoint. Construction management as a separate discipline has grown in recent years, but is still most commonly used for fairly large or complicated projects, or by an owner who has many projects to administer at once (such as several branch libraries under design and construction at the same time).

The costs for construction management services vary depending on the scope of services to be provided, the size and complexity of the job, the quality and reputation of the firm, and the marketplace. A typical range of fees is from 1 to 5 percent of the construction contract cost with the service generally running about 3 percent. Fees may be broken down and quoted separately for varying levels of services; they may also be calculated on a per-project basis, where the number of staff hours for each activity is estimated and a per-hour or per-diem rate is utilized to provide clients with a lump-sum cost quote. Again, services for a construction management firm can be obtained through a request for proposal process.

Professional Cost Estimator

Traditionally, the architect and engineers provide the owner with cost estimates as plans develop. This assumes first that the architect and engineers are good cost estimators, and second, that they can be objective about their own work and the cost of the project. Most architectural firms still offer in-house cost estimating services, but many architects subcontract this out to other firms. Some owners may want to take this process out of the hands of the architectural firm and contract independently with another professional. This approach assures the greatest independence and objectivity on the part of the cost estimator and frequently provides a more accurate cost estimate.

In addition to the preliminary project cost estimate put together by the library planners, updated cost estimates should be obtained at the three main plans review stages (schematic, design development and working drawings). Athough, cost estimates provided at the schematic plans stage will be rough compared to later estimates, financing for a library project is often based on the estimate provided at this stage. Because of this, project contingencies for these projects should be reasonable. Most estimates at the schematic stage will be based on square footage. In other words, the construction estimator will make assumptions of how much the various components of the building (electrical, HVAC, structural, etc.) will cost per square foot and provide an estimate in the format shown in Table 2-10. These estimates will be based on construction contracts and/or regional cost figures. Most cost estimators today have at their disposal a great deal of information either in database or spreadsheet form. The computerized approach to cost estimating has greatly increased its speed and to some extent its accuracy. However, local experience is an important consideration in cost estimating, especially in the later stages.

As the architectural plans are developed and better defined, the accuracy of the cost estimate should increase because the cost estimator has more information regarding the actual materials and quantities that will be utilized. At the design development stage, the cost estimate becomes more specific and by the final working

Table 2-10. Schematic Cost Per Square Foot Estimate*
(for a 10,000-square-foot building)

Building Item	Cost per Sq. Ft.	Total Cost
Mechanical	$15.00	$ 150,000
Plumbing	5.00	50,000
Electrical	11.00	110,000
Equipment	9.00	90,000

*Cost figures are for illustration only.

drawing stage it should be very specific and quite accurate. Professionally prepared construction cost estimates at both the design development and working drawings stage should provide planners with a detailed cost estimate and a summary based on the actual cost of materials and labor for the various building systems. This can be done by using the Construction Specifications Institute (CSI) masterformat divisions (site work, concrete, masonry, metals, finishes, mechanical, electrical etc.) or a similar estimating system that provides a detailed cost breakdown. The cost estimate should provide line items including quantities, unit costs, and total quantity costs as in Table 2-11. Only when the cost estimate gets down to this level of detail can library planners and funding agencies begin to feel confident about the accuracy of the estimates (assuming the unit cost figures are accurate to begin with).

The cost of preparing estimates of this type depends upon the size, nature, and complexity of the construction project. Just as with architectural fees, cost estimating fees are proportionately higher for smaller jobs and for remodeling work. Professional cost estimators usually work on a percentage basis, and their fee is often quoted as a percentage of either the architect's fees or the construction cost. For a "full service," high-quality estimate for all three major stages of design, cost stimating firms often charge a fee of between 8

and 12 percent of the A&E fees. On average, 10 percent of the A&E fee is reasonable for a professional quality cost estimate; however, cost estimating firms can calculate the cost of an estimate on an hourly basis or as a percentage of the estimated construction contract if requested. The corresponding percentage of the construction contract is approximately .8 percent for a professional cost estimate with some variation up or down depending upon the size and complexity of the job.

Because of the expense of these estimates, it is often tempting to skip them and simply trust that the architectural firm will complete the building within the budget. This is an "ostrich with its head in the sand" approach to bidding projects. No one knows for sure what a building will cost (not even the architect and local contractors) until final cost quotes are in and bids are submitted, but without well-prepared and periodic cost estimates, the construction project can quickly go astray. Library planners, with their local funding agency, can find themselves with bids that are significantly over the budget. In order to avoid this embarrassment, and the loss of time, effort, and money for redesign, it is generally best to pay for a little "insurance" and have periodic "reality checks" as the project is developing.

If, in the case of "shoestring" projects, this is simply not possible, there is an alternative to consider. In small towns, it is often possible to get a retired or an inde-

Table 2-11. Sample Section of a Construction Estimate*

Description	Quantity	Unit	Unit Cost	Total Cost
ELECTRICAL				
Lighting fixture "A"	100	EA	$100	$ 10,000
Lighting fixture "B"	50	EA	125	6,250
Cellular under floor duct system	200	LF	40	8,000
Switches & dimmers	50	EA	45	2,250
TOTAL ELECTRICAL				$26,500

*Cost figures are for illustration only.

pendent contractor who will not be bidding on the job to look at the architectural plans and specifications and provide a cost estimate for a nominal fee. This is not an ideal approach, but it may provide some insight into actual costs before the project is advertised for bids. This approach can provide realistic estimates if the individuals performing the service are diligent and in touch with current costs. Further, taking this approach is certainly better than "flying blind" into the bid opening.

Library Consultant

Hiring a library consultant with library building experience is another form of "insurance" which is money well spent. Library administrators, boards, and local government officials who will probably face only one or two library building projects in their lifetime frequently call upon professional librarians who have considerable experience and knowledge in planning and executing a library building project. Most library building consultants gain their library building planning experience as library directors involved in building a library in their own communities. Some individuals gain experience in regional library systems or as state library consultants.

Usually they are asked by colleagues to advise on a building project, or they may respond to a Request for Proposal (RFP) solicitation and successfully gain a contract. Generally, if they have been involved in executing a successful library building project, their experience is noted and their time is frequently in demand by those with less knowledge and experience. Many consultants work on a part-time basis and hold full-time positions. Some consultants become successful enough to go into the business full time, set up consulting partnerships or sole proprietorships, advertise in national trade journals, and appear frequently at professional conferences.

American Library Association's Library Building Consultant List

While there are many individuals practicing various forms of library consulting at the regional and state level, it is important to know that the American Library Association (ALA) maintains a directory of nationally recognized library building consultants.[8] This directory provides the name, address, and telephone number of library building consultants practicing around the country, a list of recent consulting projects, a description of the services provided by the consultant, and their availability and preferred fee structure. For legal reasons, ALA does not endorse individuals but it does provide the profession with a tool to obtain quality consulting services by publishing the directory and keeping it current. A copy of the directory is available from ALA for a nominal fee by calling the toll free number: (800) 545-2433 and asking for the Library Administration and Management Association.

In order to avoid costly mistakes and the loss of time, the decision to hire a library consultant should be made as early in the library planning process as possible. The experience that a well-qualified library consultant brings to the project in terms of saving costs will usually more than make up for his or her fee. This is particularly true today, since the cost of construction is so high that one minor mistake can cost a jurisdiction thousands of dollars not only in the capital budget, but over many years in wasted operating funds.

Most nationally recognized library consultants have experience in all aspects of planning a library building: needs assessment, facility master plans, site selection, building programming, architectural plans review, project financing, and budget preparation. Jurisdictions may want to hire a consultant to work on specific parts of the process or to advise them throughout the entire process. The process of hiring a consultant in most cases will be dictated by the local jurisdiction's procedures regarding the acquisition of professional services.

In some cases, this process may be as simple as a telephone call, or an interview with a prospective consultant who has been recommended by a colleague. In other cases, the jurisdiction may wish to mail out formal RFPs and review the responses before interviewing and hiring. In any case, it is extremely important to obtain references for recent projects as well as examples of the consultant's work—copies of building programs, master plans, etc. Further, library planners should interview the consultant to make sure that they can work easily with that individual. Finally, regardless of who is hired, a consulting contract should be drawn up describing as precisely as possible what the consultant is to do and at what expense to the local jurisdiction.

Request for Proposal (RFP)

One advantage of doing an RFP is that it allows many consultants to make a proposal. This provides the local jurisdiction with an opportunity to better understand the type and quality of consulting services available. It is important to recognize that the quality of the proposals received from consultants will often reflect the quality of the RFP itself. It is up to the prospective client to define the problem as clearly and concisely as possible and to provide a format for the RFP that requires the consultant to give a clear picture of his or her experience and methodology. Many jurisdictions have standard RFP formats that can be adapted to the library project. If none is available, the following outline can be used for an RFP for library building consulting services.

General Information: This section provides the consultant with general information about submitting the proposal: the number of copies to submit; the method by which the proposal should be submitted; the address to which it should be submitted; and the date and time by which it must be received. This section should also contain the name, address, and telephone number of a contact person.

Further, the local project coordinator should be identified and the method of payment given, along with an anticipated schedule of payments. The type of contract (fixed fee, etc.) resulting from a successful proposal should be specified as well as criteria for awarding the contract (lowest price, or best overall proposal). The RFP should always state that the issuing agency has the right to reject any and all proposals.

Although optional, it is sometimes helpful to state in the RFP if there is a cost constraint or a maximum amount of funding available for the consulting contract. Finally, if there are any other specific local bidding and contracting requirements, they should be clearly stated.

Statement of the Problem: The prospective client should carefully define the problem that needs to be solved. For example, the library is too small and is out of space, but the jurisdiction is unsure if the solution is a building expansion, a new building, or several branches. Further, it may be uncertain that there is enough land available to expand, or which of several possible sites would be best to build upon. As part of this section, it is wise to include a reasonable amount of background material regarding the library and any previous management studies, building plans, or associated planning activities. Finally, this section should ask the consultant to concisely restate the problem in the proposal.

Work Product: The RFP should clearly state what the local jurisdiction expects to receive as a final product—a report, presentations, etc. The number of reports or presentations needed should be stated. It is also important to specify what constitutes an acceptable report or presentation.

Work Plan and Timetable: This section should ask the consultant to describe a plan for accomplishing the work assignment. If the jurisdiction has a specific deadline for completing the work, it should be stated here. Further, the consultant should be asked to indicate the number of hours expected to be allocated to each task. The response will normally be in the form of a chronology of events which describe, step by step, when the consultant will perform the proposed work. The response should also outline in detail the services the consultant will provide.

Experience, Education, and Publications: This section should identify the key consulting staff who will work on the project and ask the consultant to provide a resume including his or her educational experience and pertinent publications. Most importantly, the consultant should be asked to provide descriptions of similar projects carried out in recent years. References for each project should be identified by name and title, with a telephone number and address. Finally, a sample of the consultant's work, such as a recent building program, can be requested to be returned to the consultant upon request.

Cost Analysis: This section may require the consultant to provide a brief breakdown of costs for the services to be provided along with a total bid for the project. Staff costs, supplies, direct costs such as telecommunications, transportation costs, and general administrative overhead can be detailed, or a simple lump sum may be stated. Most consulting firms prefer the latter since it allows them more flexibility, but still provides the client with an overall "ceiling" for the cost of the contract. If additional work beyond that provided in the proposal is potentially desirable, it will be useful to require the consultant to provide a fixed per diem which can be utilized at the local jurisdiction's discretion.

Additional Information and Exceptions: This section provides the consultant the opportunity to include any other pertinent information not asked for elsewhere in the RFP. This section also allows the consultant the opportunity to state if the proposal contains any exceptions to the requirements of the RFP.

Signature of Consultant: The section should require the consultant to sign and date the proposal.

For jurisdictions with the time and inclination to evaluate numerous proposals, the RFP process is a good way to select a consulting firm. However, this approach may miss some of the best and/or busiest consultants who do not have the time or inclination to respond to an RFP. In some cases, if the reputation of a consultant is well known, the best arrangement can be made through a simple negotiation which reduces the workload for both the prospective client and the consultant.

Fees

Fee structures for library consultants vary tremendously depending on the consultant's experience and the nature of the consulting contract. If the RFP process is used, the consultant can provide the local jurisdiction with a lump-sum price for the work specified in the proposal along with a stipulation in the contract that if the local jurisdiction requires additional work, the consultant will work at a specified per diem. In some cases, consultants work on a percentage of the project basis, like architects, and in other cases the work is at a per-diem or hourly rate. Sabsay[9] and Dahlgren[10] indicate that a library building consultant's fee should be estimated at approximately 1 percent of construction or total project costs. However, consulting has become more competitive in recent years and contracts for less than this amount are certainly possible. The hourly or daily rate charged depends on the consultant's experience and availability. In 1992, if demand was high, some consultants could request and get $80 to $100 per hour or more plus reimbursables. If a consultant is just starting out and demand is low, rates of $25 to $50 per hour can sometimes be obtained. Regardless of the rate charged, the old adage "you get what you pay for" is true for library consultants. In most cases, fees can be negotiated depending upon the client's and consultant's needs.

Library Automation Consultant

Frequently during the planning of a library building, the library administration is also planning for some new form of computerized library automation, from CD-ROM systems and public access microcomputers to full online bibliographic access providing public access to a book catalog, automated circulation, and acquisition of library materials. It is frequently

necessary to hire a library automation consultant to assist with the planning, acquisition, and implementation of the system. An RFP process similar to that used for the library building consultant can be used for the library automation consultant. Fees for automation consultants vary widely and are specific to the type and scope of work performed along with the amount of on-site travel.

The per-diem fees for library automation consultants range from $300 to $400 plus expenses up to $500 to $600 or more. Small contracts with limited involvement may run only a few thousand dollars, but full-service efforts on major contracts may run in the tens of thousands of dollars. It is best to contact individual consultants and provide a description of the scope of work planned and obtain estimates for that work when preparing the preliminary budget. It is usually best to get a fixed price or lump sum quote. Library automation consultants may well save library managment the cost of their fees in the savings on the acquisition and use of automated systems.

Audiovisual Consultant

Occasionally, the planning of a library building will require the services of an audiovisual consultant to provide current technical information regarding equipment and services. This is particularly true if the library management plans to provide sophisticated video production services in the new facility. Technical experts in this field can usually be found through the project's architect or the telephone directory in major metropolitan areas. The fees for these consultants are not well established and vary tremendously depending upon their expertise and the scope of work necessary for the project. However, several telephone calls to various firms will usually provide either per-diem or lump-sum estimates of fees.

Interior Designer

Many library projects are designed and built with the assistance of interior designers; many are planned without them. In most cases, a good interior designer can actually save project funds and at the same time improve the quality of the library's furnishings and equipment. Not only are they aware of many different lines and manufacturers of furnishings and equipment, but many also command special attention and pricing because of their high volume of work. Because of their broad knowledge of the furnishings marketplace, interior designers are not limited in selecting the library's furnishings from library furniture vendors alone. There are, for example, many manufacturers of office furniture and equipment whose products work as well in libraries as items offered by library suppliers.

In the case of tables, chairs, carrels, and service desks, for example, it is of utmost importance that the person responsible for specifying and bidding the contract understands how high-quality, durable furniture should be made. Just as architects and engineers prepare detailed specifications for a building, interior designers prepare detailed specifications for the furnishing and equipment contract for bidding purposes. In the case of a high-quality performance specification (as opposed to a single item or sole source specification), any manufacturer who can meet the specification can bid on the project. An interior designer can save project funds by increasing the number of potential bidders, which increases the competition for the job and thus provides the best possible prices for the library furnishings.

Interior designers can frequently improve the quality of the building's interior casework design as well. While many architects are good designers of casework, some are not. There is a strong case to be made for high-quality built-in furnishings and equipment such as public service desks, public access catalog units, display shelving for special collections, and the like. Just as high-quality design for the building itself is important, so is high-quality design for the building's interior, particularly if the building is to function well as a library. Remember, while it is important to have a building that is pleasing to look at on the exterior, it is equally important for the library to provide a unique and pleasing experience for those who use it or work in it. Good interior design can go a long way toward making this a reality, and if successful, the library will tend to be used more frequently. This should be one of the primary goals of any building program. Interior designers can also reduce the need for future maintenance and replacement costs by selecting durable, easily maintained furniture and building finishes with a long life.

It is best to hire the interior designer early in the project. It is appropriate, for example, to select the interior designer at the same time as the architect so that the interior designer can have input into the project as early as the conceptual design stage, and certainly no later than the schematic stage. A good interior designer will do more than just select furniture and colors (like an interior decorator), but provide innovative design for interior furnishings, casework, signage, light fixtures, etc. The interior designer may be part of the architectural design firm, or may be an independent professional. Both instances have advantages and disadvantages, but either will work as long as the individuals are competent and able to work effectively together. One way to ensure this is to clearly define each professional's role early in the design process and specify which aspects of the project are in the building contract and which are in the interior design contract.

Fees for interior design services vary just as architectural fees do. Interior design contracts for libraries are generally either a percentage of the furnishings and equipment (F&E) budget, performed on a cost-per-square-foot basis, or a negotiated lump sum based on time and out-of-pocket expenses. A fairly standard percentage is between 7 and 9 percent of the F&E contract. However, some interior designers command much higher percentages if they are well known and in demand. Fees quoted on a cost-per-square-foot basis "presently range from less than $1.50 per square foot to more than $3.00 per square foot depending upon the responsibilities delegated to the interior designer and the complexity of the project."[11] Interior design contracts can frequently be negotiated depending on the amount of work in the marketplace, the type and size of the job, the project timetable, and other factors. Lump-sum or per-diem contracts are possible depending upon various circumstances.

Furnishings and Equipment (F&E) Contract

The cost of the interior furnishings and equipment for the library is a very significant consideration when calculating the project's cost estimate. It is also one of the most difficult to estimate. Far too often this figure is ignored or grossly underestimated at the beginning of the project. This results in a new, beautiful library building and an interior that is unsatisfactory in appearance and functionality. Sometimes the library planners must go back to the funding agency toward the end of the construction phase to ask for additional funds to furnish (and finish) the building. These scenarios should be avoided by including an adequate furnishings and equipment budget in the preliminary cost estimate.

There can be significant differences in the furnishings and equipment budgets for

public library projects. As much as the construction cost per square foot varies for library buildings, the cost per square foot for library furnishings and equipment varies even more. There are several factors at play in this equation:

- The quality of the furnishings and equipment to be acquired (quality can be measured in terms of materials used, design, and durability);
- The size of the project (larger projects will cost less per square foot for comparable furnishings and equipment because of volume discounting);
- The extent of use of electronic equipment such as microcomputers, CD-ROM readers, microform readers, and full-fledged library automation systems (online catalogs, circulation control, acquisitions, etc.);
- The amount of built-in casework that will be bid in the construction contract;
- Whether or not signage along with floor and wall coverings are included in the construction contract;
- The amount of task lighting for workstations and library shelving which will be bid in the furnishings and equipment contract;
- The extent to which existing furnishings will be used in the new building;
- The amount of furnishings and equipment that will be acquired out of the first year's operating budget rather than the project budget; and finally
- Whether or not various kinds of equipment are planned and purchased for the project (for example, some libraries will buy globes, rocking chairs, and playpens for the children's room).

This variation, as well as the different methods utilized in reporting the costs of library furnishings and equipment to *Library Journal*, makes the problem of estimating the F&E contract extremely difficult. It should also be remembered that as with the construction cost data, there is a time lag between when the furnishings and equipment contract is bid and when the information is reported.

F&E Costs as a Percentage of the Total Project Costs

Nevertheless, in preparing the preliminary budget estimate, it is essential to come up with a rough cost figure for furnishings and equipment which can be refined once the building program has been completed and an interior designer has been selected. Begin by looking at comparative data from recently completed projects. Perhaps library buildings have been recently constructed nearby and information about the cost of furnishings and equipment is available from the project administrators. However, it is best to obtain information from a variety of sources in order to get a broad picture of what is possible and what is typical. One of the best ways to do this is to review the data collected in *Library Journal* regarding furnishings and equipment costs for public library buildings. The historical data on what has been happening year after year provides some insight. Table 2-12 shows the percent of the total project costs expended by year for furnishings and equipment for all new public library construction projects.

Over the 24-year period that the construction statistics have been collected, the furnishings and equipment costs have averaged approximately 10 percent of the total project costs for all public library construction projects reported. However, in the last five years, this average has increased to approximately 11 percent. This change may in part be accounted for by the increased acquisition of more costly electronic equipment for use in the library by patrons and staff. This increase may also have to do with a demand for higher quality furnishings and equipment or it may simply be the fact that the inflationary increase in furnishings and equipment over recent years has exceeded that of construction and other project-related costs. The range over the 24 year period for the furnishings and equipment percentage is from a low of 7.9

Table 2-12. Average Percent of Total Project Costs for Furnishings and Equipment (based on *Library Journal* statistics)

Fiscal Year	F&E Cost as a Percentage of Total Project
1991	10.6%
1990	9.6
1989	9.2
1988	14.2
1987	13.1
1986	10.0
1985	9.3
1984	8.2
1983	10.0
1982	10.3
1981	10.5
1980	9.5
1979	11.0
1978	10.0
1977	9.4
1976	9.4
1975	9.4
1974	7.9
1973	8.1
1972	7.9
1971	9.2
1970	9.6
1969	9.6
1968	9.8

©Reed Publishing

percent in 1972 and 1974 to highs of 13.1 percent and 14.2 percent in 1987 and 1988. It is obvious from the statistics that individual projects display even wider ranges for the percentage of furnishings and equipment costs.

F&E Costs as a Percentage of the Construction Costs

Another method of using percentages to determine the cost of furnishings and equipment is to calculate the cost of the F&E contract as a percentage of the construction contract. This approach has been used by a number of library consultants over the years to obtain preliminary cost estimates for the F&E contract once the construction cost has been estimated.

David Sabsay provides the argument for the linkage between the F&E and the construction contract:

At an early stage, one can estimate the total furniture and equipment budget as a percentage of the construction cost. This relationship makes good sense when one considers that the latter represents current material and labor costs (although ones which fluctuate more than do general consumer goods) and the size of the building to be furnished. There is also a logical relationship between the quality of the structure and the quality of its furnishings.[12]

Table 2-13 shows the results of dividing the total amount of funds reported for furnishings and equipment by the construction costs for each year since the *Library Journal* statistics started:

Table 2-13. Furnishings and Equipment Contract as a Percentage of Construction Cost (based on *Library Journal* statistics)

Fiscal Year	F&E Percent of Construction
1991	15.26%
1990	13.20
1989	12.08
1988	20.29
1987	17.78
1986	13.41
1985	12.47
1984	10.02
1983	13.18
1982	13.51
1981	14.01
1980	12.14
1979	13.89
1978	13.64
1977	12.48
1976	12.37
1975	12.40
1974	10.52
1973	10.57
1972	10.97
1971	12.40
1970	13.06
1969	13.06
1968	12.13

The range for this percentage is from a low of 10 percent in 1984 to a high of 20 percent in 1988. The average for all 24 years is approximately 13.5 percent, but more importantly, the average is 15.25 percent for the five most recent years. Three out of the last five years have shown percentages over 15 percent, and two of these years were records with the highest percentages reported (17.78 percent for 1987 and 20.29 percent for 1988). There does appear to have been a significant shift in the data for furnishings and equipment costs in the last few years. It will be important for those planning new library projects to continue to monitor this statistic in the upcoming years to see if this trend continues, levels off, or reverses.

Average Library F&E Costs Per Square Foot

When estimating project costs, the cost per square foot for furnishings and equipment is also an important statistic to consider. Table 2-14 shows the average cost per square foot for furnishings and equipment for all of the new construction projects reported in *Library Journal*.

There has been a definite change in these statistics over the years. Obviously libraries can't be furnished and equipped for just over $2 per square foot anymore! The two years that produced the highest percentage figures also produced the highest cost per square foot for furnishings and equipment of $13.10 in 1987 and $14.14 in 1988. The range for furnishings and equipment costs is from a low of $2.38 per square foot in 1968 to a high of $14.14 in 1988. The average for the most recent five years is $12.23. For further analysis, Figure 2-9 shows the cost per square foot information in Table 2-14 in graphic form.

As can be seen from the graph, furnishings and equipment costs have been increasing throughout the 24-year period. Based on the graph, this increase is on average an annual inflation rate of just under

Table 2-14. Average Cost per Square Foot
for Furnishings and Equipment
(based on *Library Journal* statistics)

Fiscal Year	F&E Cost Per Square Foot
1991	$12.24
1990	10.62
1989	11.05
1988	14.14
1987	13.10
1986	8.58
1985	7.72
1984	8.06
1983	7.69
1982	7.08
1981	7.98
1980	5.84
1979	4.60
1978	5.49
1977	5.11
1976	4.52
1975	4.06
1974	3.28
1973	3.03
1972	3.03
1971	2.96
1970	3.06
1969	2.87
1968	2.38

©Reed Publishing

8 percent per year for library furnishings and equipment. From 1968 to 1978 the climb was relatively slow and stable, but in recent years the progression has become more erratic with dramatic increases and decreases in the cost per-square-foot. The per square foot cost for furnishings and equipment peaked in 1988 at $14.14 and dropped off in 1989 and 1990 to only $11.05 and $10.62. This recent drop is probably a pause like a "stock market correction" which adjusts the very rapid cost per square foot increases reported during the 1987 and 1988 projects. The 1991 figure jumped back up some and subsequent years will probably see a continued rise in overall furnishings and equipment costs. However, how much the rise will be and when will it occur is difficult to predict.

Variable Factors in F&E Costs

One of the problems with using the *Library Journal* statistics is that the method of reporting furnishings and equipment costs varies tremendously from project to project. There is no way to tell from these statistics how much money for custom built-in desks, counters, and cabinets is included in the furnishings and equipment category and how much is reported in the construction costs. Although the data collection form for the *Library Journal* statistics is standardized, the way various jurisdictions bid and report their projects is not.

For example, in some projects the public service desks are built-in, but in others they are not. This means in one case the cost of these desks may come under the construction contract and in another it may be under the F&E contract. This is, by the way, often a point of contention between architects and interior designers, and it should be clarified by library planners early on so that both parties don't assume the other is handling the item in "their" budget allocation. While a case can be made to bid casework as part of the F&E contract, as a general rule, it is often best to have items that will be fastened to the structure of the building included in the general construction contract. This helps with lining up service desks with electrical and data outlets as well as with the inevitable coordination problems between the general contractor and furnishings and equipment vendors. If the general contractor is ultimately responsible for the critical alignment of these fixtures, the library planners have one individual who will resolve a problem, not two or three. However, there are exceptions to this rule, and library public service desks are frequently bid outside of the construction contract. To a large extent this issue is fairly job specific.

In addition to built-in furnishings,

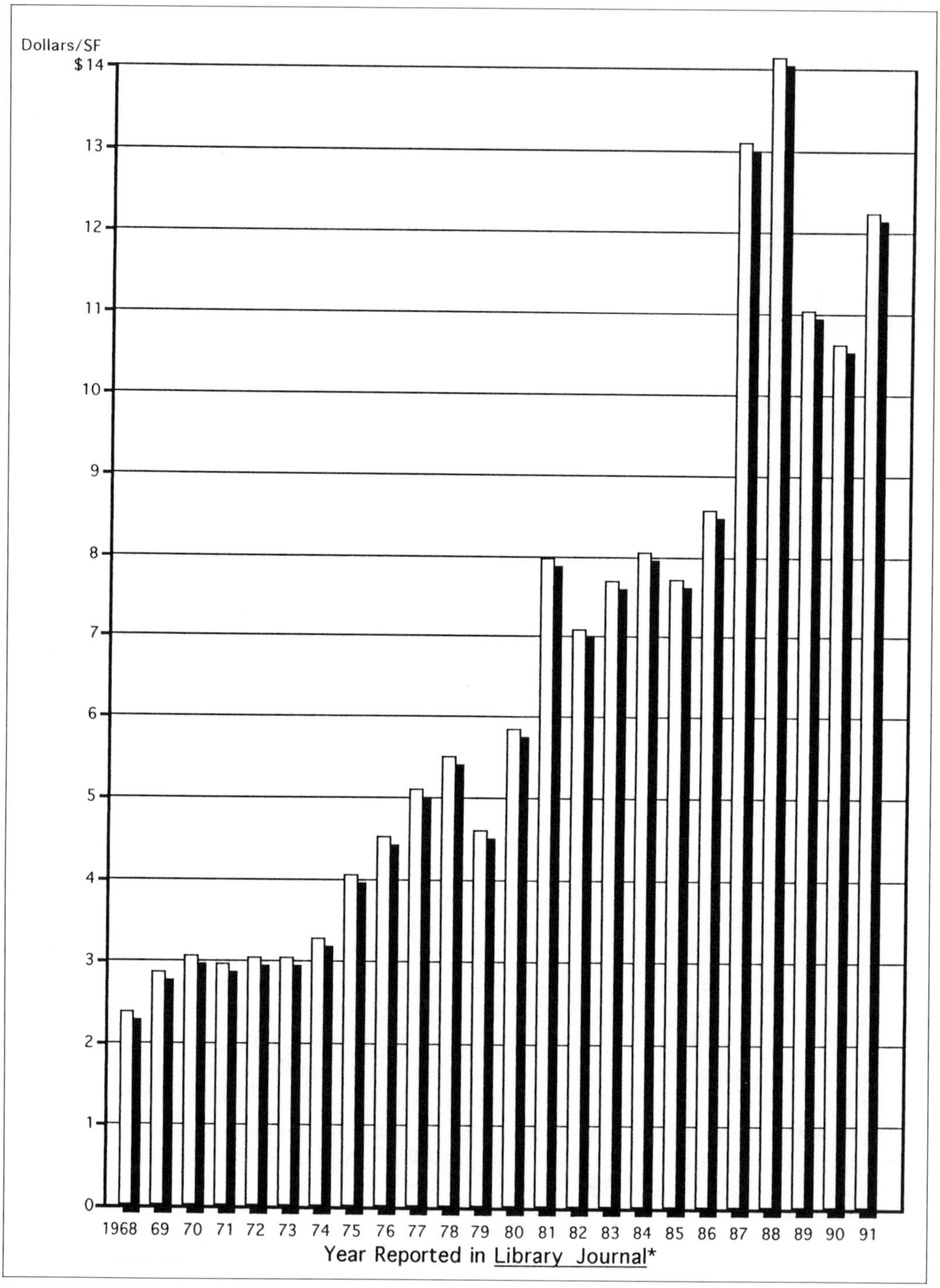

Fig. 2-9. Average F&E Costs per Square Foot for Public Libraries

* ©Reed Publishing

Fig. 2-10. Interior view of library furnishings, Wesley Chapel Branch, Dekalb County Public Library, Decatur, Georgia.

library shelving is sometimes bid as part of the construction contract because it needs to be fixed to the structure of the building, as in California, which has strict seismic requirements. In most states without seismic concerns, shelving is frequently bid separately as part of the F&E contract in order to save on the general contractor's overhead and profit mark-up. Often high-quality casework for special displays in a local historical collection room is bid as part of the construction contract, but it may be specified in the F&E contract equally well. Carpeting, wall coverings, signage, and window treatment may also be points of contention between the construction and F&E contracts. Library planners must not only resolve early on where these items will be bid, but must make cer-

tain that funds have been provided in the project cost estimate to cover all items.

Another problem is that frequently the budget for furnishings and equipment is sacrificed for the good of the building. This often occurs when the bids for the building come in high and the owner is unable to reduce the costs of the construction contract. What frequently occurs is a raid on the furnishings and equipment budget to ensure the building will be built. The rationale is usually, "We must get all the building that we can now, since we can always furnish and equip it later." While there is some logic to this approach, unfortunately, the money to adequately furnish and equip the building later frequently isn't forthcoming. Or it may be obtained in later years' operating budgets and is not reported in the *Library Journal* statistics as part of the project's furnishings and equipment costs. This approach often results in a new library building that is inadequately equipped and cannot function well, or is equipped with furnishings and equipment that have been brought from the old facility. The resulting picture of old, worn-out furnishings in a new, contemporary building is sad at best and often embarrassing.

Because of these problems, and the fact that library furnishings and equipment budgets are frequently not well-planned at the beginning of a project, the F&E contract amount often ends up being "whatever is left over after the building is complete." This problem sets up a vicious cycle because, unfortunately, these inadequate budgets subsequently get reported and the problem is perpetuated from project to project. The bottom line: it is important to take time in the beginning to plan the costs of the interior of the library building as carefully as the building itself. Once the building program has been completed, a list of the needed furnishings and equipment can be extracted and an item-by-item cost estimate can be performed.

Detailed F&E Cost Estimate: Unit and extended cost estimates can be prepared on an item-by-item basis from manufacturers' catalogs using list prices. However, it should be remembered that there will be discounts typically ranging from 30 to 40 percent depending on the size of the job. Larger projects will get higher discounts and therefore cost less per square foot to furnish and equip. This process can be tedious and it is usually best to turn it over to someone familiar with costs in the industry such as an interior designer or a library consultant who specializes in this area. In some cases, furnishings and equipment vendors are willing to perform this function in the hope of getting the F&E contract. Their obvious lack of objectivity is often a deterrent to having vendors perform cost estimates, but reasonably accurate estimates can sometimes be obtained in this manner assuming the vendors are reputable.

A detailed cost estimate for furnishings and equipment looks similar to the final cost estimates for the building. Table 2-15 shows a simplified version of what should be prepared for the F&E contract estimate:

Table 2-15. Sample Sections of a Furnishings and Equipment Estimate*

Item	Quantity	Unit	Unit Cost	Total Cost
CASEWORK				
Circulation desk	30	LF	$300	$ 9,000
Wall cabinets	20	LF	125	2,500
BOOK SHELVING				
90" double faced sections	100	EA	250	25,000
42" double faced sections	20	EA	150	3,000
SEATING				
Adult chairs	40	EA	400	16,000
Adult tables	10	EA	750	7,500
TOTAL F&E:				$63,000

*Cost figures are for illustration only.

Once the building program is completed, this kind of estimate can be made relatively early. It will be based upon generic units and catalog unit costs, and then refined later by the interior designer, who will specify actual manufacturers and model numbers for the various items. Only when specific furnishings and equipment are selected can the issue of quality be addressed. As with construction costs, all things are not equal with furnishings and equipment for libraries. In addition to the variety of materials available (marble counter tops will cost more than formica, for example), there are definite differences in the quality of construction and the durability of finishes and fabrics as well as the ability of the furniture and equipment to hold up for the life of the building.[13] The quality of design is also a consideration. Some older "institutional" library lines do not work well in library buildings with more contemporary designs. In these cases, it may be important to custom design some items or to specify more stylistic "office lines" which are found in private office buildings. These can offer very functional and modern items for libraries such as office landscape panel systems that can be used as workstations, quiet study "rooms," "electronic carrels," and even as public service desks in some instances.

Traditionally, libraries did not have the amount or variety of electronic equipment that is available today. It is now commonplace for libraries to house microform readers, photocopy machines, microcomputers for public and staff use, CD-ROM readers, online public access terminals with printers, minicomputers, multiplexers, surge protectors, audiovisual equipment, facsimile machines, and other innovative equipment through which the library can disseminate information. Some library projects are still built with a minimum of this type of equipment, but increasingly, this is unusual. The cost of this equipment is substantial and must be estimated along with the traditional tables, chairs, and bookstacks if funds are to be available for these items. The cost of these items often does not appear in the *Library Journal* statistics because they are purchased out of separate special fund accounts or out of the library's operating budget. If these alternative fund sources are not an option and this kind of equipment is desired, then library planners must be careful to include these costs in the project budget estimate as well.

Given all these considerations, it is obvious that even the most recent average costs for furnishings and equipment cited in *Library Journal* are below what should be used for most projects. The question is, How low are they? One way to answer this question is to look at a few specific examples of furnishings and equipment purchases for recently built projects around the nation. While there will be some variation in quality and quantities among projects, these figures provide what the author feels is a more accurate accounting of the real costs for library furnishings and equipment during the late 1980s and early 1990s.

Recent Library F&E Costs

The first case to consider is the Dekalb County Public Library, in Decatur, Georgia. For the 13 projects completed in recent years, the average cost per square foot for furnishings and equipment for these buildings was approximately $23 with a range from $15 to $29. These figures do not include built-ins or electronic equipment. Dekalb County is not an especially affluent community but is generally considered solidly middle class overall. As mentioned earlier, the buildings cost $74 per square on average; with site development costs added, the average went up to approximately $93 per square foot. Neither the buildings nor the furnishings and equipment could be considered ostentatious, although they were comfortable, durable, and of

Fig. 2-11. Interior view of library furnishings, Chula Vista Library, Chula Vista, CA.

good quality. The King County Library System in Seattle is in the process of building 18 public libraries and the costs for furnishings and equipment are remarkably similar to the Dekalb County projects. The average cost per square foot is projected to run a little over $23 for all projects when completed; the range is from $15 to $26 per square foot. In King County the public service desks, which are built-in, are in the construction contract and only a minimal amount of electronic equipment is included in the above figures.

Another West Coast project completed in 1992 is the new 160,000-square-foot central library in Sacramento, California. The furnishings and equipment budget was approximately $28 per square foot and included casework for public service desks as well as some electronic equipment. The furnishings and equipment cost figures for the projects recently funded with state bonds in California are also interesting to compare. The costs per square foot for movable furnishings and equipment averaged $16 but ranged from $4/SF to of $38. When the costs for built-in equipment and shelving (which are fastened to the building in California because of seismic considerations) are added to movable furnishings and equipment, the average cost rises to $25 with a range between $8 and $54. Most of these projects will have been bid by 1994 and it will be interesting to see what the final furnishings and equipment figures are, particularly given the highly competitive bidding environment brought on by the recession.

Based on this recent project information, as well as the *Library Journal* statistics, how does one develop a preliminary estimate for library furnishings and equipment costs? Trying to come up with an approximate figure sometimes feels a little like a game of roulette: "pick a number, any number." However, the author has consulted with several interior design firms with extensive experience in bidding library fur-

Table 2-16. 1992 Library Furnishings and Equipment Cost Estimates (excluding electronic equipment)

Range of Cost Per Sq. Ft.		
High	*Medium*	*Low*
$38	$25	$16

nishings and equipment. The cost estimates in Table 2-16 are based on their combined experience as well as the data reported earlier.

These figures exclude all electronic equipment, wall coverings and floor coverings, but include the following:

- Shelving (bookstacks, canopy tops, end panels, book ends, dividers etc.);
- Custom/built-in furniture (service desks, counters, cabinets, display shelving, children's story-hour seating/specialized play area, OPAC carrels/counters, etc.);
- General furniture (tables, chairs, benches, stools, carrels, atlas and dictionary stands, card catalogs, office landscape panel systems, office desks, credenzas, etc.);
- Miscellaneous equipment (kick step-stools, dollies, booktrucks, AV and paperback display, AV carts, book return systems, wastebaskets, sand urns, clocks, display case, conference center, lectern, tack boards, vacuum cleaner, ladder, safe, security mirror, AV and microform storage cabinets, vertical or lateral file cabinets, map cases, lockers, etc.);
- Signage (shelving, rooms, directional, directory, plaques, etc.);
- Window treatments (blinds, drapes, sun shades, etc.)
- Banners and hangings (decorative, acoustical, etc.)

The area of electronic furnishings and equipment for public libraries is a particularly difficult one for which to provide a preliminary estimate because there is so much variation in what is planned for each facility. While it is hard to imagine building a library today without a telephone or photocopy machine, not all libraries will

Fig. 2-12. Alameda, California, Public Library VDT terminals.

open their doors with new CD-ROM units, satellite dishes, or online catalogs supported by central processing units. Library planners will want to examine this aspect of the budget particularly carefully especially if they desire a fully automated, state-of-the-art facility. Table 2-17 offers rough estimates for electronic equipment for public libraries, which includes the following items: microform reader/printers, photocopy machines, typewriters, CD-ROM readers, microcomputers, printers,

calculators, cash registers, charging machines, AV projectors, book theft detection systems, facsimile machines, AV listening/viewing stations, TDD, surge protectors, computer terminals, telephones, video production equipment, people counters, and satellite dishes.

The range is wide because many small rural libraries on the low end of the scale do not tend to acquire much of this type of equipment, while urban and suburban libraries frequently buy a significant amount. The cost of central processing units and cabling has been excluded because it is unique to each library project as well as to the type of system and the manufacturer. Estimates for this equipment will have to be handled by consultation between the library technical services staff and library automation companies and/or consultants. Table 2-18 shows the combined figures for Tables 2-16 and 2-17,

Table 2-17. 1992 Library Electronic
Equipment Cost Estimates
*(excluding CPUs and cabling for online
library automation systems)*

Range of Cost Per Sq. Ft.		
High	*Medium*	*Low*
$10	$ 5	$ 2

Table 2-18. 1992 Library Furnishings and Equipment Cost Estimates *(excluding CPUs and cabling for online library automation systems)*

Range of Cost Per Sq. Ft.		
High	*Medium*	*Low*
$48	$30	$18

and provides a summary of all library furnishings and equipment costs excluding central processing units and cabling for online library automation systems.

Projected Library F&E Costs

Based on these 1992 cost estimates, Tables 2-19 and 2-20 provide cost projections for library furnishings and equipment (with and without electronic equipment) based on a nominal 5 percent increase per year for inflation (the inflation rate can vary from no increase to 10 percent or more in any given year depending on the volatility of the market and the bidding environment). These tables can be used by library planners to determine approximate square footage costs for furnishings and equipment based on the year a project's furnishings and equipment contract will be bid. To use the tables, find the year it is anticipated that the furnishings and equipment contract will be bid and then read to the right to determine the range of average cost-per-square-foot estimates for the F&E contract.

Again, this type of extrapolation is risky since it assumes a "straight line" cost rise which may actually be closer to an upward curve. In any event, the author feels the figures can help provide a preliminary cost estimate for library furnishings and equipment with the standard disclaimer that library planners will need to make adjustments based on local conditions as well as quantity and quality determinations. Appropriate amounts will need to be subtracted from the furnishings and equipment

budget if, for example, it is decided to include some built-in equipment or shelving in the construction contract or if funds will be available for library automation from some other source. It must be emphasized once again that these figures are only rough estimates that will have to be verified by a carefully detailed item-by-item cost estimate as the project develops. It should also be recognized that all cost-per-square-foot estimates provided are based on library buildings in the 10,000- to 20,000-square foot range and increases of 5 to 10 percent up or down will likely be experienced for significantly smaller or larger projects, respectively.

Table 2-19. Suggested Furnishings and Equipment Cost Projections *(excluding electronic equipment)*

	Range of Cost Per Sq. Ft.		
Year	*High*	*Medium*	*Low*
1994	$41.90	$27.56	$17.64
1995	43.99	28.94	18.52
1996	46.19	30.39	19.45
1997	48.50	31.91	20.42
1998	50.93	33.51	21.44
1999	53.47	35.19	22.51
2000	56.14	36.95	23.69

Table 2-20. Suggested Furnishings and Equipment Cost Projections *(including electronic equipment, except CPUs and cabling for online library automation systems)*

	Range of Cost Per Sq. Ft.		
Year	*High*	*Medium*	*Low*
1994	$52.92	$33.08	$19.85
1995	55.57	34.73	20.84
1996	58.35	36.47	21.88
1997	61.27	38.29	22.97
1998	64.33	40.20	24.12
1999	67.55	42.21	25.32
2000	70.93	44.32	26.59

After reviewing these figures and calculating some preliminary costs for furnishings and equipment based on the numbers, some readers may feel "they can do it for less." This is certainly the case in many situations. However, don't use a "low-ball" figure picked out of the air for furnishings and equipment just because it is felt that the funding officials or the public will not accept higher figures. This simply puts library planners in the uncomfortable position at the beginning of the project of planning for something that they can't deliver. Above all, be realistic! Analyze as carefully as possible what the real costs are likely to be. Before the cost estimate is set in concrete, do a unit cost breakdown based on all the furnishings and equipment in the building program, and don't fudge. It is the author's contention that the real costs for library furnishings and equipment are considerably more than many in the library profession have been willing to acknowledge.

Works of Art

In addition to all the items considered as furnishings and equipment, many public library projects include works of art, since the library is a major cultural institution and often one of the more prominent public buildings in the community. The art work may be for both the interior of the library and the exterior grounds. The amount of funds allocated for this purpose is entirely up to the local jurisdiction. Many grant programs and a number of local jurisdictions allow for or require works of art to be budgeted as a percentage of the construction budget. The percentage range usually runs between 1 and 2 percent of construction. If a specific work of art is desired from a famous artist or if the local jurisdiction wishes to commission artwork, the cost could be higher if the work is significant.

Art Consultant

If the acquisition of artwork will be a significant portion of the budget, it may be necessary to hire an art consultant to assist with selection or commissioning. This individual can help library planners acquire artwork of value and prestige at a reasonable value. Fees for such consultants vary and are highly specific to the project locale.

Legal Counsel

In addition to the legal costs associated with land acquisition, there may be other project-related legal expenses. For example, there are frequently questions regarding the financing of the project including assistance with the sale of bonds or other debt instruments, fundraising and campaign reporting activities, election procedures for referenda, compliance with environmental laws, compliance with public advertising for bids (including the cost to advertise in the local newspaper), compliance with state or federal grant program regulations, and possibly construction contract litigation. Many jurisdictions have attorneys on staff who will handle the routine day-to-day legal questions and again, a standard internal charge-back fee may be assessed against the project.

However, if legal counsel is not readily available from the funding agency, or if there is major construction contract litigation, it may be necessary to retain a private attorney with extensive construction contract litigation experience. It is difficult to estimate these kinds of legal costs up front when establishing the budget since some projects will need only a few hundred dollars of assistance and others may require several thousand dollars for extensive litigation. This is why these costs are usually included as part of a standard percentage charged for public administration. It is possible that these costs may be covered by project contingency funds. Further, if the library construction project will require the sale of bonds or other debt instruments, it is very likely that the services of a bond counsel will be required for this rather complex transaction. Again, if necessary, estimates of legal fees for specific activities, such as services of a bond counsel or contract litigation, may be obtained by contacting a legal firm directly.

Financial Consultant

In addition to a bond counsel, it is often useful for a local jurisdiction to hire a financial consultant to assist with the issuance of general obligation bonds or other debt securities. There are firms that specialize in financial planning for local governments and their services often include working with clients to help them get the best possible deal in the complicated securities marketplace. "Fees for this service can take many forms: a flat fee; hourly charges based on services rendered; or a percentage of the total dollar amount of the financing. All three are commonly used as well as combinations and variations. About the safest course a library can follow is to ask around, either informally or formally through a request for proposal."[14]

Auditor

Once the project is completed, there will need to be an audit of all project funds expended. In addition to any local requirements for an audit, it is likely that there will be audit requirements if state or federal funds are involved in the project. To determine the audit requirements and the resulting costs, contact the appropriate local, state, and federal agencies. In some cases, an "internal" audit performed by the staff auditors of the funding agency will suffice; however, when state and federal

agencies are involved, it may be necessary to obtain an independent audit performed by a certified public accountant.

If this is the case, the audit will probably cost more. In any event, the cost of the audit will depend on the size and complexity of the project as well as the type of audit required. If the funding agency requires a compliance audit in addition to a fiscal audit, the cost will increase significantly. Once the requirements of the audit are determined, library planners can usually obtain cost estimates for its preparation from auditing firms or its internal audit department which is usually reimbursed on a charge-back basis.

Generally, a straight fiscal audit will review all project receipts and expenditures to verify that documentation exists to support the transactions. The final audit will certify that funds were received and expended in specific amounts in the given line items that form the project budget. In most cases, all funds will be allocated to a line-item expenditure from the contingency category, but if there are any funds left in the contingency line at the end of the project, this money is considered unexpended surplus funds and returned to the appropriate funding agencies on a pro-rata basis. The contingency should be spent down to as little as possible by the end of the project.

Contingency Fund

One mistake often made by library planners who have little or no experience with construction projects is to under-estimate (or overlook entirely) an amount for a project contingency fund. Occasionally, taxpayers and government officials look at contingencies as "slush funds" that should be severely limited or eliminated altogether. This perspective is understandable if these individuals are charged with trying to keep costs under control, but construction projects that are planned without an adequate contingency fund are a disaster waiting to happen. This is because it is simply impossible to plan for all the possible unknowns that can arise during a construction project. There are so many potential pitfalls—from economic cycles to unforseen soil problems—that a construction project without an adequate contingency is likely to fail in some significant way. On the other hand, it is important for library planners to manage the project in a fiscally sound manner by handling contingency funds appropriately, and not as "extra money" that can be spent frivolously at the end of the project.

Imagine the level of credibility achieved by library planners who have managed their construction project soundly and can return contingency funds to the local funding agency at the end of the project! In most cases, the government officials will probably allow the library planners to add a few prudent embellishments to the building or allocate the funds to the book budget for an opening-day collection if the money can be spent in this manner. In either event, if the government officials feel the library planners have effectively managed the capital project funds, they are more likely to grant a request for increased operating funds for the new building. However, if the library planning team comes back to the local funding agency asking for additional money to finish the project because the contingency was exhausted early on, the team's fiscal management skills will undoubtedly be questioned.

Therefore, it is important for library planners to utilize the contingency carefully and appropriately to meet unexpected expenses. It should be understood from the outset that the contingency is a *project* contingency and therefore can be spent on *any* aspect of the project, but that the majority of problems with unexpected costs will come in the execution of the con-

struction contract. This is why most contingencies are calculated on the basis of the amount planned for construction and/or remodeling work. At the preliminary cost estimate stage a reasonable project contingency is between 10 and 15 percent for new construction and 15 to 20 percent for any remodeling work, depending on the size and complexity of the project. If possible, the high end of the ranges for both new construction and remodeling should be utilized.

These contingency levels should be maintained through the design process up until the project is bid. They may be lowered somewhat if necessary after the construction bids have been opened in order to obtain a construction contract if bids are high. However, there should be a reasonable (10 percent for new construction and 15 percent for remodeling) contingency level maintained well into the construction project. Sometimes even these amounts will not be adequate if particularly severe circumstances are encountered. It is not infrequent that soil problems, for example, are discovered which can require several hundred thousand dollars to solve. Or difficulties may arise with a remodeling project where additional asbestos is discovered when demolition is performed. This may require the general contract to be placed on hold and an asbestos contractor brought in to remove the toxic materials. This process can be very costly, and if contingency funds are not available, the project could be jeopardized.

Once the site work is completed and all the major structural and mechanical systems of the building are in place (and all of the demolition work completed for a remodeling project), the contingency may be dropped to approximately 5 percent for new construction and 10 percent for remodeling projects. These levels should be maintained until the very end of the project and either returned to the funding agencies or used to upgrade the F&E contract, building finishes, or possibly land-scaping. However available contingency funds are expended, library planners should emphasize improvements that will enhance the long-term durability of the facility as well as lower maintenance costs over the long run. The library building should be viewed as a community asset, and the funds expended at this time should be viewed as an investment for the long term.

OTHER ADMINISTRATIVE CONSIDERATIONS AND COSTS

Life Cycle Costs

The concept of life cycle costs should be kept in mind by library planners from the very beginning of a project cost estimate. This approach views the costs of acquiring capital assets such as buildings and equipment from the perspective of the long term. The real cost of a project includes the cost of operating and maintaining the facility over its expected lifetime as well as the capital costs to build it. When operating costs are factored into the equation, there can be a very definite impact on the project cost estimate. Generally this means that higher quality materials and equipment will need to be used in the building, and this will frequently increase the project's budget.

This extra up front cost may significantly reduce the long-term cost of owning the facility because of savings in energy costs, maintenance, and even staff. Careful development of plans by the architect and engineers can produce a building that may be slightly more expensive initially but less expensive to operate over the years. This is particularly true in the area of energy efficiency. While there has been tremendous progress in the implementation of building codes in this area in the last two decades, there are still many ways in which a building can be made more or less energy effi-

cient by the decisions of the architect and engineers. From passive solar building design to the specification of more efficient mechanical and lighting systems or advanced insulation materials and techniques, the energy efficiency of the library building can be significantly affected by the designers. Good professional architects and engineers will try to provide owners with efficient buildings, but only the owners can choose to accept this advice or, better, inform the designers at the beginning of the project that this is a priority.

At the stage of selecting an architect, this can become a criterion and negotiating point. What successful approaches has the architect utilized in the past to reduce the operating costs of buildings? Will the architect provide a life cycle cost estimate study as part of the fee? If so, how will the study be done, and does the architect have examples of previous studies? The goal is to find a report form detailed enough to ensure accuracy, but easily accessible to lay people so that the true life cycle costs of the building's various systems of can be clearly understood. This will allow library planners to make informed and intelligent decisions regarding the energy efficiency of the building and its major systems.

Another area in which substantial life cycle savings may be obtained is in the specification of the quality of the materials used in the building. Usually, the easier it is to maintain the building, the lower the long-term costs will be. Materials that require little or no maintenance are preferable. This is true for both exterior and interior surfaces. For example, floor and wall coverings that are durable and easy to clean are obviously preferable to those that soil easily and are difficult to clean. Durable fixtures that resist vandalism are usually better for the long term. The building's exterior of the building is particularly important because the materials must withstand the elements. The actual materials, of course, will vary from library to library, and planners should not impose inflexible materials selections on the project architect since it is his or her job to keep abreast of the best materials on the market.

Library planners should understand that market conditions sometimes change dramatically in ways that affect the architects choice of building materials. For example, in many environments copper or slate roofs are likely to last longer than other alternatives. However, the architect may know that, because of recent increases in the cost of copper or in the labor costs for applying the slate roof, neither of these two alternatives is economically viable even for the long run. Changes in market conditions can go both ways. A local jurisdiction may not think that it can afford anything other than the "typical" roofing system recently used in several public works projects. However, the architect may be able to specify that a copper roof be bid as an alternate and the jurisdiction may be able to obtain it because of a quick and short-lived drop in the price of copper.

Earlier in the chapter "value engineering" for a project was mentioned. As the term implies, this is the process of looking at architectural plans and specifications from the standpoint of increasing value and the cost benefit ratios. In other words, trying to follow the specifications in a way that reduces costs. Design schemes as well as materials may be questioned; occasionally, untested "cutting edge" technologies may be eliminated. Value engineering can highlight attractive but expensive features of the building that may be costing the owner more than realized. The owner must then decide what is prudent and desirable for the public facility and the community. Savings can be realized not only in the aesthetic design of the building, but also in the functional design of the library.

Sometimes by careful planning and an eye toward efficiency in the layout of the library, savings can be realized even without an increase in the initial capital budget. This is one of the reasons why a qualified library building consultant can often save a local jurisdiction money. During the review of architectural plans, library consultants can often suggest changes that will promote efficiencies in the long-term operation of the building. Further, through the preparation of a building program that effectively guides the architect in the design of a functionally efficient library, a library building consultant may help produce a building that can be operated with less staff. Since staffing costs account for 60 to 70 percent of most library operating budgets, even a 10 percent reduction in staff could produce substantial savings over the 20- to 30-year lifetime of a library building.

The Projected Operating Budget

In almost all cases, a new or expanded library building will normally cost more to operate than the existing facility, if only because the new building is usually considerably larger. It is critical to think about the costs of operating the library as the preliminary planning documents are prepared. The needs assessment, facilities master plan, and building program will determine the type and scope of services offered at the new facilities. As library planners develop these planning documents as well as the capital project budget, the library management should develop an operational budget projection in parallel. This approach will help prevent surprises at the end of the project and the obvious embarrassment of having completed a wonderful new or improved library facility without adequate funding to open the doors and operate it.

The operating budget projection will need to consider many factors such as staff, utilities, and maintenance and should be updated as the project develops. Preparing a preliminary operational budget projection becomes increasingly important when the project budget is submitted to the funding agency officials and they ask what it will cost to operate the new facility. Further, once the facility is funded and the construction begins, the library administration will need to create budget proposals for the library board and the local funding agency in order to get of the funds necessary for a smooth transition to the new or expanded building.

There is much to consider in an operating budget for a new facility. Because the building is larger it will probably require more staff. The new building will also have greatly increased use, which means more materials circulated, more reference questions asked, and therefore a higher demand on staff time. Library use often increases as much as 50 to 100 percent when a new building is opened. There will also be increased demand for new books and other library materials, so an increased annual materials budget will be necessary. While the new building may be more energy-efficient than the old one, it probably will cost more for utilities because it is a larger facility. Many other line items will increase, including costs for insurance, maintenance, and supplies. The library management is responsible for keeping board members and local funding agency officials apprised of the projected operating costs. However, there will be a fair number of "unknowns" until the building is open and has gone through a "shakedown" period of six months to a year. A reasonable contingency during the first year of operation is suggested.

Moving Expenses

In addition to operating budgets, the library management must consider other administrative costs that are not considered part of the project's "capital" budget but may be important to the completion of the project. For example, there will be moving expenses and possibly space rental costs if the library must be moved from the existing building and placed in temporary quarters during construction. Once the project is completed, there will be another move into the new facility. These expenses can sometimes be absorbed by normal operating budgets, but if the project is sizable, it may be necessary to estimate the costs and seek a special appropriation.

Unless the library project will be a completely new facility and not replace an existing library, it will be necessary to move books, materials, and some furniture and equipment from the existing building to the new one. This may be handled in a number of ways. If the library is not too large, the move can frequently be turned into a public relations activity by involving the general community along with various services clubs (Key Club, Boy Scouts) in the actual physical move. While not particularly efficient, human book conveyors with people lined up side by side for several blocks and moving the books one at a time hand-over-hand, make great pictures in the local newspaper and raise community awareness that the new library is about to open. However, if the library is sizable, the move will probably have to be organized more professionally. If the job is too big to be handled easily as a community effort, perhaps the local jurisdiction can provide some staff assigned to occasional "mover duty." If this is not feasible, then an RFP may be issued to various moving companies.

At the planning stage, moving companies can be called for a rough estimate. As long as the library planners know the distance of the move and can reasonably estimate what needs to be moved (number of books, magazines, stack units, tables, chairs, filing cabinets, etc.), how much time is available for the move, how much cleaning will be necessary, how much of the library staff will be involved, and other conditions like the availability of elevators and loading docks, then a moving company should be able to provide a ballpark estimate. Keep in mind that these estimates are "soft" and subject to seasonal variations as well as other business cycles such as recessions. In addition to local moving companies there are several national library moving companies that advertise in library trade journals. A move of moderate size can probably be handled by a local moving company, but if the move is sizable it may be best to hire a company that specializes in moving libraries. In either case, it is wise to obtain competitive bids in order to get the best price, but be sure to have a tightly written request for proposal (RFP) or request for quote (RFQ). For preliminary planning purposes, a cost of between 30 and 50 cents per book to be moved is a reasonable budgetary range.

Ceremonial Expenses

Ceremonial expenses are one area of costs frequently overlooked during the development of a project. While these expenses are usually covered by the library friends group or other private sources, they do need to be planned for. Most library building projects have a "groundbreaking" or "topping out" ceremony or both. These events are usually not particularly expensive, but they may require purchasing or borrowing some shovels and hard hats. They will probably require a microphone if the crowd will be large, and it may be desirable to provide refreshments.

Finally, most libraries hold a building dedication ceremony at the completion of the project. This is important in order to thank everyone involved for their contributions of money and hard work. The dedication is usually a more formal event than a groundbreaking ceremony and will probably require a raised platform and microphones, as there may be several speakers. There is usually a dedication brochure to be designed and printed. Sometimes it is desirable to find funds to pay for a keynote speaker if the planners of the event want to make it special. Again, funds for refreshments may be necessary if the event is large enough to be catered, or the friends group may be able to handle the event with donated baked goods and drinks.

Private Fund Raising and/or Referendum Campaign Expenses

Another area where private funds are often used is to support either a referendum campaign or a private fundraising campaign for the capital improvement project. Raising the sizable amount of funds needed for a major construction project usually requires either a substantial private fundraising campaign, a major referendum campaign, or both. Both forms of campaigns take a reasonable amount of money to engage in. Estimates must be prepared for any kind of campaign at the local level since every community is different and the size of the project will affect the scope and intensity of the campaign. Campaign planners will need to develop preliminary campaign budgets to cover the costs of mailings, printing, telephones, computers, etc., and possibly fundraising or political consultants.

It may be helpful to hire a fundraising or political consultant (or both) to help obtain the necessary funding for the construction project. Normally, the fees for these consultants cannot come from public sources; money to cover the costs must be raised privately. A fundraising consultant will assist library planners in putting together a private fundraising drive, and a political consultant will help plan and execute a political campaign for a referendum. Fees are usually determined through negotiation.

Most political consultants work on a fixed-fee basis, although they can occasionally be hired on a retainer basis for a per diem. The hourly cost for political consultants can vary from a low of $65 up to $275 or more. Fees also depend upon whether or not the consultants will receive media advertising commissions. Most fundraising consultants work for a fixed fee for a specified amount of work or on a per-diem fee basis since working on a percentage of the funds raised is prohibited by the ethical codes of most national fundraising associations. Again, per diems range widely from a low of around $500 to a high of $1,500 or more for nationally-known firms. Again, most firms prefer to specify the amount of work to be performed (like a feasibility study) and then provide a set fee for the service.

Collection of New Books and Materials

Another area often overlooked when budgeting for a new library building is the cost of new books and other materials for an appropriate opening-day collection. Usually when a new library building is opened, the public expects to see new books and materials on the shelves. Further, it is essential to acquire a substantial number of new books and materials if the library being built is not replacing an existing one. Acquiring an entire core collection for a new public library, even for a small library building, involves a significant outlay of funds. In order to provide a cost estimate for this line item, it is best to start with the number of volumes of books, magazines, and audiovisual materials needed in order to open the library. To generate a budget estimate, the library administration can use an average cost per book, magazine subscription, or audiovisual unit to extrapolate overall costs for the collection. This collection can, of course, be supplemented with books loaned from other libraries in the jurisdiction or from "backup" collections.

The costs of books and other library materials are often not considered to be capital outlay and therefore not included in the project cost estimate, particularly if bond proceeds cannot be expended for their acquisition. However, if these materials must be purchased for the project, they must be budgeted somewhere—either in the library's operating budget or the project budget. Frequently, this is a good project for the library's friends group. They can raise private funds for the acquisition of new books for the new library through any number of activities. This not only helps to pay for the new books and materials, but also helps to further involve the community in the library project.

PLANNING FORMS

If the reader carefully follows the steps laid out in this chapter, the process of obtaining a reasonable budget should be successful. However, a word of warning. Estimating a construction project is like shooting at a moving target because the project budget keeps changing as the project develops. Just when library planners feel they have one aspect of the budget finalized, something will occur in another part of the budget to affect the line items just completed. This is to be expected throughout the project. However, if a proper contingency has been planned the problem will not be cause for alarm.

The following forms may be photocopied as worksheets to assist the reader in estimating a project budget. There are four forms to be used with the four basic types of projects:

1. New building
2. Remodeling of an existing library
3. Conversion of an existing building into a library
4. Addition and remodeling of an existing library

Following the forms section is a discussion of a hypothetical library planning committee's efforts to develop a project budget for a new building in "Anytown, USA" utilizing one of the forms as an example.

LIBRARY CONSTRUCTION COST ESTIMATE PLANNING FORM
(NEW BUILDING PROJECT)

NEW BUILDING CONSTRUCTION CONTRACT:		$ _____
PURCHASE PRICE OF SITE:		$ _____
Option Agreement:	$ _____	
SITE DEMOLITION:		$ _____
SITE DEVELOPMENT:		$ _____
RELOCATION OF BUSINESSES OR RESIDENCES:		$ _____
FURNISHINGS & EQUIPMENT:		$ _____
WORKS OF ART:		$ _____
PROFESSIONAL FEES:		$ _____
Architect & Engineers:	$ _____	
Construction Management:	$ _____	
Interior Designer:	$ _____	
Library Building Consultant:	$ _____	
Library Automation Consultant:	$ _____	
Telecommunications Consultant:	$ _____	
Cost Estimator:	$ _____	
Soil Engineering:	$ _____	
Traffic Engineering:	$ _____	
Environmental Analysis:	$ _____	
Appraisal:	$ _____	
Surveyor:	$ _____	
Legal Counsel:	$ _____	
Title Report & Insurance:	$ _____	
Audiovisual Consultant:	$ _____	
Acoustical Engineer:	$ _____	
Signage Consultant:	$ _____	
Art Consultant:	$ _____	
Financial Consultant:	$ _____	
Auditor:	$ _____	
Others:	$ _____	
OTHER (MISCELLANEOUS) COSTS:		$ _____
CONTINGENCY:		$ _____
TOTAL PROJECT COSTS:		$ _____
OTHER ADMINISTRATIVE COSTS:		$ _____
Campaign/Fundraising Expenses:	$ _____	
Moving Expenses:	$ _____	
Ceremonial Expenses:	$ _____	
Library Materials Collection:	$ _____	
Other Costs:		$ _____
TOTAL PROJECT-RELATED COSTS:		$ _____

Fig. 2-13.

LIBRARY CONSTRUCTION COST ESTIMATE PLANNING FORM
(REMODELING PROJECT)

BUILDING DEMOLITION & REMODELING COSTS:		$ _____
FURNISHINGS & EQUIPMENT:		$ _____
WORKS OF ART:		$ _____
PROFESSIONAL FEES:		$ _____
Structural Engineering Study:	$ _____	
Asbestos Study:	$ _____	
Energy Audit:	$ _____	
Architect & Engineers:	$ _____	
Construction Management:	$ _____	
Interior Designer:	$ _____	
Library Building Consultant:	$ _____	
Library Automation Consultant:	$ _____	
Telecommunications Consultant:	$ _____	
Cost Estimator:	$ _____	
Environmental Analysis:	$ _____	
Traffic Engineering:	$ _____	
Legal Counsel:	$ _____	
Title Report & Insurance:	$ _____	
Audiovisual Consultant:	$ _____	
Acoustical Engineer:	$ _____	
Signage Consultant:	$ _____	
Art Consultant:	$ _____	
Financial Consultant:	$ _____	
Auditor:	$ _____	
Others:	$ _____	
OTHER (MISCELLANEOUS) COSTS:		$ _____
CONTINGENCY:	$ _____	
TOTAL PROJECT COSTS:		$ _____
OTHER ADMINISTRATIVE COSTS:		$ _____
Campaign/Fundraising Expenses:	$ _____	
Moving Expenses:	$ _____	
Ceremonial Expenses:	$ _____	
Library Materials Collection:	$ _____	
Other Costs:	$ _____	
TOTAL PROJECT-RELATED COSTS:		$ _____

Fig. 2-14.

LIBRARY CONSTRUCTION COST ESTIMATE PLANNING FORM
(CONVERSION PROJECT)

PURCHASE PRICE OF SITE & BUILDING FOR CONVERSION: $ _____
Option Agreement: $ _____
RELOCATION OF BUSINESSES OR RESIDENCES: $ _____
SITE DEVELOPMENT: $ _____
SITE DEMOLITION: $ _____
BUILDING DEMOLITION & REMODELING COSTS: $ _____
NEW CONSTRUCTION COSTS: $ _____
FURNISHINGS & EQUIPMENT: $ _____
WORKS OF ART: $ _____
PROFESSIONAL FEES: $ _____
Structural Engineering Study: $ _____
Asbestos Study: $ _____
Energy Audit: $ _____
Architect & Engineers: $ _____
Construction Management: $ _____
Interior Designer: $ _____
Library Building Consultant: $ _____
Library Automation Consultant: $ _____
Telecommunications Consultant: $ _____
Cost Estimator: $ _____
Soil Engineering: $ _____
Traffic Engineering: $ _____
Environmental Analysis: $ _____
Appraisal: $ _____
Surveyor: $ _____
Legal Counsel: $ _____
Title Report & Insurance: $ _____
Audiovisual Consultant: $ _____
Acoustical Engineer: $ _____
Signage Consultant: $ _____
Art Consultant: $ _____
Financial Consultant: $ _____
Auditor: $ _____
Others: $ _____
OTHER (MISCELLANEOUS) COSTS: $ _____
CONTINGENCY: $ _____
                          TOTAL PROJECT COSTS: $ _____

OTHER ADMINISTRATIVE COSTS: $ _____
Campaign/Fundraising Expenses: $ _____
Moving Expenses: $ _____
Ceremonial Expenses: $ _____
Library Materials Collection: $ _____
Other Costs: $ _____
TOTAL PROJECT-RELATED COSTS: $ _____

Fig. 2-15.

LIBRARY CONSTRUCTION COST ESTIMATE PLANNING FORM
(ADDITION & REMODELING PROJECT)

PURCHASE PRICE OF SITE FOR EXPANSION:		$ _____
Option Agreement:	$ _____	
RELOCATION OF BUSINESSES OR RESIDENCES:		$ _____
SITE DEVELOPMENT:		$ _____
SITE DEMOLITION:		$ _____
BUILDING DEMOLITION & REMODELING COSTS:		$ _____
NEW CONSTRUCTION COSTS:		$ _____
FURNISHINGS & EQUIPMENT:		$ _____
WORKS OF ART:		$ _____
PROFESSIONAL FEES:		$ _____
Structural Engineering Study:	$ _____	
Asbestos Study:	$ _____	
Energy Audit:	$ _____	
Architect & Engineers:	$ _____	
Construction Management:	$ _____	
Interior Designer:	$ _____	
Library Building Consultant:	$ _____	
Library Automation Consultant:	$ _____	
Telecommunications Consultant:	$ _____	
Cost Estimator:	$ _____	
Soil Engineering:	$ _____	
Traffic Engineering:	$ _____	
Environmental Analysis:	$ _____	
Appraisal:	$ _____	
Surveyor:	$ _____	
Legal Counsel:	$ _____	
Title Report & Insurance:	$ _____	
Audiovisual Consultant:	$ _____	
Acoustical Engineer:	$ _____	
Signage Consultant:	$ _____	
Art Consultant:	$ _____	
Financial Consultant:	$ _____	
Auditor:	$ _____	
Others:	$ _____	
OTHER (MISCELLANEOUS) COSTS:	$ _____	
CONTINGENCY:	$ _____	
TOTAL PROJECT COSTS:		$ _____
OTHER ADMINISTRATIVE COSTS:		$ _____
Campaign/Fundraising Expenses:	$ _____	
Moving Expenses:	$ _____	
Ceremonial Expenses:	$ _____	
Library Materials Collection:	$ _____	
Other Costs:	$ _____	
TOTAL PROJECT-RELATED COSTS:		$ _____

Fig. 2-16.

HYPOTHETICAL PROJECT PRELIMINARY COST ESTIMATE: ANYTOWN, USA

The following is a description of the preliminary project cost estimate process for a new library project in the hypothetical Anytown, USA. The narrative illustrates that developing a project estimate takes time and effort to do accurately. The estimate does not come about in one meeting. The cost figures in this example evolved over time as more and more information was obtained by the diligent library planners in Anytown, USA. All cost figures used in this section (even though sources like *Library Journal* are cited) are hypothetical and used for the purpose of illustration only.

The Initial Cost Estimate

In most communities, the overall cost of a project—the bottom line—is the most important figure in the minds of many taxpayers and local governing officials. The Anytown library planning officials started their search for the total project cost using *Library Journal* construction statistics. They found from the most recent statistics that the average total cost (everything included) for public libraries was about $118 per square foot. Based on a recently completed needs assessment, they also knew they wanted to build a new library that was approximately 30,000 square feet. They were tempted to take the $118-per-square-foot figure (or less) and multiply it by 30,000 square feet to come up with a number, but they knew that the lag time in the publication of the *Library Journal* data meant that figure was approximately three years old. Further, they knew they wouldn't be able to bid their construction contract for at least another two years, so they needed to factor in an additional two years of inflation.

Based on this, it was likely the national average for library construction projects bid two years from now would be about $137 per-square-foot, so they multiplied this figure by 30,000 square feet and came up with a total project cost of $4,110,000. After they got over the initial shock of such a substantial figure, they began to wonder why the library project would cost so much and how they could justify the costs to the city manager and other local officials, let alone their neighbors. They also knew that until they could substantiate the costs—whatever they may be—they better not let this figure out into the community.

To better understand the total cost of the project, the Anytown planners began to look at its various parts. They took the most recent five-year averages for the *Library Journal* categorical statistics and came up with the following rough breakdown of project costs:

Construction Contract (73%)	$3,000,000
Furnishings & Equipment (11%)	452,000
Site Acquisition (7%)	288,000
Other Costs (9%)	370,000
Total Project Cost	$4,110,000

They understood that these were just rough numbers that needed to be further refined to get an actual budget estimate. They also knew that Anytown, USA is not an "average" community even though it is not "rich" either. So, they began their analysis of every possible expense for the new library building.

Building Construction Contract

The starting point for most projects is the cost of construction for the building, and this was no exception in Anytown. From the *Library Journal* statistics they saw that the national average for the most recent year was $86 per square foot for construction costs. However, they remembered the three-year lag as well as the need to project another two years into the future for when they planned to bid their construction contract. From this figure of five years, they projected the *Library Journal* statistics to come up with a construction cost per square foot figure of approximately $100.

One member of the planning team was aghast at this figure and was sure that they could build it for less. Some on the planning team agreed, but others were not so sure. One pointed out that a nearby town, Middletown, recently built a public library at a cost of about $94 per square foot. He knew there were other libraries built nearby in recent years as well, but didn't know what they cost. Another member indicated that the cost of the post office which was completed the previous year was about $95 per square foot and the bank building just recently bid was about $120. The chairperson of the group thought the local public works official might have some information on the subject and assigned various members to explore the cost comparisons further.

After collecting additional data on the cost of nearby libraries as well as construction costs in general, the planning team met again. Two more nearby libraries, one in Hightown and one in Pitsville were visited. The library in Hightown cost about $140 per square foot, but it was a real "Taj Mahal." The library in Pitsville cost about $70, but it certainly wasn't up to the standards of Anytown. The local public works director indicated that public schools could be built for about $70 to $80 per square foot, but "relatively good quality" commercial buildings were currently costing between $90 and $95. One member had researched some building industry indexes and came up with cost projections two years into the future ranging from $102 to $105 per square foot for library buildings. Another member pointed out that a new office building in a large commercial mall development was being planned for about $130 per square foot and they were planning on bidding the project next year.

It was obvious that the planning team had a lot of information, but certainly no consensus on what the library building would cost. Everyone agreed they didn't want a library like Pitsville's, but they also couldn't afford or justify one like Hightown's. They agreed to take another look at the *Library Journal* figure and start there. It seemed like a lot of money, but maybe it wasn't so high compared to what other projects were costing. After all, the post office cost $95 per square foot last year and they certainly wanted the library to look as good and last at least as long as the post office. Adding three years worth of inflation to the post office cost brought the figure up to about $108 per square foot. Everyone agreed that if they built the library along the lines of the bank building they would probably be run out of town. However, one member indicated that one reason the bank building cost what it did was because of the construction of the vault.

The public works director's estimate that commercial construction averaged $90 to $95 per square foot was interesting to the team, particularly when two years of inflation was factored in to bring the figures up to $99 to $105. It was pointed out that this wasn't far from the *Library Journal*-based figure of $100. The Middletown library was also discussed further. It was bid one year ago and came in at $94 per square foot, and the planning team members who had seen the building felt it was exactly what Anytown needed. One year old, plus two more years into the future for their bid date meant that inflation at 5 percent per year for three years would bring the cost figure up to about $109 per square foot. The planning team summarized the pertinent information about construction costs per square foot two years in the future as follows:

Library Journal national average
  $100

Post office projection
$108
Local planning director's projections
$99 to $105
Middletown library's projection
$109
Building index projections
$102 to $105

"It looks as though we are somewhere between $99 and $109," the chairperson announced. "Before we go on, is there any other information we need to consider?" One member pointed out that two out of three of the sites that were currently under consideration were downtown and near a new development that was being planned. He also pointed out that this development was going to be very upscale for Anytown and would set a new market trend in town. Given this, he felt that the construction cost estimate should be set at the upper end of the range, and possibly even higher. Others felt that the library wasn't competing with commercial concerns and shouldn't try to "keep up with the Joneses."

Another member disagreed, saying in effect that the library facility must be attractive in order to interest people in the service: "The library building itself is one of the best ways to advertise library service." Another member felt the library building would be projecting a kind of "self-image" for Anytown for years to come. Didn't the community want to project a positive, growth-oriented image to attract new business and industry? The public library should demonstrate the community's commitment to educating its people and supporting cultural enhancements that improve the quality of life. Besides, we wouldn't want Middletown to have a better library than we have, would we?

After further discussion, it was decided that the library should be budgeted between $105 and $110 per square foot, with emphasis on the latter figure until more information could be obtained by an archi-

tect. The $110 figure multiplied times the 30,000-square-foot building projection came to a total of $3.3 million. For some reason, this figure didn't seem as high to the planning members as the original $3 million cost that was based on the $100-per-square-foot figure, even though it was obviously more money. They reflected that they now knew a lot more about the real costs of construction in their community, and because of this, they felt better prepared to justify and defend the project's construction costs.

Purchase Price of a Site

At the next meeting, the planning members took up the topic of the cost of a site. They knew that $288,000 in their community would not buy them much of a site, at least not one in a location they wanted. The planning members had a pretty good idea of commercial property costs in their town ($4 per square foot) and they had their eye on several parcels. One in particular interested them and they felt with further study it could become the library site. The site was on the main street and close to the center of town as well as to the new development being planned. The planning team felt that the property would make a particularly good library site because of its high visibility and accessibility.

Its value was considerable. Information from the Anytown public works department and the tax assessor's clerk indicated that the property was probably worth between $400,000 and $500,000 based on recent comparable sales. The site was owned by Mrs. Smith, a widow whose husband had been the town's doctor and was also a well-known local philanthropist. One of the planning team members had been a close personal friend of Dr. Smith's and knew Mrs. Smith very well. He thought it might be possible to get her to donate the site, but he wasn't certain she was in a position to do it. He said he would be willing to ask her to donate the site if the team decided it would be the best site for the library.

The planning committee decided to hire a library building consultant to perform a site selection study and write a building program. They all felt that once the site study was completed, this matter should be explored further. They also felt they wanted to have a site for the library at least as good as Mrs. Smith's property, so they decided tentatively to allocate at least $500,000 for the cost of land. If they found out in the future that the site could be obtained for free, they could always adjust the budget downward.

After the site selection study was completed, it was determined that Mrs. Smith's site would be the best place for the library. The site was certainly well located and it was large enough to accommodate the library, parking, and a modest future expansion. The planning committee contacted Mrs. Smith to ask if she was interested in selling or donating the site to the library. She indicated that she would be interested in selling the site, but wasn't sure about donating it and would have to discuss it with her children, her attorney and her accountant. She did, however, give the planning team the go-ahead to have the property surveyed and "whatever else was necessary in order to acquire it." Feeling they now had a good working relationship with her, the planning team ordered a boundary and locational survey and contacted a professional to appraise the property. Finally, the planning committee went to the city attorney's office and requested a title search.

Site Demolition

At this point, the library planners hired an architect to help with the preliminary planning, and the architectural firm was assisting with the cost estimate. The site was a level vacant lot with only a few trees

and an old barn on it. The architect felt that most of the trees could be saved, but a few would have to be removed. The barn was an eyesore with no historical value. The cost estimate to remove the trees and the barn was approximately $8,000.

Site Development

Someone on the planning committee remembered that many years ago there might have been a county maintenance yard located on the property, but she wasn't sure. Another recalled that his grandfather told him about how he used to look for arrowheads in the gulley that ran through that property when he was a young boy. The lot certainly looked good on the surface, but the library planners had no idea of what was below the surface. While soil conditions were generally good in their community, there were some locations where bedrock was close to the surface.

Because of this, they decided to have a soil engineering report prepared along with an environmental assessment. The architectural firm decided on the placement of soil borings and worked with the soil engineering firm to study the site. The soil report came back with some bad news. A good bit of the site contained fill dirt which was not structurally sound and would have to be removed. The architect estimated it would cost approximately $100,000 to remove this dirt and replace it with structural fill. Further, there was some bedrock near the surface on one end of the site that probably would have to be blasted. This could cost as much as $10,000. Fortunately, the soil tests indicated no sign of toxic chemicals on the site, and the environmental assessment turned up nothing conclusive although the state archaeological office indicated that all of Anytown had potentially held archaeologically significant artifacts.

The architect was working on a conceptual plan for the library building and site and estimated another $190,000 worth of site development cost associated with the parking lot, required deceleration lane, landscaping, signage, sidewalks, patios, and exterior lighting. This was not a firm figure, but the architect did not feel it would require more than this amount for the site improvements. They indicated they would be able to provide more precise estimates as the plans developed and a professional cost estimator became involved.

Furnishings and Equipment

The library planning team knew that the most recent *Library Journal* cost figure for furnishings and equipment was about $12 per square foot. However, in talking with the library director of Middletown, they discovered the F&E contract for that library was closer to $26 per square foot, but it included "everything from service desks to microcomputers." In Middletown's case, they kept almost all furnishings and equipment out of the construction bid except for a few counters and cabinets in the mail room and technical processing. According to the Middletown library director, everything in the library was new; nothing from the old building was brought into the new one. The Anytown planners liked what they saw in Middletown and were determined to get a state-of-the-art library in Anytown.

In discussing the matter with their library director, they were pleased to learn that she felt the library should have all new furnishings and equipment, with the exception of the recently acquired computer system. In addition to tables, chairs, public service desks, and office furniture, the library would need all new shelving and a number of new items of automated equipment like CD-ROM readers and microcomputers. The director felt the estimate of $26 per square foot might be reasonable,

but she wanted to discuss it further with the library consultant.

The library consultant was still in the process of completing the building program which would specify all necessary pieces of furnishings and equipment for the new building. The consultant's experience gave him reason to believe the F&E contract would probably be somewhere between $20 and $30 per square foot depending upon a number of variables, most notably the quality level specified, the final program requirements, and the bidding climate when the F&E contract was advertised.

Because the F&E contract would be bid two to three years in the future, and because the economy was "heating up," the library planners decided to take the higher end of the cost range for preliminary planning purposes and allocated $30 per square foot for the F&E contract. When the building program was complete, the interior designer developed a complete furnishings and equipment list that included all custom casework for built-in service desks, all movable furnishings and equipment, window treatments, and signage as well as a number of electronic information delivery units. The interior designer consulted with the architectural firm, and they agreed to leave the wall and floor coverings in the general contract, but to allow input from the interior designer in the selection of each.

From this list, the interior designer made preliminary selections and presented them to the library planning committee along with a preliminary itemized unit cost estimate. The cost estimate indicated that the F&E contract would probably run about $28 per square foot. The library planners decided they wanted a few changes made in the interior designer's plan, which she thought would run about $30,000. This resulted in an estimate of $29 per square foot, and an F&E contract amount was set at $870,000 for the 30,000-square-foot-building.

Works of Art

Anytown did not have a local policy supporting public art, and since the library planners were getting nervous about the cost of the project and felt that they wanted to put their emphasis on good quality furnishings and equipment, no allocation for artwork was made.

Professional Fees

Architect and Engineers: Before hiring their architect, the library planning committee did some research and learned that most projects built in the Anytown area were charged somewhere between 7 and 8 percent for architectural and engineering fees. The committee distributed a request for proposals, screened the proposals, and short-listed five firms for an interview. After the interview, the firm of Avant & Garde was hired. The planning committee was very impressed with their background and experience as well as their obvious flair for building design. The firm came highly recommended and had a history of bringing projects in under budget. The principals who interviewed had done their homework and it was obvious they had listened well to what the library committee wanted. Their services, however, were not cheap. They demanded and got an 8 percent fee for their services plus reimbursables for a total of approximately $300,000.

Construction Management: After talking further with the local public works director, the library planning committee felt the project would be in good hands if the public works department performed the construction management for the project. It was a policy of the jurisdiction that the public works department "charged back" for service to other agencies. The charge-back fee ran about 3 percent of the construction contract which came to about $108,000.

Interior Designer: Middletown had hired an interior designer to help with the selection, writing of specifications, and bidding of the F&E contract, and Anytown felt they needed the same kind of help. The library planners issued an RFP for an interior designer. After interviewing several firms the Anytown library committee decided to hire the interior designer who did the Middletown library because she obviously had solid recent experience with a library and they loved what she had done there. Further, the Middletown people had been pleased with her work and felt she had saved them a lot of money on furnishings and equipment.

The interior design firm worked on a percentage of the contract basis and charged 8 percent of the F&E contract plus reimbursables which was at that time estimated to be $870,000. Eight percent of this figure was $69,600. Reimbursables were estimated at about $5,400 for travel since the firm was located several states away. The total interior design contract was set at $75,000.

Library Building Consultant: The planning committee member decided they needed the assistance of a library consultant who was familiar with planning public libraries. After issuing an RFP, and interviewing three consultants, the planning committee hired the consulting firm of "Libraries-R-Us." This firm had a national reputation of quality customized work and was retained to assist with the needs assessment process, perform a site selection study, write the building program, and perform reviews of the architectural plans as they developed. The firm provided a lump-sum fee proposal of $50,000.

Library Automation Consultant: The library had recently finished an library automation plan and acquired a new computer system providing on-line catalog access as well as circulation control. The system was expandable and could be moved into the new building. A library automation consultant was still under contract, but funds for this contract came from the operating budget.

Telecommunications Consultant: The library planners felt they could get adequate help in selecting a telephone system for the new building and did not need a telecommunications consultant for the project.

Professional Cost Estimator: The library committee negotiated the A&E contract to include the services of the cost estimator. The architectural firm subcontracted with the cost estimating firm, and the library planning committee was provided with a cost estimate at the schematic, design development, and working drawing stages. The first estimate was on a square-foot basis and was produced after the architect's schematic plans were reviewed. At this point the project would cost approximately $110 per square foot.

Soil Engineering: Based on a request for a quote (RFQ), the library planners in consultation with the local public works department and the project architect obtained a price quote of $7,000 for the soil engineering report. Additional soil testing would be necessary during construction to make certain that the compaction of the fill was satisfactory. This amounted to another $5,000.

Traffic Engineering: The architect felt the site plan was relatively straightforward and traffic patterns were not difficult to deal with. Traffic analysis was not required as part of the environmental assessment, so no funds were set aside for this purpose.

Environmental Assessment: Because of a state law requirement, the library planners performed an environmental assessment in consultation with the local funding agency and the architect. A couple of specialists

were called upon briefly, but for the most part the work was done by the local public works department and the local planning department. The charge-back fee for this relatively minimal study was $3,000.

Appraisal: The library planning team and site owner Mrs. Smith were both eager to determine the fair market value of the property, and so they agreed to split the cost of an appraisal. In search of a high-quality appraisal, they hired an appraiser with considerable experience in commercial property and nationally recognized credentials. The appraisal report cost $6,000; the library committee's share was $3,000.

Surveys: The library committee decided to have a boundary and locational survey performed. The low price quote from local surveyors was $4,000. In addition, they negotiated the price for a topographical survey at a later time for $3,000.

Legal Counsel: An agreement was reached with the local funding agency that all routine legal work would be done by the Anytown city attorney. The attorney's office estimated that the charge-back would probably run between $3,000 and $5,000 for title work and occasional consultation, including advice on holding a referendum to finance the building. The legal department advised that it was standard practice in Anytown to simply increase the amount of any bond sale by the amount necessary to cover the costs of the sale of bonds, so the library planners did not need to try to estimate these costs at that time. The library committee decided to allot $5,000 for legal fees.

Title Report and Insurance: The city attorney's office estimated the cost of a title report and title insurance for the project would be approximately $4,000.

Audiovisual Consultant: The library planners were unsure if they would need an AV consultant. They discussed the matter with the library administration, the library consultant, and the architect and discovered that the planned program of service probably wouldn't require the services of an AV consultant.

Acoustical Engineer: Based on the architect's recommendation the library planners did not provide funds for an acoustical engineer.

Signage Consultant: After consultation with the architect, library consultant, and interior designer, the library committee decided to allocate $3,000 for a signage consultant. They felt it was very important to have good quality signage to help patrons locate library materials and find their way around the building without constantly asking staff.

Art Consultant: Since there was no allocation for artwork, the library committee did not allocate funds for an art consultant.

Financial Consultant: After consulting with Anytown's finance department, the library committee decided the finance officer would provide them with adequate assistance and a financial consultant was not necessary. The finance department indicated that any additional assistance that might be required would be covered in their regular operating budget.

Auditor: After talking with the Anytown's financial director, the library planners realized that all project funds would have to be audited during and at the end of the project. The finance director gave them an estimate of $5,000 in charge-back fees for auditing.

Other Fees: The Anytown library planners knew they wanted good landscaping with low-maintenance plantings, so they set aside an extra $5,000 for a landscape architect after talking with the project architect. They could not think of other professional fees that would be necessary for the project.

Contingency Fund

The Anytown planning committee was concerned about running out of money part-way through the project. They knew that they would have to go to the voters of Anytown and pass a referendum to obtain the large sum needed for the library project, and they wanted to make sure they wouldn't have to go back a second time. There was much discussion over what a reasonable contingency would be. Some argued for a figure as low as 5 percent of construction; others felt that 10 or even 15 percent was necessary.

The committee members discussed the matter with the public works director as well as the architect. The public works director reported that while the soil conditions in the Anytown area were fairly stable, the fact that rock was discovered on the site was of concern. The architect pointed out, that the amount of fill required was just an early estimate, and until the contractor started to remove the dirt and testing was performed, they wouldn't know what the actual cost would be. The architect also indicated that while the firm believed $110 per square foot would be adequate for constructing the building, the building market was "heating up" and prices could increase more than anticipated before the bid date.

Based on these discussions, the library planning committee decided to play it safe and opted for a 15 percent contingency. The estimated cost of the construction contract (construction plus site development and demolition) was $3,608,000. Fifteen percent of this figure was $541,200. The planning team rounded this figure off to $542,000 and added it to the cost estimate.

Total of Project Capital Outlay Costs

The process of developing the preliminary cost estimate was long. The site selection study was completed, the building program was done, architectural plans had developed to the schematic stage, and both the interior designer and the architect had provided preliminary cost estimates. This planning, along with all the other hard work by the planning team, came together in the form of a total project cost estimate that the library planners felt they could propose to the Anytown City Council. The capital outlay budget now stood at $6,100,000 which was, as one member put it "a far cry from our original estimate of just over $4 million." Committee members were asked if there was anything in the budget they would like to see removed or reduced, but they felt that they could defend every line item. As a result, the budget was adopted (Figure 2-17). A date was set to present it to City Council and request a library bond issue to be placed on the ballot in the amount of $6,100,000.

Other Administrative Costs

Campaign/Fundraising Expenses: In addition to the capital outlay costs, the library committee knew there would be more project-related costs such as the funds necessary to run a political campaign. They talked with several other groups that had recently run referendum campaigns in Anytown and discovered they would probably need anywhere from $15,000 to $25,000 of private funds to ensure a victory. The Anytown library supporters felt they needed the assistance of a political consultant, and they wanted to do some polling in addition to other routine campaign expenses, so they budgeted $25,000 for campaign expenses.

Moving Expenses: In consultation with the library director, the library committee decided to save on moving expenses by enlisting the help of local volunteer organizations. The Anytown library collection was not large, and since they did not plan to move any furniture or equipment from the old building to the new one, the move would not be too difficult.

Ceremonial Expenses: The library friends group offered to handle any expenses for a groundbreaking or dedication ceremony. They decided to get together to provide goodies and a local fast-food restaurant offered to donate the drinks.

Library Materials Collection: The library committee and the library director were both concerned that the existing collection would be a public relations problem when the new building opened. Based on a recommendation from the library director in consultation with the library consultant, the library committee decided to raise about $375,000 for new books and library materials for an opening-day collection supplement. Since bond proceeds could not be expended for this purpose in their state, the friends group agreed to take this activity on as a fundraising effort so that books could be acquired and processed before the library opened.

The committee members knew they would have to raise the additional $400,000 from private sources. Once they succeeded at presenting the project to the Anytown City Council and securing a place on the fall ballot, the library committee began to reorganize by forming a campaign steering committee and preparing for the private fundraising and referendum campaign.

Fortunately, the Anytown library planners had a clear understanding of where funds for the new library would come from. However, this is not the case in many communities. Often a major part of developing a project budget is determining the source of funds. Assessing potential funding sources for a capital project is the subject of the next chapter.

LIBRARY CONSTRUCTION COST ESTIMATE PLANNING FOR ANYTOWN, USA

NEW BUILDING CONSTRUCTION CONTRACT:			$	3,300,000
PURCHASE PRICE OF SITE:			$	500,000
Option Agreement:	$	N/A		
SITE DEMOLITION:			$	8,000
SITE DEVELOPMENT:			$	300,000
RELOCATION OF BUSINESSES OR RESIDENCES:			$	N/A
FURNISHINGS & EQUIPMENT:			$	870,000
WORKS OF ART:			$	N/A
PROFESSIONAL FEES:			$	580,000
Architect & Engineers:	$	300,000		
Construction Management:	$	108,000		
Interior Designer:	$	75,000		
Library Building Consultant:	$	50,000		
Library Automation Consultant:	$	N/A		
Telecommunications Consultant:	$	N/A		
Cost Estimator:	$	N/A		
Soil Engineering:	$	12,000		
Traffic Engineering:	$	N/A		
Environmental Analysis:	$	3,000		
Appraisal:	$	3,000		
Surveyor:	$	7,000		
Legal Counsel:	$	5,000		
Title Report & Insurance:	$	4,000		
Audiovisual Consultant:	$	N/A		
Acoustical Engineer:	$	N/A		
Signage Consultant:	$	3,000		
Art Consultant:	$	N/A		
Financial Consultant:	$	N/A		
Auditor:	$	5,000		
Other: (Landscape Architect)	$	5,000		
CONTINGENCY:			$	542,000
TOTAL OF PROJECT CAPITAL OUTLAY COSTS:			$	6,100,000
OTHER ADMINISTRATIVE COSTS:			$	400,000
Campaign/Fundraising Expenses:	$	25,000		
Moving Expenses:	$	N/A		
Ceremonial Expenses:	$	N/A		
Library Materials Collection:	$	375,000		
Other Costs:			$	N/A
TOTAL PROJECT RELATED COSTS:			$	6,500,000

Fig. 2-17.

REFERENCES

1. Data from December issues of *Library Journal* 1968–1991 © 1989 by Reed Publishing, USA. Reprinted with permission.
2. Joseph L. Wheeler, "The Effective Location of Public Library Buildings," *Occasional Papers* No. 12, (University of Illinois, Graduate School of Library Science, July 1958).
3. Hoyt Galvin, "Public Library Parking Needs," *Library Journal* 15 November 1978, pp. 2310-13
4. Uniform Relocation Assistance and Real Property Acquisitions Act of 1970 (PL 91-646).
5. *Marshall Valuation Service* (Los Angeles: Marshall & Swift, Inc.) Quarterly.
6. *Means Square Foot Costs; Means Building Construction Cost Data; Means Assemblies Cost Data* (Kingston, Mass.: R. S. Means Co.), Annual
7. Raymond M. Holt, (2nd rev. ed. by Anders C. Dahlgren) *Wisconsin Library Building Project Handbook* (Madison, Wisc.: Wisconsin Department of Public Instruction, 1990), p. 110.
8. *Library Buildings Consultant List* American Library Association, (Chicago: Library Administration and Management Association), Bi-Annual.
9. David Sabsay, "Estimating Library Building Project Costs at an Early Stage," in *Talking Buildings: A Practical Dialogue on Programming and Planning Library Buildings* (Sacramento: California State Library, 1986) p. 100.
10. Holt, p. 111.
11. Holt, Raymond M. *Planning Library Buildings and Facilities: From Concept to Completion.* (Metuchen, N.J.: Scarecrow Press, 1989), p. 74.
12. Sabsay, p. 101.
13. Carol R. Brown, *Selecting Library Furniture: A Guide for Librarians, Designers, and Architects.* (Phoenix: Oryx Press, 1989).
14. Steve H. Larson, "The Role of the Financial Consultant in a Library Building Program" *Illinois Libraries* 69, (November 1987), p. 630.

Potential Funding Sources 3

Once the project cost estimate includes enough detail so that one may have a reasonable degree of confidence in it, it is necessary to survey the landscape for potential funding sources. There are many approaches to funding a public library in this country, but the key to success is to find the source (or combination of sources) that best fits the project. Many projects are funded from a single source such as a general obligation bond issue, while others combine local bonds, private fundraising, state and federal grants, etc. All kinds of combinations are possible, depending on the project.

ASSESSING THE POSSIBILITIES

There are a number of considerations when assessing potential funding sources. Is the project large or small? Does it need a sizable amount of money or relatively little? Is the timetable flexible enough to be compatible with application cycles for state or federal grant programs? Are state and federal funds available, and if so, what are their advantages and disadvantages? Is it feasible to raise all or some of the project funds from the private sector? Could the funds to be raised by a referendum? Would the community support this approach, and could the library supporters mount an effective campaign? Are there "creative" financing methods available such as lease-

purchase agreements or development agreements and fees? What are the inherent limitations of these alternative approaches?

In order to find the best funding source, library planners must become aware of all potential sources of funding, assess the likelihood of funds from each, and evaluate the pros and cons of any given approach. Each possibility has trade-offs, some of which can make a major difference. The accurate assessment of potential conflicts or drawbacks to any given funding source can be crucial to the project's success or failure. Finally, it is important to consider which options are the most cost effective, that is, which financing methods cost the community the least in time, effort, interest, and lost revenues.

Local Funds

To a large extent, finding an adequate funding source is the process of narrowing down the possibilities. For example, if the project is a large building in a metropolitan area, it is unlikely that all of the funding can be raised from private sources. However, in some communities that have a history of effective private fundraising efforts, the money for a small to medium-sized project may well be raised primarily from private donations. If it is not feasible to raise all the funds from gifts and donations, it may be possible to raise funds for some part of the project, for example, a children's wing or meeting room, or the furnishings and equipment for the new building.

If private fundraising methods aren't feasible, there are a many methods of financing library projects out of the local tax base. Some small projects are funded directly out of the operating budget for any given year, but most major capital projects will require more than one year's appropriation of funds. Consequently, many local jurisdictions use general obligation bonds, while others use certificates of participation, lease revenue bonds, mortgages, special taxes, sales taxes, excise taxes, development fees, tax increment financing, or any number of possible alternatives. Many local jurisdictions have financial consultants on staff or on retainer who can be consulted when assessing potential financial instruments. Library planners should seek out this expertise early on.

State and Federal Funds

Beyond the immediate community, there is always the prospect of state or federal funds. Some states have active state matching programs specifically for public library construction. A telephone call to the state library will tell. If there is a state program, it is usually worth requesting program requirements and application forms, and visiting with the program officer either by telephone or in person after a brief review of the program information. State libraries also administer the federal Library Services and Construction Act (LSCA) program of which Title II is dedicated to funding public library construction. Along with LSCA Title II funding, there are other possibilities for federal funding to explore, such as Community Development Block Grants (CDBG), Challenge Grants from the National Endowment for the Humanities (NEH), and loans from the Rural Development Administration (RDA) (formerly Farmers Home Administration), as well as other federal sources that become available from time to time.

Some of these sources have been used more frequently in the past than now, but all have a role to play in the development of public libraries. In recent years, many new financing methods have been developed to assist with the funding of infrastructure such as public library facilities. These may be helpful, but many of the "tried and true" methods like referendum and private fundraising campaigns still work and have a lot to offer in terms of building up a constituency to support the library's ongoing operations. There is a strong interrelationship among the different funding sources, and the use of one source will often stimulate the use of others.

THE HISTORICAL PERSPECTIVE

The Early Years

To better understand current sources of funds for public library construction, it is helpful to review the history of such funding. The generous contributions of Andrew Carnegie around the turn of the century were to a large extent the beginning of the development of the modern public library system in the United States. Carnegie did more for public library facilities than any other single individual, and his legacy will not be forgotten. Within three decades Carnegie had "donated $56,162,622 for the construction of 2,509 library buildings throughout the English-speaking world. More than $40 million of this amount was given to build 1,679 public libraries in 1,412 communities in the United States."[1]

The tradition of private giving for public library construction, however, did not start with Andrew Carnegie. A number of public libraries were built prior to the Carnegie era, and records show that approxi-

Table 3-1. Sources of Funds for Large Public Libraries, 1850 to 1989[2]

Date	Number	Cost	Source of Funds Public	Private
1850–1893	28	$ 7,500,000	25%	75%
1894–1918	60	36,500,000	40%	60%
1919–1945	28	37,600,000	85%	15%
1946–1969	26	122,400,000	90%	10%
1970–1989	31	356,500,000	90%	10%

Table 3-2. Public Libraries Constructed by Date

Date	Main Buildings	Branch Buildings
Pre-1865	82	
1865–1900	529	
1901–1910	841	
1911–1920	715	
1921–1930	448	1,167 (Pre-1931)
1931–1940	504	363
1941–1950	297	436
1951–1953	192	
1954–1956	213	
1957–1959	248	
1960	85	1,149 (1951–1960)
1961	85	
1962	80	
Unspecified		2,601

mately 75 percent of their funding came from private sources. This is demonstrated in Table 3-1 which is reproduced from Donald E. Oehlerts's book on the history of the building of large main public libraries in the United States.

Shortly after the turn of the century the predominance of private funding began to wane. It began to slip, in part, as Carnegie's private-sector stimulation of public funding for public libraries started to take effect. Local jurisdictions, required by the terms of the gifts to maintain the buildings, began financing public libraries with local funds. In a 1930 article Simeon E. Leland provided a list of over 150 local bond issues for public library buildings from 1899 to 1927.[3] This report appears to chronicle the beginning of what in time became a substantial contribution of local public funds for public library construction. As Table 3-1 shows, sometime in the 1920's the public sector overtook private donors as the primary source of public library financing.

Over the years, there have been intermittent attempts to chronicle the construction and capital expenditures for public library buildings in the United States. In 1968, Hoyt Galvin reported that

Henry T. Drennan of the Library Services branch of the U.S. Office of Education tabulated data for the fiscal year ending 1962 on public library buildings in the 50 states and the District of Columbia by date of initial construction. He received reports on 4,319 central library buildings and 5,707 branch buildings as follows:[4]

Donald Oehlerts provides the following estimates for main public libraries built from 1850 to 1989 based on various surveys and reports in *Library Journal:*

Table 3-3. Main Public Library Buildings, 1850 to 1989[5]

Date	Estimated Number Completed	Estimated Total Cost
1850–1893	500	$ 15,000,000
1894–1918	1,500	80,000,000
1919–1945	1,000	60,000,000
1946–1969	2,000	500,000,000
1970–1989	1,000	2,800,000,000
Total	6,000	$3,455,000,000

1945 to 1965

Unfortunately, other than Oehlerts's estimate for large public libraries, there are no comprehensive figures for the different types of funds spent for public library buildings during this period. The only other source of this kind of information is a 1966 report by Nathan M. Cohen of the U.S. Office of Education to the Subcommittee on Economic Progress of the Joint Eco-

Table 3-4. Capital Outlay, Public Libraries, by Source for Selected Years 1945–65 (In millions of dollars)

Year	Total	Local	State	Federal	Private
1965	103.0	70.9	0.5	29.9	1.7
1964	61.3	60.1			1.2
1962	27.7	26.8			.9
1956	12.3	11.7			.6
1950	4.4	4.1			.3
1946	1.8	1.6			.2
1945	1.2	1.0			.2

nomic Committee of the Congress of the United States.[6] Table 3-4 shows the data tabulated back to 1945 and broken down into four main sources of funds: local, state, federal, and private.

Capital outlay funds for public library buildings increased from $1.2 million in 1945 to $103 million in 1965. To a large extent, this increase is accounted for by the rise in local funding from $1 million in 1945 to $70.9 million in 1965. The increased growth rate for all funds was further accelerated by the introduction of $29.9 million in federal funds in 1965. Private funds represented 17 percent of the total in 1945, but only 1.7 percent in 1965, a ten-fold decrease. In 1945, 83 percent of all construction funds were local public funds, while in 1965, local funds accounted for 69 percent. Of the total $70.9 million in local funds in 1965, approximately $15.2 million (21 percent) came from local general obligation bond issues. The remaining local funds came from other kinds of bonds and local direct tax appropriations. While federal funds were just beginning, state funds for public library construction during this time period were negligible.

In the mid-1960's, a nationally sponsored survey of public library buildings resulted from the inclusion of Title II, Public Library Construction, in the expanded fed-

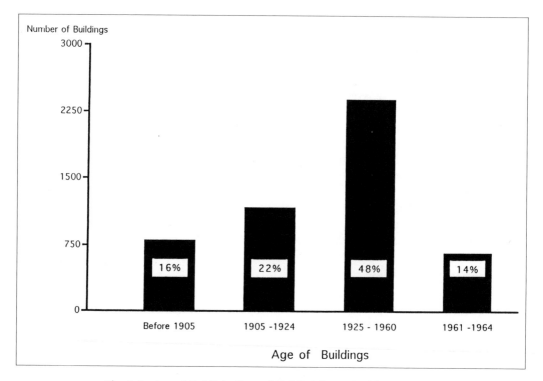

Fig. 3-1. Age of Publicly Owned Public Library Buildings, 1964.

eral Library Services and Construction Act (LSCA) of 1964. Figure 3-1 is based on the extrapolation of unpublished data from the U.S. Office of Education's *Survey of Public Library Building Facilities, Fiscal 1963.*[7] In this survey, reports from local libraries to the U.S. Office of Education indicated that 38 percent of publicly owned public library buildings were more than forty years old. The largest percentage of buildings (48 percent) were built from 1925 to 1960; only 14 percent were constructed in the early 1960s.

This survey showed that in 1965, local public libraries occupied approximately 55 million square feet of space and reported the need for an additional 40 million square feet at an estimated cost of approximately $1 billion. An extrapolation of this data revealed an overall need of approximately $1.9 billion in capital outlay funds for an additional 68 million square feet of public library space from 1966 to 1975.

RECENT INFORMATION: *LIBRARY JOURNAL'S* ARCHITECTURAL ISSUE

Shortly after the publication of the U.S. Office of Education's reports, which supported the continuation of LSCA Title II federal funds for public library construction, the library profession began to report statistics covering recently built public library buildings. Since 1968, the main source of consistently reliable information has been the annual architectural issue of *Library Journal.* The profession is indebted to library building consultant Hoyt Galvin, who first developed this consistent method of collecting library construction data in conjunction with *Library Journal.* While the data in the *Library Journal* report are not completely comprehensive because reporting is voluntary for local libraries, the process does provide a significant statistical sample showing the

general trend of increasing funds for public library construction over the last 24 years.

The Growth in Total Annual Expenditures

The total funds expended for public library construction has steadily increased as can be seen in Figure 3-2. This increase, a little over 5 percent per year, reflects the substantial growth in funds available for public library construction since the beginning of the *Library Journal* data collection. For the 24-year period, the reported average annual expenditure for public library construction was $149 million. For many of the early years, annual amounts hovered around $100 million. However, since the surge in funding in 1979, when the amount increased to almost $200 million, things have never been the same, and except for 1983, total funds have consistently exceeded $100 million. Beginning in 1984, the growth rate has been nothing short of phenomenal. With the exception of 1990, the total funds available for public library construction have increased steadily and significantly. Since 1987, total funds have exceeded $200 million each year, and, in 1990 and 1991, the total amount has averaged over $300 million.

The significance of the recent increase in capital spending is obvious when it is understood that the last eight years of funding represents over 50 percent of all funds reported during the 24-year history of the *Library Journal* construction statistics. Unfortunately, it is impossible to predict the future. The recent growth rate does appear positive, but during the early years of data collection there were significant fluctuations in the income stream for public library construction, and these vacillations in the level of funding may reappear when the effect of the recession of the early-1990's begins to show up in the data reports.

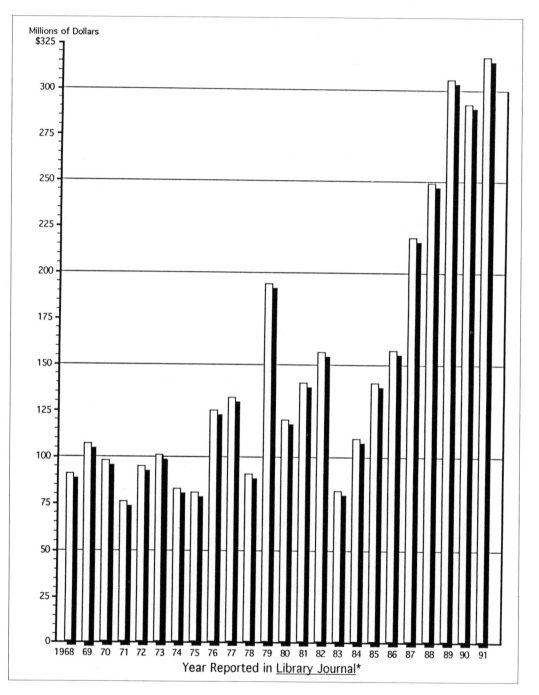

Fig. 3-2. Total Funds Expended for Public Library Construction By Year

* ©Reed Publishing

Table 3-5. Public Library Construction Funds by Source* (In millions of dollars)

FY	Total	State	Federal	Local	Private
1991	318	25.8	14.7	250.0	27.4
1990	292	36.8	17.6	208.5	29.0
1989	306**	14.2**	16.4	246.4	28.6
1988	249	20.8	14.7	191.4	21.9
1987	219	13.0	10.4	181.2	13.9
1986	158	8.9	11.1	117.0	20.8
1985	140	5.8	17.9	97.0	19.3
1984	110	7.1	4.5	94.0	4.0
1983	82	11.3	5.5	58.2	7.1
1982	157**	4.3**	17.4	112.6	22.9
1981	140	4.9	22.4	100.7	12.1
1980	120	4.8	33.3	73.1	9.1
1979	194	15.3	81.8	83.9	12.8
1978	91	6.9	17.4	57.6	9.1
1977	132	7.1	20.4	95.6	8.6
1976	125	7.5	27.4	77.4	12.4
1975	81	2.8	11.5	58.9	7.7
1974	83	1.8	7.6	67.4	6.1
1973	101	2.6	8.7	77.5	11.9
1972	95	1.4	11.8	74.1	7.2
1971	76	3.2	13.4	53.1	6.5
1970	98	3.1	22.9	58.3	13.3
1969	107	1.1	26.6	74.1	5.4
1968	91	.9	20.8	68.9	N/A
TOTAL:	3,565	211.4	456.2	2,576.9	317.1
AVERAGE:	149	8.8	19.0	107.4	13.2
PERCENTAGE:	100%	5.9%	12.8%	72.3%	8.9%
ROUND-OFF	100%	6%	13%	72%	9%

*Compiled from 6-year cost summaries of *Library Journal* December issues.
**State Library Buildings deleted from data in 1982 and 1989.
©Reed Publishing

Funding by Source

Much information may be gained from analyzing the various sources of funds from public library construction reports. Table 3-5 summarizes the total dollars expended for public library construction and provides a breakdown by funding source (state, federal, local, and private). This table chronicles the major trends in public library construction expenditures since 1968.

Figure 3-3 contains the same information as Table 3-5 in the form of a graph. It is easy to see that the amount of money going into public library construction from various sources has varied over the years. Table 3-5 shows that for the 24-year per-iod over 90 percent of all capital develop-ment funds have come from the public sec-tor (local, state, and federal combined), with the majority of funds (72 percent) coming from the local public sector. On average, state funds have accounted for 6 percent and private funds 9 percent of all construction funds. Federal funds have var-ied significantly over the years but on aver-age have accounted for about 13. The spe-cifics for each funding source will be re-viewed in detail in the following chapters.

Trends in Funding by Source

Table 3-6 shows a comparison of the amount of funds going into public library

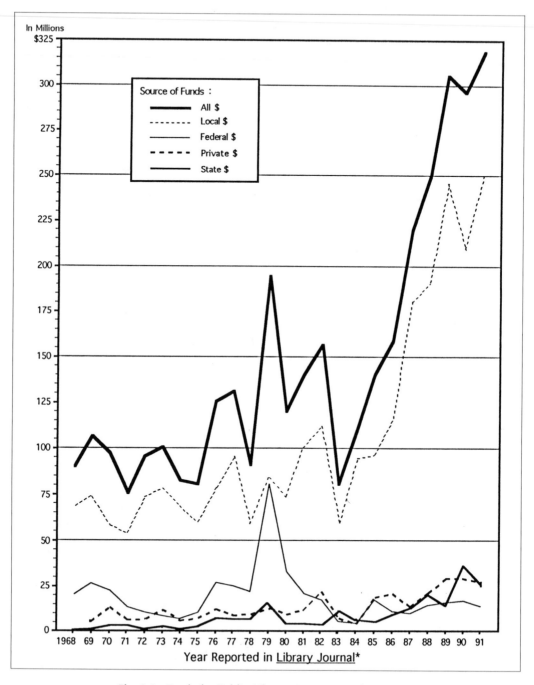

Fig. 3-3. Funds for Public Library Construction by Source

* ©Reed Publishing

Table 3-6. Trends in Funding by Source (average dollars expended per year, in millions)

Year	Total	State	Federal	Local	Private
1968 to	149	8.8	19.0	107.4	13.2
1991	100%	6%	13%	72%	9%
1968 to	106	4.5	22.5	70.6	8.4
1979	100%	4%	21%	67%	8%
1980 to	191	13.1	15.5	144.2	18.0
1991	100%	7%	8%	76%	9%
1987 to	277	22.1	14.8	215.5	24.2
1991	100%	8%	5%	78%	9%

©Reed Publishing

construction from the various sources during different time periods. The first row contains data for all years, the second row for the first 12 years of data collection, the third for last 12 years, and the fourth for the last 5 years.

Local Funds

Local funds have remained the major source of money for public library projects. As mentioned, over the 24 years of data collection, local sources have accounted for an average of 72 percent of all funds. In the early years, this figure was only 67 percent, with approximately $71 million per year of local funds going into public library construction. However, in the last 12 years, local funds jumped to 76 percent of the total by doubling to over $144 million per year. This trend is obviously continuing when only the last five years of data are analyzed. During this time period, 78 percent of all funds came from local sources, a total of more than $215 million per year. While local sources have always been the main contributor to public library construction, it appears the percentage of local funds is continuing to increase. This trend is important for library supporters to recognize. The days of looking beyond local horizons for significant funding may be waning, because the engine that is driving

public library construction definitely appears to be local funding.

Private Funds

The private sector has remained the most stable source of funds over the last 24 years. For these years, it has accounted for approximately 9 percent of all funds, averaging just over $13 million per year. In the early years, private sources accounted for approximately 8 percent of all funds and averaged a little over $8 million per year. In the latter years, the percentage increased slightly to 9 percent while averaging $18 million per year. In the last five years, private funding has accounted for 9 percent of all funds, averaging $24 million per year. While it appears that the level of private funding that flourished during the Carnegie era may never return, private funds since the 60s have provided a stable although relatively modest source of funds for public library construction.

Federal Funds

While federal funds have provided approximately 13 percent of all funds over the 24-year period, they are currently on the decline. During the early years (corresponding in part to the beginning of the LSCA Title II program), federal funds accounted for 21 percent of all funds and averaged over $22 million per year. However, in the later years, the federal share dropped dramatically to almost one third of its former level. For the last 12 years, federal funds have accounted for only 8 percent of all funds with an average annual allocation of less than $16 million. There has been not only a significant drop in the percentage of federal funds, but an actual dollar drop which is even more significant considering the inflationary pressures during that period. In the last five years the federal share dropped to 5 percent—less than one quarter of what it was in the early years. Finally, the actual funds provided dropped again to a level of less than $15 million per year on average. Given this trend, it seems unlikely that large federal appropriations will return soon unless there are major federal policy shifts toward public library construction or infrastructure financing.

State Funds

While federal funds have been on the decline, state funds have been on the increase, but unfortunately not as dramatically. For all years, state funds have accounted for 6 percent of all funds expended for public library construction. During the early years, state funds accounted for only 4 percent of all funds with an average annual appropriation of only $4.5 million per year. By the last 12 years, the state's share had increased to 7 percent and state funds on average accounted for $13 million per year. During a time when the total amount of funds going into public library construction nearly doubled, state funds almost tripled. In the last five years, this trend has continued with the state's share increasing to 8 percent and the average annual appropriation going up to over $22 million per year. The $110 million generated from state sources in the last five years accounts for over half of all the state funds expended for public library construction in the last 24 years.

The problem is that while state funds have been on the increase they have not kept up with the decline in federal funds. During the early years, the two sources accounted for 25 percent of all funds and provided on average $27 million per year out of $106 million total. During the last 12 years, the combined percentage for these two funding sources dropped dramatically to only 15 percent. Even though the amount provided by both sources increased slightly to an average of over $28 million per year, this rate of increase did not keep up with the dramatic growth of all funds to over $190 million per year which nearly doubled from the first 12 years average.

This trend appears to be continuing since the percentage for these two sources has dropped again in the last five years to 13 percent of the total funds expended for public library construction. While these two sources account for approximately $37 million per year, the growth in overall funds to $277 million per year has outpaced the combined growth rate of state and federal funds.

Summary

While federal funds have been declining significantly, state funds have been increasing, but not enough to make up the difference. The remainder has been made up by local public sources since private sources have remained relatively stable over the years. Library planners should keep these facts in mind when deciding how to finance the proposed project budget. In the last five years, 87 percent of all funds have come from local sources including both private and public funds. In most cases, the funds will come from sources "close to home," but state and federal sources should not be ignored. It is always worth looking into these prospects, but it should be done with realism and practicality. For the most part, the federal "pot of gold" is not as accessible as it once was; and while state sources have increased, they are limited to only a handful of states that currently have active library construction grant programs. However, since there may be an opportunity to tap into some of the $37 million allocated annually from state and federal funds, it is important to review the existing state and federal programs in the next two chapters.

REFERENCES

1. George S. Bobinski, *Carnegie Libraries: Their History and Impact on American Public Library Development* (Chicago: 1969, American Library Association), p. 3.

2. Donald E. Oehlerts, *Books and Blueprints: Building America's Public Libraries* (Westport, Conn.: Greenwood Press, 1991), p. 130.

3. Simeon E. Leland, "The Financing of Library Construction Through Bond Issues" *Library Journal* 15 January 1930, pp. 54-55

4. Hoyt R. Galvin, "Public Library Buildings in 1968" *Library Journal* 1 December 1968, p. 4498.

5. Oehlerts, p. 129.

6. Nathan M. Cohen, "Public Libraries," in *State and Local Public Facility Needs and Financing* (Study prepared for the Subcommittee on Economic Progress of the Joint Economic Committee, Congress of the United States) Volume 1, *Public Facility Needs* (Washington: Government Printing Office, 1966), p. 623

7. John C. Frantz and Nathan M. Cohen, "The Federal Government and Public Libraries: A Ten-Year Partnership, 1957-65" in *Survey of Public Library Building Facilities, Fiscal 1963-64.* (Washington: Government Printing Office, 1966), p. 17.

Federal Funding Sources

OVERVIEW OF FEDERAL FUNDING

During the past 24 years, federal funding has provided over $456 million for public library construction in the United States averaging over $19 million per year. This accounts for approximately 13 percent of all funds expended for that purpose. Figure 4-1 shows the annual federal funding amounts reported for public library construction.

Federal funding for many programs tends to be unstable from year to year, and public library construction is no exception. Federal funds accounted for as much as $81 million in 1979 and as little as $4.5 million in 1984. In the first three years of data collection, federal funds accounted for over $20 million per year but tapered off in the mid-seventies. Federal funds rebounded to over $20 million per year in 1976 and then spiked upward to over $80 million in 1979. Unfortunately, federal funds began a "free fall" that year until bottoming out in 1984. Since that time, federal funds have climbed back into the mid-teens and wavered there for the last seven years.

Along with the variation in the actual amount of federal funding, the percentage of total funds accounted for by the federal funds has varied tremendously. Figure 4-2 shows the federal funds reported each year as a percentage of the total amount of funds available for public library construction:

Federal sources have the greatest range of any of the four main funding sources. As Figure 4-2 shows, federal funding has accounted for a very wide range of funding percentages over the years, from around 4 percent in 1984 to just over 42 percent in 1979. The two graphs are similar except in the most recent years because for many years the total amount of public library construction funding mirrored the availability of federal funds. This has changed since the percentage of federal funds dropped off from the early years. In the first 12 years, federal funding accounted for approximately 21 percent of all funds for public library construction, but in the last five years, it has accounted for only 5 percent.

What has happened over the last 24 years to cause such significant change? The figures for 1979 are the most unusual, for in that year a total of $194 million was expended for public library construction with an astounding $81.8 million coming from the federal government. This figure is approximately four times the usual amount coming from this source and resulted from the convergence of two federal funding initiatives.

The first was the appropriation of $6 billion in federal funds from the Local Public Works Program of the Public Works Employment Act of 1976 and 1977 (PL 94-369 and PL 95-28). These funds, which had a ninety day start-up requirement, were administered through the Economic Development Administration (EDA) at the

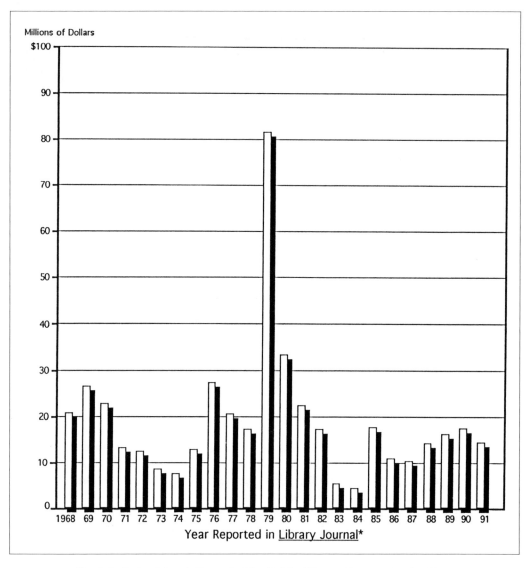

Millions of Dollars

Year Reported in <u>Library Journal</u>*

Fig. 4-1. Federal Funds Expended for Public Library Construction by Year.
*©Reed Publishing

end of the Ford administration and the beginning of the Carter administration. Of the $6 billion of public works funds, 192 public library building projects received over $133 million.[1] For communities that could begin construction immediately, this federal program was a bonanza. The program required little or no local matching funds, and public libraries were reasonably successful in competing for these funds at the local level. In addition to the public works funds, congressional approval of an extension of the State and Local Fiscal Assistance Act (PL 94-488) provided authorization of over $25 billion of federal revenue-sharing funds during this time period, and a major stimulus for public library capital projects.

Percent of Total Funds

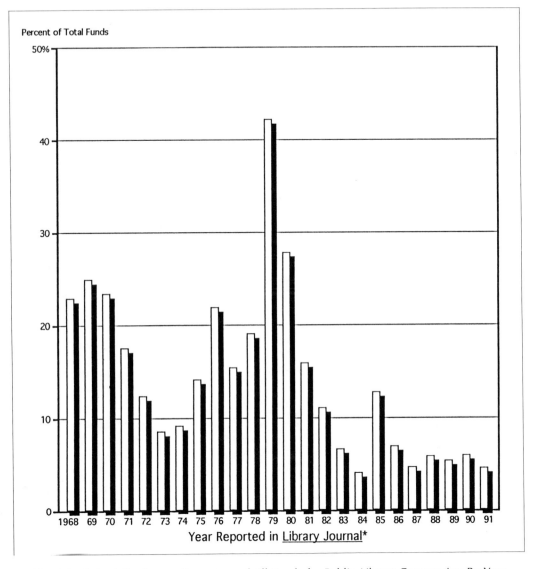

Fig. 4-2. Federal Funds as a Percentage of All Funds for Public Library Construction By Year
* ©Reed Publishing

From 1973 to 1986, when federal revenue sharing funds were available, this source accounted for a substantial amount of the federal funds going to public library construction, but unfortunately there was never any consistent collection of data to show the exact amount or the percentage. In 1976, Hoyt Galvin[2] reported that approximately 73 percent of all federal funds

came from general revenue-sharing funds during that year, but unfortunately the *Library Journal* statistics do not typically report the specific source of federal funds received for public library construction projects. Without consistent data collection for federal funds used in public library construction projects, the profession may never know the exact amount or program source of federal monies expended for this purpose.

The peak of federal capital funding for public libraries appears to have been from 1975 to 1982. During this eight-year period, over $230 million of federal funds poured into public library construction. This amount is more than half of all the federal funding for public library construction during the 24 years that *Library Journal* has collected statistics. Unfortunately, this level of federal participation may never be repeated. The federal percentage dropped to its lowest point in 1984 largely because of substantial reductions in the federal revenue-sharing program. Finally, in 1985, federal funds recovered somewhat with the revitalization of LSCA Title II program because of the pass-through of $50 million from the federal 1983 Emergency Jobs Act (PL 98-8). Even though direct appropriations had not been available for Title II since the early 1970s, the wisdom of the efforts of the ALA Washington Office to keep the title "on the books" was evident. Because the enabling legislation for Title II was still in force, the jobs bill funds could be easily and quickly passed through the Title II "financing shell" to public libraries in need of construction funding.

Fortunately, because this pass-through funding of the jobs bill generated increased interest in the federal LSCA Title II program, it was reinstated in 1985. Since that time, there has been a gradual increase (except for 1990) in federal funding supported by the reauthorizations of LSCA Title II. However, even with this reinstatement, the percentages for federal funds have remained low in recent years because of the tremendous growth in local, state and private funds for public library capital development. However, the important "spark plug" effect of the federal LSCA Title II program on the development of public library facilities country cannot be underestimated.

LIBRARY SERVICES AND CONSTRUCTION ACT (LSCA) TITLE II

Over the years the most important source of federal funds for public library facilities has been the LSCA Title II public library construction program.

The Library Services and Construction Act (LSCA) was signed into law by President Johnson on February 11, 1964. Its overall purpose was to promote the extension of public libraries to all areas without such services or with inadequate services; to provide for the construction of new public library buildings or the improvement of existing library facilities.[3]

LSCA began as Public Law 88-269 and has been amended numerous times over the years (PL 101-254 is the most recent), but its intent has remained the same: to foster the development and enhancement of public library facilities.

When LSCA Title II began in the mid-1960's, 38 percent of all public libraries had been built before 1925 (see Chapter 3, Figure 3-1). The need was further supported by survey results indicating that local public libraries had reported the need of an additional 40 million square feet of space at a cost of approximately $1 billion.[4] Fortunately, Congress responded by providing $30 million for LSCA Title II in 1965, the first year of appropriations.

Despite the 11-year hiatus in the funding of the program between 1973 and 1985 — largely compensated for by other federal funding sources as explained above — there has been a reasonable if varied level of appropriations of federal LSCA Title II funds over the years.

As shown, the total amount of federal funding for LSCA Title II is just over $340 million, but with additional pass-through funding for the program such as funds from the Emergency Jobs Act and the Appalachian Regional Commission (ARC), LSCA Title II has been responsible for disbursing approximately $400 million in federal

Table 4-1. LSCA Title II Appropriations by Fiscal Year[5]

Fiscal Year	Appropriations
1992	$16,383,640
1991	18,833,395
1990	18,572,036
1989	21,877,520
1988	22,143,100
1987	22,050,000
1986	21,102,000
1985	24,500,000
1984	0
1983	0
1982	0
1981	0
1980	0
1979	0
1978	0
1977	0
1976	0
1975	0
1974	0
1973	15,000,000
1972	9,500,000
1971	7,092,500
1970	7,807,250
1969	9,185,000
1968	27,185,000
1967	40,000,000
1966	30,000,000
1965	30,000,000
Total:	$341,231,441

funds for public library construction. When other federal sources are taken into account, such as federal revenue sharing, EDA public works, HUD block grants, and NEH, the total amount of federal funding of public library construction in the last 28 years is probably over $1 billion. The difference between this figure and the one shown in the *Library Journal* statistics ($456 million in 24 years) is due to three factors. The first is the variable amount of time it takes to distribute federal funds through the state agencies to local jurisdictions, along with the variable lengths of time for local planning and construction. In short, not all funds that have been appropriated have been reported yet because the projects have not been completed. Se-

condly, the reporting mechanism to *Library Journal* is entirely voluntary, and every year some projects go unreported. Finally, the time span of the *Library Journal* data collection is four years less than the 28-year span of the LSCA Title II program.

The funding for the LSCA Title II program can be discussed in three distinct phases, the first of which ran from 1965 to 1973, the second from 1974 to 1984, and the third from 1985 to the present time. Each phase is unique and provides a different perspective on federal funding for public library construction.

LSCA Phase I (1965-1973)

The first phase of the LSCA Title II program lasted for 9 years. Over $175 million was appropriated, averaging $19.5 million per year. These first years saw some of the largest annual appropriations for the program ($30 to $40 million). Demonstrating the importance of LSCA Title II and federal funding in general, the document entitled *Public Library Construction 1965-1978*[6] reported that LSCA Title II funded 1,917 library construction projects. This federal funding stimulated the investment of $528,893,615 in state and local matching funds which generated a total of $724 million for public library construction during this time period. Over 88 million people were affected by this expansion in library services, and nearly 25 million square feet of public library space were added or remodeled. Almost 200,000 new reader and meeting-room seats were added and the capacity to hold almost 72 million books was added to public libraries.

This first phase of the LSCA Title II program gave a tremendous boost to the development of public library buildings. Every federal dollar going into public library construction in those years stimulated $2.70 of state and local funding. This new federal partnership was in many ways akin to the role that Andrew Carnegie played for public libraries around the turn of the century, and created a renaissance for the funding of public library buildings. Unfortunately, this trend did not last long, and in 1973 funding for the program ceased. With the cessation of Title II appropriations, the general revenue-sharing program became the most significant source of federal funds for public library capital development.

LSCA Phase II (1974-1984)

The second phase was an 11-year period when only pass through funding was appropriated from other federal sources and disbursed through the LSCA Title II program. The majority of the money came through in 1983 with the jobs bill allocation of $50 million. However, some funding trickled down from the Appalachian Regional Commission and other agencies as well.

It is ironic that the largest expenditures for public library construction from federal sources were made during this period of relatively little federal funding through Title II. As noted earlier, the source of this federal funding was mostly from federal revenue sharing and the public works program administered through EDA. These funds were not specifically earmarked for public libraries and had to be fought for with competing local needs. This demonstrated that when public library planners were ready to proceed with projects quickly and willing to lobby local officials in an effective manner, they could be and often were successful in obtaining federal funds in competition with other agencies.

Even so, it is extremely important for the steady development of public library facilities to have a dedicated stream of federal funds to spur public library construction. This funding provides continuity and allows local library officials to prod local funding officials to action secure in the knowledge that there are federal funds available specifically for public library

projects. With this in mind, and because there were no current appropriations for LSCA Title II, Senator Jacob Javits proposed an appropriation level of $150 million per year for Title III of the National Library and Information Services Act which he sponsored in 1980. To support this legislation, the library community through the assistance of state library agencies attempted to determine the national need for new public library space. This 1980 survey showed the need for over 2,900 public library building projects costing in excess of $2.3 billion over the five-year period from 1981 to 1985.[7]

Although, this legislation never became law, the results of the survey were used again by the ALA Washington Office to support the need for library construction funds when the Emergency Jobs Act was proposed. The Emergency Jobs Act program initiated "500 public library construction projects of which 346 were reported to have been completed as of February 1, 1987."[8] The $50 million of federal jobs bill funds triggered the use of $100 million of state and local funding for public library construction as well. This supported the intent of the jobs bill which was to target areas where unemployment was highest and most entrenched.[9] Federal and state agencies were to utilize the funds where they would have the greatest impact on employment through the immediate creation of new jobs. Because of this mandate, approximately 70 percent of the library projects funded were either remodeling or addition and remodeling projects; only 30 percent were new building projects. The jobs bill funding had a very positive impact not only on the creation of jobs, but also stimulating renewed interest in federal funds for public library construction.

LSCA Phase III (1985 - Present)

The third phase witnessed the rebirth of appropriations for LSCA Title II with $24.5 million in 1985. During the eight year period from 1985 until 1992, LSCA Title II appropriations amounted to over $165 million, an average of about $20.7 million per year. It is interesting to note that this is only slightly more than the average of the first phase, and with the devaluation of the dollar during this time actually results in a serious decline in terms of real spending power. Nonetheless, this resurrection of federal public library construction is most welcome since a review of the most recent statistics indicates these Title II-administered federal funds have stimulated almost one-and-one-half times their amount in state and local matching funds.[10]

The story does not end here, the LSCA Title II program has recently been re-authorized and annual appropriations appear to be ongoing although the library community must fight for them each year. While the appropriation levels have declined in recent years (from the mid-twenty-million range down to the mid-teen-million dollar range), it may be that the employment difficulties caused by the recession of the early 1990s will result in another jobs-bill allocation that can be used for public library construction. In January 1992, Senators Kennedy and Wellstone introduced the Emergency Anti-Recession Act of 1992 which if passed would add $60 million in additional funding for Title II of LSCA. Possibly this effort, or another like it, which recognizes the positive impact of federal funds for public library construction, will usher in increased levels of federal funding in the future.

How to Apply for LSCA Title II Funds

If a jurisdiction is interested in pursuing a grant from the LSCA Title II program, the first step is usually to contact the state library agency. The program officer responsible for administering the Title II funds can provide potential applicants with program requirements and application forms along with the timetable for application.

Although the LSCA law and Title II federal regulations are the same for every state, the states administer the program based on their own state plan, which provides for a good deal of latitude within federal program requirements.

Eligible Costs

The current version of LSCA Title II states that grants can be used for the construction and technology enhancement of public libraries. The term "construction" is defined to include:

construction of new buildings and acquisition, expansion, remodeling, and alteration of existing buildings, and for the purchase, lease, and installation of equipment of any such buildings, or any combination of such activities (including architect's fees and the cost of acquisition of land). Such term includes remodeling to meet standards under the Act of August 12, 1968, commonly known as the "Architectural Barriers Act of 1968," remodeling designed to ensure safe working environments and to conserve energy, renovation or remodeling to accommodate new technologies, and the purchase of existing historic buildings for conversion to public libraries. For the purposes of this paragraph, the term "equipment" includes information and building technologies, video and telecommunications equipment, machinery, utilities, and built-in equipment and any necessary enclosures or structures to house them; and such term includes all other items necessary for the functioning of a particular facility as a facility for the provision of library services.[11]

All of these types of "construction" are eligible under the LSCA Title II program, although they may not all be eligible in every state. The state may decide to exclude an item, e.g., the cost of acquiring land is excluded in the state of Georgia. Further, certain types of construction may be given priority over other types. For example, some states may emphasize remodeling for disabled access or technology improvements, while others may emphasize new construction. The administration of

LSCA Title II is strongly rooted in the states and has been influenced by state library staff members who implement the program by requesting applications, approving grants, and providing technical assistance to grant recipients. Some states, like California, even go beyond the terms prescribed in the law and introduce other state-based priorities into the administration of the program, such giving high priority to eligible projects "serving communities whose minority population significantly exceed the state average."

It should be noted that for the first time in the history of the program, the acquisition of technology necessary to provide access to information (computerized equipment), may be a project in and of itself. It does not have to be part of a remodeling or a new construction project. In recent years, many states have sought to provide Title II funds for remodeling for disabled access, energy conservation, new technologies, and health and safety (removal of asbestos and other toxic materials, for example). However, the program does not allow Title II funds to be expended for general repair or maintenance of an existing building.

Fund Allocations

Each year that LSCA Title II funds are appropriated, they are available until expended. The national appropriation is allocated to states according to a formula. State fund allocations vary since the formula is, in part, based on the state's population. Further, while the federal share of eligible costs may not exceed 50 percent, it is often the case that more than 50 percent of the project's costs are provided by state and local governments. Many states impose maximum and minimum grants to "spread the money around" as well as reduce the administrative overhead. The program is flexible, and potential applicants should become familiar with the recent fund allocation trends.

The Application

Because of the limited amount of Title II funding available, in most states the program is competitive each year. Local jurisdictions that have the legal authority to apply to state library agencies must do so in competition with other jurisdictions. It also usually means that good projects go unfunded each year in most states. It is extremely important for potential applicants to understand the program's funding criteria and complete the application forms in the manner prescribed by the state library program officer or state librarian. Most Title II applications will ask for such basic project information as the amount of square footage to be built or remodeled as well as the size of the current facility, the number and kinds of materials and seats to be housed in the new or improved facility, and a brief description of the service to be provided.

This is frequently supplemented by requests for planning documents such as needs assessments, facility master plans, building programs, and occasionally architectural plans, outline specifications, and cost estimates prepared by architects and engineers. In almost all cases, a detailed project budget is required showing the projected costs as well as the sources of funds including federal, state, and local shares with some form of commitment for the local matching funds. The applicant must also state that funds are available to operate the facility as a library, since grant recipients are required to operate and maintain the library facility built or remodeled with Title II funds for 20 years or else repay the federal government's interest in the project. Generally, a timetable for the project's completion is also required. Some states have rather rigid requirements about how soon the project must be under construction; others are more lenient.

The Grant Decision

Once the application has been submitted, the state library will review it for accuracy and compliance with the program requirements. There are various methods the states use to make grant determinations. Some states actively involve their LSCA advisory committee, while in others the decision may be made by the state librarian alone. In any case, all states must allow the applicant a hearing if a grant is denied. This, or a less formal review, may help potential applicants determine how their application could be improved for resubmission in the future. It may take several tries for a jurisdiction to succeed in obtaining a grant.

Program Compliance Requirements

If a jurisdiction is fortunate enough to receive a Title II grant award, it must follow a number of requirements for the planning, design, contract administration, and operation of the library. While the following discussion is not comprehensive, it will outline the major points of concern. The reader is advised to seek this information from both state and federal program documents and reminded that Title II projects are administered differently by each state. Grantees must be accountable regarding the project's records and program compliance requirements and furnish progress reports, use appropriate fiscal accounting procedures, provide state and federal officials access to the project records, and retain the records for five years. The grantee's employees must observe the provision of the Hatch Act and may not use their position for personal gain or create situations that could be considered a conflict of interest. Further, the grantee must certify that it has adopted a policy of maintaining a drug-free workplace.

During the planning and design of the project, a professional library building consultant must be hired to write a building program and a registered architect must be hired to design the building as well as provide competent and adequate engineering supervision at the construction site. The design of the building must meet current building codes and regulations such as those for energy conservation, disabled access, and health and safety. The grantee must provide relocation assistance under the Uniform Relocation Assistance and Real Property Acquisition Policies Act if any persons or businesses are displaced by the project. Executive Order 11988 regarding flood plain management must be adhered to, and if the project lies in a flood plain, flood insurance must be purchased for the lifetime of the project under the Flood Disaster Protection Act of 1973. If the project will affect properties that are listed in or eligible for inclusion in the National Register of Historic Places, then the preservation requirements in the National Historic Preservation Act of 1966 must be followed. If there is the possibility of the loss of archaeological artifacts, the requirements of the Archeological Preservation Act of 1960 must be implemented. Further, a Title II project must not be listed on the Environmental Protection Agency's list of violating facilities.

With respect to construction administration, all federally funded Title II projects must be bid competitively and the contract awarded to the lowest responsible bidder. Except for projects that are exclusively for technology enhancement, the provisions of the Davis Bacon Act apply, which means the prevailing federal wage rates must be paid to the various trades used on the construction job. These rate determinations must be posted at the job site and the grantee must retain contractor payrolls for five years in case of an audit. The provisions of Equal Employment Opportunity must be adhered to as specified in Executive Order 11246 and amended by Executive Order 11375. The provisions of the Copeland Anti-Kickback Act are in effect, as are those of the Clean Air and Clean Water

Acts for contracts over $100,000. There must be potable water at the construction site and the construction contract must comply with the Contract Work Hours and Safety Standards Act. Finally, the grantee must provide access to the construction site for state and federal officials during the construction of the building and post a sign on the job site that indicates that funds were provided from the LSCA Title II program as well as provide a building plaque that indicates the same whenever the building is finished.

Once the facility is completed, the grantee must ensure that it is used and operated under the nondiscrimination provision of Title VI of the Civil Rights Act of 1964 as well as other applicable laws. While these requirements may seem excessive, they are all fairly basic provisions to any federally funded construction program and are usually not difficult to adhere to as long as the grant recipient understands them from the beginning. In most cases the planning requirements have had a positive effect on the library buildings built with Title II funds and have resulted in better facilities than might have been otherwise constructed. In some cases, however, it can be documented that some of these requirements (particularly the Davis Bacon Act) have increased the costs for the project in some locales.

Finally, it should be noted that while there are state variations in how payments of the federal funds are made to grant recipients, payments are usually made at major milestones in the project's planning and construction. States may provide, for example, 25 percent of the federal funds when 25 percent of the construction contract is complete, 50 percent of the funds when 50 percent of the contract is complete, etc. Most states usually hold out a small percentage of the federal funds (often 10 percent) until after the project is completed and the final auditing has been performed and accepted. This provides some

leverage which is frequently necessary to see that projects are in fact completed and closed out.

In summary, the LSCA Title II program remains an effective method of federal funding for public library construction. Many public library facilities in the nation desperately need state and federal assistance for development, and the Title II program helps meet that need. However, it is at present severely underfunded compared to the need. In 1980, Raymond M. Holt stated at the New York American Library Association annual conference, "For the future, the problem of achieving adequate public library facilities appears to be of such dimensions that it can be solved only by dependable, long-term federal participation."[12] It must be added that the annual funding level must be adequate to begin making substantial progress toward bringing the nation's library facilities up to a reasonable standard of service for all individuals of the society regardless of where they live and what socioeconomic level they represent. Adequate public libraries are an integral part of every American's "pursuit of happiness." Access to books and information in all forms is critical to providing social equality and stability, and public library facilities have an important role in this process.

OTHER FEDERAL SOURCES

While the LSCA Title II program provides a dedicated revenue stream for public library facilities, because of the relatively low levels of appropriation, it must at present be supplemented with other state and federal funding sources. Over the years numerous federal agencies have contributed funds toward public library construction. The following is a brief description of other sources of federal funds available for public library construction. Some of these programs are still active and some are not. New programs may develop in the future that will provide federal funds for public library construction.

It is prudent for local jurisdictions to monitor the federal budget and be prepared to pursue potential federal funding. Preparedness usually means understanding the need for library service and facilities in a community and having current planning documents such as needs assessments, facility master plans, building programs, and even in some cases preliminary architectural plans and specifications. If complete plans and specifications for the entire building are not ready, sometimes library planners can still qualify for quick-start-up programs if they can get construction contracts going for the project's site work including demolition, rough grading, etc. They could then buy more planning time for a second contract that would include the construction or remodeling of the building with final site work. This approach is not always feasible, but it may occasionally be useful if speed is of the essence.

While preparedness is important, not all federal programs require a quick start-up. The following section provides an overview of the various federal funding programs that have provided funds for public library construction. Programs are listed alphabetically by the name of the federal agency that administers them.

Agriculture Department

Rural Development Administration
Community Facility Loans (formerly Farmers Home Administration (FHA) program)

The Community Facility Loans program of the Rural Development Administration (RDA) provides low-interest loans and loan guarantees to local jurisdictions to construct, expand, or otherwise improve community facilities including public libraries. This program was authorized by Section 306 of the Consolidated Farm and (Rural Development Act of 1972 (PL 92-419) and most recently amended by the Food, Agriculture, Conservation, and Trade Act of 1990 (PL 101-624). The RDA provides insured loans that are available up to 40 years for relatively low interest rates. Loans are available to communities of less than 20,000 population; however, priority is given to more rural communities (under 5,000 and 2,500). Recently, the direct loan program has been funded at about $100 million per year, which usually generates 200 to 300 loans per year. However, increases in the program are scheduled which may bring the program up to a total of $200 million per year when "guaranteed" loans are included at the $100 million per year level as well. In addition to actually lending money to local jurisdictions, the guaranteed loan program backs loans up to 90 percent of the value provided by commercial banks and loan institutions.

Over the years public libraries have been reasonably successful in receiving loans from this program. Approximately 70 loans have been made for public libraries since the mid-seventies for a total of approximately $28 million. These loans have ranged from $30,000 to $2.7 million, with an average of about $400,000. Nine communities have received loans of over $1 million for public libraries:

East Hampton, Conn.	$2,000,000
Killingly, Conn.	2,215,000
Fulton County, Ind.	1,000,000
Jennings County, Ind.	2,776,000
New Carlisle & Olive Township, Ind.	1,450,000
Starke County, Ind.	1,700,000
Tipton County, Ind.	1,150,000
Westfield, Ind.	1,200,000
Queen Annes County, Md.	1,060,600

Obviously, public libraries in the state of Indiana have had a good deal of success with this program. Not only have they received six of the nine largest loans, but Indiana leads the nation with the number of loans at 12, followed by Rhode Island with eight loans, Connecticut with six loans and Mississippi with five loans. While specific information about the program in each state is available at the various district and state RDA offices, a complete list of RDA loans made to public libraries nationwide as well as general information about the program is available from:

John R. Bowles, Director
Community Facilities Division
Rural Development Administration
U.S. Department of Agriculture
Room 6304, South Building
Washington, DC 20250
(202) 382-1490

Appalachian Regional Commission (ARC)

Created by the Appalachian Regional Commission Act of 1965 (PL 89-4), the Appalachian Regional Commission (ARC) strives to raise the standard of living for individuals in the economically depressed area of the Appalachian Mountains, and promote economic growth in portions of the following 13 states: Alabama, Georgia, Kentucky, Maryland, Mississippi, New York, North Carolina, Ohio, Pennsylvania, South Carolina, Tennessee, Virginia, and West Virginia. Information regarding ARC programs can be obtained at state offices in those states or at:

Appalachian Regional Commission
1666 Connecticut Ave., N.W.
Washington, DC 20235
(202) 673-7868

Many of these states have received ARC funds to build public library projects, and some states have been quite successful, notably Alabama, Georgia, New York, North Carolina, Pennsylvania, Tennessee, and West Virginia. In the late seventies and early eighties the state of Georgia success-

fully combined ARC funds with a state library construction program to bring the local share down to as low as 20 percent in some projects.

The supplemental grants component of ARC's program raises the federal share in grant-in-aid programs for the construction of basic public facilities to up to 80 percent of construction costs. In this way, a state or community can participate in a program by putting up as little as 20 percent. ARC also awards first-dollar grants to qualified applicants who have been rejected by another federal agency and whose project fits into ARC's guidelines.[13]

ARC funding for public library projects is channeled through the LSCA Title II program and administered as pass-through funding.

Over the years ARC has made 197 grants for public library construction, furnishing, and equipment amounting to appropriations of just over $21 million. The total federal ARC appropriations in each state for public library capital outlay are as follows:

Alabama	$1,639,658
Georgia	2,831,059
Kentucky	441,563
Maryland	473,796
Mississippi	565,374
New York	1,898,175
North Carolina	3,245,144
Ohio	286,351
Pennsylvania	1,602,543
South Carolina	424,760
Tennessee	1,660,356
Virginia	1,311,603
West Virginia	4,942,111

Unfortunately, ARC funding for public library construction waned in the early to mid-eighties when program priorities shifted. However, there is still potential for ARC funding of public library construction, and funding priorities may change back if enough grassroots local pressure is applied in favor of funding public libraries.

Commerce Department

Economic Development Administration (EDA)

General Revenue Sharing Program: The federal General Revenue Sharing Program began in the early seventies with the enactment of the State and Local Fiscal Assistance Act of 1972 (PL 92-512). This act provided $30.2 billion to state and local governments from 1973 to 1976. The State and Local Fiscal Assistance Amendment of 1976 (PL 94-488) extended revenue sharing through fiscal year 1980 by adding another $25.6 billion. The revenue-sharing program was extended a third time with PL 96-604 through 1983, providing $4.6 billion annually. PL 98-185 extended the program a fourth time for 1984 through 1986 for an additional $4.6 billion annually. The total federal expenditures for the general revenue-sharing program amounted to over $66 billion for the 14-year duration of the program.[14]

Designed to provide maximum flexibility in financing state and local programs, the revenue-sharing program funneled federal funds to states and local jurisdictions; based on local priorities, these agencies determined how to spend the funds. This meant that public libraries had to compete for the funds with other government activities and convince local funding agencies that their particular needs were the most worthwhile. Public libraries were successful at obtaining revenue-sharing funding, but not overwhelmingly so. Public library projects often took a back seat to potholes in roads, broken water mains, and other "crisis" projects. However, when competing against other social programs, libraries usually performed fairly well. In 1980, Raymond Holt succinctly stated the matter: "Libraries which have strong, highly visible programs and can articulate their building needs fluently to officials and to the

public stand a good chance to secure a high priority for revenue-sharing funds."[15]

It is unknown exactly how much general revenue-sharing funds were spent during the existence of the program on public library programs generally or more specifically on public library capital projects; however, the Department of Commerce has provided some data regarding public library expenditures for some of the years the program was active. From 1973 to 1983, the Commerce Department reported that approximately $600 million had gone into public library programs.[16] Table 4-2 provides the revenue-sharing expenditures by state and local governments for public library programs. If the six years for which the Commerce Department data are not available (1978–1980 and 1984–1986) are estimated at $75 million each, then the overall amount of revenue sharing funds for public libraries would be just over $1 billion.

The program was very popular with local government officials since the revenue-sharing funds came with few federal controls. Unfortunately, this source of federal funding is no longer available for public library construction.

Table 4-2. State and Local General Revenue-Sharing Expenditures for Public Library Programs from 1973 to 1983[17] (in millions of dollars)

Fiscal Year	Revenue Sharing Funds for Public Libraries
1983	$75.95
1982	75.86
1981	74.64
1980	N/A
1979	N/A
1978	N/A
1977	79.72
1976	97.95
1975	95.01
1974	82.27
1973	19.60

Local Public Works Program: Another program administered by the EDA was the Local Public Works (LPW) program authorized by the Public Works Employment Act of 1976 and 1977 (PL 94-369 and 95-28). Similar to the public works programs of the Works Progress Administration (WPA) in the 1930s, this program provided federal capital for public projects in an attempt to stimulate the economy and lower unemployment lingering from the 1973-1975 recession. This program provided $6 billion of federal funds of which approximately $133 million was obtained by 192 public library projects for capital improvements. As noted earlier, this infusion of federal capital was partially responsible for the largest one-time annual report of federal funds in *Library Journal* at over $81 million in 1979. The LPW program was extremely popular with Congress and with local library officials who could meet the 90 day start-up requirement. In this program, preparedness paid off enormously.

Unfortunately the LPW program lapsed in 1978 with no further appropriations, but during its very short life public libraries received a great deal of benefit from it. The lesson is that during recessionary times, it is always worthwhile for local library planners to be prepared for programs that are occasionally passed by Congress to stimulate the economy. Constant monitoring of the federal budget is essential for library planners who want to be in a position to respond should a windfall of federal public-works funding become available.

Defense Department

Although an infrequent provider of funds for public library construction, the Department of Defense does occasionally provide capital "impact funds" to local communities that are experiencing rapid growth due to the proximity of major military installations. While records of such appropriations over the years have not been kept, one example of a project that received federal Department of Defense funds is in Georgia. When the Naval Submarine base was built in the late eighties in Camden County, Georgia, a public library in Kingsland was fortunate enough to receive $333,000 of federal funds which it used for the construction of a new building. It is prudent for library planners to monitor impact-fund allocations if there is growth in a locale due to a new or expanded military base.

Housing and Urban Development (HUD) Department

Community Development Block Grants (CDBG)

The Community Development Block Grant (CDBG) program is one of the most important programs providing federal funds to local jurisdictions since the cessation of the federal General Revenue Sharing program. Administered by the Department of Housing and Urban Development (HUD), Community Development Block Grants are authorized by the Housing and Community Development Act, Title I 1974 (PL 93-383) as amended. The grants are provided in two forms. The first is an entitlement grant for large cities and urban counties. The second is a competitive grant for small cities. While there is no matching funds requirement, these grants are intended to encourage public-private partnerships by providing public funds to stimulate private investment to develop "viable" urban communities. The federal funds are allocated to provide "decent" housing for a "suitable living environment," to expand economic development opportunities, and to improve local community facilities and services, all of which should be directed primarily towards persons of low and moderate income.

All CDBG projects must address one of the three national objectives:

1. Benefit low- and moderate-income persons;
2. Eliminate or prevent slums and blight; or
3. Meet other urgent community development needs because of a threat to the health and welfare of the community.

Within these three categories, funds may be used for a wide range of projects, so competition is often significant at the local level. Funds can be used for operational expenditures or for capital outlay for new or improved community facilities, the last of which is particularly significant for the purpose of public library construction.

CDBG funds may be used to purchase facilities to serve the public, including acquisition of land and buildings for conversion into public facilities such as public libraries. The rehabilitation of existing buildings may include funds for demolition, historic preservation, energy conservation, removal of architectural barriers for the disabled, relocation assistance, and the like. Projects that are specifically for routine maintenance and repair are not eligible. Funds may also be used for the construction of new facilities (including the acquisition of land) that provide public services like public library buildings. While library projects that address the elimination of slums or blight in a downtown area can qualify, neighborhood branch libraries that serve a distinct clientele of low- to moderate-income people are the most successful in competing for the grants. While this program recognizes a connection between economic development and the improvement of public institutions like libraries, library planners must make the case through strong advocacy. Library planners in search of capital funds for new buildings or for remodeling projects such as those needed to comply with the Americans with Disabilities Act (ADA) may wish to explore this potential funding source.

Large Cities and Urban Counties Entitlement Grants: Cities with populations over 50,000, urban counties over 200,000 (excluding any entitlement cities), and cities with populations under 50,000 which are central cities in Standard Metropolitan Statistical Areas (SMSAs) are eligible for entitlement grants. HUD provides funds on a formula basis to approximately 750 cities and 125 counties in this manner. The local jurisdictions have a great deal of control over how the funds are spent. HUD monitors the program to make certain the projects are eligible for the CDBG funds. Recent nationwide federal appropriations have been in the $2.3 billion range, and approximately 20 to 25 percent of the entitlement CDBG funds go towards public works.

Small Cities Competitive Grants: In most cases, HUD provides formula grants to the states, which then distribute the CDBG funds to local jurisdictions on a competitive application basis. This means there is usually a good deal of statewide competition for the funds. Some states establish set-asides in particular funding categories such as public facilities, economic development, and housing. Local municipalities then compete for funds for projects in each of these categories. Recent federal CDBG fund appropriations have been in the $1 billion range for the small cities program, with approximately 50 percent of the funds going public works.

Public Library Grant Recipients: Public libraries are eligible for CDBG funds and a number have been funded in both large urban areas as well as small municipalities. However, it appears that public libraries have been more successful in obtaining funding from the entitlement program for the larger metropolitan areas. HUD has not kept national statistics regarding the number of public libraries funded through either the small cities or entitlement program, so it is not known what has occurred over the life of the program. The competition is often difficult, and strong community support is necessary for success. Public libraries have not had a high rate of success, but a fair number have received CDBG funds. Communities with public library facility needs in areas with a high number of low- to moderate-income residents can be successful in obtaining CDBG funds.

San Diego recently received $2,450,000 in CDBG funds to assist in the construction of the new Valencia Park public library. Because of the low income levels in the area as well as the low literacy rates, the city was able to obtain not only a CDBG grant, but also a $3 million state grant, which when combined with other local funds will provide the money needed to build a new branch library. Fresno County, California, has funded several projects (Easton, San Joaquin, Parlier, and Bear Mountain) wholly or partially with CDBG funds. Kern County, California, has also received funding for several library projects (Lamont, Arvin, and Baker branches) totaling over $1.5 million of CDBG funds. The Los Angeles Public Library system received over $14.5 million in CDBG funds for public library construction in the mid-eighties for numerous branch projects. Those interested in pursuing CDBG grants should contact their local government officials, particularly community development directors, since most are familiar with the CDBG program. Assistance can also be obtained from state, regional, and national HUD offices.

Interior Department

National Park Service

Historic Preservation Grants-In-Aid: The National Historic Preservation Act of 1966 (PL 89-665), as amended, provides funds to local jurisdictions for the acquisition, preservation or development of properties listed in the National Register of Historic Places. Funds may be used for architectural and engineering studies (including plans and specifications) as well as reconstruction of historically significant buildings as long as their historic character is preserved and the public is allowed some access to the facility. Projects must adhere to rather strict technical specifications (the Secretary of the Interior's Standards for Historic Preservation Projects[18]) during reconstruction, and alteration of the original building is strongly discouraged; however, tax incentives are provided. Funding is limited for actual reconstruction work, with the largest recent cash flow occurring during the transfer of $25 million of Emergency Jobs Bill funds in 1983. Recent national appropriation levels for the program have been about $27 million. States have a good deal of flexibility in administering the program. The majority of funding in most states currently goes toward identification of properties with potential for inclusion in the National Register and not for actual development of the properties. When funds are available for reconstruction work, the federal match is for no more than 50 percent. However, the federal match may be as high as 70 percent for survey and planning grants. For information regarding the program, the State Historic Preservation Officer (SHPO) should be contacted.

National Endowment for the Humanities (NEH)

Challenge Grants Program

The National Endowment for the Humanities (NEH) was established "to support research, education, and public programs in the humanities"[19] and is authorized by the National Foundation on the Arts and the Humanities Act of 1965 (PL 89-209), as amended. NEH makes challenge grants available on a three-to-one matching basis (three local to one federal) to libraries and other nonprofit organizations. Applications are accepted once a year (usually in May) and notification of awards comes before the end of the year. Samples of successful applications are available from the program's lending library on request at the following address:

Harold C. Cannon, Director
National Endowment for the Humanities
Office of Challenge Grants, Room 429
1100 Pennsylvania Ave., N.W.
Washington, DC 20506
(202) 786-0361

"Endowment challenge grants are designed to assist institutions in finding new sources of support for humanities programs."[20] Funds may be used to generate income from endowments to support humanities programs, "Grant funds may also be used for direct expenditures where the benefits are long-term, for example, orientation exhibits, construction or renovation of buildings."[21] While there is a limit of $250,000 specified for direct expenditures such as construction, NEH may waive this limit and fund "bricks and mortar" projects up to the grant program ceiling of $1 million. Funds may also be used for retirement of debt, preservation and conservation of collections, renovation for climate control, and equipment purchases. Section 45.013 of the *Catalog of Federal Domestic Assistance* (June 1993, 27th ed.) indicates that "All applications involving capital improvements are reviewed for design excellence, appropriateness of the proposed design to the applicant's objectives and compliance with Federal law regarding access for people with disabilities and local and national historic preservational standards."

Although in many cases the historic preservation aspects of a building project are extremely important, funds may be requested for new buildings as well as additions.

Applicants requesting support for the construction of a free-standing structure, for building renovations, or for additions to buildings of any age are required to consult with their state historic preservation officer (SHPO) to determine if a property or site is listed, or is eligible for listing, in the National Register of Historic Places. The opinion of the preservation officer about whether or not the property is eligible for listing in the National Register should be forwarded to the Endowment as an appendix to the application. If it is determined that a property is eligible for listing, the applicant should also forward the written comments of the preservation officer as to the proposed project's effect on the building or site according to the guidelines set forth in the Secretary of Interior's "Standards for Rehabilitation and Guidelines for Rehabilitating Historic Buildings." A description and/or map of the property, architectural plans, and any other such documents suggested by the preservation officer should be included in the supporting materials.[22]

If a grant award is made, NEH will transmit this application information to the Advisory Council for Historic Preservation.

Public libraries with Carnegie-era buildings or other facilities that deserve historic preservation may be very interested in this program. Grants for the facility needs of public libraries are not common, but they are possible if the NEH can be persuaded that the project will foster the humanities. The recent federal appropriations for the challenge-grants program have been in the $12 to $15 million range per year. Grants range from several thousand up to $1 million, with the average grant about $440,000. The application process is highly competitive; only one in seven applications is funded each year. Unsuccessful applicants may request information about the shortcomings of their application to improve them for resubmittal. For successful applicants, the local matching funds may come from contributors in the form of cash, pledges (paid in cash during the grant period), nonfederal grants, marketable securities, real estate, in-kind gifts, or donated services. Income from deferred gifts, bequests, and planned giving is not eligible.

Other NEH requirements are similar to those of other federal programs. A narrative report must be provided each year as well as a final report within 90 days of the end of the grant period. The grantee must maintain financial accounts and records in accordance with generally accepted accounting principles (GAAP). Financial records must be kept for at least three years after the project's completion. There are the typical requirements regarding discrimination against the handicapped, provision of equal opportunity, and compliance with the Davis Bacon Act when construction or remodeling is involved. None of these is onerous unless local nonunion wage rates are so low that the addition of federal funds into the project causes a cost escalation for more than the amount of the federal grant.

A review of successful challenge grants since the late 1970s shows that approximately $6 million of federal funds have been granted to public libraries for construction projects as well as for furnishings, equipment, and fundraising efforts for capital campaign efforts. The following 28 projects received grants ranging from $5,000 to $1 million and averaging a little over $200,000 per grant:

ALABAMA

Andalusia Public Library: To renovate and equip an Assembly/Learning Center

Homewood Public Library: To support the humanities-related portion of the costs to remodel a 10-year-old church building to serve as a new facility.

Monroe County Public Library: To assist in the acquisition and conversion of a former hotel into a new library.

CONNECTICUT

Scoville Memorial Library: To renovate and expand the building to modernize services.

DELAWARE

Frankford Public Library: To renovate a former bank building to house the library.

FLORIDA

Friends of the Islamorada Branch Library: To assist in effort to expand current facility.

ILLINOIS

Chicago Public Library: To assist in the renovation of the Goldblatt building for a new central library; to build an endowment for preservation and acquisitions.

MAINE

Portland Public Library: To purchase furnishings and equipment for a new facility.

MARYLAND

Enoch Pratt Free Library: To launch the library's first major capital campaign in order to renovate the Central library and several branches and to augment endowment for humanities.

MASSACHUSETTS

Concord Public Library: To renovate existing space and enhance automation.

Reading Public Library: To assist with the renovation of a historic school building as a new library facility.

Springfield Library and Museums Association: Part of a $6 million campaign to renovate and restore the Association's historic Quadrangle building which houses the Central Library.

MICHIGAN

Durand Memorial Library: To renovate and expand the existing library facility.

MISSOURI

St. Louis Public Library: To spearhead a major campaign for the repair and refurbishment of the main library.

NEW JERSEY

Matawan-Aberdeen Public Library: To purchase shelving and furniture for the expanded library.

NEW YORK

Penn Yan Public Library: Portion of the costs to expand the building.

OHIO

Public Library of Cincinnati and Hamilton County: To renovate the Main Library Department of Rare Books and special collections.

PENNSYLVANIA

Carnegie Library of Pittsburgh: To purchase and install computerized information system; security systems for library checkout; acquisitions.

Eva K. Bowlby Public Library: To renovate and expand the library facility.

Dimmick Memorial Library: To restore a historic turn-of-the-century library facility.

Ludington Public Library: To expand, renovate, and reorganize the library facilities.

Meadville Public Library: To enlarge children's room and replace worn collections.

Murrysville Public Library: To expand and renovate the present library building to improve collection development and accessibility.

Township of Shaler North Hills Library: To renovate and expand the building and purchase furnishings and equipment.

RHODE ISLAND

Providence Public Library: To assist in the renovation of the historic central library, reducing the number of floors from 17 to 9 and providing climate control, improved security, and better utilization of space and access to collections.

TEXAS

Dallas Public Library: To support acquisitions to strengthen humanities collections; renovate storage facilities, etc.

VIRGINIA

Central Rappahannock Regional Library: To renovate an old school building.

WYOMING

Albany County Public Library: Portion of the costs to construct and equip a new building.

While these projects successfully received funds for capital expenses related to public library construction, it is wise to remember that in each case the application was justified and supported by activities relating to the humanities. NEH is not just a construction grant source. The project must relate directly to the purpose of fostering the humanities. While $6 million is not a lot of federal funding over the years, it was significant to those 28 libraries that had facility improvement projects that fit the scope of the challenge-grants program. Further, it is important to keep in mind that most federal funding programs have been created to provide assistance to state and local governments and nonprofit organizations in order to stimulate state and local financial participation.

THE STIMULATION OF STATE AND LOCAL FUNDS

Given the inherent instability of federal funding programs, it is little wonder that state and local library administrators are concerned what will come from Congressional action in Washington each year. Federal programs come and go. It is difficult to predict what the future will bring for federal funding for public library construction, but the recent trend has unfortunately been downward. While federal funds through the LSCA Title II program, or from any federal program, have provided a significant share of public library construction funds over the years, it does not appear that they can ever be relied upon to provide the lion's share of funding to meet the on-going need for capital outlay funds. The federal LSCA Title II program has been, and is, tremendous capital development tool for public libraries, but as the past has shown, there is no guarantee that it will be in effect from year to year.

In addition to providing an important revenue stream for public library construction, perhaps the greatest impact of federal funding has been the stimulation of local and state funds for the capital development of public libraries. There is ample evidence that, especially in the early years of the LSCA Title II program, federal funds stimulated much of the local matching funds which probably would not have otherwise been spent for public library buildings. Over the years, federal LSCA Title II funds have stimulated two to three dollars of state and local funds for every federal dol-lar expended. Further, there is evidence that many state construction programs were stimulated by either the temporary demise of the LSCA Title II program in 1973 or by its resurrection in the 1980s.[23] The Georgia, Florida, Kentucky, Mississippi, New Jersey, and Connecticut state public library construction programs were all stimulated in the early 1970s by the cessation of LSCA Title II funding, and the state programs in Illinois, Tennessee, Connecticut, Florida, New York, and West Virginia were stimulated or further affected by the reinstatement of Title II in the 1980s. The fact that the LSCA Title II program has been administered through the state library agencies certainly contributes to this interrelationship between state and federal construction funding.

The LSCA program stimulates not only local dollars for the individual projects funded during each year's allocation, but also state and local funding sources for public library construction in general. Often the introduction of a federal funding program that provides seed money will stimulate much broader interest in that program activity at the local level. This is the case with public library construction. There are many examples of public library buildings funded entirely with local money where the original interest in the project was stimulated by the possibility of federal funding. Sometimes this increased level of spending at the local level continues for many years and results in higher state and local appropriations even after federal funds have lessened. This has been the case with the LSCA Title II program.

It appears that this federal program has done exactly what was intended for the long term as well as the short term: stimulated state and local support for public library construction. This is not an argument for its discontinuance, because some of federal funding is necessary for this trend to continue, but a recognition that LSCA Title II is a federal capital outlay program that really works! Nevertheless, the fate of LSCA Title II is always in question, and state and local-library administrators should be prepared for the program's possible cessation in the future.

To this end, prudent state library administrators and local public library supporters should make note of the role of the state in the development of public library services as described by Carleton Joeckel many years ago:

> Since education is a state concern and the library is a part of the educational system or at least supplementary to the schools, it also is a concern of the state. In any event, the public library must be raised to a level higher than that of purely local interest. The process will doubtless be gradual, but it must be definite if the library is to be successful either in extending its service to all people of the state, or in raising the quality of service to anything like a uniform standard.[24]

Given this perspective, it may well be that the only effective substitute for the LSCA Title II program (or for waning federal funding in general) is the development of an ongoing state grants program for public library capital outlay. The following chapter discusses in detail current and past state library construction programs as well as considerations for establishing one.

REFERENCES

1. Frank William Goudy, "The Local Public Works Program: Impact on Public, School, and Academic Libraries" *Public Library Quarterly* 3 (Spring/Summer 1982), p. 56.
2. Hoyt R.Galvin, and Barbara N. Asbury, "Public Library Buildings in 1976" *Library Journal* 1 December 1976, p. 2440.
3. Ann M. Erteschik et al., comps. *Public Library Construction 1965-1978: The Federal Contribution Through the Library Services and Construction Act.* (Washington Office of Libraries and Learning Resources, Office of Education, 1978), p. 1.
4. Nathan M. Cohen, "Public Libraries" *Illinois Libraries* 50, (February 1968), p. 179.
5. Based on information provided by Don Fork, Coordinator of LSCA Title II, Office of Library Programs, Public Library Support Staff, Office of Educational Research and Improvement, U. S. Department of Education, Washington, D.C.
6. Erteschik et al., p. 16.
7. Raymond M. Holt, "Buildings" in *The ALA Yearbook*, ed. Robert Wedgeworth. (Chicago: American Library Association, 1982) p. 82.
8. Donald J. Fork, "Public Library Construction" in *Library Programs—LSCA Programs: An Action Report.* (Washington: Office of Educational Research and Improvement, U.S. Department of Education, January 1988), p. 40.
9. Donald J. Fork, "Public Library Construction: An Overview and Analysis, Fiscal Year 1987" in *Library Programs* (Washington: Office of Educational Research and Improvement, U.S. Department of Education, September 1990), p. 2.
10. Ibid, p. 6.
11. Library Services and Construction Act, as amended (PL 101-254), Part IX, Section 3. (2) "Construction."
12. Raymond M. Holt, "Federal Sources" in *Facilities Funding Finesse: Financing and Promotion of Public Library Facilities* Richard B. Hall, ed. (Chicago: American Library Association, LAMA, 1982), p. 37.
13. "Appalachian Regional Commission" in *Guide to Federal Resources for Economic Development.* (Washington: Northeast-Midwest Institute, 1981), p. 107.
14. Frank Goudy "A Piece of the Pie: Libraries and General Revenue Sharing" *Wilson Library Bulletin* 60, (December 1985), pp. 15-16.
15. Holt, "Federal Sources," p. 33.
16. Goudy, "A Piece of the Pie," pp. 15-18.
17. Ibid, p. 16.
18. W. Brown Morton III, and Gary L. Hume, *The Secretary of the Interior's Standards for Historic Preservation Projects.* (Washington:

U.S. Department of the Interior, National Park Service, Preservation Assistance Division), 1985.

19. *Challenge Grants: Guidelines, Application Materials, and Administrative Requirements.* (Washington: National Endowment for the Humanities, Office of Challenge Grants, 1991), p. 2.

20. Ibid.

21. Ibid, p. 3.

22. Ibid, p. 20.

23. Richard B. Hall, "LSCA Title II & State Aid" *Interface* 7 (Spring 1985), p. 4.

24. John G. Lorenz, "Successful Methods of Financing Public Library Improvement in Other States" *Wisconsin Library Bulletin* 58, (July 1962), p. 287.

State Funding Sources 5

THE INTERRELATIONSHIP OF STATE AND FEDERAL FUNDS

The Stimulation of Funds

One of the main things state and federal funding programs have in common is the role of stimulating the expenditure of local funds for public library construction. LSCA Title II stimulated numerous state library construction programs, the most notable being the one in Georgia, the nation's longest-running state-based funding program for public library construction. The seeds planted by the temporary demise of the LSCA Title II program in 1973 have blossomed many times over in other states, as well.

Although the lack of federal funding triggered state funding programs in some states, the reinstatement of LSCA Title II funding in the early eighties also stimulated interest in state-based programs, partly by alerting many local public officials to the inadequacy of their library facilities. Subsequently, many applications for federal grants were not funded because of the limited availability of the funds. This, in turn, stimulated further interest in state-based library construction programs to meet the need that had been "created" by the federal program's reauthorization.

Over the years, state capital outlay programs have fulfilled an important role acting as seed money for local fundraising similar to the way federal funds have stimulated both state and local construction funds. These local funds have been from both public and private sources. Their exact amount is unknown; however, like federal funds, state funds stimulate considerably more local funding than the amount of state funds expended for public library construction.

State programs stimulate local funds in a number of ways. For one, most state programs require a specific local match. This is usually based on a formula, which may require the local match to be anywhere between 10 and 90 percent, but most require between 25 and 75 percent of the funding to be local, with the federal LSCA Title II formula of 50 percent widely adopted. In almost all cases, state grants are made contingent upon local appropriations. If the local agency does not perform, the state grant is rescinded. This is a powerful tool for stimulating local funds, particularly if the local match depends on the passage of a referendum. In many communities, this dangling of the state funds "carrot" is just enough to push a local campaign over the top to success.

Another way state and federal funding programs for library construction stimulate local funds is simply by raising awareness of local officials and the public. Sometimes library officials have been unable for many years to get the attention of local officials regarding the library's space problems, but when the possibility of "free" state or federal funding presents itself, the matter is examined seriously. Combined with grassroots community support, this can bring forth a grant application. Even if the grant is not awarded, the project is much likelier to be funded with local funds because the problem has been identified, the planning has been done, and "everyone knows we need to do something about the library." There are many public libraries that have been built only because of state funds. If for no other reason, state-based construction programs for libraries should be promoted by library supporters throughout the nation.

OVERVIEW OF STATE FUNDING

State Library Grant Programs

The state library is usually the best starting point when searching for possible state funds. A call to the state librarian or the state library's development office will determine if a state construction program is currently active and, if not, what other state sources are available. If a state program is active, the enabling legislation and the program's policies, regulations, and guidelines, along with an application form, should be requested early in the planning process for the project.

Other State Agency Sources

Occasionally, states provide construction funds for some specific purposes like energy retrofit, seismic retrofit, accessibility for the disabled, or historical remodeling. These funds may be available through state agencies other than the state library agency. Funds for energy audits and conversion are sometimes available from state energy commissions and occasionally from local utility companies. Sometimes the funds are not outright grants but loans that must be repaid. In the case of energy retrofits, the repayment may be made from the savings realized through energy conservation.

Executive and Legislative Sources

In many states, the governor's office has an emergency or contingency fund that can be allocated at the governor's discretion. Library projects have been known to tap this funding source occasionally to make urgent repairs, or when a budget shortfall created a need for funds to complete a project such as finishing a parking lot or buying additional furnishings and equipment. Occasionally, local library jurisdictions are able to convince powerful legislators to provide one-time single-line-item appropriations for specific projects. This "pork barrel" approach may be frowned upon, but could be the only effective method of producing capital funds for public library construction when no other state sources exist. It may be possible to obtain special legislation for a very large construction project if a case can be made that the library will become a regional or state resource center and benefit a great number of citizens.

State Bond Banks and Revolving Loan Programs

In addition to outright grants, many states have begun to look at bond banks and revolving loan programs to offer local jurisdictions low-interest capital loans for public facilities. This approach may become more popular in the future if federal, state, and local capital revenue sources continue to tighten. State bond banks provide local jurisdictions with access to the debt market at better rates than they can obtain on their own. Instead of the local jurisdiction issuing bonds for capital improvements, the state with its higher credit rating issues bonds or other debt instruments at lower interest rates that are then passed on to the jurisdiction.

This approach is supported by a state financing authority that secures the state bonds by acquiring the project's property (land and building) through a lease-purchase agreement. The lease payments from the local jurisdiction are used by the state authority to repay the principal and interest on the bonds as well as any state administrative costs. Since the interest rate obtained through the sale of state bonds is lower than that for local municipal bonds, there is a savings to the local jurisdiction. Once the state bonds have been paid, the local jurisdiction may reacquire title to the facility by exercising the purchase option for a nominal one dollar sum.

The state of Illinois currently has such a program, which can be used for financing the capital outlay needs of public libraries. The Illinois Development Finance Authority (IFDA) is a state-level financing authority that assists municipalities by arranging financing for lease-purchase agreements for projects.

> Since the program provides financing for capital equipment and real estate, a public library could finance the purchase of land for new construction, as well as an existing building which will be remodeled for library purposes; lease purchase of furnishings and equipment, including automation equipment and book security systems; and the purchase of a "turnkey" library facility, which includes the construction of the facility, furnishings and equipment.[1]

One of the advantages of this program is that no referendum is required assuming the municipal libraries are willing to finance the project for less than a ten-year time period. The finance authority provides capital funds by issuing certificates of participation (COPs). These certificates are retired by payments covering principal and interest from annual appropriations by the local municipalities.

Other states with bond banks and loan programs that can assist public library construction include Indiana,[2] Wisconsin,[3]

and Wyoming.[4] While relatively few public libraries have been built using state-financed bond or infrastructure banks, there are definite advantages to consider in such a program.

One of the attractions of an infrastructure bank is that it represents a long-term commitment to dealing with the capital infrastructure dilemma. It is an implicit guarantee of permanent attention to public capital needs. Once a bank has been created and endowed with professional staff, it is unlikely to disappear. Loans will have to be repaid and the bank will have to be there to receive them. If the initial legislation establishes a revolving fund, so that loans that are repaid are recycled to new infrastructure users, a second generation of lending activity can be ensured.

Permanence, visibility, and professionalism are the critical arguments in favor of an infrastructure bank. It is not that below-market loans to support public capital spending represent a magical or costless source of financing, but rather that an infrastructure bank is a tangible, long-term commitment, more difficult to disavow than a new federal block grant program.[5]

It might well be that bond banks and revolving loan programs could represent a longer-term solution than outright grants from the state. While a grant is better than a loan from the local perspective, state grant programs are difficult to operate from year to year since they require an ongoing infusion of capital from the state. The advantage of bond banks as well as revolving loan funds is that once they are initially capitalized, they can continue operating without a continued stream of state revenues other than to support their administrative costs.

Revolving loan funds are particularly interesting because they offer a potentially powerful tool for stimulating local funds for public library construction. To start a revolving loan program, a state legislature could appropriate to the fund a specific amount of money, for example, $10 mil-

lion. Instead of granting this money to local jurisdictions to build public libraries,
it would be made available as a loan to be
repaid over time with interest. A number
of financing methods can be used with a
revolving loan fund, but "a common thread
is a base of capital that is lent to a borrow-
er for use in purchasing an asset and that,
upon being repaid, 'revolves' or is lent again
for another use."[6] In this way, the revolving fund program continues from year to
year, providing low-interest loans to local
jurisdictions for public library construction. The program is limited only by the
amount of the original appropriation, the
interest rates, and the number of interested jurisdictions. Obviously, the higher the
original appropriation, the more loans that
can be made each year.

Regardless the method used to finance
public library construction, there does
seem to be an increased interest in using
state funds to assist at the local level. In
recent years, while federal funds for public library construction have been on the
decline, state funds have increased to an
average of eight percent expended nationally in the last five years.

Library Journal Statistics

Table 5-1 shows the amount of state
funds reported each year in *Library Journal.* Figure 5-1 shows the same data in
graph form. As was discussed in Chapter
3 and as can be seen in the following table,
state funding for public library construction has increased in recent years. There
is considerable evidence that this trend
will continue because a number of states,
including California, Massachusetts,
Georgia, and Mississippi, have recently
received sizable appropriations for public
library construction.

A review of 24 years of *Library Journal*
statistics reveals that approximately 60
percent of U.S. states have provided some

Table 5-1. State Funds For Public
Library Construction

Fiscal Year	State Funds
1991	25,789,278
1990	36,766,149
1989	14,212,687**
1988	20,771,413
1987	13,021,558
1986	8,917,953
1985	5,746,952
1984	7,124,956
1983	11,335,489
1982	4,331,802**
1981	4,880,422
1980	4,761,981
1979	15,301,477
1978	6,899,585
1977	7,138,772
1976	7,506,352
1975	2,778,979
1974	1,766,183
1973	2,637,831
1972	1,388,094
1971	3,156,112
1970	3,107,030
1969	1,056,232
1968	895,941
TOTAL:	$211,293,228

**State library buildings deleted from data for con-
sistency.
©Reed Publishing

funding for public construction. 40 percent
of the states have never provided any funding. In many cases, the state appropriation
may have been a one-time "pork barrel"
line-item appropriation provided to a fa-
vored locale by a powerful legislator which
was never repeated. In other cases, state
programs provided annual appropriations
for public library construction for a number of years, but it has been difficult for all
but a few to maintain this for any length
of time. Table 5-2 summarizes the most
significant state appropriations for public
library construction. Of these, about a
dozen programs are currently active and
granting reasonably significant amounts of
state funding to local public library
projects.

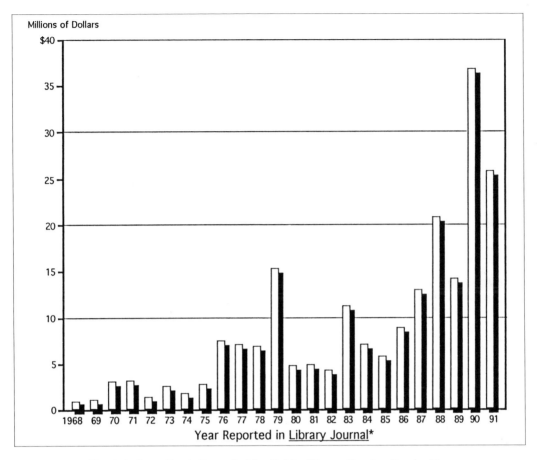

Fig. 5-1. State Funds Expended for Public Library Construction by Year

*©Reed Publishing

The major state construction programs have provided over $427 million of state funds for 1,883 projects in the last 25 years. This figure is higher than the $211 million reported in *Library Journal* because a substantial portion of the $427 million has been appropriated for construction projects that have not yet been completed and reported. This attests to the fact that a significant amount of state funding has been appropriated in recent years. For example, almost all of the $75 million of the California appropriation, the $35 million of the Massachusetts appropriation, and a substantial amount of the recent appropria-

tions from Georgia have not been reported.

Of all of the state library construction programs, Georgia's has been the most consistent and longest running and has provided the most state funds. The Georgia program has continuously funded public library construction for 20 years, providing in excess of $120 million for 232 projects. California follows Georgia in total state funds appropriated, with $75 million—the largest one-time appropriation of state funds for public library construction in any fiscal year. California is followed by Illinois with $47 million of state funds and Massachusetts with $35 million. Kentucky has

Table 5-2. Significant State Programs for Public Library Construction

State	Dollars (in millions)	Number of Projects
Alabama	$ 3	35
Alaska	6	75
California	75	22
Connecticut	20	101
Delaware	3	6
Florida	9	61
Georgia	121	232
Illinois	47	93
Kentucky	28	300
Maryland	3.5	34
Massachusetts	35	59
Mississippi	18	202
Nevada	10	18
New Jersey	5	24
New York	5	292
North Carolina	4	124
Rhode Island	21	56
Tennessee	1	21
West Virginia	12	125
Wyoming	.5	3
TOTALS	$427	1,883

made the most grants (300), followed by New York (292), Georgia (232), Mississippi (202), West Virginia (125), North Carolina (124), Connecticut (101), Illinois (93), and Florida (61). Each state construction program is unique. Analysis of the programs reveals numerous ways that a state program can be structured, but it also provides insight into some similarities. The following section describes the major state library construction programs that have been active in the last 20 years.

MAJOR STATE PROGRAMS

Alabama

In 1986, the Alabama legislature included $3 million for public library construction in an education bond issue. This one-time special fund appropriation was administered by the Alabama State Library in cooperation with the Alabama Public School and College Authority. A total of 35 grants were made, ranging from $2,895 to $154,400. The projects included accessibility for the disabled, expansion and renovation, and new construction. Maintenance projects were excluded from the program.

The total expenditure for the 35 projects was approximately $18.5 million. This means that the $3 million of state funds stimulated over $15 million in local matching funds. While one major project accounted for over half the total appropriations, almost $6 million in local funds was generated by the remaining 34 projects.

Although new construction was given priority, only six of the projects were new buildings. Five were for the construction of additions to buildings. Another six projects were for first-time renovation of existing buildings for use as public libraries. The remaining projects were primarily for renovations including expansion into basements, second floors, and space previously used as storage. At completion, all buildings were handicapped-accessible.

Alaska

The establishment of LSCA Title II in the mid-1960s provided the impetus for Alaska to begin a state-funded public library construction grant program through the state library in 1966. The state passed legislation that specifically addressed public library construction grants in 1970. These statutes set out the local matching requirements and directed the Division of State Libraries to establish guidelines for administering the program. Cities with populations of more than 2,000 must provide at least 40 percent of the total project costs. Rural communities, whether incorporated or not, must provide at least ten percent of the total project cost. The municipality's matching share may be in the form of money, land, or services, but money has been the prevalent form of local match. Grants may be used for construction of new facilities, renovation or expansion of existing buildings, and equipping or furnishing a library facility.

Although the state library administered the program and awarded grants beginning in 1966, it did not implement written regulations until 1989. The regulations require the applicant to present a project proposal that meets the anticipated needs of the library service area for at least ten years. Site, design, space, and layout must conform to the general recommendations cited in an appropriate publication, such as Anders Dahlgren's *Planning the Small Public Library Building*, published by the American Library Association. The regulations include standards for minimum space requirements, shelving, and furniture. Compliance with all applicable state and federal accessibility standards is mandatory. The applicant must demonstrate an ability to operate and maintain the proposed project after completion.

The state library awarded the first grants in 1966, but the source of funding of the early projects is unknown. In 1974 and 1980, the state funded the program through general obligation bonds. In 1982, 1984, and 1987, the program was funded with general funds. Over the years, the legislature has generally replenished the grant program when available funds were expended; however, no new money has been appropriated since 1987 in spite of requests from the library community, so the program is currently dormant.

Since this has been an ongoing program, there is no specific application cycle; public libraries apply for grants at any time. The state library reviews the application and awards the grant if the application meets the program's requirements. The program is not intended to be competitive; it would be competitive only if limited funds remained and several applicants were being considered for them. The State Library provides consulting services to the applicants during the application process.

Table 5-3. State Grants for Public Library Construction in Alaska

Fiscal Year	State Grant Appropriations	Number of Projects
1987	527,000	9
1984	500,000	11
1980-1982	553,170	11
1974	3,013,732	26
1966-1973	$1,091,580	22
Totals:	$5,685,482	75*

*Due to projects being funded from more than one account, the total number of separate projects is 75, rather than 79.

Table 5.3 shows the state grants awarded since the beginning of the program.

Over the last 25 years, the state has provided $5,685,482 for public library construction through the grant program administered by the state library. However, it has provided much more through direct legislative grants. In the mid-1970s, the state began allocating part of the capital budget to each legislative district. Each legislator could decide which local requests to fund from his or her allocation. Projects funded this way are administered by a state agency in the sense that the money is passed through the agency's budget. However, the agency of record exercises little control over the grant. In some cases, the Division of State Libraries was the administrator of record for direct legislative grants for public library construction. Libraries have fared relatively well in this process. The most notable was a succession of grants totaling about $27.5 million to Anchorage for the construction of its $43 million main library in the mid-1980s. However, there were many others ranging from a few thousand dollars to several million dollars.

California

It could be said that the genesis of the California Library Construction and Renovation Bond Act of 1988 was the local taxpayer revolt that culminated in Proposition 13. As a result of that limitation in the local tax base, as well as a two-thirds majority vote requirement for local referenda, it became necessary for the state of California to develop alternative funding vehicles, including state-based financing for public construction projects. In the eighties, a number of publicly funded agencies such as schools, libraries, and parks attempted to place large bond acts on a state-wide ballot. This approach succeeded in part because a state-wide referendum in California requires only a majority vote instead of the two-thirds "supermajority" required at the local level.

The California State Library supported an effort to develop a bond act for public libraries by performing a state-wide public library facility needs assessment as well as helping draft the legislation and working with a key legislator who had a special interest in the issue. The legislator was a member of the leadership and while there were specific library projects for which he wanted funding, he also had a strong commitment to developing public libraries state-wide. Unfortunately, his view was not shared by the majority of the legislature or the governor at that time. The bill was not placed on a state-wide ballot until 1988.

In the meantime, unfortunately, the amount of the Bond Act was reduced from $300 million to $75 million. This is still a significant amount of funding, and it is actually the nation's largest one-time annual appropriation of state capital outlay funds for public libraries. However, this is tempered by the size of the state and a ten-year backlog of public library construction projects resulting from the passage of Proposition 13. When the state library called for a "notice of intent to apply," it received close to 200 responses requesting approximately $425 million of state funds! After the referendum was passed, the state library needed to take two regulatory actions in order to support the bond act. The first was "Bond Act Building Standards,"[7] which provided a basis in the California Code of Regulations for specific requirements for public library buildings such as floor loading, fire safety, and seismic requirements. These standards also established the method the state library would use to approve architectural plans, specifications, and change orders.

The next regulatory action had to do with interpreting and making specific the bond act's financial aspects and providing assistance with the application process.[8] The latter meant that the application form itself became part of the program regulations. In the state of California, regulations are developed through a rigid process requiring a high degree of public scrutiny. For example, after the regulations are first proposed, a time period is allowed for public comment and a public hearing. The state library has to respond to all applicable comments, make necessary revisions, and offer the revised regulations for additional public comment. After the public comment period closes, the regulations are further reviewed by an internal state agency staffed by attorneys who read the regulations for clarity, necessity, consistency, and legality.

The program regulations were finally completed in the fall of 1990, and the state library called for preapplications. The library community responded with just over 100 preapplications requesting approximately $350 million of state funds. The environment was highly competitive to say the least, and the problem facing the state library and the California Library Construction and Renovation Board was how to allocate the grant funds fairly. Since partial grants could not be made, the board was required to allocate to an applicant all or none of the state match of 65 percent of the eligible project costs.

Earlier, the state librarian and board had developed an evaluation process that was reflected in the information requested in the application form. The board had to consider five factors in the bond act when evaluating applications:

1. Needs of urban and rural areas
2. Projected population growth
3. Changing concepts of public library service.
4. Distance of the proposed project from other existing and proposed facilities
5. Age and condition of the facility

From these five categories, the state librarian devised a methodology to evaluate applications. A review team of readers from the state library's library development staff read and commented on the elibible applications. Objective numerical factors were calculated. The objective and subjective perspectives were merged and the state librarian provided findings to the board which categorized applications as exceptionally competitive, very competitive, competitive, somewhat competitive, less than competitive, rejected, or ineligible.

From these findings, the board selected applications for grant approval. The board's composition was determined by the bond act itself; it included two legislators, the state treasurer, the head of the Department of Finance, and the state librarian. Applications were called for in two cycles and the board allocated half of the bond act funds ($37 million) at each cycle. During the first cycle, the state library received approximately 50 applications requesting approximately $250 million, and the board awarded eight grants totalling $37 million. During the second cycle, the state library again received approximately 50 applications requesting approximately $200 million of state funds, and the Board awarded 16 grants totalling the remaining $37 million. In all, 24 projects were funded which will add approximately half a million square feet of public library space in the state of California in the early to mid-nineties.

The $75 million of state funds stimulated approximately $50 million of local matching and supplemental funds. While the bond act's match was 65 percent state funds to 35 percent local, it was applied only to eligible project costs. In most cases, there were ineligible project costs that had to be funded with supplemental local funds. These included general remodeling (although remodeling for disabled accessibility, energy conservation, and health and safety were eligible), movable equipment, local code plan checking and code compliance inspections, appraisals, and audits. Based on the total funds needed for the projects ($125 million) by including the ineligible costs, the actual state-to-local ratio turned out to be closer to 60 percent state to 40 percent local. The average cost per square foot for construction alone (not including site development, demolition), furnishings and equipment etc.) was approximately $115 ($145 including site development and demolition. When all project costs (eligible and ineligible) were factored, in, including the value of land., the average cost per square foot came to approximately $250.

The cost of acquiring land was an eligible cost in the program, which reflects the extremely high value of land in California. The average value of the land in a project was just under $800,000. Site costs ranged from $29,000 to $2,700,000. These costs not only drove up the project's total costs, but also the state's share, and so reduced the number of projects that received state grants. However, excluding the value of land as an eligible cost would have greatly reduced the state's participation in a project, and in some instances would have meant the difference between being able to make application or not.

Unfortunately, because of the limited amount of state funds available from the bond act, many well-developed and deserving projects did not receive grants. This kind of competitive atmosphere does not tend to build political consensus. Because of the continued need for state funds, the California library community attempted to place another bond act on the November 1992 ballot. Meetings were held to obtain input on how to amend and improve the 1988 bond act. Draft amendments were incorporated by the original bond act's sponsor who agreed to carry the bill again. Amendments included an attempt to "guarantee" funding for projects that had already been submitted and were considered "highly competitive" or better. Unfortunately, the bill did not receive the support necessary to place the issue on the ballot.

There are undoubtedly a number of reasons for this occurrence, but the primary one was the extremely deep recessionary period that California was experiencing then, which produced a nearly $12 billion state budget deficit. Even though the bill's proponents attempted to utilize a "jobs bill" approach to support the measure, the concern over the economy and California's slipping bond rating was too much to overcome. Chances for another try may be improved assuming the economy improves in the future. Further, supporters will be able to point to recently constructed new public libraries as examples of what a state and local partnership can mean for public library facility development.

Connecticut

In 1974, the state of Connecticut enacted a statute to help fund public library construction which after numerous revisions has ultimately come to be the following:

Sec. 11-24c. Construction cost grants. Priority list. The state library board shall make construction grants to public libraries established pursuant to this chapter. The board shall: (1) Establish criteria for the purpose of developing a priority listing of all construction projects and (2) grant an amount equal to one-third of the total construction cost, not to exceed three hundred fifty thousand dollars for

each approved project within the limits of the available appropriation for such projects. In the event that the appropriation is insufficient to fund projects as provided above, projects remaining on the priority list shall be included in the priority listing for the next fiscal year. Each application for such grant shall be filed on or before September first, annually, on forms to be prescribed by said board.

Originally, the maximum grant was for $100,000. In 1980, the maximum grant was increased from $100,000 to $200,000, and the portion of the grant was increased from one-quarter to one-third of the project's total cost. In 1985, the maximum grant was increased to $350,000. The minimum grant is $3,333 which means the total cost of the project has to be at least $10,000. From a practical standpoint, most grant applicants apply for both State and LSCA Title II public library construction grants for the same project. Since the maximum LSCA Title II grant in Connecticut is $100,000, the maximum combined state and federal grants is $450,000. Table 5-4 shows the history of state construction grants in Connecticut.

Table 5-4. State Grants for Public Library Construction in Connecticut

Fiscal Year	Amount Authorized*	Amount Awarded	No. of Grants
1991	$ 3,429,787	$ 1,751,120	8
1990	4,250,029	2,789,155	16
1989	2,532,754	2,274,391	12
1988	4,000,000	3,559,568	18
1987	1,295,000	1,295,000	5
1986	1,513,161	1,513,161	6
1985	1,000,000	486,839	6
1984	800,000	797,208	7
1979	1,250,000	1,250,000	8
1978	500,000	500,000	7
1975	700,000	700,000	8
TOTAL	$21,270,731	$16,916,442	101

*Includes carryover funds from previous years or returned grants to be reassigned.

The 1992–1993 state budget contains no funds for public library construction. However $2,113,087 in carryover funds from previous years is available. The approximately $17 million in state funds combined with approximately $2 million in federal LSCA Title II funds have stimulated local matching funds of approximately $126 million for the 101 projects. In Connecticut, grant applicants do not have to have their local matching funds in hand when they apply for state funds; however they must acquire these funds within 18 months after the state approves of the grant. Unexpended funds from previous years may be carried forward to subsequent years for reallocation.

The state library construction grant program is funded by state bond issues. Annual budget requests are based on a state library survey of potential applicants. Because not all potential applicants respond, or because applicants sometimes apply at the last minute, the budget request is not always adequate to cover all applications, resulting in a lower state appropriation than what is needed. The state library is considering establishing more detailed regulations, but at present the program is administered by guidelines that change yearly.

Ninety percent of the state funds go into projects for either new buildings or additions with some renovation, but approximately ten percent of the funds are used for smaller remodeling projects to retrofit for building and fire-code violations, handicapped accessibility, energy conservation, technology enhancements, or simply improved space design.

Application requirements include schematic plans; a project timeline; a deed to the site; certification of structural soundness of the building when expanding, converting, or renovating; a certification of accessibility and usability by the physically handicapped; a building program; and a subsurface soil analysis for new buildings and additions. Applications are reviewed by the state library staff for completeness and ranked according to priorities related to the project's ability to meet the library's 20-year projected space need. The ranked grant applications go to the State Library Board and State Bond Commission for approval in November.

A 1991 state library survey showed that 88 out of 196 public libraries in Connecticut are not fully handicapped accessible and that 61 public libraries were planning to expand or renovate in the next few years. The need for additional funds is evident even though the current recession has had a negative impact on state capital funding programs.

Delaware

On July 19, 1990, the governor of Delaware signed into law the Delaware Public Library Construction Assistance Act, providing funds for acquisition, construction, alteration, remodeling, or enlargement of library buildings; the acquisition or installation of equipment; or the acquisition of land, including improvement of sites, construction of sidewalks, sewers, or water mains needed to connect the public library building to a publicly owned system. Up to 40 percent of the total cost of a project may be applied for, with the remaining 60 percent of the cost available from local or any other nonstate source. Before 1990, state funds were available for public library construction on a case by case basis. From fiscal year 1989 through 1993, six public library projects received $2,668,300 in state funding as can be seen from Table 5-5. In Delaware, these state funds were acquired from the sale of state bonds.

Any public library in Delaware must submit a written application to the state library agency requesting state funds. The agency reviews the applications and makes its recommendation based on the need, scope, total cost, and local funding avail-

Table 5-5. State Grants for Public Library Construction in Delaware

Fiscal Year	State Grant Appropriations
1993	$ 170,600
1992	760,700
1991	837,000
1990	300,000
1989	600,000
Total:	$2,668,300

able. Recommended applications are then forwarded to the Delaware Department of State and the Delaware Council on Libraries for their comments. The allocation of funds is based on recommendations from the governor to the General Assembly. Each application is assessed on its merits. No funds are set aside for particular types of projects, nor are there detailed standards or specifications for the program.

In 1988, King Research, Inc., prepared a needs assessment report for the Delaware state library agency recommending an immediate increase of 96,600 to 251,900 square feet of public library space to bring the state up to nationally accepted guidelines to meet minimum levels of services. In addition, the "Delaware Standards and Guidelines for Public Libraries, 1991–1995," includes a formula for determining the minimum square footage of library space recommended for the population served. Of 27 public libraries in Delaware, 17 do not meet recommended minimum amount of space.

Florida

From 1965 until the federal LSCA Title II program was discontinued in 1973, Florida used only LSCA funds for public library construction. In order to continue its goal of providing adequate public library facilities for all residents of Florida, the state began a program to make state funds avail-

able for public library construction during 1976. Public library construction grants are currently available to eligible government agencies for the construction of new buildings, site acquisition, and the acquisition, expansion or remodeling of existing buildings to be used for public library services. Eligible governmental agencies include the 67 county general governments, the incorporated municipalities, and special districts or special tax districts that establish or maintain a public library and provide free library service.

Since the program started in 1976, $9,190,232 in state funds have been used for 61 public library construction projects. Of the 61 projects funded with state funds, 40 were new libraries, 13 were for expansion projects, four were for remodeling, and four were a combination of expansion and remodeling. The $9 million of state funds stimulated approximately $59 million of local matching funds. Table 5-6 shows the breakdown of state funds by fiscal year.

Table 5-6. State grants for Public Library Construction in Florida

Fiscal Year	No. of Projects	State Grant Appropriations
1992	5	$ 1,364,180
1991	6	1,292,052
1990	4	600,000
1989	6	1,025,000
1988	4	510,000
1987	6	890,000
1986	5	420,000
1985	7	863,500
1984	1	200,000
1983	3	315,000
1982	2	240,000
1981	2	100,000
1980	0	0
1979	2	400,000
1978	5	715,000
1977	0	0
1976	3	255,500
Totals:	61	$ 9,190,232

Eligible government agencies submit applications to the state library each year. The applications are made prior to the state appropriation. State library staff then review all applications for eligibility and completeness in accordance with Florida's rules for evaluating and ranking grant applications. The criteria used include type of construction, population of the applicant's service area, size of the total library building, type of library building, building program, and project narrative. When evaluating the narrative and the building program, staff look at how library functions relate to one another in terms of space, work-flow patterns, plans for future expansion or growth, etc. If the application has any deficiencies, the applicant is given 30 days to correct them.

After the grant applications are evaluated, they are ranked by score. The funds requested in each application then become part of the state library's legislative budget request. When funds become available, they are allocated to the projects that receive the highest scores. This continues until all allocated funds have been awarded. The maximum grant an applicant may receive is $400,000; the minimum is $10,000. The state matching grant may not exceed 50 percent of the allowable project costs, and local funds must be unencumbered at the time of the award. In order to receive funds, the library facility must be at least 3,000 square feet. Once the grant is awarded and an agreement executed, the library has 270 days to enter into a lump-sum contract for the construction. Funds for a library construction grant can be used to cover costs for architectural services, acquisition of land, new construction, expansion, remodeling, site preparation, legal and engineering costs, and initial equipment.

Rules were established for the library construction program in 1982 and substantially amended in 1986. Prior to 1986, applicants submitted notification of intent to the state library. The projects were then placed in the state library's legislative budget request and were either funded or not. The rule change in 1986 provided a level of objectivity by adding criteria for evaluating and ranking library construction grants based on the rules. If an applicant receives a grant, it will be for the full amount requested. Florida has always encouraged strong local support of its library program through its state funding programs, as can be seen by the $59 million in local funds generated by the state funded projects.

Georgia

The temporary cessation of federal LSCA Title II funding in 1973 provided the stimulus for Georgia's capital outlay funding for public library construction. When the federal funds ran out, several projects were left without promised federal assistance. Two of these happened to be in the district of a very influential Georgia state legislator. Several politically savvy public library directors arranged a meeting with this legislator, and after discussing the needs of public libraries and the impact of the federal program on library development, they effectively came out of the meeting with a state construction program. In 1973, nine library projects (including the two in the friendly legislator's district) were funded with approximately $1 million of state funds matching local appropriations.

From this initial expenditure, an annual allocation of state funds for public library construction developed and continues to this time. Table 5-7 shows the number of projects funded and the state appropriations by fiscal year.

What is remarkable about the Georgia library construction program is that over a 20-year period, the state has had the will, resources, and vision to provide a relatively stable and consistent revenue stream for

Table 5-7. State grants for Public Library Construction in Georgia

Fiscal Year	No. of Projects	State Grant Appropriations
1992	22	$ 13,280,000
1991	20	12,925,000
1990	17	14,700,000
1989	0	0*
1988	25	19,250.000
1987	26	16,688,468
1986	45	28,046,532
1985	5	2,061,822
1984	2	441,955
1983	3	1,155,000
1982	1	587,000
1981	7	2,516,336
1980	13	3,551,084
1979	8	1,207,720
1978	7	1,029,200
1977	0	0*
1976	1	10,000
1975	10	1,488,891
1974	11	1,154,645
1973	9	1,041,000
TOTALS:	232	$121,134,653

*While no funds were allocated in these fiscal years, the program was actually continuously funded every calendar year because of the use of the state supplemental budget.

capital funding that library planners and politicians could count on year after year. This program is a "cultural pork barrel" in the most positive sense. It has allowed state legislators to provide local communities with more than just roads, sewers, and streetlights. The program has supporters at all levels of Georgia government, but is one of the least "political" programs, in the negative sense, of any state library construction program. During the 20 years of the program, Georgia funded 100 percent of all bona fide grant applications that met the program's requirements. However, while the funding source has been active each year, the requirements did not remain static. The program has evolved and adapted to the changing political climate and responded to the needs of grant applicants.

In the beginning, state funding was appropriated annually, and projects were developed through an application process. Funds were made available on a first-come-first-served basis. Jurisdictions that completed all the application requirements first received the available funds. In the early days, the funding formula was a one-to-one match with a ceiling of $250,000 of state funds per project. This formula remained in place for several years and was adequate to meet the need of relatively small rural projects of which Georgia has a preponderance. Of course, it should be remembered that at this time public libraries could be built in this region for $25 to $30 a square foot.

As time went on, there were several significant changes in the construction program. In the mid-1980s the cash flow for the program increased from $2 million to $20 million per year. This increase resulted from several factors. First, the ceiling of $250,000 was causing a problem. While it was originally intended to keep large urban projects from using up substantial amounts of the available funds, it was causing a problem even for small to medium sized projects because construction costs had escalated significantly during the seventies. A $1 million dollar project at $50 per square foot for construction built only about 14,000 square feet of library space in the early eighties in Georgia. In this case, the state provided the ceiling of $250,000 and the local jurisdiction came up with $750,000. The supposed 50 percent match from the state had become effectively only a 25 percent match because of the ceiling.

In addition, funds at the local level were getting very tight because of the recession of the early eighties. The state construction program almost ceased one year not because for lack of state funds, but because there were few projects that could come up the required local matching funds. Consequently, several formula revisions increased the state match up to two to one and eventually nine to one for small projects. The most notable of the revisions resulted in the following formula:

> On all library projects, the state will fund 90 percent of the first $500,000 of the total project, and 66.6 percent of any additional project cost above $500,000.

> No library system may receive more than $3 million of public library capital outlay funds in any given year.

The formula allocated nine state dollars for every local dollar for projects under $500,000. This formula was actually proposed by another powerful rural legislator to assist with a library construction project in his district. However, with broad support, it became a permanent policy of the State Board of Education, which is the governing board for public libraries in Georgia. The formula was of tremendous benefit to small rural projects, but it also provided a significant stimulus to suburban and even urban projects, which could still get 90 percent of the first $500,000 and two-thirds of the remaining project costs up to a ceiling of $3 million.

This was particularly important because it fit the social and political zeitgeist perfectly. While Georgia was predominantly controlled by a large group of rural legislators, the state's major growth was in the metropolitan Atlanta area. This formula allocation forged a balanced alliance between the legislature's rural members and those who represented high growth interests. Further, much of this growth was from snowbelt "immigrants" who expected and demanded good public library service. Since the majority of these people were settling in the metropolitan Atlanta area, the increased demand for local funds to provide improved library services was no surprise. It is interesting to note that this social trend also resulted in the passage of six major local bond referenda in the metropolitan area during the late eighties.

This resulted in even more pressure on the state construction program to provide funds to match these locally generated funds for public library construction.

There was another significant change which had a long term impact on the success of the program. In the early days of the program, a set amount of state funds was appropriated by the legislature and the state library accepted applications for the funding on a first-come-first-served basis. This approach worked well when the demand was low, but as it increased there was greater pressure for more state funds. Fortunately, the state library began developing project applications in advance of each legislative appropriation. With the cooperation of many local library jurisdictions, the exact amount of funding needed for any given year was known by the state library, the governor's office, and the legislature before the legislative session.

Eventually, application development for each year began as soon as the legislature had appropriated the previous year's funding. This meant that each spring, at the close of the legislative session, the state library called for preapplications for the next year's projects. The construction consulting staff then began developing the applications by calling for, reviewing, and approving building programs, site selection studies, and finally a formal application including a very specific project budget and funding commitments from the local agencies. This process took approximately six months and was virtually the same each year, so local library directors could become familiar with it and depend upon its consistency.

By fall, a specific project list developed by the state library was formally transmitted to the governor's office and the legislature as part of the Department of Education's budget package. This worked well because it not only provided the politicians with a specific and well-defined list of projects and the amount of state funding needed, but it also allowed the local project supporters to develop and focus a grass-roots lobbying effort in support of their projects. Further, the application process provided substantial credibility for each project. Local officials knew exactly how much money they needed, and the state request was backed up by a commitment for the local matching funds. Further, they had a well-planned building and had identified a specific site on which to build the project.

These powerful tools created a strong local vested interest in the project and were used effectively to compete at the state level for ever scarcer dollars. This approach of developing projects in advance may be one of the Georgia program's most important aspects. Its effectiveness has been demonstrated year after year with annual appropriations that allocate significant amounts of state capital to local public library construction projects. Because of the success of this method, other state library agencies should consider this approach when setting up a state-based capital outlay program.

After ten years of surplus revenues, the state of Georgia experienced a revenue shortfall in fiscal year 1983. Up until this time, the library construction program had been financed with cash, but in an eleventh-hour budget amendment the library construction projects were placed on the "bond side of the budget." This appeared to be of little consequence until it was discovered that there was no authority in the state constitution to allow for the sale of state bonds for public libraries. However, there was authority to sell state bonds for "educational facilities" to be administered by local school boards. Given this authority, the state bonds were sold and the library projects were administered by local school boards under a cooperative understanding between the school boards and the library boards.

The recognition by all at both the state and local level that this was not desirable resulted in a proposed constitutional

amendment that was passed by Georgia voters in the fall of 1984. For a full description of the campaign to pass the amendment, which provided a firm basis upon which state bonds could be sold to directly fund public libraries, see the *Library Journal* article "Passing a Constitutional Amendment: To Help Finance Georgia Public Library Buildings with State Bonds."[9] The amendment was passed by a 60-40 margin, and with this kind of public mandate, the governor and the legislature responded appropriately by increasing state funding for public library construction significantly

Armed with the authority to receive state bond funding directly, a state-wide public mandate, a generous and politically shrewd allocation formula, a consistent, responsive, and fair project development process in advance of the legislative session, and an increased demand for library construction funds at the local level, the state library and local library supporters were able to obtain every dollar requested in state assistance for public library capital outlay throughout the eighties and into the nineties. Since this has been the case, the priorities established by state board policy have rarely been used. The state library staff evaluations of the applications are specific to the individual projects since the projects are not in competition for funding. The upshot is a considerably improved relationship between the state library staff and local library officials.

If there is a downside to the program it may be that its strengths are also its greatest weaknesses. While the program has been very successful at obtaining state funds for library construction, the funds necessary to provide library service in the completed facilities at a level commensurate with the quality of the building have not always been forthcoming. While small communities can come up with the ten percent match, they are not always as successful at finding funds for staff, programs, and collections. Sometimes this is due to difficult local fiscal conditions, but sometimes to the lack of a well-documented community needs assessment prepared in conjunction with the building program.

This problem has probably been aggravated by a recent formula revision that was tied to new space standards that have several levels of "quality" and which provide state funds at different levels. Projects in jurisdictions under the "minimum" space standards still get the generous formula discussed earlier, but projects being planned over this level up to an "optimal" level are provided with a straight 60 percent state match. Projects being planned over the optimal level do not get any state assistance at all. Unfortunately, sometimes it is the standards and the resulting formula that drive the planning, rather than the actual needs of a community. This is probably an inherent problem with any state or federal program and can only be overcome by local officials who take an honest, practical look at their community's need for library buildings and then make application based on that need, not on how much money they can get.

The goal for the Georgia program is to maintain reasonable funding levels in the face of increasing state and local budget deficits. As was projected, the program has begun to taper off somewhat because of a number of factors. First, there is no longer a tremendous need since many projects in both urban and rural areas have been completed. Over the last 20 years, Georgia has built new or improved 232 public libraries out of approximately 368 outlets in the state. This means that over 70 percent of the library buildings have been either built, or enhanced by the construction program, but there are still projects which are in need of state funds. Soon, some of the projects built in the program's early years will need to be expanded or remodeled. Assuming the economy at both the state and local levels improves, Georgia's library construction program should continue

to meet the needs of its citizens well into the next century.

As a final note, the $120 million investment the state of Georgia has made in its public libraries has stimulated approximately $60 million of local matching funds. Based on a total project expenditure of approximately $180 million, the state and local matching ratio for all of the projects over the 20-year period is approximately one-third local to two-thirds state dollars. However, it should be noted that the Georgia program does not allow local jurisdictions to consider land acquisition an eligible cost for matching purposes. When the value of land is included, the matching ratio is probably closer to 40 percent local to 60 percent state over the duration of the program. This inability to include land costs has created some difficulties with the quality of sites acquired for projects. As will be discussed later in this chapter, the question of whether or not to include site costs in the formula for matching funds is a difficult one. The practice of not including land costs may be one of the greatest weaknesses of the Georgia program. However, it has kept the local commitment in the projects at a higher level than the formula might otherwise indicate.

Illinois

The state public library construction program in Illinois was initiated as a result of the federal government's jobs bill in 1983. Another major boost occurred in 1985 when the state embarked upon the "Build Illinois" program, a capital development initiative that included a significant amount of funding for library construction as well as other forms of public infrastructure. The Build Illinois Bond Act was "intended to improve the state's business climate and create thousands of new jobs by financing capital improvements at universities and libraries, rehabilitating sewers and roads, expanding conservation

Table 5-8. State grants for Public Library Construction in Illinois

Fiscal Year	State Grant Appropriations	State Grant Award	No. of Projects
1991	$ 0	$30,890,685	31
1990	12,500,000	100,000	1
1989	20,000,000	3,138,974	10
1988		697,862	7
1987	2,000,000	2,264,131	9
1986	7,530,000	5,271,011	24
1985	0	422,280	5
1984	2,250,000	1,810,829	6
1983	2,500,000	0	0
TOTAL:	$46,780,000	44,595,872	93

and environmental programs, and by making financial assistance available to businesses."[10] Bonds issued from this program were limited obligation bonds supported by revenues from a tax on nondealer used-car sales as well as other taxes already in place. Including the new Illinois State Library building and the new Central Library building of the Chicago Public Library, the program financed approximately 30 public libraries in Illinois in the mid-eighties. Table 5-8 provides an overview of all state funds for public library construction, including the Build Illinois program.

Grant funds available state-wide from the Illinois State Library are provided through appropriations by the Illinois General Assembly. The money is generated through state bond sales funded through various revenue sources, including a computer software sales tax. The rules for the state construction grant program require local matching funds to be provided by the applicant public library. The awarded state funds of approximately $45 million have stimulated approximately $60 million in local matching funds. These are generated primarily through bond issue referenda, investments, fundraising, support from the library's corporate authority, and mortgage loans. In some cases, most or all of the

project costs are provided through special appropriations by the state legislature. Special appropriations provided $18.5 million in 1990 and $10 million in 1991 to the Chicago Public Library for the construction, remodeling, and renovation of 14 branches.

From 1984 through 1991, the funding priorities were in order: remodeling to promote accessibility for people with disabilities, new construction, additions to existing buildings, and remodeling. Of the 93 projects during that period, 19 were for accessibility, 34 for new construction, 20 for additions, and 20 for remodeling. A grant award for an accessibility project may be up to $75,000. The matching formula is 50 percent grant funds to 50 percent local funds. To qualify as an accessibility project, at least 70 percent of the work has to be related to remodeling for accessibility. A grant awarded for new construction, an addition to an existing building, or remodeling may be in the range of $25,000 to $250,000; the matching formula is 40 percent grant funds to 60 percent local funds.

After the legislature appropriates funds for construction grants, the state library calls for letters of intent and applications. Local public libraries must apply to the state library for grants. To qualify, a public library must meet state per-capita grant requirements and participate in interlibrary system reciprocal borrowing. The applications are reviewed in priority order by the Illinois State Library Advisory Committee (ISLAC)'s Subcommittee for Library Construction.

The subcommittee reviews a detailed building program, architectural schematic drawings, an indication of readiness to build, commitment of local matching funds, the project budget, the applicant's finances and operating budget, and how the project addresses Illinois's public library standards, "Avenues to Excellence II." Projects must adhere to the Illinois Accessibility Code and the Americans with Disabilities Act (ADA). For projects over $150,000, a building consultant is necessary; an architect registered in Illinois is required for all projects. Also, all projects require a sign-off from the state's preservation agency.

If a project meets the criteria for funding, the subcommittee recommends to ISLAC that it be funded. The grant program is competitive, but efforts are made to fund as many projects as possible. If there is a shortage of funds, a library may be offered a smaller grant than requested. Occasionally, a library will receive a grant combining both state funds and LSCA Title II funds. ISLAC makes its funding recommendations to the state library and the Illinois secretary of state, the constitutional officer who is the official state librarian.

Since the program's inception, the state library has striven to reduce the amount of paperwork in the application and grant-reporting process. Over the years, the application form has been streamlined. The number of copies of applications and building programs submitted to the state library has been cut in half, and the amount of documentation to be submitted during construction also has been reduced. In order to expedite the construction phase, the state library's prior approval of change orders is not necessary unless they exceed $10,000. When the program was established, the state library's approval was needed for change orders over $1,000.

The matching amount for accessibility projects has increased over the years. Originally, the formula was 50 percent state to 50 percent local funds with a grant award up to $50,000. In order to stimulate more libraries to remodel for accessibility, the formula was changed in 1988 to an 80 percent state grant matching 20 percent local funds for a grant award up to $100,000. The matching formula was changed again in 1991 to 50 percent grant funds to 50 per-

cent local funds for a grant award up to $75,000 in order to stretch state grant funds.

In 1992, the Subcommittee for Library Construction and ISLAC recommended new funding priorities. Accessibility projects remained the first priority, and new construction, additions, and remodeling were combined into the second priority. The third priority is for public library construction planning grants. Unfortunately, the demand for construction grants exceeds the supply of funds available. Over three dozen letters of intent requesting over $3 million in construction grants were submitted by libraries in both 1991 and 1992 when less than $750,000 of LSCA Title II funds and no state funds were available in each of those years.

A 1991 survey indicated that of the 624 public libraries in Illinois, 116 were planning to become accessible to people with disabilities; 53 were planning new buildings; and 147 were planning to expand and remodel. The survey also indicated less than half the public libraries in Illinois were physically accessible to people with disabilities. To qualify for a state per-capita grant in fiscal year 1994, public libraries will be required to submit their ADA self-evaluations. ADA will lead to structural changes in many library facilities, which further demonstrates the need for additional state support for public library construction.

Kentucky

The Kentucky state library is fortunate to have had a program for state-funded public library construction since 1968. Utilizing the seed money of LSCA Title II, the state library was able to convince the governor and the legislature that public library buildings were a priority need, and those funds were allocated for that purpose during the 1968 general assembly. The program subsequently became a line item in the state library's budget and has continued to be funded annually.

Because of the large number of counties (120) in Kentucky, the state library has advocated county-wide public library systems in its development program. To date, 118 counties offer public library services. Of those, 105 counties have received construction project funds through the state library from either state or federal sources. More than 300 state-funded grants have been made to assist the county-wide libraries with their facility needs.

The initial state-funded construction program was unique in design and was called the amortization program. Eligible libraries were awarded grants to be funded over a 20-year period, which were matched with local funds. The libraries borrowed the amounts needed to construct their buildings, and the long-term debt was retired through the yearly grant. This program design was utilized for six years (1968 to 1970 and 1972 to 1974), producing 37 new or fully renovated buildings costing over $5 million. The state's yearly budget allocation for that program was $493,600.

In 1975, an additional $500,000 was allocated, which began the current program design. Grants are made during the state's fiscal year to projects that can completely obligate their costs within the year. These can be new buildings, additions, renovations, or repair projects. Since 1975, approximately $1 million has been allocated to the state construction program annually (which includes the amortization program). A one-time windfall allocation of $1.5 million was also made that year, generating numerous projects. Approximately $28 million in public library construction projects has been generated over these 25 years.

The funding formulas have paralleled LSCA guidelines for local matching funds. Originally, the state share was 65 percent of project costs up to a maximum grant of $250,000. The maximum state grant was raised to $350,000 in 1979. The state share was changed to 50 percent of the project costs up to $350,000 in 1987 to parallel the LSCA matching formula.

In 1979, a repair grant program was initiated with the premise that the state library should support the county libraries in maintaining their facilities as well as constructing them. The program encourages preventive maintenance as well as providing help for potential emergency conditions. Libraries may be reimbursed on a matching basis for major repairs, such as roof, HVAC, or carpet replacements. The maximum reimbursement is $30,000 for total repair projects of $60,000 and above. A minimum reimbursement of $1,500 can be made for a project of $3,000. Approximately $100,000 per year is expended for this program from the state library's construction budget.

The state's dollars have been well spent on public library buildings, producing functional and efficient facilities. In many small counties, the library building is the gathering point for all types of community activities and is the most attractive building in town. When the program began, buildings were designed to accommodate 20 years of growth. The early projects are now starting to show their age and the local counties returning to the state library for grants to expand the buildings.

Maryland

In Maryland, the state aid program, in which all 24 library systems participate, requires a county and state coordinated minimum library program for the support and growth of public libraries. Through the state aid program, the state of Maryland shares in the county library systems' operating and capital expenses. In the *Laws of Maryland Relating to Public Libraries, 1990 Edition* issued by the Maryland State Department of Education, capital expenses include principal and interest payments or

Table 5-9. State grants for Public Library Construction in Maryland

Fiscal Year	State Grant Appropriations	No. of Projects
1984	$ 1,163,493	3
1983	637,041	1
1982	326,407	8
1981	0	0
1980	644,367	6
1979	0*	0*
1978	0*	0*
1977	0*	0*
1976	0*	0*
1975	18,489	1
1974	0	0
1973	78,250	1
1972	189,278	1
1971	16,263	1
1970	45,000	1
1969	8,400	1
1968	159,148	1
1967	0	0
1966	119,150	5
1965	99,914	4
Totals:	$ 3,505,200	34

*Data unavailable for these years.

current capital spending or accumulation for the purchase of land for libraries; the purchase and construction of library buildings; remodeling and adding to library buildings; and the purchase of equipment and furniture for libraries. The capital expense is not less than 20 percent of the cost of the minimum program in any county.

State aid and construction were merged in the state budget as a single line item in the mid-1980s. This means that in actual practice, capital expenses have not been used for construction in recent years. Libraries in the state have found other ways of acquiring building money including LSCA Title II funds and floating bonds at the county level. This prevents using or having to set aside construction money out of operating budgets in lean economic times. The formula for allocation of state funds varies from year to year. Allotments are derived from a formula based on each

year's population and assessed property value. There are no priorities set at the state level except for the allocation of LSCA Title II funds. State allocations for public library construction in Maryland prior to the mid-eighties are listed in Table 5-9.

Massachusetts

Despite the establishment of the Massachusetts Board of Library Commissioners in 1891, the commonwealth of Massachusetts had played no funding role in the construction of buildings until 1987. The board's mission was to advise local librarians and trustees on book selection, standard library practices, and general administration. Board members and their consultants made regular visits to each library to offer professional advice, and board files from the early part of this century reveal a lively consultation program involved in every aspect of library service, including space planning, but no state funds were ever made available for construction.

A survey of public libraries and library branches in Massachusetts conducted in late 1987 revealed that of the 367 respondents, 256 libraries needed renovation, an addition, or a new building. Another 31 respondents needed handicapped-accessibility projects of varying types but otherwise had satisfactory facilities. At the time of the survey, therefore, 67 percent of existing library facilities were in need of construction to meet minimum health, safety, and service needs in their communities. In 1987, after four years of lobbying efforts by local library trustees, the Massachusetts Library Association, and library users throughout the state, "An Act to Improve Public Libraries" (MGL Chapter 478, Acts of 1987) moved successfully through the legislative process and was signed into law, establishing the Massachusetts Public Library Construction Program and authorizing the allocation of $35 million in capital funding for library construction and repair.

An extremely competitive state grant round, patterned after the existing federal LSCA Title II program, drew 94 applications eligible for $127 million in funding. Grants ranged from token awards in communities that had proceeded with construction projects on their own to awards of up to 65 percent of a proposed project's eligible costs. Of the $35 million appropriated, $7 million was dedicated to the Boston Public Library toward its $21 million Phase I reconstruction of the McKim Building. Constructed in 1895 and known as one of the three great buildings of Boston, the McKim Building had been as neglected over the years as its counterparts throughout the state. Phase I of the restoration was to include structural repairs, a new heating system, full handicapped accessibility except to the closed stacks, and complete rewiring. Restoration of marble, frescoes, murals, and ceramic and wood finishes was to be funded privately.

The remaining $28 million was allocated to construction of nine new buildings, 46 renovations and additions to old buildings, and three planning projects. $3.1 million was allocated for reimbursement to 23 cities and towns that had already funded their libraries locally after July 1, 1986. The full $35 million has been included in Governor William Weld's Five-Year Capital Plan, with final projects scheduled to begin in 1995 for a total of 59 projects. The state money stimulated over $120 million of local matching funds.

The legislature and the library community at this writing, are exploring the possibility of continuing funding at the established level of $6 to $9 million beyond fiscal year 1995, particularly in light of safety issues and the requirements of both state and federal accessibility laws, as well as the need to update buildings in order to house new technologies and new media. The McKim Building of the Boston Public

Library is in need of a further $30 million Phase II project to complete its renovation. The Johnson Building of the Boston Public Library is 20 years old and beginning to show its age, and 200 or so aging and inadequate Massachusetts library buildings are still in need of varying degrees of renovation.

In this context, the federal LSCA Title II program, which makes available about $400,000 each year for library construction in Massachusetts is a highly valued inducement to library trustees to consult with the Massachusetts Board of Library Commissioners about their building projects. But the two or three Title II awards given out each year are only a token in a situation that requires a regular, consistent, multiyear program of state aid for public library construction.

Mississippi

State funding for public library construction began in Mississippi in 1974, when the legislature appropriated $3 million in federal revenue-sharing funds to the library commission for public library construction. An additional $4 million was appropriated in 1975 and $2.5 million in 1977. The 1975 and 1977 funds included money to assist the commission in administering the program. Table 5-10 shows a summary of state grants for public library construction by fiscal year.

Table 5-10. State grants for Public Library Construction in Mississippi

Fiscal Year	State Grant Appropriations	No. of Projects
1992	$ 8,700,000	108
1977	2,500,000	26
1975	4,000,000	37
1974	3,000,000	31
TOTAL:	$18,200,000	202

The revenue-sharing construction program began when the LSCA Title II program experienced a ten-year hiatus starting in 1973. Many of the criteria developed for the LSCA program were used in the revenue-sharing projects. For example, the program required a dollar-for-dollar match with the maximum state grant at $200,000.

The first grants funded by the state library were made in 1975. Thirty-one libraries were funded (26 new buildings and five additions/renovations). The $3 million of state funds generated approximately $3.2 of local funds. The maximum state grant was $200,000 and the minimum $6,533. Local matching funds came from a combination of revenue sharing, general funds, mill levies, and private contributions. In fiscal year 1976, another 37 projects were funded, including 26 new buildings and 11 additions or renovations. The $4 million of state funds stimulated approximately $7.5 million of local funds. Twenty-six libraries received funds in fiscal year 1978. In addition, two libraries that had received grants in 1978 were given additional money to complete their projects. Of the 26 grants awarded, 13 were for new libraries and 13 for additions or renovations. The $2.5 million dollars in state funds stimulated over $5 million of local matching funds.

Because adequate facilities for public libraries were in great demand during the 1970s in Mississippi, applications were awarded on a first-come, first-served basis. Applications were made at any time during the year by a library system with the city and/or county providing the matching funds. Completed applications were date-stamped and placed in line for receipt of funds by the library commission. Each library funded with state revenue-sharing funds had to meet certain eligibility criteria concerning the organizational structure of the library, financial support of the public library system, and service standards.

The program's major strength was its emphasis on building and developing public library systems. A library could not receive funds unless it was affiliated with a public library system. The program also required the library system to be funded at certain levels in order to maintain the buildings constructed. Since applicants were not required to have matching local funds available at the time of application, the projects moved forward more slowly than desirable in some cases.

In fiscal year 1991 to 1992, public library systems in Mississippi were asked to submit preapplications for capital improvement needs which formed the basis of a state-wide needs assessment and were used to justify a state bond issue for public libraries. The preapplications indicated a need for 57 construction projects (new, renovations, and conversions) for an approximate total of $13.9 million. Continuing the state maximum grant at $200,000, the state's share to fund these projects was approximately $5.8 million. Fortunately, the state bond issue passed during the 1992 regular legislative session, providing $8.7 million for public library construction, automation, and improvements. After a 14-year haitus, state funding for public library construction is once again available in Mississippi.

Nevada

In 1983, the Nevada legislature passed an act (Nevada Revised Statutes, Chapter 328) directing that a proposal to issue state general obligation bonds for building and expanding public libraries be submitted to a vote of the people. At a general election in November, 1984, voters approved $10 million for this purpose. Regulations based on the statute were written by the library development division of the state library in cooperation with the Legislative Council Bureau to facilitate the process for application and disbursal of the bonds. In

January, 1986, applications were sent to all Nevada public library directors. Returned applications were initially reviewed by the state library and evaluated for compliance with the regulations. The state librarian forwarded qualifying applications to the Nevada Council on Libraries. Recommendations to fund library building construction and expansion projects then went to the Interim Finance Committee of the Nevada legislature which had final authority to approve grants.

To qualify for the funding, local governments were required to provide an adjusted share computed according to the following formula:

1. The total assessed valuation of the local government entity divided by the population of that entity to determine the local assessed valuation per capita.
2. The total assessed valuation of the state divided by the population of the state to determine the state-wide assessed valuation per capita.
3. The local assessed valuation per capita divided by the state-wide assessed valuation per capita.
4. The basic local share (50 percent of the estimated total project cost) multiplied by the quotient from No. 3 to determine the adjusted local share.

Qualifying applications were approved and funding disbursed from the office of the state librarian beginning in October of 1986. By the summer of 1989, more than $9.5 million had been expended in the construction of 11 new libraries and the renovation or expansion of eight public libraries in all corners of the state including $450,000 reserved for rural libraries. As of 1992 only $52,803 of the $10 million remained and was expected to fund the completion of a rural library building in Lyon County. The maximum state grant award was $2,447,261 for construction of the new Las Vegas Library which also houses a children's museum. The minimum award was $7,990 for expansion of the rural Beatty Community Library.

New Jersey

State funds for public library construction were first provided in New Jersey in 1974: an appropriation of $190,000 was used to fund one library. After an eight-year hiatus, state funds were once again available in 1983, and then after another interruption of two years the program began again and provided state funds for four consecutive years as Table 5-11 shows.

During the six years that the program was active, 24 public library construction projects received over $5 million of state funds. The program provided a minimum of 20 percent of the construction costs based on square footage costs determined by the state librarian. The maximum grant was $500,000 and the minimum $70,000. Eligible projects included new construction, acquisition of an existing building, addition to an existing building, or rehabilitation of an existing building.

Eligible applicants must submit a written community analysis, building program, schematic plans, outline specifications, and cost estimates prepared by an architect, and show evidence of local matching

Table 5-11. State grants for Public Library Construction in New Jersey

Fiscal Year	State Grant Appropriations	State Grant Award	No. of Projects
1989	$ 1,500,000	$ 1,385,703	5
1988	1,000,000	921,248	5
1987	1,000,000	1,000,000	6
1986	1,000,000	980,000	4
1985	0	0	0
1984	0	0	0
1983	680,000	655,700	3
1982	0	0	0
1981	0	0	0
1980	0	0	0
1979	0	0	0
1978	0	0	0
1977	0	0	0
1976	0	0	0
1975	0	0	0
1974	190,000	182,170	1
Totals:	$ 5,370,000	$ 5,124,828	24

funds. Applicants are ranked by the municipality's per-capita wealth, and priority is given to municipalities with the least financial resources. Project applications are reviewed by three consultants with expertise in library construction and applicants may be required to revise plans based on the review.

Currently funding is unavailable through the program, but a recent 1991 survey indicated that at least 27 public library projects were in the planning stages and potentially in need of state funds.

New York

The state of New York has had two rounds of state funding for public library construction in fiscal years 1984 and 1986 as can be seen in Table 5-12. Between the two years, state funds in the amount of $5 million were provided to a total of 292 projects, many of which were renovation or rehabilitation projects for disabled accessibility, energy conservation, or technology retrofits. Not only remodeling projects but also expansion projects and new buildings received funding. State grants ranged from a minimum of $287 to a high of $188,831. Local funding must be a minimum of 50 percent, since the state grant cannot exceed 50 percent of the project's total cost. However, in many cases the local funding far exceeded the local matching requirement.

After the appropriations were set, library jurisdictions made application to the library system to which they belong. The library system evaluated the grant application based on a plan previously submitted to the state library. The applications were forwarded to the state library, where final determinations were made. Generally, funding decisions were not rigorous if the application was correctly completed. Grants were awarded according to a rather complicated formula based on a prorata share of the funds related to the population served by the library. There was no funding determination by established priorities, which meant that if the application was eligible and complete, the applicant received some amount of funding based on the formula.

New York has not received any state library construction funds for the last few years, but is once again proposing the need for additional state funding. A 1991 survey indicated that 185 public library construction projects were in the planning stages and seeking funding. The projects reportedly would cost approximately $211 million and require $98 million of state aid.

North Carolina

Since 1980, there have been two separate periods of major state-funded public library construction in North Carolina. The first occurred during the early eighties and the second during the late eighties. As Table 5-13 shows, 124 public library projects received a total of $4 million in state funds. This funding was matched with close to $50 million of local funds.

Table 5-12. State Grants for Public Library Construction in New York

Fiscal Year	State Grant Appropriations	No. of Projects
1986	$ 2,000,000	129
1985	0	0
1984	3,000,000	163
Totals:	$ 5,000,000	292

Table 5-13. State grants for Public Library Construction in North Carolina

Fiscal Year	State Grant Appropriations	No. of Projects
1989	$ 500,000	13
1988	1,250,000	16
1987	1,250,000	13
1980	1,000,000	8
Totals	$ 4,000,000	124

1980–1982

In 1980, the North Carolina General Assembly appropriated $1 million from general state funds for the construction, expansion, or renovation of public library buildings. This was part of an overall $102,276,716 appropriation for general capital improvements for all state agencies. There is not much information available as to how this request originally came about; however, in a brief review of this program prepared in June 1982, the state library noted the influence of Robert Ladd's supplement to the *National Inventory of Library Needs* in providing background information on space needs.

Under this fund, grants were limited to a maximum of $100,000 per application and were to be equally matched by each library. The reality was that the maximum grant made was for $30,150 (the minimum grant was for $2,500) and local funds in many cases accounted for more than 50 percent of the project. The total amount of local funds stimulated by the state grant program was at least $1,950,000. The state library had the primary responsibility for verifying applications. Grants were to be recommended by the Department of Cultural Resources (of which the state library was a constituent agency) and were subject to the approval of the state's Advisory Budget Commission and the governor.

1987–90

Starting in 1987, the general assembly appropriated $1.25 million for public library construction for each of the state fiscal years 1987–88 and 1989–90. These appropriations were in response to building needs identified and voiced by the state's public libraries and the state library agency. For both years of the biennium, this authorization limited grants to a maximum of ten percent ($125,000) of the total amount appropriated each year. At least 50 percent of the costs for projects funded

with these appropriations came from local matching funds; however, several large projects provided a significant overmatch of local funds. The state library was responsible for administering the money and it devised procedures, guidelines, and forms for applicants to use based on LSCA Title II criteria (need, service area, and project readiness). Projects were reviewed and evaluated by state library staff and members of the state library commission.

In state fiscal year 1989–90, the general assembly again voted $500,000 for public library construction. In addition to the 1987–89 rules, the authorizing legislation added a provision that the value of the land used for a public library building could satisfy the in-kind matching requirement. The state library also made some changes in its guidelines for applicants: allowing only libraries that qualified for North Carolina's state aid to public libraries fund to apply, defining the terms "renovation" and "addition," and requiring libraries to present a legal appraisal of the actual value of land used for matching purposes.

Since the 1989–90 appropriation, there have been no further state funds for public library construction. However, the state library has undertaken a special study of North Carolina's public libraries during state fiscal year 1992–1993. This study includes an assessment of current library construction needs. In summary, state funds, with their local matching requirements, have provided a strong impetus to local communities to upgrade or build new public library facilities. These funds have especially helped smaller projects since they are administered with less paperwork and regulation than LSCA Title II funds. If there is a drawback to the program, it is that allowing the value of land to match state money sometimes results in fewer local dollars being available for actual construction purposes.

Rhode Island

The state of Rhode Island has allocated state funds for public library construction since 1965, and this program, like many others was stimulated by the inception of LSCA Title II. The two programs have been closely intertwined over the years since many of the construction projects have obtained both state and federal grants. The Rhode Island program funds all types of construction projects, including new buildings, additions, remodelings, and conversions. In the past, applications from local jurisdictions have been accepted on an ongoing, noncompetitive basis and reviewed

Table 5-14. State Grants for Public Library Construction in Rhode Island

Fiscal Year	State Grant Funds *	No. of Projects
1991	$1,203,746	2
1990	5,234,151	5
1989	841,002	2
1988	661,550	1
1987	6,250,000	2
1986	1,408,475	4
1985	950,000	1
1984	208,189	2
1983	0	0
1982	0	0
1981	0	0
1980	89,200	1
1979	1,610,000	2
1978	42,500	1
1977	270,000	1
1976	375,000	1
1975	150,000	2
1974	180,223	1
1973	540,561	1
1972	346,519	1
1971	1,000	1
1970	26,248	2
1969	5,000	3
1968	15,240	1
1967	406,014	4
1966	46,560	7
1965	175,600	8
	$21,036,778	56

*State grant funds listed do not include the repayment of interest incurred in borrowing the state share, since interest rates change over the grant period.

at the state library. As long as the project is eligible for funds, a state allocation is made based on the cost of the state share. The state allocation covers up to 50 percent of the total project costs including the interest incurred from borrowing the state share. The state funds are disbursed to the local jurisdictions over five to 20 years in the form of payments after the completion of the project. Many communities in Rhode Island use this state revenue stream to repay the principal and interest on bonds, mortgages from commercial banks, or other debt instruments. Table 5-14 shows the state grant funds committed each year since the beginning of the program. (Note that the amounts listed for each year are the total committed by the state, not necessarily the amount paid during that particular year.)

There have been no state allocations since 1991 because of recent fiscal restraints and an increase in state debt payments for the program. However, it is anticipated that the program will start up again in fiscal year 1995 when the debt load drops below $2 million per year. The state library is considering implementing new regulations for the program at that time. This state construction program has performed a significant role in developing public libraries in Rhode Island and will probably to do so in the future.

Tennessee

As Table 5-15 shows, the state of Tennessee has had three appropriations for public library construction. The 1989 appropriation bill included a list of 29 libraries eligible to apply for the funds and specified that the state funds were to be used as part of the local match for LSCA Title II grants. The 1990 and 1991 appropriations were given to three libraries that were in the process of applying for LSCA Title II funds. Award or authorization to use the state funds was

Table 5-15. State Grants for Public Library Construction in Tennessee

Fiscal Year	State Grant Appropriations	No. of Projects
1991	$ 30,000	1*
1990	50,000	2
1989	906,600	19
TOTAL:	$986,600	22

*A second grant was given to one of the projects receiving funds from the 1989 appropriation.

contingent on an application for LSCA Title II funds being approved by the Tennessee State Library and Archives Management Board and the secretary of state. Libraries were eligible for federal grants for 50 percent of the cost of a project, not to exceed $100,000. Brief guidelines written for the state funds made the library projects subject to the provisions of the Tennessee Long Range Program for Library Development.

The funds have been reappropriated annually, as necessary, to maintain their availability for eligible libraries. The reappropriation bills have given the management board authority to allocate the funds to additional locations as libraries originally designated as eligible have declared they would not utilize the funds. As of the spring of 1992, 21 projects received state funding totaling $771,896. Sixteen of the state grants have been for $35,784. Funding for the 21 projects includes $1,816,175 of LSCA Title II funds and an estimated $4,468,790 of local funds. The $214,704 balance of state funds will be used for three libraries from the original group which are still eligible or reallocated to additional libraries.

The request for state funds resulted from interest in public library construction stimulated by federal LSCA Title II funding available since 1983. Most of the original libraries designated as eligible for the funds were located in rural parts of Ten-

nessee with less ability to provide the matching share necessary for the federal LSCA Title II grants. The availability of the funds has helped stimulate projects and resulted in larger and better buildings for many of the funded projects. However, the limitation on the size of the grants is a weakness of the program.

West Virginia

West Virginia has a long history of allocating state funds for public library construction. The program was stimulated by the presence of LSCA Title II funds and the lack of local matching funds. Projects frequently get both state and federal grants. Table 5-16 shows that from 1970 to 1987, the state of West Virginia appropriated over $11 million and funded 125 public library projects. These state funds stimulated over $13.6 million in local matching funds.

Projects ranged from equipment acqui-

Table 5-16. State Grants for Public Library Construction in West Virginia

Fiscal Year	State Grant Appropriations
1987	$ 390,000
1986	20,000
1985	20,000
1984	388,000
1983	100,000
1982	0
1981	0
1980	1,200,000
1979	1,350,000
1978	1,000,000
1977	1,500,000
1976	1,500,000
1975	1,500,000
1974	1,250,000
1973	700,000
1972	250,000
1971	0
1970	500,000
Total:	$11,668,000

sition to expansion and remodeling to major new construction projects. The West Virginia program is also known for financing "instant" and "outpost" libraries which are modular self-contained buildings designed specifically for library use. There is no established formula for the state match since the applicant's ability to pay is the prime consideration. The state rarely grants more than 80 percent of the project costs, and most often the state grant does not exceed 60 percent for smaller projects or 40 percent for more expensive projects.

Applications must be submitted by a local library board which has been created under West Virginia Code Chapter 10 or a special act of the legislature. The state library does not grant directly to county commissions, city councils, or boards of education. Interested communities are encouraged to submit a letter of intent when they are serious about a construction project. A formal application is requested by the state library when planning for the project is near completion. Applications are evaluated by the state librarian and a recommendation is made to the West Virginia Library Commission. If the commission agrees to consider a project, the applicant's library board is invited to attend a commission meeting for an interview. Projects are then considered on a case-by-case basis. Need and ability to pay are the prime considerations. To prevent a community from tying-up funds for a long period of time, construction must begin within six months of project approval. The applicant may ask for an extension, for which acceptable reasons must be given.

While there have been no state funds appropriated since 1987, the need remains for state funding of public library facilities in West Virginia. Based on a recent needs assessment, the state library has a list of 32 potential projects in need of $5.9 million in state funds.

Wyoming

While the state of Wyoming does not have a formal program of state grants specifically for public library construction, funds are available to cities, counties, and other political subdivisions for capital construction and infrastructure development through the government grants and loans program of the Wyoming State Land and Farm Loan Office. This program was established in 1974 utilizing revenues generated from use of minerals on state lands. The amount of funds set aside for grants and loans is determined by the legislature biennially.

Grants for construction projects are awarded on a competitive basis. Awards of up to 50 percent of the construction costs of the project may be granted. Applications consist of a letter requesting funds supported by appropriate architectural plans, county commission support, and building construction cost documents. The grant applications are reviewed by the staff in the government grant and loan program with recommendations made to the state Farm Loan Board. The awards are made by the Farm Loan Board which comprises the top five elected state officials (governor, secretary of state, treasurer, auditor, superintendent of public instruction). Each application competes with all others. Sewer and bridge projects, for example, compete against public libraries in the same round of applications. No single type of project takes priority. The staff recommendations may exceed available funds so the board eliminates projects to reach the fundable number. While this is not a structured grant process, grants are usually awarded twice each year in January and July.

Only three public libraries have utilized this grant program to date. Until the first award was made in 1988 no other library thought it was eligible under the general categories of grants. Table 5-17 shows a summary of grants for public library construction.

Table 5-17. State grants for Public Library Construction in Wyoming

Fiscal Year	State Grant Appropriations	No. of Projects
1991	$135,000	1
1990	40,000	1
1988	250,000	1
TOTAL:	$425,000	3

Many applicants lobby the board and many attend the meeting when awards are made. This unofficial process demonstrates local interest in the project and valued importance (one library believes that the apple pie made for the governor by a local pie shop helped with their project). A recent state library survey of possible building projects identified 14 library projects varying from disabled accessibility to new buildings. It is possible that three of these projects might apply for grants under this state program over the next three to five years.

A COMPARATIVE ANALYSIS OF STATE PROGRAMS

The preceding descriptions document the significant past and present state programs for library construction across the nation. It is obvious that there are many possible variations. The following section attempts to analyze some of the similarities and differences in the programs. This analysis is for potential applicants for state grants as well as for state library officials who are interested in creating a state-based program for public library construction or modifying an existing one.

Authorization

Most state-based library construction programs have a statutory basis of some form. Further, they have program require-ments that govern the allocation of state funds which are spelled out in policies, regulations, procedures, guidelines, or application forms. In most cases, the appropriation of funds is by the legislature on an annual basis; however, in California and Nevada, state bond funding authorization must be placed on a state-wide ballot for approval by the electorate after approval by the legislature and governor. Many states have the authorization to use state bond funds; however, many states use general revenues or other special funds.

Eligibility

Programs vary regarding which agencies are eligible to apply for and receive state library construction funds. In California, as in many other states, eligible applicants are cities, counties, and special districts. However, in Georgia, only library systems are eligible to apply, while in West Virginia only the local library board may make application. In Illinois and Mississippi, applicants must be either a member of or affiliated with a library system. Numerous other eligibility requirements vary from state to state. In some states, the projects must meet minimum standards of some kind (e.g., square footage, operating budget) in order to be eligible. In California, a project was not eligible to make application if it had already been advertised to bid. This requirement was put in the law to prevent state funds from supplanting local funds for projects that were already financed.

The kind of library project a community may apply for varies as well. Most states support new construction and expansion projects. Guidelines for remodeling projects vary tremendously. Some states, like California, provided state funds only for specific types of remodeling such as accessibility for the disabled, energy conservation, and health and safety purposes, but excluded general remodeling. Georgia allowed state funds for any form of remodeling, but excluded "partial" projects which were for remodeling only with no new square footage added to the building. These projects were allocated to the federal LSCA Title II program in Georgia. Some states (including California) allow for buildings to be purchased and converted into public libraries; some states, such as Georgia, do not. Building maintenance like roof repairs are often excluded; however, the Kentucky program has in recent years turned into a program specifically for maintenance. Some states, such as Illinois, allow for "planning grants." Some states (Florida and California) provided funds for site acquisition, and other states (Georgia) do not. The eligibility of furnishings and equipment varies throughout the different state programs as do other miscellaneous project-related costs such as architect's fees, site demolition and development, and building consultants.

In summary, there is no one right way to determine what should be eligible in a state grants program for library construction, but numerous considerations can help to fit the program to state and local needs. If the state's libraries are all old and inadequate, funds for remodeling are probably not the answer, but funds for new construction would make a lot of sense. If the state's library infrastructure is fairly well developed, then funds for repairs, general remodeling, and specialized remodeling make a great deal of sense. While it may be desirable to have library furnishings and equipment as an eligible cost, the state's bond codes may not permit it. If good library sites are very expensive, it may be necessary to include land acquisition as an eligible cost in order to encourage the use of high-quality sites. In the end, it is usually helpful to be as permissive as possible with what is eligible, and to make it as simple as possible to understand and calculate in order to avoid confusion during the grant application process. There is real-ly nothing wrong with allowing essentially everything required for a "turnkey" library building to be an eligible cost. If the cost to the state is the concern, this can be controlled by a matching formula or a ceiling grant amount.

Maximums and Minimums

In many states, maximum and minimum grants have been established for a number of reasons. Maximum grants control the allocation of funds so that a few large projects don't use up all the available funds in a given funding cycle. This approach tends to spread the money around so that many areas of the state benefit and is usually helpful in developing and maintaining state-wide support for a construction program. Maximum grants can be established on a project basis or on a library jurisdiction basis. In Georgia, library systems can receive no more than $2 million per fiscal year; however, they may fund any number of projects with that $2 million. While grant ceilings can be helpful, it should be kept in mind that they need to be raised occasionally to keep up with inflation and the escalation of project costs. Minimum grants are usually set because it is believed that below a certain dollar amount it is not worth the time and effort to prepare and process a grant application. However, this figure varies tremendously from state to state. Some states even set minimums on the project size. In Florida, for example, projects of less than 3,000 square feet are not eligible.

Formulas

Most states have established formulas to govern the allocation of the state matching funds. These formulas are usually on a percentage basis, e.g., 50 percent state to 50 percent local funds. Georgia and Alaska probably have two of the most generous formulas and give up to 90 percent of the project costs in certain situations. Some states, like West Virginia, do not have a set formula, but instead have a process of negotiation to determine the state amount. In West Virginia, the state librarian has the power to adjust the state's match up or down based on need and financial abilities. This approach can be effectively used to see that the state funds go where they are most needed. However, the advantage to fixed formulas is that the grant applicant can rely on an exact amount from the state based on a simple calculation. This is very helpful during the planning process and avoids the problem of a jurisdiction receiving a state grant for less than is necessary to build the facility in the manner planned, or at all.

Formulas may be set up in any number of ways. Nevada used a formula based on local and state assessed property values. New York used a complicated formula based on a prorata share of the funds related to the population served by the library. The options are many, but it is usually best to establish a formula that is not only equitable and politically well balanced but also simple to understand and calculate. Unnecessary and arbitrary aspects of any formula should be eliminated. It should always be kept in mind that the larger the state's share in a project, naturally, the greater the state's voice in the development and approval of the project. Another consideration in any formula is what can be included as an eligible project cost or what can be included as part of the local match.

The Value of Land

The cost of the library site can be a substantial expense in some locations. In California, Florida, Illinois, North Carolina, and other states, the acquisition of land is an eligible cost and used when the formula is applied and the state and local matching shares are calculated. Facing up to the cost of land as a legitimate part of a

project's cost is important particularly if the state library wishes to influence where the library will be placed. Good library sites are usually expensive, and they are seldom given away by local officials or even private benefactors. If the land value is included as part of the project, the state administrators will probably have more involvement in site selection and development. If the land value is not included in the eligible project cost, as in Georgia, it is difficult to turn down a proposed library site. Some local officials may be tempted to provide sites that are sometimes less than desirable for library locations. This can have a negative long-term impact on library development state-wide if repeated in numerous communities.

Application Deadlines

Every state program, should have a clearly defined grant application process. In most cases, application is made to the state library by a specified deadline. Grant submittal deadlines can be very important to potential applicants. In highly competitive programs, the grant deadline is similar to the bid deadline for a construction contract. If the agency accepting the late submittal does not reject it, that agency may well be sued for noncompliance with its own regulations. Multimillion-dollar projects that represent substantial time and expense to the grant applicant have been rejected by state agencies when they were submitted only a few minutes after a deadline! It is wise for potential grant applicants to know the program deadlines and submit the application well in advance to allow for last-minute problems and delays.

Application Requirements

Almost all grant programs use an official application form, in which the project, applicant, and local officials are identified along with a detailed description of pertinent project information. This information may be extensive or relatively simple depending on the program. Applications also usually include a project budget, a timetable for completion, and sometimes additional information about the size of the building, the site, and even the design.

Along with the actual application form, program requirements may call for additional supporting documents. These may include a needs assessment, community analysis, or library facilities master plan; a building program with a detailed facility space analysis; or various engineering reports such as studies for structural integrity of an existing building or an asbestos survey if the project is for remodeling. Many states, (e.g., California, Florida, and Connecticut) require architectural plans and outline specifications to be submitted with the application, and some states require a supporting cost estimate prepared by an architect or cost estimator. Frequently, a relatively extensive site analysis is required as well.

Information on the library's potential site may also be required in the application, including its general location, use potential, availability of parking, visibility, accessibility, availability of utilities, topography, drainage, size, configuration, and potential site demolition and development costs. The evaluation process may consider any of these factors, and if so, the information must be collected and submitted with the application. Some states, such as California, require substantial environmental analysis for any public construction project. Applicants for library construction grants there had to comply with the California Environmental Quality Act (CEQA) which created a substantial amount of work for applicants. Generally, boundary surveys are required with applications, along with soil testing and a legal opinion regarding the title to the property. It is usually necessary for the applicant to

have some form of control over the site prior to the application for state funds. This may mean ownership, an option to purchase, a court order of possession, a lease, or lease-purchase agreement. Finally, if the value of the land is an eligible cost, an appraisal will likely be required with the application as well.

Once all this planning information has been pulled together, it is usually also necessary to have the application officially certified by the applicant's governing board. Some form of financial statement committing to the required local matching funds for the project should be attached. This approval usually needs to be made at an official meeting of the board of the governing agency. Some programs, such as those in California and Georgia, also require the applicant to indicate a willingness to operate the completed facility. In almost all cases, projects funded with state funds will be required to comply with various state building codes (disabled accessibility, energy, fire safety, etc.) and the public contracts code that governs competitive bidding in the state.

Priorities

Along with eligibility and application requirements, most state programs have pre-established priorities. In many programs, all forms of construction are allowed but only certain types are given a priority. Some states emphasize new construction, while others (New York and Illinois) emphasize various forms of remodeling. Some states, like Connecticut, give priority to projects that do the best job at meeting needs based upon standards. "Need" is often emphasized both from a standpoint of needed space as well as financial need. While need is often subjective and difficult to ascertain objectively, the California program grappled with the issue and came up with an approach utilizing both objective data and subjective qualitative factors. As was discovered, genuine need is not easy to ascertain in a highly competitive process involving many communities.

Any potential grant applicant should become familiar with the state program's priorities early in the application process and assess the chances for success. One way to do this is to inquire about projects that have been funded in the past as well as those that have not. Armed with this information, a community can objectively assess its chances of being funded. Some states will provide a statement of competitiveness based on preliminary project information. California provided a preapplication process whereby potential applicants submitted a six-page project summary to receive an early assessment of the project's competitiveness from the state library staff and state librarian. A ranking list was developed and sent to all potential applicants. This information was used by local jurisdictions to assess their chances and helped them decide whether or not to spend the time and effort required to make a full application.

The Availability of Local Funds and the Start of Construction

State programs vary tremendously on the issue of when the local matching funds should be available for the construction project. Some states give priority to projects that have the money in an account at the time of application, reasoning that this demonstrates the applicant's commitment and readiness to begin construction immediately. Others allow the applicant to manage the cash flow of the project and have no specific time when all of the funds must be available. The California bond act did not require the state funds to be expended by any specific date, but the grant recipient's contract with the state library specified that construction must begin within one year of the date stated in the application. The availability of local funds

was considered a local issue with the grant recipient expected to monitor the project's cash flow requirements and make certain that funds were available to pay bills.

In Mississippi, the fact that applicants were not required to have the local match in hand at the time of application was considered a reason that projects developed more slowly than desirable. In Georgia, construction is expected to begin within six months of the grant award (although extensions are provided), but the grant recipient is not allowed to sign a construction contract without demonstrating that all the local funds are available in the form of cash, or an investment instrument, and under the control of the library system. Similarly, Florida and most other states require that projects start construction within a specified amount of time after the grant is awarded. This is to make sure that state funds are put to work in the economy as soon as possible and don't lie around losing effectiveness because of inflation. It is also usually very important to the health of a state program for state-funded projects to move forward without delay. This is one of the secrets of the success of the Georgia program. While the application process takes approximately a year, once the grant is awarded the projects are free to move forward very quickly with plans development and construction. Legislators generally respond positively when state funds do not languish and projects are built quickly after their approval.

Who determines the Grant Award?

In most states, the state library staff and frequently the state librarian review the applications. In a few instances, the state librarian makes the final decisions regarding grant awards; however, in most cases the final decision lies with a board, a commission for some governing body of state officials. In almost all cases, the state library staff reviews the applications for eligibility, accuracy, and program compliance. In reviewing the applications, the staff may look at any number of items depending on the program requirements and the evaluation process. Fairness and credibility are two of the most important issues. It is important, if possible, to make the grant award decisions on the basis of professional review of stated criteria and priorities and keep the determinations outside the arena of pork barrel politics. However, this is often easier said than done.

Sometimes "political realities" come into play and projects that may be less desirable get funded ahead of or in lieu of others in a state program. Sometimes this is necessary for the good of the program; sometimes it's simply a political payoff. It can be frustrating and even maddening, but occasionally it really is for the best in the long run. Sometimes making sure that a project gets funded for a particularly influential legislator can ensure the continuing success of an entire program, which will mean many more new library buildings for many communities over time. This is not an advocacy or apology for power politics or the "good old boy" approach to state appropriations, but it is a reality that state officials and lobbyists must contend with periodically. Hard ethical and practical decisions like this are often faced by state librarians and state board members in administering a library construction program. Potential grant applicants should be aware of this fact, and to some extent, understanding of the difficulty of these officials' position.

Evaluation Criteria

The criteria on which an application will be evaluated should be clearly and precisely stated well in advance of the application deadline. While it limits flexibility, it is only fair for potential applicants to be able to assess their chances of success. The criteria that are used in different state programs vary tremendously, but again they usually address issues of need, readiness, and the quality of planning for the project. The state of Florida's criteria include the type of construction, the population of the applicant's service area, the type and total size of the library building, the building program, the project narrative, and the like. New Jersey ranked projects on a per-capita wealth basis, with the lowest given the highest priority.

The evaluation process for the California program was very detailed. A relational database was established which ranked projects based on a dozen objective factors ranging from the distance in miles between the proposed project site and the nearest library building to the age of the library facility to be replaced. The information and ranking of projects based on these factors was then weighed with the rest of the application. The narrative application information required was extensive and included the quality of the needs assessment performed as well as the applicant's ideas for addressing "changing concepts in public library service." The evaluation of the applications was very thorough, and the projects that were ultimately funded closely met the criteria stated in the bond act.

Some state grant programs don't, in effect, evaluate applications at all. In the New York program, the applications were reviewed by staff for accuracy, but all eligible applicants got some money regardless of the project as long as the application was complete and accurate. This approach produced numerous grants, and many small ones, but it effectively spread the available money around the state. Mississippi felt it had so much demand that it simply awarded grants on a first-come-first-served basis. This approach certainly reduces the pressure on the state officials, but it adds pressure to local officials to get applications in quickly, and one certainly has to be concerned about the quality of the project under these circumstances.

Competitive Versus
Noncompetitive Programs

This brings up the issue of the desirability of competitive programs versus noncompetitive programs. Competitive programs usually require local jurisdictions to compete for limited state funding by submitting an application after a certain amount of state money is appopriated. This amount is usually far less than is needed state-wide. If the gap is wide between the available funding and the need, the competition is fierce (as with the California program). One of the major disadvantages of a competitive program is that not all applicants will receive funds. This can be particularly hard when a lot of time, effort, and money have gone into preparing the application, and the local jurisdiction perceives the need for a new library as very important. Sometimes an applicant does not receive state funds for a good reason, i.e., because the project has not been well planned. In these cases, it may be to the losers' advantage in the long run to be turned down and required to make application again in another year.

State library officials often point to deficient applications as justification for a competitive evaluation process. It provides leverage for the state library staff to seek improvement and a mechanism whereby the state library can influence the project's development. State library control over a project's development may be desirable from a state perspective, but this view is not always shared by local officials. Unfortunately, the fundamental problem with competitive programs is that they do not build political consensus and cooperation in the library community, which is a requirement for the development of an ongoing state-wide program.

One reason for the success of Georgia's program is its noncompetitive nature. The state consultants are able to provide a good deal of positive input into the development of the projects at an early stage. This enhances good planning for the project and develops a scnse of credibility for the state library as well as a sense of trust. The evaluation of a project is in essence done along the way, with the approval of various planning documents such as building programs and site applications. In this way, the state library has a positive impact on the development of the projects and ensures a certain degree of quality control. Further, the state library staff's evaluation of an application is specific to that project and not comparative to other projects since the projects are not competing for funding. The upshot is good communication and rapport among all parties: state library staff, other state officials, local library officials, local citizens, and legislators.

When the state-wide library community can work together instead of competing with itself, a positive sense of community can develop at the state level allowing projects to be funded over a number of years. State legislators respond well to this because they know their vote this year for a colleague's project may well result next year in that colleague's vote for a project in their own district. The process builds momentum that can be sustained for many years as long as there are no major embarrassments caused by any of the projects. Embarrassing a state legislator or the governor should be avoided at all costs if a state program is to remain healthy. There are always problems that must be worked through in any program and most programs will need to make a number of adjustments over the years, but this is a strength rather than a weakness.

Good interaction is much more likely in a noncompetitive environment than a competitive one. Unfortunately, it is usually easier to get a competitive program started than a noncompetitive one because it is difficult to get local officials to apply for funds for a program that is not already established. Usually the closest a state library can come is to perform a state-wide needs assessment for public library facilities. However, if a competitive program is in place, it may be possible to change the program in mid-stream, as Georgia did many years ago, and turn it into a noncompetitive program.

HOW TO START A STATE-BASED LIBRARY CONSTRUCTION PROGRAM

If state library construction funding does not already exist in a state, how does one start such a program? Besides the obvious need for some draft legislation, the library community needs to work hard to present the need for such a program and obtain funding. Legislation alone doesn't count for much. North Dakota has had enabling legislation for library construction for many years, but has never been able to get funding. What is the best way to ensure that funding will be forthcoming? The approach that seems to work best is for the state library (or a consultant hired by the state library) to perform a state-wide inventory and needs assessment of all public library facilities.

State-wide Inventory and Needs Assessment

State libraries know that in many cases local public library facilities are inadequate, but they don't always have convincing proof of this. They may well be able to run calculations based on standards which show that the overall square footage existing for public libraries is below what it should be, but they often do not have the hard data to back up the figures. It is easy enough to take the state population and multiply it by an appropriate standard-square-foot-per-capita figure (such as .5 square feet per capita) to get an overall amount of square footage that the state should have in library space. However,

even when this figure is compared to what currently exists, the difference (the needed square footage) is still just an abstract number.

This is a good first step and it may suffice for fiscal types, but it rarely stirs the blood of politicians. In order to get their attention, it is usually necessary to cite specific library projects, preferably in their district, which need funding. Further, a reasonable amount of detail about each library building project is desirable. What is its name? Where is it located? Is it a new building or a remodeling? How much square footage needs to be built or remodeled? What will it cost and how much state and local funding is needed assuming a given state formula for allocation? How soon are the funds needed? A list of projects can be developed by the library community to be used with individual legislators state-wide. In addition, overall figures can be generated which help to demonstrate and justify the state-wide need. These figures can be used with fiscal officers at the state level, but now they are backed up by data collected from the local level which gives them more credibility. In this way, the needs assessment can move out of the abstract and into the concrete.

This approach was used to a limited extent in the development of the California program, although it took several needs assessments and several years to get the bill through the legislature. Recently, the Commonwealth of Virginia produced a space needs study of public libraries in Virginia[12] that demonstrates the need for new public library space. One thing to keep in mind is that the actual process of preparing the needs assessment may be more important than the numbers it generates in building support for a state-wide program. In other words, it is important to get the local community involved in the needs assessment process and not just have a form filled out in the library director's office.

Along with results, one of the main purposes of a needs assessment is to build support for the individual projects at the grassroots level. Supporters can be built into a state-wide coalition to present a united front when the issue is taken to the legislature and the governor's office. Nothing is more powerful at the state level than an honest and forceful "buy-in" by local project supporters who are influential in their communities.

The needs assessment is not an end in itself, but a call to awaken the troops and identify lenders for the upcoming battle for funds. Some communities may do an in-depth needs assessment, and others may do less, but local individuals and officials from all segments of the community should be involved if possible. The library board and friends group should provide initiative and leadership, vision and enthusiasm, but influential people from all community groups should be asked to participate. When the time comes to approach legislators, it is best to have county commissioners, city council members, mayors, school superintendents, and corporate CEOs making the case along with the "average citizen" and library board member. The earlier these people are involved in the project, the better they understand it, and the more convincing they can be if they have the facts and figures about the project readily available. It is usually helpful to get the state library association and its lobbyist involved in the needs assessment process and the lobbying effort. However, library professionals will not usually be as effective with legislators as lay people because they are often perceived as being self-serving.

Making the Case for State Construction Funds

Once the needs assessment is complete, it is necessary to begin making the case for state funds for a library construction program. As with all campaigns, this effort needs to be well organized. The state library may be able to provide some assistance but will probably be limited because of the prohibition against lobbying placed on most civil service state employees. However, individuals working in this capacity usually can provide information if asked by private citizens or legislators. Higher-level officials such as state librarians are frequently not prohibited from actively supporting such efforts for state grants programs. Usually a combination of the state library staff, state library association members and a political action committee or library advocates group is needed to develop effective leadership to plan and organize the effort to obtain the state funds. Once the organization is in place, a strategy must be set and the case for state funding for library construction made.

If the library community can effectively band together, there is always the possibility of convincing the "powers that be" to fund library buildings. Remember, politicians love buildings even more than babies. Once a building is built, they get to stand in front of it, have their pictures taken at the dedication, and claim credit for it. Further, the building is a permanent reminder to the community that "Senator Jones got that library for us." A smart politician will generally support state funds for a program that has such broad appeal among constituents as a public library. However, if there is no program in place for state funding for libraries, the "sell" may be difficult. Frederick Glazer, the state librarian of West Virginia, describes what he calls the "foot in the door" approach:

> Your supporters can get in and get out with their request before the legislator has a chance to say "But why *state* construction money for libraries?" We always say "Why not?" when they do think to ask us, and they're really not sure why not. Just because it's not been done before or "the money's not there" is not a good answer. The money is never there, just as the time is never right.

There is a limited amount of money available during any given year and they have to determine who gets it and how it will be spent.[13]

The longer answer is that libraries today form a network of resources that affect the economic, social, and educational health of the *entire* state. They are no longer a purely local issue for a population as mobile as ours.

If the state is fortunate enough to already have state funds for library operational expenses, so much the better. If the state is willing to help operate library facilities, it is not such a gigantic step to consider that it should invest capital funds in the development of library infrastructure, i.e., the buildings and equipment. It is interesting to note that library supporters are often concerned that a state capital outlay program may damage the funding levels of a program providing operating funds. Experience has shown in most states that this is not the case. Legislators rarely make comparisons between the general operating budget and the capital outlay bond budget. Moreover, in many states that have both types of funding, the two programs tend to support each other because they bring more library supporters to the capitol on library legislative day and each program tends to provide awareness for the other.

Further, if a state has a history of government support for education—particularly if the state has a well-supported program of capital outlay for schools or universities—the idea of state funds for public library construction is not so foreign. Often state library construction funds become available through a broad-based capital outlay program providing for various types of construction such as the recent "Build Illinois" program, which financed approximately 30 public libraries, in addition to other types of public infrastructure projects such as roads and sewers. Many times state officials can be convinced to fund public library buildings because of a basic obligation to provide educational support for the citizens of the state, particularly in areas that can least afford threm. They can often be sold on this concept when it is demonstrated that strong state support in the form of seed money for capital outlay often results in improved local support for operating budgets. This is the case in most states with construction programs, which is why state capital outlay programs for public library construction are such a valuable tool for library development.

Another approach is the economic argument. Libraries are good for the economy. By increasing the quality of life in a community, they increase property values and attract business and industry to invest there. Further, with access to improved informational resources, the workforce is more productive and has a better opportunity to be competitive in the marketplace. In recessionary times, it should never be forgotten that a library project, like any other construction project, creates jobs. Many state fiscal offices can provide conversion factors to calculate the number of construction jobs created by a given amount of construction dollars. These figures can be used with legislators and local officials to convince them of the wisdom of starting a state-based program in order to stimulate the economy. Finally, if nothing else will work, wrap the library issue in the flag, mom, and apple pie. Even in today's sophisticated political environment, this approach still plays well for libraries, because as Jefferson, Madison and the other founders knew and said so often, education and information are the life blood of democracy and life long learning is the watchword of today and the future.

Regardless of how well developed the arguments are, the program won't happen if no one will listen, so it is usually necessary to enlist the help of a powerful political ally. This individual can be any one in the legislature who is a well-respected member of the leadership. In Georgia, it was the Speaker of the House; in California it was the Senate majority leader. It could certainly be a governor or any other elected official who has the power to make things happen. It is also important to obtain bipartisan support for the program; if two powerful legislators, one from each party, can coauthor the bill, so much the better. One of the first places to start looking for support for the program is among the House and Senate appropriations committee members. Because they have direct and intimate involvement with the budget process, library projects in their districts will usually get noticed. The library community should certainly target these individuals as well as others in the legislature who need library buildings in their districts. Those legislators with the most projects cited as needful in the needs assessment survey should be made aware of the unique "opportunities" that a state-based program would provide them.

Possibly the first round of state funding will be only a few projects, but it's a start. These projects may be leveraged by library supporters into more projects next year because "everyone wants a piece of the pie." It is amazing how often library projects develop in nearby communities soon after a state-funded library building goes up, particularly in a rural area. Community pride and rivalry account for a great deal in the political process. With each new library building coming online, there is increased visibility for the state-wide program which helps to reinforce its existence. Fred Glazer accurately observed:

> Once you get a program started, you find that you will have people coming to you with support. When they talk to their legislators it's the "Well, they got theirs, why can't we get ours?" syndrome. They want to know why the senator from District A was able to get a library built there—"Aren't you, the senator from District B, just as effective as he is?[14]

Getting a program started is usually harder than keeping it going unless the state gets into economic straits due to a recession or a bad bond rating. The program will quickly become popular with both local and state politicians and will be meeting the needs of many citizens statewide who are interested in improved local access to information. It is critical to generate and maintain broad support from the field for any state program. This usually means appealing to a wide variety of local situations, being flexible with the program, and working to improve it every year. Priority issues such as fairness, rural versus urban, small projects versus large ones must constantly be attended to for long-term success. Finally, make certain that legislators who have assisted with the program or a specific project are recognized and thanked. Be sure to give credit where credit is due to all involved, but make certain that the local legislators and the governor are at the dedication as keynote speaker or ribbon-cutter. Those who are successful in getting state funds for library construction are those who understand politics and are not afraid to get out and participate in the political process.

ADVANTAGES OF STATE LIBRARY CONSTRUCTION PROGRAMS

Besides the obvious advantage of having an additional revenue stream from state sources for funding library projects, there are other advantages to state library construction programs. A state-based program is a direct partnership between the state and its citizenry through local governments. Once a state government recognizes and commits to the obligation to improve its citizens educational advancement, the idea of a state library construction program makes a great deal of sense. It is a way to provide the state's citizens with opportunities that will affect all aspects of their daily lives. It is natural that state and local governments should cooperate in developing public library facilities through some form of grant or loan program. In the best of situations, this cooperative attitude can create an atmosphere of "we" and "us" building the libraries instead of the adversarial "they" and "them." This approach during the grant application and administration process can be achieved, but it takes a lot of effort on the part of both state and local officials.

A big advantage to a state-based program is that it shows the return of public tax dollars to local communities in a highly visible manner. This is good not only for state politicians, but also local politicians and administrators. Careers (as well as salaries) can be enhanced at the local level when a local grant administrator or library director succeeds in obtaining a large state grant that will be spent in the community to build a library building, create jobs, and stimulate local sales-tax revenues. Further, a state-based library construction program encourages cooperation between local funding agencies and library officials to create a higher awareness of the need for library service. This in itself is an effective way to promote library development.

A state-based library construction program is a powerful tool for library development in many ways. The use of state seed money for infrastructure has long been held an effective way of stimulating local support for any program, and public libraries are no exception. The requirement for local matching funds in a project strengthens the commitment not only to the project at hand, but also to the long-term health of the service, i.e., there is a vested local interest. This interest has been created by the infusion of state funds, and it might not have been developed if the state funds had not been available. With assistance from the state, and the local matching funds, the project can be built and the program of service created or improved for the long term.

The "carrot" of state funds often creates intense local interest in a public library. Often private funds and local public funds are raised simply because the state has challenged local communities with a grant. Private donors who might never have thought to donate to the library come forward, and frequently referenda are passed because local supporters can cry "Don't let us lose this multi-million dollar grant— help us pass this referendum!" The thought of losing money, particularly if it will be lost to another community, is often a tremendous stimulus to a campaign.

Another often overlooked advantage is the potential positive effect of a state library agency administering the program. Through effective leadership of a consulting staff, a state library can guide local libraries in planning their building projects. This frequently results in new library facilities that more effectively serve their communities. Many communities only build one library building every 20 years or so. State library staff, experienced with many projects, can often help local communities avoid the pitfalls that others have experienced. This can be done through developing reasonable policies and regulations and through simple consultation and advising of grant applicants. Good program management at the state level usually will save more money than it costs, although it is difficult to quantify and prove this fact.

Through the use of state standards, a state library can often bring local communities up to a higher level of service than they would have thought possible without outside involvement. Many communities tend to underestimate their long-term needs and build library facilities that are soon inadequate. State library consulting staff can often assist with the needs assessment and building program development to help avoid this. They can also review the architectural plans and point out changes that will help the building function more effectively as a library. Finally, through careful monitoring of the program, state staff can often help to avoid misuse or abuse of funds which could become an embarrassment to the program or the community involved.

There are advantages to having the program administered by the state rather than the federal government. State-based programs are generally easier than federal programs to administer and to influence because their managers are closer to home. State government's proximity to local government enhances its ability respond to local needs, so programs change and grow over time. Finally, because of this closeness, it is less likely that the state-based program will end abruptly.

THE DECISION TO APPLY
FOR STATE FUNDS

Local officials often wonder if they should apply to their state-based library construction program for a grant. This decision is not an easy one, because in order to obtain the state funds, local officials will have to give up a certain amount of control over the project. The question always is, Is the money worth it? The answer depends on the requirements of the state program, the amount of money available, and the particular circumstances of the proposed project. The first issue to resolve is how compatible the state program requirements are with the needs of the local community and the project. The first step is to obtain from the state library all the available information about the program. Next, it is wise to talk with recent grant applicants, both successful and unsuccessful. How do they feel about the program? Did they feel they were treated fairly? After local officials have read the program requirements, it is often helpful to contact the program manager by telephone or schedule a meeting and discuss the state program and the local project. This will

provide valuable information on how the state program is administered, and also help the local applicant begin to develop a relationship with the grant administrator. Most grant administrators are responsive to this kind of early contact because they want potential applicants to be as informed as possible about the grant program. They know that when a problem arises during a grant application, it is often because the applicant did not understand a critical aspect of the program. This kind of failure of an application is not an advantage to anyone, and most grant administrators work to keep this from happening, but it is ultimately the applicant's responsibility to understand the requirements of the grant program.

One of the most common conflicts that local projects have with a state program is the timeline. Frequently, the project is developing faster or slower than the timetable required for the state program. There is often a good deal of flexibility built into some aspects of a state program, but there are also usually specific deadlines (like the application deadline) which cannot be changed. One of the first assessments that must be made is, Can the timetable for the project be meshed with the state program's timetable? If so, is it worth the delay or rush to do so? Along with the application deadline, there are other deadlines that should be reviewed. Must the project be under construction by any specific date? Must the project funds be expended within a given period? Must a final closeout audit be submitted by a given date? All these considerations may affect the local applicant's decision to apply for a state grant.

Sometimes state program requirements are not acceptable to or compatible with local jurisdictions. In this case, the local jurisdiction must decide either to pass on the grant program or work to get the problem requirements changed. The latter option may be relatively simple if the problem is minor, or it may be a very time consuming process. The local jurisdiction must then weigh if the time and effort are worth the possible funding. Local jurisdictions often feel they should be given the funds with no strings attached. Many states work to reduce the amount of paperwork in state-based programs, but it must be understood that any state-wide government program will have some requirements no matter how streamlined it is. Generally, the more money the state puts into a project, the more involvement the state is likely to have in the project. This is not always undesirable and may in some circumstances be a decided benefit to the local jurisdiction and the future of its library.

Grant recipients often complain that the biggest loss they face is the loss of flexibility and the ability to move quickly to make changes in projects. In some state programs, making changes is not difficult, but in others (especially those which were highly competitive ones) it may be very difficult, time-consuming, and in some cases not allowed without the loss of the grant. In almost all state programs a series of approvals must be obtained in order to move on to the next phase of the project. During project development, planning documents such as building programs, community needs assessments, and facilities master plans must often be submitted for review and approval. State programs often require extensive information prior to approving the site upon which the building will be built.

Once the application has been accepted, architectural plans, specifications, and cost estimates must often be approved before the project can be bid. Most states have public contract codes or program regulations mandating how the construction contract will have to be awarded and administered. Often any change orders to the project as well as resulting budget amendments will have to be approved by the state. Payment requests will typically have to be approved before the state will release funds. State payment procedures vary widely, with some programs providing relatively large payments for completion of various stages of the project and others requiring payment requests that are supported by individual invoices and then partially reimbursed. Finally, most state programs will require some form of final audit and a final inspection report covering the completed facility in order to close out the project.

While the preceding list of hoops to jump through may be daunting to many, most of these steps will have to be taken by the local jurisdiction anyway in the development of the project; and having the state involved at each step may not be as bad in reality as is often feared, and may afford significant protection to the locality.

The final decision to apply for state funds is ultimately a local one. As a general rule, no one in state government twists anybody's arm to apply for state funds, particularly when they are difficult to come by. The final determination of whether to apply for a state grant usually comes down to how much state money the project can reasonably expect to get, and how badly it is needed. If it is decided that the best course is not to pursue state or federal grant funds, local library planners will need to analyze carefully all possible sources of local funds. There are many options open for library construction funding at the local level as will be seen in the next chapter.

REFERENCES

1. Joe Natale, "Alternative Financing for Capital Projects." *Illinois Libraries*. Vol. 75, No. 1 p. 27.

2. Kurt C. Zorn, "Financing Infrastructure to Promote Economic Development in the East North Central Region" *Government Finance Review* 2, (April 1986), p. 30.

3. Raymond M. Holt (2nd ed. by Anders C.

Dahlgren) *Wisconsin Library Building Project Handbook.* (Madison: Wisconsin Department of Public Instruction, 1990), p. 113.

4. See the program description under "Wyoming" in this chapter.

5. George E. Peterson, "Financing the Nation's Infrastructure Requirements" in *Perspectives on Urban Infrastructure* (Washington: National Academy Press, 1984), p. 128.

6. Roger D. Feldman et al, "Financing Infrastructure with Revolving Loan Funds" in *Financing Infrastructure Tools for the Future* (New York: Executive Enterprises, 1988), p. 91.

7. Cy H. Silver, "Construction Standards for California Public Libraries" in *Library Administration and Management,* 4 (Spring 1990), pp. 82-86.

8. "Final Adopted Library Bond Act Regulations" *California Code of Regulations:* Title 5, Division 2, Chapter 1, Sections 20410–20426. (Sacramento: California Library Construction and Renovation Board, November 1990).

9. Richard B. Hall, "Passing a Constitutional Amendment: To Help Finance Georgia Public Library Buildings with State Bonds" *Library Journal* 15 June 1985, pp. 32–33.

10. Philip S. Howe and Elizabeth M. Vogt, ed. "Funding for Libraries and Their Services" *Illinois Libraries* 72, (May 1990), p. 445.

11. Richard B. Hall, "The State Library Bond Act Evaluation Process" *California State Library Newsletter* 118, (October 1990), 118, pp. 8–24.

12. *Report of the Library Board Virginia State Library and Archives on Space Needs Study of Public Libraries in Virginia* House Document No. 5 (Richmond: Commonwealth of Virginia, 1992.)

13. Frederick Glazer, "State Sources" in *Facilities Funding Finesse: Financing and Promotion of Public Library Facilities,* ed. Richard B. Hall (Chicago: American Library Association, Library Administration and Management Association, 1982), p. 28.

14. Ibid., p. 27

Local Funding Sources 6

Regardless of the recent developments in state and federal funding sources, the major source of funding for public library construction in the post-Carnegie era, has been local public revenues. Over the past 24 years of *Library Journal* statistics, over 70 percent of all funds expended for public library construction have consistently come from local public revenues, and in recent years, the percentage appears to be approaching 80 percent.

Table 6-1 and Figure 6-1 show that there has been a virtual explosion in local funds available for public library construction in the last five years. Local agencies have supplied over $1 billion of capital outlay funds for public library construction since 1987. It took 14 years from 1968 to 1981 for the first $1 billion of local funds to be reported for public library construction. This feat was replicated in the last five years alone!

Since local public funds account for such a high percentage of funding for public library buildings, it is important to consider in detail the various financing methods utilized at the local level.

Public agencies may use any number of local financing methods to fund public library buildings. Local jurisdictions may opt to use the "pay as you go" method of paying cash for library capital improvements from general or special revenue sources. If this approach is not feasible, local jurisdictions may choose debt financing methods such as general obligation bonds, special tax bonds, tax allocation bonds, etc. Additional alternatives include the use of lease-purchase agreements utilizing lease-revenue bonds and certificates of participation (COPs), or entering into public-private partnership joint ventures. There are many vehicles by which these various financing methods can be delivered, including the use of referenda, the formation of special financing districts in conjunction with the use of special assessments, the establishment of redevelopment agencies, the use of sales or excise taxes, or the establishment of development fees and exactions. The many methods of funding public library facilities are like different bands of color in the spectrum: they are distinct, but they all come from the same source and may be combined and blended to produce an endless variety of possibilities.

Regardless of the approach used, the goal is to find a fair and equitable method of assessing local taxpayers for the cost of the public library facility. The possible options listed here imply no endorsement of any specific approach. Each approach has advantages and disadvantages. There is no inherently right way to finance public library buildings. Each jurisdiction must assess the possibilities and determine the most cost-effective and beneficial method for its own particular project.

Table 6-1. Local Funds as a Percentage of Total Public Library Construction

Fiscal Year	Local Percentage	Local Funds
1991	78.6%	$249,965,890
1990	71.4	208,459,281
1989	80.5	246,403,145
1988	76.9	191,427,737
1987	82.7	181,186,229
1986	74.1	116,969,907
1985	69.3	97,010,901
1984	85.5	93,964,773
1983	71.0	58,184,924
1982	71.7	112,546,992
1981	71.9	100,698,102
1980	60.9	73,089,175
1979	43.2	83,849,534
1978	63.3	57,557,957
1977	72.4	95,553,190
1976	61.9	77,402,334
1975	72.7	58,862,450
1974	81.2	67,398,403
1973	76.7	77,487,948
1972	78.0	74,064,674
1971	69.9	53,052,707
1970	59.5	58,264,129
1969	69.3	74,126,091
1968	75.7	68,939,755
Average:	72.2	

GENERAL REVENUE APPROPRIATIONS

Traditionally, public library facilities have been funded from general fund revenues, most notably property taxes. As with other forms of infrastructure, public libraries have been typically considered "common property." Since citizens expected to have equal access to the use of the facility, it followed that they should also expect to share equally in the method of paying for it from the general fund. This made a great deal of sense in small towns where the public library facility needs were adequately met with one modest building in the middle of town. However, as the size of communities has increased and library programs have expanded to include multiple branches, the concept became less widely supported since individuals on the outskirts of the city often did not visit the central library.

Regardless of this natural progression caused by growth, many public library facilities are still financed from the general fund. When library projects require relatively small amounts of local funds because of state or federal matching funds or simply because of the size of the building, communities are occasionally able to handle the capital improvement project from the regular annual collection of tax revenues. These local general revenues may come from any number of sources, including property taxes, sales taxes, income taxes, and excise taxes. Property taxes still remain the primary source of funds for library buildings as well as many other local facilities, but other forms of general revenue funds such as sales taxes should not be overlooked for public library construction.

Sales Taxes

In addition to property taxes, local governments may use the receipts from sales taxes for capital improvements and equipment acquisition. In some states, such as Georgia, state legislators have provided counties with the option of implementing local-option sales tax ordinances by the use of a referendum. In recent years, several library facilities have been financed utilizing this method in the communities of Conyers, Athens, Savannah, Waycross, and Sparta, Georgia. Once the supporting state legislation was in place, county officials still had to be convinced to authorize a county-wide referendum, and library supporters had to generate a majority vote at the polls in order to be successful. When the necessary votes were obtained, the county would begin the collection of sales taxes and accumulate them over time. It was then only necessary to schedule the design and construction of recipient projects so as to maintain a posi-

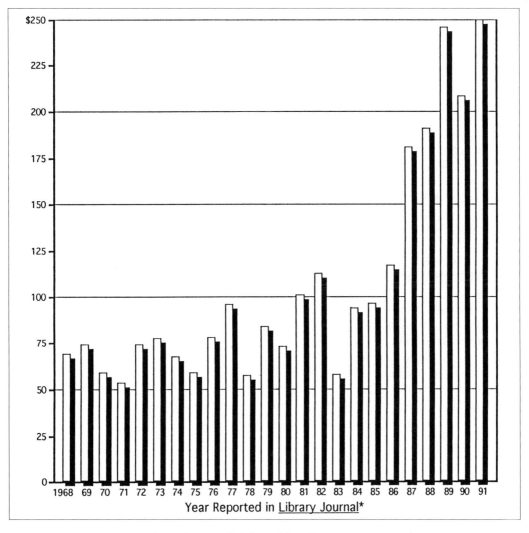

Fig. 6-1. Local Funds Expended for Public Library Construction by Year

*©Reed Publishing

tive cash flow for the projects from the sales tax receipts.

This method can be used in any state that has similar enabling legislation for a local sales tax. Further, in some states it is possible for local jurisdictions to issue sales tax revenue bonds. This allows the jurisdiction to obtain the capital necessary to build the projects early in the process (avoiding careful monitoring of cash flow and potential delays). The bonds are sold to investors, and the repayment of principal and interest is guaranteed by the sales tax revenue stream authorized by the voters. This approach works well assuming the economy remains strong enough to ensure adequate receipt of sales tax revenues to meet the debt payments. Because of this added risk to investors, sales tax revenue bonds usually require slightly higher interest rates than general obligation bonds.

Excise Taxes

Excise tax is best known as the tax the federal government imposes on such items as tobacco, alcohol, firearms, and motor fuel. However, in some states local governments have the authority to impose excise taxes. The U.S. Supreme Court considers an excise tax to be "a tax imposed upon a particular use of property or the exercise of a single power over property incidental to ownership." (*Bromley v. McCaughn,* 280 U.S. 124 [1929]). In order to explain what an excise tax is, it is useful to discuss what an excise tax is not. An excise tax is not a property tax, a special tax, a special assessment, or a development fee. Care must be taken by local jurisdictions not to allow a proposed excise tax to take on the characteristics of any of these other methods of raising revenue or they risk having the tax invalidated and thrown out by the courts.

Property taxes have several distinguishing characteristics. "Traditionally, the courts have recognized several factors which would characterize a tax as a property tax. These include: (1) the tax is imposed on the only or one of a limited number of uses of the property; (2) the measure of the tax is based upon the valuation of the property; (3) the unpaid tax is secured by a lien on the property; and (4) the tax is levied by reason of ownership."[1] In order not to be considered a property tax, an excise tax must not have these characteristics. However, "A property tax can be described as a tax levied by reason of the ownership of property, regardless of the use to which the property is put. Accordingly, a property tax is collected annually at a predetermined time. In contrast, an excise tax is imposed on a particular use of the property, regardless of ownership. An excise tax 'is generally due and payable only when the taxed privilege is exercised.' (*City of Oakland v. Richard Digre* (1988) 205 Cal. App. 3d 99."[2]

A special tax is collected for a specific purpose and unlike an excise tax, must be placed in a separate account from the general fund. As long as the funds generated from an excise tax are placed in the general fund rather than a separate account, the tax is considered a general (excise) tax and not a special tax. This is important, in part, to avoid the referendum requirement which in California's requires a supermajority vote of the electorate. Further, an excise tax is not a special assessment because it does not provide special benefit only to a limited number of landowners in the jurisdiction. The excise tax will normally be applied jurisdiction-wide and not to just a few landowners.

Finally, in order to avoid being classified as a development fee, an excise tax cannot be imposed on developers based on the local jurisdiction's regulatory approval powers over land development. Unlike development fees, excise taxes do not have to maintain a linkage between the proposed public improvements and the area being developed.

> An excise tax is not subject to "reasonable relationship," "needs nexus," or "rational nexus" tests; therefore, monies collected need not be earmarked, do not need to relate specifically to needs created or benefits accruing to a particular development, and are not subject to geographic or temporal nexus requirements. The purpose of a tax is to raise revenues. In contrast, an exaction or impact fee must have a principal regulatory purpose, even though it may have an incidental revenue-raising component.[3]

If an excise tax is imposed on the business activity of land development, and approval of a development is not made contingent upon payment of the tax, the tax should be able to withstand the challenge of being considered a development fee.

Since excise taxes can be imposed on a particular use of property or on some form of business activity, they can be used, in certain circumstances, to finance public library facilities as was recently the case in Vacaville, California:

> An excise tax is an "activity" tax levied on the availability and privilege of using certain

services or facilities. It is not a tax on the ownership of property. In this instance, the tax is levied for the privilege of having the new cultural center (including a public library), play fields, and streets available for use by the occupant of property. . . . The $5/month tax on all residential units is collected on the water and sewer bill. Business pays a flat amount based on the number of employees as a surcharge on the semi-annual business license. . . . As a tax on the occupancy of property (collected for convenience on the water and sewer bill), it cannot be collected with the property tax bill. The city does not have the ability to lien property for non-payment.[4]

Even though in most states that allow local excise taxes the establishment of an excise tax does not require a referendum, in Vacaville's case, an advisory ballot referendum was held because the city council believed in the concept of majority rule. The city accepted a simple majority in determining the issue in lieu of the supermajority approval rate required in California for other taxation referenda. An excise tax can be used to raise general revenues to help pay for capital improvements such as a public library as long as those being taxed are receiving some benefit from the construction of the facility. In Vacaville's case, the facilities were built with the proceeds of the sale of $11 million in certificates of participation. The collection of the excise tax provides a revenue source to pay off the principal and interest on the certificates.

In addition to excise taxes, public libraries have been built with all forms of funding coming into the general funds. How local politicians and financing officials decide to earmark general revenues for public library facilities is often not apparent to the general public or library supporters. However, this is not really critical as long as the funding is forthcoming and based on well-established legal authority. A local jurisdiction's power to collect taxes of any kind is not inherent, but provided by the state constitution or statutes

with the exception of home-rule jurisdictions. Some states, such as Illinois, provide local jurisdictions with specific authority to raise revenues for public library construction through tax levies. In Illinois, the "Construction, site development and maintenance tax,"[5] "capital improvement, repair or replacement tax,"[6] "working cash fund tax,"[7] and "restoration tax"[8] all allow for the raising of property tax revenues for public library capital outlay purposes. One of the unique features of several of these Illinois statutes is that they specifically provide the authority to levy these taxes without a referendum unless a petition is filed with signatures from ten percent of the voters in the last general election. If the latter does occur, then a "back door referendum"[9] must be held in order to approve the tax levy.

In addition to having the authority to tax, a local jurisdiction must determine whether or not to utilize debt instruments in financing its public facilities. While most library buildings are built utilizing some form of debt instrument, a significant number have been built with direct one-time appropriations from the annual operating budget, especially in windfall situations where there is a large influx of funds for a given year. Library agencies that have planned in advance and have a project that is ready to go are often successful in obtaining large one-time allocations from the general fund. Unfortunately, windfall situations are not common. Most library agencies must plan to finance their capital improvement projects using whatever funds are available during normal economic times and budgetary cycles.

"Pay As You Go" Versus "Pay As You Use"

Regardless of the source of funds, there are two basic approaches to financing capital projects: "pay as you go" or "pay as you use." Payment of the costs of public facilities from currently available general or special fund revenues is commonly called "pay as you go." This approach keeps down the cost of financing a project because no money has been borrowed by the local jurisdiction and therefore there is no interest charged. The biggest problem with this method is that local jurisdictions seldom have an adequate annual revenue stream to pay for all of the capital needs, particularly when the community is growing fast. Another drawback is that this method places the burden of payment completely on current taxpayers. This contrasts with the "pay as you use" philosophy which allows the use of debt instruments so the facility can be built "up front" and payment takes place over time by all of the facility's users. In this way, the cost of the facility is paid by both present and future users. This approach makes sense particularly if the community has a high growth or mobility rate. Since this is the case in many areas of the country today, various forms of the "pay as you use" method will be discussed in detail later in this chapter.

Occasionally, local jurisdictions use a form of cash accrual as a variant of the "pay as you go" approach. This allows for a specific amount of cash to be set aside each year toward the day when enough has been accumulated to purchase a site, build a building, and pay for the entire capital improvement at one time. While still workable, this approach was more popular in the first half of the century. There is specific legislation in the State of Illinois, for example, that allows library jurisdictions to establish a tax levy to set aside funds for public library construction, but this approach can be used without special legislation in many states. Funds are simply allocated annually from the general fund or some specially designated revenue source over a specific time period depending on the total cost of the project.

With small library projects, this approach may work well, particularly if the planning and construction are phased. Once a reasonable amount has been saved,

the preliminary expenditure of funds can go toward planning the project, such as hiring a library consultant and an architect. Next, it may be possible to secure the library site by obtaining an option to purchase and eventually buying the site. When sufficient funds have accumulated, the construction project can be bid and a contract awarded. Later, funds can be used for the acquisition of furnishings and equipment as well as moving costs. While this approach works well with relatively small projects and is often used in rural areas, it usually is not feasible for larger projects since it takes such a long time to accumulate enough funds to execute the project. During this lengthy wait, the community goes without adequate library service and the cost of construction increases because of inflation.

Some smaller jurisdictions have found that this "pay as you go" method works so well that as soon as a new building is built, they immediately set up a capital reserve fund and begin making annual contributions of funds which, with interest, will be available for capital improvements at the end of, say, 20 years when a new building or expansion may be necessary. This approach saves interest paid to service debt, but it does tie up a funds for a significant amount of time so that they are not available for other uses. In most cases, especially with larger projects, needed construction funds are raised through debt financing and paid back plus interest over time. This approach frees up funds for the general operating budgets of the community's public agencies. Another advantage of "pay as you use" is that the payments in the later years of the obligation are made with dollars that are worth less because of inflation.

Mortgages

A typical example of the "pay as you use" approach is the use of a mortgage. Some states provide statutory authority that allows mortgages as financial instruments for financing public library construction. For example, municipal libraries and special library districts in Illinois can make use of mortgages by borrowing funds from commercial banks against the future collection of special taxes. Under the provisions of the "mortgage tax," "trustees with corporate approval now can mortgage a library site owned or being purchased and a library being built in addition to mortgaging an existing library building. The loan can be up to 75 percent of the value. But it must be used exclusively for building, buying, repairing, remodeling or improving a library."[10] In most cases, a referendum is required to utilize the mortgage tax in Illinois; however, municipalities with home-rule powers can use the tax without a referendum. Several Illinois communities have utilized mortgages to finance public library construction projects including Zion, Morton, and Sugar Grove. States such as Rhode Island and New York provide the authority for the use of mortgages as well. There are many other financing mechanisms that can be used with the "pay as you use" approach, the most well-known and commonly used of which is the sale of general obligation bonds.

LOCAL GENERAL OBLIGATION BONDS

Although there are a few exceptions, in most states and localities, the issuance of general obligation bonds, requires approval of the electorate through a referendum. While a referendum may be held to allocate funds from any number of sources such as sales taxes, special taxes, property taxes etc., the majority of local referenda for public library construction result in the issuance of general obligation bonds.[11] General obligation bonds are most commonly used because they provide the least expensive method public agencies can use to incur large amounts of debt over long periods of time. This is the case, in part, because the full taxing authority or the

"full faith and credit" of the funding agency stands behind the debt instrument. Given this high degree of security for the bonds issued, the bond purchasers are usually willing to accept a lower interest rate, thereby providing what is essentially a low-cost, long-term loan that is guaranteed by a local jurisdiction's taxing authority over its entire tax base. The actual cost of the bonds depends on such variables as the interest rate at the time the bonds are issued and the rating of the bonds. However, general obligation bonds are frequently one-quarter to a full percentage point lower in terms of the interest rate charged than other debt instruments which are not backed by the full faith and credit of the jurisdiction. General obligation bonds are also attractive to investors since they are usually structured as tax-exempt sources of income.

In most states, limits are set on the amount of debt that a local government agency may incur. This is usually between five and 15 percent of the total value of the taxable assets within the jurisdiction. Many local governments never approach this limit, but occasionally jurisdictions are prohibited from issuing additional bonds until their debt load is reduced. It is wise to check with the local funding agency's fiscal officer to determine not only the current level of debt, but also the historical level carried by the jurisdiction. These figures will give a good idea of the feasibility of pursuing a funding mechanism that will add to the debt load. If debt financing is eventually decided upon, the government fiscal officer will become an invaluable ally.

Selling bonds of any kind is a complex process requiring financial finesse as well as the assistance of attorneys specializing in that area. These attorneys are commonly referred to as the bond counsel. If the local jurisdiction is small and does not routinely handle the sale of bonds, it may be wise to employ a financial consultant in addition to a bond counsel. These individuals, along with the funding agency's fiscal officer, can project the local revenue stream and structure the debt instrument in the manner most beneficial to the funding agency. The bond counsel will then assist in selling the bonds to individuals and financial institutions through an underwriter when funds are needed for the project. The timing of the sale of bonds is important in order to get the lowest possible interest rate, but also because of federal arbitrage laws and regulations. The arbitrage rules require funds obtained through the sale of bonds to be expended for the project within certain time periods. The interest that can be earned on these funds is limited so that local jurisdictions do not abuse their bonding authority. Once the bonds are sold, the project must move forward and the bond funds spent expeditiously to avoid the assessment of penalties.

The timing of the bond sale may affect other funding methods and sources used in conjunction with bond issues. For example, it may be necessary to expend funds raised from the private sector early in the project for planning purposes and hold off on the bond sale as long as possible until the local jurisdiction is ready to bid the project. General obligation bond issues may be combined with other financing methods and funding sources such as private funds, as well as state and federal matching programs. This approach becomes particularly significant in states where the use of bonds for the acquisition of furnishings, equipment, and books is prohibited. Some of these items may not be appropriate for bond security because they are not considered capital outlay. State statutes may require the useful life of the asset acquired with bond funds to be equal to or greater than the duration of the bond. This is often not the case with equipment if the bond is for ten years or more. This requirement provides further security for the bond holders in the form of a tangible asset that can be repossessed if the bonds are not paid off by the issuing agen-

cy. It is prudent to check with a bond counsel during the development of the preliminary budget to determine if furnishings, equipment, or books may be acquired with general obligation bond funds. If a significant portion of the proposed project may not be paid for out of these funds then another funding mechanism must be utilized in conjunction with the bond proceeds.

The greatest number of projects that have funds from only one source are funded by local public bond issues. These tend to be large projects or part of a bond issue that funds numerous smaller library buildings. While it is impossible to determine the exact percentage of local funds raised by public bond issues compared to those raised from direct operating revenues or other local approaches, the local general obligation bond issue has clearly been the most common method of raising large amounts of capital for public library improvements over the years. However, this may be changing to some extent, especially in high-growth states such as California, or in other states where taxpayer revolts have imposed debt limitations on local jurisdictions.

Unfortunately, the library profession has never seriously attempted to analyze the percentage of funding coming from bond issues compared to other local sources. This is true for the years that the *Library Journal* statistics have been collected as well as back to the turn of the century "It appears, however, from an analysis of such data as are available that the majority of libraries, excluding those financed by gifts, have been constructed from the proceeds of bond issues. No statistics are available to show the exact amount of construction by one method or another, so that the data upon which this conclusion is based results from the patching together of scattered bits of information."[12] Further, there have been only a few attempts to analyze the reasons local library bond issues succeed or fail. A literature search on the subject reveals that prior to the 1980s, the most serious articles comparing the success and failure of referenda had been written by Guy Garrison. His studies of library elections in Illinois from 1953 to 1963[13] and again from 1963 to 1968[14] are classics and provide invaluable insight into the results of library bond issues held for the purpose of library construction during that time period.

The major finding in these two reports was that in the state of Illinois from 1953 to 1968, the chances of getting a library bond issue approved were better than two to one. This percentage certainly attests to the importance of libraries to the Illinois voter. More recently, Dr. Herbert Goldhor reported that over two-thirds of the library bond issues held in Illinois from 1980 to 1985 were successful. This encouragingly high rate of voter approval for library bond issues was further supported by data from Dr. Goldhor's unpublished national survey of "Public Library Referenda in 1985." Again, about two-thirds of all local bond issues held were successful in the states participating in the survey.

Not all research into library bond issues has shown such positive results. As reported by Albert C. Lake[15] in a speech given at an American Library Association preconference on library buildings in the early 1970s, an unpublished research study by Howard M. Rowe entitled "A Study of Public Library Bond Issue Campaigns in the State of California During the Period 1945–1962" showed that two-thirds of all library bond issues held in California during that period failed. However, it must be remembered that the reason library bond issues are so speculative in California is the requirement of a two-thirds majority in order to pass bond referenda.

Other than these documents and the publications of Guy Garrison,[16] William Berner[17] and Ruth G. Lindahl,[18] research into the reasons for success or failure of local referenda has been limited in library literature. A comprehensive search of library literature turns up numerous accounts of individual success (and failure) stories, but as Guy Garrison notes:

> When planning such campaigns, librarians frequently depend on local experience on similar projects, on the advice of other librarians who have gone through such elections, either successfully or not, and on the meager amount of reliable information that is available to them in published accounts of library elections.
>
> The written material that exists is not only scattered widely but is largely reportorial in nature. The conclusions drawn, if any, are based more on opinions than on facts. There are too many libraries and too many kinds of local political situations to allow safe generalizations about library elections from articles of this type.[19]

William S. Berner provides a similar lament in his survey of the literature regarding the planning of a library referendum campaign:

> Unfortunately it is difficult to determine how representative the experiences described in recent articles on library referendums may be. They represent only a few instances, and no systematic comparison has been made between successful and unsuccessful library referendum campaigns.[20]

Unfortunately, there has never been an ongoing and comprehensive accounting of referenda for financing public library buildings by local bond issues or other methods. Historically, the only documentation that exists other than some analysis in Oehlerts[21] is the 1930 article regarding the use of local bond issues for financing public library construction. In this article Simeon E. Leland lists over 150 local bond issues for public library buildings from 1899 to 1927 which was complied from Moody's *Manual of Investments, Governments and Municipals, 1928.*[22]

Library Journal Survey of Referenda for Public Library Buildings

In 1986, the author, with the cooperation of *Library Journal* and the 50 state library agencies, began a data collection effort to

Table 6-2. Referenda for Public Library Buildings 1987–1991***

Community	Library	Vote For	Against	Amount of Referendum	Gen/ Spec	Other Ballot Items
ALABAMA						
1990						
Birmingham	Birmingham Public Library	73%	27%	$ 3,000,000	G	Y
ALASKA						
1989						
Soldotna	Soldotna Public Library	75	25	1,100,000	G	N
ARIZONA						
1988						
Phoenix	Phoenix Public Library	58	42	55,000,000	S	Y
1987						
Glendale	Glendale Public Library	56	44	9,698,000	S	Y
ARKANSAS						
1988						
Little Rock	Central Arkansas Library System	60	40	2,000,000	S	Y
CALIFORNIA**						
1991						
Los Altos	Santa Clara County Library	74	26	3,715,000	G	Y
Oakland	Oakland Public Library	81	19	1,500,000	G	Y
Rolling Hills Estates	Palos Verdes Library	70	30	16,000,000	G	N
1990						
Davis	Davis Branch Library	78	22	4,100,000	G	Y
Menlo Park	Menlo Park Library	83	17	5,000,000	G	N
Salinas	Monterey County Free Library	51	49	7,558,000	G	Y
1989						
Livermore	Livermore Public Library	61	39	760,000	G	Y
Los Angeles*	Los Angeles Public Library	62	38	90,000,000	G	Y
Los Angeles	Los Angeles Public Library	68	32	53,400,000	G	Y
San Francisco	San Francisco Public Library	76	24	109,500,000	G	Y
Vacaville	Vacaville P.L./Solano County Lib.	52	48	2,900,000	G	Y
COLORADO						
1991						
Denver	Denver Public Library	75	25	91,600,000	G	Y
1987						
Steamboat Springs	Bud Werner Memorial Library	67	33	575,000	S	N
CONNECTICUT						
1988						
Ashford*	Babcock Library	43	57	1,420,000	S	N
Niantic	East Lyme Public Library	98	2	1,500,000	S	N
1987						
Anonymous	Anonymous	86	14	350,000	S	N
Harwinton	T.A. Hungerford Memorial Lib.	51	49	855,000	S	Y
FLORIDA						
1991						
New Smyrna Beach*	New Smyrna Beach Brannon Lib.	31	69	3,400,000	S	N
Ocala*	Central Florida Regional Library	30	70	14,100,000	G	N
Port Orange*	Port Orange Regional Library	42	58	3,100,000	S	N
1987						
New Port Richey	Pasco County Library	52	48	10,000,000	G	Y
West Palm Beach	Palm Beach County Library	67	33	20,000,000	G	Y

Continued

Table 6-2. *Continued*

Community	Library	Vote For	Against	Amount of Referendum	Gen/ Spec	Other Ballot Items
GEORGIA						
1991						
Quitman	Brooks County Library	57%	43%	$ 336,442	G	Y
1990						
Valdosta	Valdosta-Lowndes County P.L.	88	12	500,000	S	Y
1989						
Villa Rica	Villa Rica Public Library	66	34	50,000	S	Y
1988						
Athens	Athens Regional Library	70	30	3,750,000	G	Y
1987						
Decatur	DeKalb County Public Library	67	33	29,000,000	G	Y
Marietta	Cobb County Public Library	71	29	7,160,000	G	Y
Sparta	Hancock County Public Library	99	1	735,000	S	N
IDAHO**						
1991						
Hayden	Kootenai County Libraries	83	17	2,400,000	S	N
Council Bluffs*	Free Public Library	46	54	4,900,000	S	N
1990						
Twin Falls	Twin Falls Public Library	71	29	1,965,000	S	N
1988						
Pocatello*	Pocatello Public Library	46	54	1,500,000	S	N
ILLINOIS						
1990						
Barrington	Barrington Public Library District	60	40	5,325,000	G	Y
Coal City	Coal City Public Library District	61	39	1,850,000	G	N
Eldorado	Eldorado Memorial P.L. District	54	46	550,000	G	N
Lacon	Lacon Public Library District	80	20	68,151	G	N
Midlothian	Midlothian Public Library	78	22	1,700,000	G	N
Palatine	Palatine Public Library	52	48	15,500,000	G	N
Westmont	Westmont Public Library	59	41	3,900,000	G	N
1989						
Lake Zurich	Ela Area Public Library	66	34	3,550,000	G	N
Prospect Hts.	Prospect Heights Public Library	67	33	2,900,000	G	N
Richmond	Nippersink Public Library	54	46	695,000	G	N
1988						
Hinsdale	Hinsdale Public Library	64	36	3,200,000	G	Y
Homewood	Homewood Public Library	54	46	2,900,000	G	N
La Grange	La Grange Park Public Library	65	35	2,200,000	G	N
Riverdale	Riverdale Public Library District	71	29	900,000	G	Y
1987						
Palos Heights	Palos Heights Public Library	54	46	639,000	G	Y
St. Charles	St. Charles Public Library	68	32	2,925,000	G	Y
Taylorville	Taylorville Public Library	55	45	300,000	G	Y
IOWA						
1991						
Boone	Ericson Public Library	71	29	2,700,000	S	Y
1990						
Anonymous	Anonymous	68	32	350,000	S	N
Newton	Newton Public Library	52	48	1,500,000	S	N

Continued

Table 6-2. *Continued*

Community	Library	Vote For	Vote Against	Amount of Referendum	Gen/ Spec	Other Ballot Items
IOWA						
1989						
Cresco	Cresco Public Library	75%	25%	$ 269,500	S	N
Nevada	Nevada Public Library	61	39	600,000	S	N
Slater*	Slater Public Library	42	58	230,000	S	N
KANSAS						
1991						
Norton	Norton Public Library	77	23	650,000	G	N
1988						
Towanda	Towanda Public Library	89	11	60,000	S	N
LOUISIANA						
1991						
St. Martinville	St. Martin Parish Library	72	28	1,825,000	G	N
1988						
Shreveport*	Shreve Memorial Library	49	51	6,000,000	G	Y
1987						
Baton Rouge	East Baton Rouge Parish Library	67	33	12,000,000	G	Y
Natchitoches*	Natchitoches Parish Library	38	62	6,280,000	G	Y
New Orleans	New Orleans Public Library	68	32	1,600,000	S	Y
MARYLAND						
1991						
Hyattsville	Prince George's Co. Memorial Lib.	75	25	12,867,000	G	Y
Towson	Baltimore County Public Library	56	44	2,050,000	G	Y
1987						
Hyattsville	Prince George's Co. Memorial Lib.	82	18	3,600,000	G	Y
Towson	Baltimore County Public Library	71	29	500,000	G	Y
MASSACHUSETTS						
1991						
Halifax	Holmes Public Library	71	29	389,000	S	Y
Kingston	Frederic C. Adams Public Library	99	1	75,000	G	Y
Weston	Weston Public Library	100	0	3,700,000	G	Y
West Tisbury	West Tisbury Free Public Library	64	36	95,000	G	Y
1990						
Anonymous*	Anonymous	38	62	2,600,000	S	Y
Anonymous*	Anonymous	49	51	102,000	G	Y
Marblehead	Abbot Public Library	92	8	340,000	S	Y
Rockland	Rockland Memorial Library	100	0	771,943	S	N
1989						
Chelmsford*	Chelmsford Public Library	49	51	1,000,000	S	N
Anonymous*	Anonymous	46	54	1,592,000	G	N
Lynnfield	Lynnfield Public Library	62	38	500,000	G	Y
North Reading	Flint Memorial Library	56	44	2,970,148	S	N
Plymouth	Plymouth Public Library	51	49	8,525,000	S	N
Spencer	Richard Sugden Public Library	61	39	455,000	S	Y
West Tisbury*	West Tisbury Free Public Library	59	41	280,000	G	Y
Westminster*	Forbush Memorial Library	48	52	1,250,000	G	Y
Williamstown*	Williamstown Public Library	57	43	310,000	S	N
1988						
Amherst	Jones Library	100	0	1,000,000	G	Y
Anonymous*	Anonymous	39	61	2,000,000	G	Y

Continued

Table 6-2. Continued

Community	Library	Vote For	Vote Against	Amount of Referendum	Gen/ Spec	Other Ballot Items
MASSACHUSETTS						
1988						
Bellingham	Bellingham Public Library	56%	44%	$ 2,000,000	S	Y
Holden	Gale Free Library	96	4	1,218,852	G	Y
Littleton	Reuben Hoar Library	92	8	487,000	G	N
Pembroke	Pembroke Public Library	82	18	2,600,000	S	N
Spencer	Richard Sugden Library	100	0	425,000	G	Y
Wareham*	Wareham Free Library	40	60	2,500,000	G	N
1987						
Eastham	Eastham Public Library	97	3	663,665	G	Y
Lincoln	Lincoln Public Library	95	5	2,250,000	S	Y
Littleton	Reuben Hoar Library	75	25	1,200,000	S	Y
Plymouth*	Plymouth Public Library	49	51	9,725,000	G	Y
Southborough	Southborough Library	62	38	1,300,000	S	N
Sterling	Conant Public Library	82	18	890,000	G	N
Wayland	Wayland Public Library	100	0	200,000	G	Y
West Bridgewater	West Bridgewater Public Library	81	19	1,600,000	G	Y
West Newbury	G.A.R. Memorial Library	93	7	850,000	G	Y
Westford	J.V. Fletcher Library	80	20	2,280,000	G	Y
MICHIGAN						
1991						
Marlette	Marlette District Library	75	25	120,000	G	N
1990						
Farmington Hills*	Farmington Community Library	49	51	14,500,000	G	N
Flushing*	Flushing Library	49	51	800,000	S	Y
Wixom	Wixom Public Library	51	49	1,500,000	S	Y
1989						
Howell	Howell Carnegie District Library	66	34	4,525,000	S	N
Rochester	Rochester Hills Public Library	56	44	10,200,000	G	N
Saginaw	Thomas Township Library	67	33	165,000	G	N
1988						
Grosse Pointe*	Grosse Pointe Public Library	41	59	8,625,000	G	Y
MINNESOTA						
1991						
Ada	Ada Public Library	58	42	250,000	S	N
Benson	Benson Public Library	54	46	250,000	S	N
Rochester	Rochester Public Library	59	41	14,000,000	G	Y
1988						
Detroit Lakes	Detroit Lakes Public Library	56	44	1,700,000	S	N
1987						
Forest Lake	Forest Lake Public Library	59	41	298,000	G	Y
NEVADA						
1991						
Las Vegas	Las Vegas/Clark County Library	51	49	70,000,000	G	Y
NEW HAMPSHIRE**						
1990						
Derry	Derry Public Library	71	29	2,345,000	S	N
Grantham*	Dunbar Free Library	49	51	275,000	G	Y
New London	Tracy Memorial Library	80	20	1,285,300	G	Y
Rye*	Rye Public Library	30	70	315,000	G	Y
Swanzey Ctr	Mt. Caesar Union Library	100	0	55,000	G	N
Temple	Mansfield Public Library	72	28	258,000	G	N
Webster	Webster Free Public Library	90	10	85,000	G	Y

Continued

Table 6-2. *Continued*

Community	Library	Vote For	Vote Against	Amount of Referendum	Gen/ Spec	Other Ballot Items
NEW HAMPSHIRE**						
1989						
Grantham*	Dunbar Free Library	49%	51%	$ 350,000	G	Y
Hampstead*	Hampstead Public Library	65	35	825,000	G	Y
Hollis*	Hollis Social Library	55	45	600,000	G	Y
New Castle	New Castle Public Library	80	20	850,000	G	N
Rye	Rye Public Library	70	30	75,000	G	Y
1988						
Hampstead*	Hampstead Public Library	57	43	950,000	G	Y
Jaffrey*	Jaffrey Public Library	58	42	1,000,000	G	Y
Raymond*	Dudley-Tucker Library	55	45	600,000	G	N
NEW MEXICO						
1989						
Clovis	Clovis-Carter Public Library	65	35	2,800,000	S	N
NEW YORK						
1991						
Farmingdale	Farmingdale Public Library	56	44	8,820,000	S	N
Hewlett	Hewlett-Woodmore Public Library	56	44	775,000	G	N
1988						
Babylon*	Babylon Public Library	29	71	2,500,000	G	Y
Bellmore	Bellmore Memorial Library	58	42	1,500,000	S	N
Cutchogue	Cutchogue Free Library	70	30	48,500	G	Y
Grand Island	Grand Island Memorial Library	64	36	1,686,250	S	N
Nanuet	Nanuet Public Library	68	32	2,500,000	S	N
1987						
Brentwood	Brentwood Public Library	76	24	7,980,000	S	N
Center Moriches	Center Moriches Free Public Lib.	54	46	1,800,000	S	N
Eden	Eden Free Library	100	0	250,000	G	N
Marlboro	Marlboro Free Library	80	20	249,000	S	N
Middle Island	Longwood Public Library	87	13	3,900,000	G	Y
Montauk	Montauk Library	65	35	985,000	S	N
Spring Valley	Finkelstein Memorial Library	73	27	3,000,000	S	N
Yorktown	John C. Hart Memorial Library	81	19	2,000,000	S	N
NORTH CAROLINA						
1991						
Chapel Hill*	Chapel Hill Public Library	49	51	3,000,000	G	N
Greensboro	Greensboro Public Library	65	35	16,060,000	G	Y
1987						
Chapel Hill	Chapel Hill Public Library	77	23	4,000,000	G	Y
NORTH DAKOTA						
1987						
Bismarck	Bismarck Veterans Memorial P.L.	73	27	3,400,000	G	Y
OHIO						
1991						
Garrettsville	Portage County District Library	54	46	910,000	G	Y
Tipp City	Tipp City Public Library	67	33	300,000	G	N
Twinsburg	Twinsburg Public Library	75	25	2,600,000	S	N
Willoughby	Willoughby-Eastlake Public Library	57	43	4,000,000	G	N

Continued

Table 6-2. *Continued*

Community	Library	Vote For	Against	Amount of Referendum	Gen/ Spec	Other Ballot Items
OHIO						
1990						
Columbiana	Columbiana Public Library	63%	37%	$ 500,000	G	N
Fairborn	Fairborn Public Library	56	44	1,750,000	G	N
Port Clinton	Port Clinton Public Library	70	30	1,200,000	G	N
1989						
Galion	Galion Public Library	67	33	900,000	G	N
Grafton	Grafton/Midview Public Library	55	45	650,000	S	N
Grove City*	Southwest Public Library	43	57	20,000,000	G	N
New Philadelphia	Tuscarawas City Library	60	40	1,500,000	G	Y
Oberlin	Oberlin Public Library	64	36	1,500,000	G	N
Shelby	Marvin Memorial Library	52	48	300,000	G	N
Zanesville	Muskingum County Public Library	51	49	5,000,000	G	Y
1988						
Brecksville	Cuyahoga County Public Library	58	42	2,500,000	G	N
Findlay*	Findlay-Hancock City Public Library	46	54	3,000,000	G	Y
Independence*	Cuyahoga County Public Library	48	52	2,500,000	G	N
London	London Public Library	58	42	650,000	G	Y
Mount Vernon	Public Library of Mt. Vernon	55	45	2,600,000	G	Y
North Ridgeville*	Lorain Public Library	42	58	1,300,000	G	Y
Orwell	Grand Valley Public Library	65	35	225,000	G	Y
1987						
Anonymous*	Anonymous	35	65	1,200,000	G	Y
Berea	Cuyahoga County Public Library	67	33	1,500,000	G	N
Columbus	Grandview Heights Public Library	66	34	4,460,000	G	Y
Columbus	P.L. of Columbus & Franklin Co.	53	47	45,000,000	G	Y
Fremont	Birchard Public Library/Sandusky Co.	56	44	3,600,000	G	N
Lebanon	Lebanon Public Library	65	35	1,350,000	G	N
Parma Heights	Cuyahoga County Public Library	57	43	1,000,000	G	N
Waynesville	Mary L. Cook Public Library	52	48	550,000	G	Y
OKLAHOMA						
1991						
Stillwater	Stillwater Public Library	67	33	4,980,000	S	N
1989						
Checotah	Checotah Jim Lucas Library	77	23	300,000	S	Y
Tulsa	Tulsa City/County Library System	66	34	4,200,000	G	N
OREGON						
1991						
Lincoln City	Driftwood Library/Lincoln City	63	37	600,000	G	N
1990						
Bend*	Deschutes County Library	47	53	8,448,000	G	Y
Corvallis	Corvallis-Benton Co. Public Library	69	31	6,850,000	G	N
Florence	Suislaw Public Library District	70	30	1,150,000	S	N
1989						
Dallas	Dallas Public Library	62	38	650,000	G	Y
Eugene*	Eugene Public Library	42	58	12,000,000	S	N
Stayton	Stayton Public Library	60	40	150,000	G	Y

Continued

Table 6-2. *Continued*

Community	Library	Vote For	Against	Amount of Referendum	Gen/ Spec	Other Ballot Items
OREGON						
1988						
Roseburg*	Douglas County Library System	46%	54%	$ 2,285,000	S	N
Sisters	Deschutes County Library	73	27	25,000	S	N
Stayton*	Stayton Public Library	46	54	275,000	S	Y
1987						
North Bend	North Bend Public Library	67	33	1,650,000	G	Y
Portland	Multnomah County Library	60	40	5,890,000	G	Y
West Linn	West Linn Public Library	64	36	1,200,000	G	Y
Wilsonville	Wilsonville Public Library	56	44	2,250,000	S	Y
PENNSYLVANIA						
1991						
Dresher*	Upper Dublin Public Library	45	55	3,500,000	G	Y
1990						
Huntingdon Valley	Huntingdon Valley Library	70	30	1,785,000	S	N
RHODE ISLAND						
1988						
South Kingstown	South Kingstown Public Library	75	25	100,000	S	Y
1987						
South Kingstown	South Kingstown Public Library	73	27	750,000	G	Y
SOUTH CAROLINA						
1991						
Conway	Horry County Public Library	100	0	4,000,000	S	Y
1989						
Columbia	Richland County Public Library	72	28	27,000,000	S	N
1987						
Charleston	Charleston County Library	76	24	15,465,234	G	N
TENNESSEE						
1991						
Kingston	Kingston City Library	61	39	564,000	G	N
TEXAS						
1991						
Baytown	Sterling Municipal	64	36	1,870,700	S	Y
Grand Prairie	Grand Prairie Memorial Library	54	46	2,700,000	S	Y
Plano	Plano Public Library	51	49	6,600,000	S	Y
San Marcos	San Marcos Public Library	53	47	2,135,000	G	Y
1990						
Angleton	Brazoria County Library System	79	21	1,020,000	S	Y
Conroe*	Montgomery County Library	46	54	17,650,000	G	Y
Coppell	William T. Cozby Public Library	64	36	2,600,000	S	Y
DeSoto	DeSoto Public Library	64	36	2,754,000	S	Y
Duncanville	Duncanville Public Library	67	33	500,000	S	Y
Pasadena	Pasadena Public Library	65	35	1,200,000	S	Y
Richmond	Fort Bend County Library	69	31	10,900,000	G	N
Weatherford	Weatherford Public Library	57	43	600,000	S	Y
1989						
Freeport	Brazoria County Library System	64	36	750,000	G	N

Continued

Table 6-2. Continued

Community	Library	Vote For	Against	Amount of Referendum	Gen/ Spec	Other Ballot Items
TEXAS						
1988						
Anonymous*	Anonymous	41%	59%	$ 600,000	G	Y
Houston	Harris City Public Library	60	40	3,500,000	G	Y
1987						
Universal City*	Universal City Library	29	71	750,000	S	N
VERMONT						
1988						
Middlebury	Ilsley Public Library	58	42	680,000	S	N
VIRGINIA						
1991						
Christiansburg*	Montgomery-Floyd Regional Library	46	54	1,400,000	G	Y
Fredericksburg	Central Rappahannock Library	56	44	1,350,000	G	Y
1990						
Fairfax	Fairfax County Public Library	62	38	39,100,000	G	Y
Fredericksburg*	Central Rappahannock Library	45	55	3,000,000	S	Y
1989						
Chesapeake	Chesapeake Public Library	58	42	10,600,000	G	N
Richmond	County of Henrico Public Library	67	33	3,000,000	S	Y
WASHINGTON						
1991						
Ferndale	Ferndale Library	63	37	1,250,000	G	Y
Spokane	Spokane Public Library	65	35	28,883,000	G	N
Vancouver	Fort Vancouver Regional Library	64	36	2,100,000	S	Y
1990						
Auburn*	Auburn Public Library	56	44	2,000,000	G	Y
Enumclaw	Enumclaw Public Library	63	37	1,250,000	G	N
Port Hadlock	Jefferson Co. Rural Library District	73	27	400,000	S	N
1989						
Enumclaw	Enumclaw Public Library	72	28	1,250,000	S	N
Kennewick*	Mid-Columbia Library	52	48	183,000	G	N
1988						
Spokane	Spokane County Library District	64	36	4,465,000	S	Y
1987						
Cheney	Cheney Community Library	79	21	275,000	G	Y
WEST VIRGINIA						
1989						
Morgantown	Morgantown Public Library	71	29	600,000	S	Y
WISCONSIN						
1989						
Stoughton	Stoughton Public Library	65	35	1,000,000	G	N
TOTALS	245 Projects	64%	36%	$1,306,338,685	G64% S36%	Y54% N46%

*Referenda that failed
**Required two-thirds approval for passage
*** Copyright © Reed Publishing

fill this void in the library literature. Each year since 1987, survey forms have been distributed to local library jurisdictions through the state library agencies to collect basic information regarding referenda for public library buildings. The data collection and subsequent articles[23,24,25,26,27] have provided basic statistical information regarding the referenda held each year as well as some analysis of that data. In recent years, the statistical reporting has been supplemented by brief case studies providing the reader with a summary of actual campaigns that were held during that year.

Five-Year Listing of Referenda for Public Library Buildings

Table 6-2 shows all the referenda reported for the five years of data collection (1987–1991), listed by state, fiscal year, and municipality. From this table, one can review the last five years of local referenda for public library construction in the U.S. The 245 referenda that are listed here are in all likelihood a representative sampling of the activity that is actually taking place nationwide.

Major Library Referenda Campaigns

Table 6-3 shows a selection of the 28 library referendum campaigns that amounted to more than $10 million each, listed by the amount of funds requested. These major campaigns account for $880 million, which is approximately two-thirds of all funds reported to have been placed before the voters during the five-year period. This means that a little over 11 percent of the campaigns held during the five year period accounted for two of every three dollars placed on ballots nationwide. Further, the top dozen (less than five percent of all campaigns) referenda accounted for approximately 50 percent of all funds requested. This is not to diminish the importance of

campaigns in smaller communities, but it does provide some perspective on the funding patterns of library referenda in this country. It is interesting to note that the pass/fail ratio for these major campaigns corresponds fairly closely to that of all referenda, which means that regardless of size, the chances for success appear to be about the same.

Table 6-3. Major Referenda Campaigns for Public Libraries

Location	Amount (in millions)	Year
San Francisco, CA	$109.5	1989
Denver, CO	91.6	1991
Los Angeles, CA*	90	1989
Las Vegas, NV	70	1991
Phoenix, AZ	55	1988
Los Angeles, CA	53.4	1989
Columbus, OH	45	1987
Fairfax, VA	39.1	1990
Decatur, GA	29	1987
Spokane, WA	28.9	1991
Columbia, SC	27	1989
West Palm Beach, FL	20	1987
Grove City, OH*	20	1989
Conroe, TX*	17.6	1990
Greensboro, NC	16	1991
Rolling Hills Estates, CA	16	1991
Palatine, IL	15.5	1990
Charleston, SC	15.5	1987
Farmington Hills, MI*	14.5	1990
Ocala, FL*	14.1	1991
Rochester, MN	14	1991
Hyattsville, MD	12.9	1991
Baton Rouge, LA	12	1987
Eugene, OR*	12	1989
Richmond, TX	10.9	1990
Chesapeake, VA	10.6	1989
Rochester, MI	10.2	1989
New Port Richey, FL	10	1987
TOTAL:	$880.3	

*Referenda that failed.
©Reed Publishing

Five-Year Summary of Referenda Funds

Table 6-4 shows a summary, by year, of the amount of funding requested by referenda nationwide along with the amount of funds that were approved and the not ap-

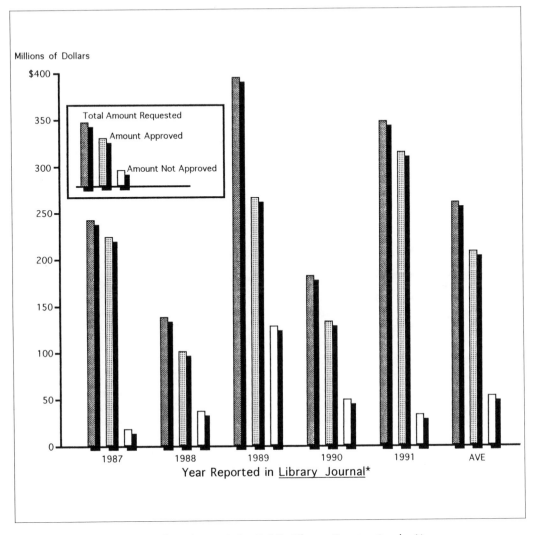

Fig. 6-2. Referenda Funds for Public Library Construction by Year.

proved. Figure 6-2 shows a graph of the information provided in Table 6-4. On average, approximately $261 million per year has been requested, with $208 million being approved and $53 million being rejected by the voters. Of the $1,306,336,033 attempted, approximately 80 percent was approved by the voters. It should be encouraging to library supporters that four-fifths of all funding attempted for public library construction by referenda in this nation is approved by the public.

Five-Year Summary of Referenda Data

Table 6-5 summarizes by year the information in Table 6-2, showing the number of referenda held each year, the percentage to pass and fail, the total amount of funds requested, the percentage of the vote "for" and "against," the percentage of referenda that were held during general elections and special elections, and the percentage of referenda that had competition from other ballot items ("yes") and those without competition ("no").

Table 6-4. Five Year Summary of Referenda Funds

Fiscal Year	Total Amount Requested	Amount Approved	Amount Not Approved
1991	$ 348,420,142	$ 315,020,142	$ 33,400,000
1990	$ 182,755,394	$ 133,065,394	$ 49,690,000
1989	$ 394,759,648*	$ 266,139,648	$128,620,000
1988	$ 138,475,602	$ 101,420,602	$ 37,055,000
1987	$ 241,927,899	$ 223,972,899	$ 17,955,000
TOTAL	$1,306,338,685	$1,039,618,685	$266,720,000
AVE	$ 261,267,737	$ 207,923,737	$ 53,344,000

*Included $75 million of public library construction funds approved in a California state-wide referendum.
©Reed Publishing

Pass/Fail Rate for Referenda for Public Library Buildings

While the reporting system is entirely voluntary, and there certainly are some campaigns that are missed by the survey method, it is encouraging to note that for those referenda reported, the chances of success for public library capital campaigns is approximately four to one. This figure may be somewhat high, assuming that those whose referenda fail are less likely to report their loss than those who succeed. Regardless, the success rate is probably still significantly higher than the rate of failure.

Voter Approval Rate

As can be seen from Table 6-5, when the percentages of votes for and against referenda are averaged, the national success rate of voter approval is 64 percent. The range in the approval rate has consistently remained between 60 and 70 percent. This enviable approval rate for public library capital campaigns is just barely short of two-thirds, which is significant in light of the number of states that require more than a majority approval rate to pass a referendum. States such as Washington and Iowa require a 60 percent approval rate; California, Idaho, Missouri, and New

Table 6-5. Five Year Summary of Referenda for Public Library Facilities

Year	#	Percentage Pass/Fail		Amount	Vote For	Con	Election Gen	Spec	Other Ballot Items Yes	No
1991	46	85%	15%	$ 348,420,142	63%	37%	65%	35%	54%	46%
1990	49	80%	20%	182,755,394	65%	35%	59%	41%	51%	49%
1989	51	75%	25%	394,759,648	61%	39%	65%	35%	41%	59%
1988	45	64%	36%	138,475,602	61%	39%	60%	40%	58%	42%
1987	54	93%	7%	241,927,899	69%	31%	69%	31%	67%	33%
ALL	245	80%	20%	$1,306,338,685	64%	36%	64%	36%	54%	46%
Average	49			261,267,737						

©Reed Publishing

Provided Courtesy of Bruder/DWL Architects

Fig. 6-3. View of the new Phoenix Central Library.

Hampshire require a two-thirds approval rate. Referenda in these states are a real challenge, but one that has been met in many cases.

Type of Election and Competition on the Ballot

For the five-year period, 64 percent of the referenda were held during general elections and 36 percent during special elections. This means that general elections are used almost twice as often as special elections. For the purposes of the survey, a general election is defined as a regularly scheduled election such as the November general election or any normal primary election. Special elections are those set up in addition to normally scheduled elections during the year. For the five-year period, 54 percent of the library referenda held had some form of competition from another capital ballot measure and 46 percent did not, which shows that almost as many library issues are decided with ballot competition as without it.

Agency Authorizing Referenda

Many kinds of local agencies can authorize referenda for public libraries; the most common is the local municipality or city. In some localities, however, counties, school and library districts, New England towns, parishes, and even special authorities may hold referenda. Table 6-6 shows

Table 6-6. Authorizing Agencies
for Library Referenda

Agency	Percentage
Municipality	42%
New England town	18%
County	16%
School district	11%
Library district	9%
Township	1%
City/county	1%
Parish	1%
Village	.5%
Special authorities	.5%

©Reed Publishing

the allocation of the referenda by the authorizing agency. For the five-year period, municipalities lead with 42 percent. When combined with New England towns, the figure increases to 60 percent. Counties, school districts, and library districts account for another 36 percent, with the remaining 4 percent spread out over miscellaneous authorities.

Types of Referenda

Over 80 percent of the referenda held during the five-year period resulted in the issuance of bonds, almost all of which were general obligation bonds, whereby the full taxing authority of the funding agency stands behind the debt instrument. In those cases where bonds were not issued, the most typical form of financing was either a limited property tax mileage or revenues from a sales tax increase for a specific period of time. Both approaches usually provided an adequate revenue stream to complete the project without having to resort to selling bonds.

Regardless of the actual method of financing, the activity of campaigning for referenda is usually very similar. The following section provides an overview of the campaign process which will be described in more detail in a forthcoming book by the author on the subject of referenda campaigns for public library buildings.

Mounting a Referendum Campaign

Going directly to the electorate has historically been, and remains to this day, one of the most sensible, democratic and equitable means of providing public funds to build public libraries. Further, an additional fringe benefit is that the community will generally be inclined to make certain that future operational budgets for the library are protected during economic down turns because of their campaign involvement and resulting high degree of commitment to the library. Given this, the science of holding a referendum and forging political consensus is extremely important to any agency endeavoring to finance, build and operate a public library.

The goal of any campaign is to convince the electorate that the new library is needed, desirable and obtainable at a reasonable cost, and then to get those people out to the polls to vote "Yes" for the issue. In order to accomplish this goal, all campaigns must begin by organizing the campaign structure, planning the campaign's strategy, raising campaign funds and then implementing the campaign through the use of various techniques based upon a campaign budget and calendar with the assistance of many campaign volunteers.

Campaign Commitment

One of the first steps in any campaign is to make certain that the necessary commitment to the project and campaign is present. From the outset, the library management and supporters should be in the game to win and should plan accordingly. In order to win, all of the library's supporters will have to make a very significant commitment of time and energy. A referendum campaign is one of the most focused and intensive activities that library supporters will face, and it will demand a good deal of personal time from each individual including the library director. There will be many late evening and weekend meetings not only for planning

ning the campaign, but also during the final weeks of the campaign when the all out effort to reach the voters is in high gear.

If commitment and consensus cannot be achieved early, the campaign should not be started until those involved can make a strong commitment to it; without strong support from the campaign organizers, the campaign is likely to fail. Library referenda frequently fail not only because of voter apathy but because of neglect and lack of commitment on the part of campaign workers.

The Steering Committee

The success of many campaigns can usually be attributed to an organized core of committed, influential individuals who form the steering committee for the campaign. The greatest of care must be taken to select the most politically savvy and influential individuals possible, who are not only committed to the campaign issue, but who can produce the desired results. These individuals must be "movers and shakers" in the community. It can't be emphasized enough how critical this step is to success since the campaign will be placed in the hands of these people.

The right people on the steering committee can mean a smooth running, effective, well thought out and successful campaign. The wrong selection of even one committee member can mean disaster or at the very least greatly hamper campaign efforts. It is particularly important to look for people who have had previous fund raising and political campaign experience. In many communities, there are individuals who are acknowledged as the "campaigners" and are selected time and again to run successful community campaigns. If library supporters can't get the most experienced "old pros," they may be able to identify individuals in a community who have the right political instincts even if the don't currently have the track record to prove it. Sometimes these individuals are the best

possible choice if they are aspiring to political office and are willing to work very hard for the library campaign to prove their effectiveness to the community and its political insiders.

Whether that person is called a campaign manager, chairperson or coordinator, it is usually best to place the campaign primarily in the hands of one person. Preferably, this person should be a recognized community leader who has previously had this kind of campaign experience, who is well known by the press, and who will be a good spokesperson for the campaign. Frequently, the busiest people make the best campaign managers.

However, it is impossible for one individual to run all aspects of a campaign. There should be several committee chairpersons, primarily responsible for the day-to-day routine duties of their individual committees. Each chairperson represents his or her committee on the overall steering committee. This type of campaign structure provides a built-in communications system. The campaign manager communicates directly with the steering committee members and these committee chairpersons then communicate with their committee members, who then can pass necessary information along to the support troops who are working on the front lines. This structure allows for communications from the "top down," but also provides a built-in mechanism for communication from the "bottom up." In this way, all campaign workers will provide an invaluable service by gathering information from the community. Such feedback can be used for adjustments and fine tuning as the campaign heats up.

Most campaigns start off with at least some of the following committees:

Financing/Fundraising
Volunteers
Public Relations
Campaign Literature
Direct Mail

Door-to-door Canvassing
Poster & Yard Signs
Speaker's Bureau
Special Events
Telephone Bank
Endorsements

It is generally best to allow people to chair or at least work on committees that they are most interested in since they will tend to do their best in these positions, but it should be up to the campaign manager to make the committee assignments. Once a steering committee has been formed, the first order of business is to come up with a strategic plan for the campaign.

Strategic Planning

The key question for campaign planners are how to identify the individual voters who are most likely to vote for the library issue, what kind of message will most effectively sway these individuals, as well as how to most effectively communicate this campaign message to them? If these questions are accurately answered, the chances of success will be immeasurably improved.

Even when funds for a campaign are low and other resources such as time and professional expertise are limited, effective campaigns can be run on a shoestring if astute strategic planning is done ahead of time. This can't be emphasized enough. Careful planning is critical to success in referendum campaigns, and it is not uncommon to spend as much time on planning as on actually campaigning.

While it is true that many of the same campaign methods will be used in many campaigns, there is no one tried-and-true approach or generic success formula that will work well in every campaign. Each community is different, and the library campaign steering committee must develop its own approach to the specific local conditions and effectively present and communicate the library issue to the electorate in a manner which best fits those who will vote in that particular election.

Early on, campaign planners should brainstorm about the campaign and then force themselves to write down a strategic plan. The plan should answer all of the "who, what, when, where, how and why" questions. The more specific campaign planners can get the better. The plan should outline in as much detail as possible the general tone and major issues of the campaign. Both the major strengths and weaknesses of the library issue should be identified. But most importantly, the primary target group(s) of likely "Yes" voters must be identified and the campaign plan should be tailored to reaching these individuals and getting them out to vote.

The campaign strategy will be different if the ballot issue will be decided at a special election versus a general election. There are significant differences in the number and type of voters in the two different elections. Special elections tend to produce smaller numbers of "habitual" voters where as general elections produce higher turnouts which consists of both habitual as well as "occasional" voters. Obviously, the number of voters who have to be reached with the campaign message increases with general elections which means that more campaign resources will need to be available to be expended in order to insure success.

In either case, campaign planners must concentrate on those likely voters who are already positively predisposed toward the library issue. It is often the case that people who will support school or other cultural issues will also support library issues. Because of this, it is wise to obtain a copy of the voting results of these previously held elections. A precinct-by-precinct analysis will often provide the answer to which areas of the community the campaign planners should focus on. This information including demographic information gleaned form census reports as well as other demographic resources should be compiled, analyzed and infused into the strategic plan.

The campaign strategy should be based upon a campaign budget and a calendar which addresses all major campaign activities and guides planners throughout the referendum process. The calendar should chronicle all major campaign activities as well as provide a "cash flow" tool so that campaign planners know when funds must be raised for specific activities. The campaign budget should identify the specific amount of money needed for each activity as well provide a plan to raise the necessary funding. The campaign plan should also detail the acquisition and training of volunteer campaign workers. Finally, once it is complete, the plan should describe all of the specific campaign methods and techniques which will be used. One method of determining which way to go with the campaign is the use of polls.

Polling

Pre-vote polls may be useful tools in determining where the library issue stands with the voters. The results help the steering committee gauge the chances of success and degree of effort that must be expended in order to be successful. In communities where funding agencies or even library boards need some convincing in order to get the library issue on the ballot, the use of a preliminary poll may prove invaluable. It is possible, however for an early poll to show that the library issue doesn't have a chance of passing no matter how well organized the campaign is. If this is the case, it is frequently wise to wait and try to assess the reasons for this sentiment along with taking any corrective steps prior to launching a referendum campaign. Another advantage to using preliminary polls is to assess the amount of funding which is likely to be approved by the voters. It may be that the referendum amount needs to be adjusted down or can be increased based on polling results.

Polling can also be used to uncover which aspects of the library campaign are the politically motivating issues to the grass roots voters. In other words, polling can be used as a mechanism for researching the issues which can be most effectively used as campaign themes or uncover the single most important issue which should become the main campaign message.

Campaign Message

How well and how frequently the library's case is presented to the voters may be one of the most important aspects of any library campaign. The case for the referendum must be made by defining the need for a new or improved library facility. What is obvious to the library administration may not always be so self-evident to the public. Once the campaign message is determined, it must be effectively communicated to the electorate, and further it must be repeatedly delivered and reinforced.

In order to do this, it is essential for the steering committee to obtain all of the pertinent "facts and figures" regarding the need and the recommended solution. If the steering committee members are uninformed on the issue, they can not hope to inform the public. The facts must be presented in a straight forward manner, but it is also important to add an emotional "hook."

Emotion

Knowing that emotional issues motivate voters is essential. A dry statistical campaign that does not touch the voter's soul in some way will often fall flat, while one that plays on the heart strings will frequently rally its constituency. Most people vote based upon their emotions as much as their logic. In order to win, it is critical to engage the potential voter with a passionate issue which he or she can bring to the polls with the strong desire to support the library issue. In many communities, urban and suburban, promoting the education of children is one of the best issues; in others, retirement communities for instance, providing services to senior citizens is more appropriate.

These areas are the basis for a visual campaign which shows children or seniors in a positive way. Regardless of the campaign, the steering committee must find the pertinent social and emotional issues which will motivate the electorate and provide sufficient impetus to vote for the library issue. In short, the campaign message must distill all of the major issues and campaign themes into one central statement, preferably with a strong emotional impact.

Campaign Methods and Techniques

Once the campaign message has been determined, the remainder of the campaign revolves around delivering the message and getting "Yes" voters to the polls. In order to win, the campaign message must be dramatic and convincing enough to get a majority of voters to pull the "Yes" lever in the voting booth. Campaign literature, community presentations, endorsements, media coverage and advertising, telephone banks, mass mailings, door-to-door canvasing and yard signs are all viable campaign techniques which should be tied in with the main campaign message. There are many methods of delivering the message, but each campaign steering committee must decide the best and most feasible techniques to be used in their community.

Personal Contact

Regardless of the techniques used, the best method of influencing voters is to personalize the message. Experience has shown that the most appropriate tool for winning over the uncommitted voter, as well as enticing the committed voter to the polls, has always been personal contact with highly committed campaign workers. Media coverage and direct mailings of campaign literature are often essential parts of many campaigns, but there is nothing better than a friendly face, a smile and a handshake to tip the scales in the right direction for the library issue. Low budget library campaigns are, for the most part, win one vote at a time through personal contact at the coffee shop, in the supermarket and even over the back yard fence. However, personal contact can come in more organized ways as well such as during speakers bureau presentations, telephone banks and one-on-one during door-to-door canvassing.

Door-to-Door Canvasing

Door-to-door canvassing takes a high degree of organization and commitment on the part of campaign planners, but it may be the single most effective campaign activity. To effectively implement a neighborhood canvassing effort, specific precincts must be targeted and an adequate number of volunteers must be assigned to walk the targeted area. Volunteers must be prepared with scripts, campaign literature, maps and voters lists which allow them to concentrate on the households which are most likely to vote.

Door-to-door campaigning is an effective way to raise awareness of library issues in an area, and while it may even occasionally work well to convert an undecided voter into the library camp, it is probably the most effective at recruiting additional campaign volunteers, fund raising for the campaign, but most importantly, identifying "Yes" voters which can later be contacted through additional door-to-door or telephone canvassing during the get-out-the-vote (GOTV) effort.

GOTV and Telephone Banks

Once likely voters have been identified as supportive of the library issue, the last few days of the campaign will be dedicated to getting those individuals out to vote for the issue. Telephone banks are particularly effective at accomplishing this just before election day by having campaign volunteers call each and every household which indicated that they were supportive of the library issue. Good GOTV efforts, particularly through the use of telephone banks, can make the difference between success and failure in close elections.

Never take the outcome of a referendum for granted. It is always best never to let up, but keep working hard right up until the polls close on election day. It is at this time, when the campaign must "pull out all the stops" and concentrate every resource, financial and personal, on getting supporters to the polls. Every campaign volunteer should be focused on a specific task which will get as many voters as possible into the voting booth. At this point, every vote should be viewed as *the* one necessary to put the campaign over the top.

Volunteers

Clearly, a referenda campaign, especially low budget grass roots campaigns, take a substantial number of committed volunteers in order to be successful. In short, there must be enough volunteers to do the work, they must be well organized and they must have a high degree of enthusiasm for the issue. It is exceedingly important to infuse emotional involvement into the campaign players and turn them into "true believers." There are many sources of campaign volunteers for library issues. Many individuals are just waiting to be asked and don't need any convincing because they already believe in the value of a public library for a community. Frequently, it simply takes someone with leadership qualities who is good at organizing people to turn them into "campaign troops."

Volunteers are the backbone of most library referenda campaigns. It is obvious that library referenda don't just happen, but are the result of a considerable amount of work by many dedicated people. While the effort to pass a referendum is no small one, the chances of success are encouraging, and success is very rewarding indeed!. How-

ever, win or lose, in the long run a referendum campaign will probably be very beneficial to the library because of the publicity gained as well as the discovery of all of the new library supporters picked up during the campaign.

Regardless of the success of referenda for library capital projects, there are a great many new and "creative financing" methods of local funding which have been developed in recent years. The following section provides a comprehensive review of innovative alternate methods of funding public library buildings.

ALTERNATIVE LOCAL FUNDING METHODS

The taxpayer revolt which spread east after the passage of California's Proposition 13 in the late 1970's and the loss of the federal revenue sharing program in the mid-eighties created a local infrastructure crisis in many parts of the country. These two events, along with the changes in the use of tax-exempt bonds brought on by the Tax Reform Act of 1986, have resulted in local jurisdictions' searching for new funding methods. In the last decade, there has been a definite shift in some states away from using general public revenue sources (such as general obligation bonds) to finance infrastructure and toward special taxes and development fees, lease-purchase financing through the issuance of certificates of participation, and other creative financing methods. This is particularly the case for fast growing sunbelt states such as California, Florida, and Texas. However, in most cases, many of these methods are transferrable to local jurisdictions in other states.

In some cases, alternative methods are used because they address new political realities in a changing world of local finance. Some of the methods have been around for quite a while, and others are relatively new, invented because of numerous pressures on local finances. Some of these approaches may fit a specific project very well; others may not. Some will not be feasible since they may require enabling legislation or constitutional authority that does not exist in a particular locale. But the library community can certainly work to incorporate such desirable authorities into the existing state statute.

Revenue Bonds

Some jurisdictions have occasionally utilized revenue bonds to fund capital improvements. This approach is not common for public library buildings since library service, for the most part, does not produce a revenue stream of immediate consequence. It is doubtful that user fees could ever generate the income necessary to support a revenue bond without a radical change in the way most public libraries are operated in this country. Revenue bonds are generally utilized to fund some form of public enterprise facility that will generate income through fees for use of services such as sewer and water systems. By charging a monthly fee for the use of the service, the jurisdiction can sell revenue bonds to be repaid over time from the revenues to pay for the construction of the sewer or water lines. Other public services such as airports, parking structures, golf courses, and bridges are frequently funded in this manner, but unless an adequate revenue stream can be identified, it is difficult to use this method for public libraries.

Further, the use of revenue bonds is not popular for "nonessential" public facilities because, unlike general obligation bonds, they are not guaranteed by the full taxing authority of the local public agency. Since the principal and interest on revenue bonds is retired by the income generated from the specific income source rather than the jurisdiction's general revenues, the risk to bond holders is higher. If this income generation is interrupted, the jurisdiction may

default on the bonds more easily than with general obligation bonds. Since the risk is greater, the interest rate paid on revenue bonds is usually higher and therefore the costs for financing the project are also higher.

In addition, there is frequently criticism over the fact that the use of revenue bonds usually does not require a referendum, and so can be dangerous for public officials. This is the case if the public perceives that revenue bonds are being used to fund projects that are unpopular with the electorate. While the use of revenue bonds is a sensitive issue, they can occasionally be used successfully for public libraries in special cases such as with redevelopment agencies where the income stream is based on tax increment or sales tax revenues or with special bonding authorities where lease revenue bonds are sold.

A lease revenue bond is a special form of revenue bond. Briefly stated, the repayment of lease revenue bonds is based on lease payments to investors for the facility from a local jurisdiction through a financing authority which is established as a separate legal entity for the purpose of financing public facilities. Revenue bonds can also be used in special assessment districts that have a built-in revenue stream from the collection of special assessments. In order to understand special assessment bonds, it is first necessary to discuss special districts.

Special Districts

Special districts are specific geographical areas usually created within the boundaries of a jurisdiction such as a city or county in order to raise funds from landowners for a specific purpose, e.g., the provision of some government service. The main criterion for a special district is that it provides a specific and usually limited service to a precisely defined service area which may or may not correspond to the boundaries of the jurisdiction which created it. Over the years, many forms of special districts have been developed by numerous states to finance public infrastructure needs as well as various services, including public library services.

Special districts may be independent or dependent. Independent special districts have governing bodies separate from the local jurisdiction within which they have been formed; in the case of dependent special districts, the jurisdiction's governing body also governs the special district. In some cases, special districts are nothing more than specialized financing vehicles created by a city or county to provide some specific service to a limited portion of the jurisdiction. "The use of special districts is determined by state laws that permit their organization and define their characteristics. It is not surprising, therefore that special districts vary widely from state to state. Some states, such as California, Washington, Texas, and Illinois, have vigorously supported the formation of spe-

cial districts for a wide range of purposes, while other states have restricted districts to a few specific purposes."[28]

In the case of the formation of special districts for the provision of public library services, the states of Washington, California, Illinois, Colorado, and others have established local library districts that have property tax authority that can be used to finance public library facility improvements. Since these special districts can collect property taxes, they usually have the ability to take on long term debt by use of general obligation bonds as well as other methods. As an example, the residents of the Palos Verdes Library District, Rolling Hills Estates, California, approved a referendum in 1991 that resulted in the issuing of general obligation bonds by that California special library district. In addition to special districts, which are just another form of local government, there are special assessment districts, which can be utilized to finance public library facilities as well.

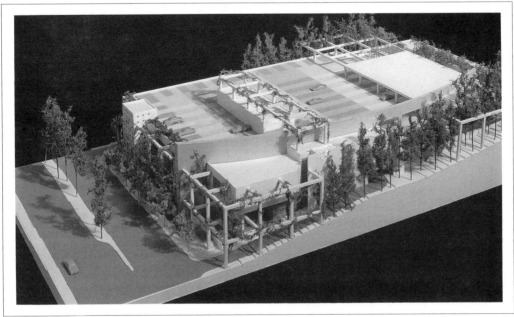

Provided Courtesy of Zimmer Gunsul Frasca Partnership

Fig. 6-4. Peninsual Center Library, Palos Verdes Library District, California.

Special Assessment Districts

Special assessment districts, also known as benefit assessment districts, are a subset of special districts and are entirely dependent upon the local jurisdiction that created them. Special assessment districts are strictly financing vehicles and have no separate governing board. "Often called public improvement districts, assessment districts are established to permit a special tax levy on property owners who benefit from specific public improvements within the district."[29] A special assessment district can be created in a number of ways, but the most frequent methods are by local ordinance or petition of landowners. In some states, a special assessment district may be established without the approval of landowners, but it is more common to obtain their approval. Special assessment districts are a method of linking landowners who directly benefit from public improvements with the costs of those improvements rather than placing the burden of infrastructure costs on all of the residents of the jurisdiction.

Special assessment districts are usually established for the provision of water, sewer, or street services, etc., but in California they can be established for the construction of transportation facilities, libraries, fire stations, public buildings and police stations in "charter cities."[30] For example, San Diego has recently instituted the use of facility benefit assessment (FBA) districts in several areas of the city which has resulted in the financing of public libraries in Carmel Valley, Scripps Ranch, and Rancho Penasquitos. In addition, several other areas of the city are planning libraries that will be funded by FBA districts. The districts are utilized primarily in areas of the city that are in the process of developing, where they finance a variety of facilities. The assessment can become substantial. "Assessments are typically levied to finance libraries, fire stations, parks, police stations, and transportation facilities within each community. Residential fees range from $1,872 to $14,761 per unit."[31]

One of the difficulties with the use of assessment districts is the development and application of an equitable formula for the assessment. The key is to demonstrate how a particular parcel that is being assessed benefits from the service being financed, in this case, a public library. The San Diego fee formula utilizes an equivalent dwelling unit (EDU) approach, whereby each residential unit is assessed a fee, but industrial and commercial development is not. The EDU formula is based on population since the need and standards for libraries in San Diego are based on population. This approach is consistent with general planning guidelines since the city develops a plan for the size of the library projects based on the population to be served. The cost of the library facility is then estimated based on the size of the proposed building. The cost per EDU is then calculated based on the number of EDUs in the FBA district and the overall cost of the needed facility. This is the benefit assessment that must subsequently be paid for each EDU. This assessment may vary from district to district depending upon the cost of the proposed library facility needed and the number of EDUs.

Special assessments may be paid in a lump sum or annually for a specific number of years. In San Diego, developers must pay the assessments in full when the building permit is issued. Further, in San Diego, FBA financing does not provide authority to issue bonds, so projects must wait to be built until adequate funds are collected from the assessments. One advantage of the use of benefit assessments is that a public referendum is usually not required. The local governing authority can on its own initiative authorize the establishment of an assessment district, but there is usually an override provision

Fig. 6-5. Rancho Penasquitos Branch, San Diego, CA.

whereby if a significant number of protests are received from landowners, the proceedings can be stopped.

In order for special assessments to be levied in most states, it must be demonstrated that a "special benefit" is being provided to the landowner who is being assessed. A special assessment may not be levied if a landowner does not receive any benefit, but if a landowner does receive some benefit the assessment must be paid. In theory, the amount of the assessment should be commensurate with the benefit the land owner receives. Benefit may be determined in a number of ways, including, the street frontage of land, square footage of the building(s) on the land, the acreage of the land, the number of quantifiable units (houses, bedrooms, bathrooms, offices, etc.) on the land, or the accessibility of the land to the public improvement.

By creating a special assessment district, a jurisdiction can often issue special assessment bonds that are repaid with assessments paid by landowners. These bonds are usually revenue bonds and are backed not only by the proceeds of the special assessment but frequently by a lien against the property held by the district's landowners. In some cases, landowners may lose their property by foreclosure if the special assessment is not paid or if the income generated by the assessment is not adequate to retire the bonds that have been issued to bondholders. Special assessment bonds may be backed by the value of the property assessed, but they are not backed by the full taxing authority (including property taxation) of the governing agency. "Special assessments are not property taxes. Unlike taxes (including special taxes), the sum of a special assessment cannot exceed the cost of the improvement or service it is financing."[32] The amount of the special assessment is determined by the benefit received, not the assessed value of the property as with property taxes. In fact, a special assessment is not a tax at all and should not be confused with property taxes or special taxes.

Special Taxes

Like special assessments, special taxes are levied for a specific public improvement or service, but special taxes do not require that landowners receive a proportional benefit from the planned improvement. Therefore, special taxes are not considered to be either fees or assessments. The use of the income from special taxes is limited to the specific program for which the tax was levied, and the proceeds must be placed in a separate account from the general fund. Special taxes are not levied on an ad-valorem basis (in proportion to property value) like property taxes, but are usually applied uniformly on a per-parcel basis and are frequently called parcel taxes. The special tax may be established at a flat rate for each parcel regardless of size, or it may be levied according to some other formula like acreage of the lot or number of bedrooms. As with special assessments, if a special tax is not paid, title to the property may be lost by the landowner through foreclosure.

In some states, local jurisdictions may sell "special tax bonds" for specific public improvement projects. These special tax bonds are secured by the jurisdiction's authority to collect the special tax as well as the property within the special tax district. Since these bonds are backed only by a portion of the jurisdiction's taxing authority and not the full faith and credit of the jurisdiction's general tax fund, the bonds are somewhat more risky for investors than general obligation bonds and therefore usually sell with a higher interest rate. The authorization to assume special-tax-supported debt may or may not require

approval from the electorate by referendum depending on the enabling legislation in any given state. In California, the implementation of one of the most prominent special tax financing mechanisms, the Mello-Roos financing district, does require approval by the electorate or landowners.

The Mello-Roos Community Facilities District Act of 1982

The Mello-Roos Community Facilities Act of 1982 (California Government Code 53311 et seq.) authorizes the creation of dependent special districts that can be used to finance a substantial number of public capital improvements as well as raise funds to operate a variety of public services, including public libraries. The act specifically enables the use of funds for library facilities (California Government Code section 53313.5[c]) and operating expenses for libraries. However, operating funds, from this source may only be used to supplement any existing service, not supplant it. This flexibility to raise funds through the levy of a special tax for both facilities and operation provides landmark status to the act. It sets a particularly important precedent for financing public libraries which frequently can find the means to build a facility, but have difficulty identifying an income stream to operate it.

The act is extremely flexible in that it allows cities, counties, special districts, school districts, joint powers authorities, or any other municipal corporation or district to establish a facilities district. Further, the facilities financed by the district do not have to be located within the district. Given this, and the fact that the district boundaries can be drawn in any manner desired, areas the local jurisdiction wishes to avoid can be easily excluded from the district. In addition, as time passes, more land may be added to the district to increase its service area. If desirable, certain properties within the district may be made exempt from the assessment of the special tax. Further, since the special tax does not have to be levied on the basis of benefit like special assessments, local jurisdictions can design the levying of the tax in the most politically advantageous manner. For example, parcels owned by senior citizens can be levied at a lower rate than others in the district. Another important feature is that facilities acquired by the district may be purchased, constructed, expanded, or rehabilitated, but they must have a useful life of at least five years. This is a particularly nonrestrictive time frame for the use of bond funds and it is likely that many forms of library furnishings and equipment will qualify unlike some other types of bonds.

From the approval of the act in 1982 until January 1992, Mello-Roos districts have issued over $3.2 billion in bonds to finance public improvements in California.[33] California is not alone in its use of Mello-Roos special districts; other states, including Arizona, Texas, Florida, and Colorado, have enacted similar approaches to financing public infrastructure. "The Mello-Roos legislation has become a model for similar legislation across the United States. The creation of special districts has enabled developers to continue the development of real estate projects without substantial increases in ad-valorem property taxes."[34] This approach to financing public libraries as well as other public improvements will undoubtedly become even more important in the future especially in high-growth areas, as pressure increases on the property-tax-based general fund.

In California, the Mello-Roos Act has recently been used to finance public library buildings in the communities of Oakland (Rockridge), Davis (Yolo County), Carlsbad, and Orange County (Santa Margarita, Aliso Viejo, and Saddleback branches). The amount of the special tax depends on a number of factors, including the cost of the facility and the number of parcels in the district. In Davis, the special tax amounts to $42 annually per parcel; in Rockridge it amounts to $25 annually per parcel. While many jurisdictions simply apply the special tax on a per-parcel basis, it can be structured in a number of ways. In theory, the tax could be levied on the number of bedrooms on each parcel, the number of water meters, the acreage of the parcel, or the square footage of the building on the land; however, it cannot be apportioned on an ad-valorem basis. Once the district is formed, a special tax lien is recorded against all the nonexempt properties in the district. This allows adequate disclosure of the tax to new property owners. This is important so that individuals who purchase homes within the district are aware that the special tax must be paid annually.

A Mello-Roos district can be created in a number of ways. The process may be initiated by the governing body of the local jurisdiction acting at the request of at least two of its members or by petition from ten percent of the registered voters in the district (or by the owners of ten percent of the land in the district). Within 90 days, the local jurisdiction must define the boundaries of the district, determine the type of facilities and services to be developed, state that a special tax will be levied annually, announce when and where a public hearing about the district will be held, and describe the voting process for the approval of the district. Prior to the public hearing, the jurisdiction must make available a report on the estimated costs of the proposed projects and services to be provided. The process of forming the district is halted for at least one year if 50 percent or more of the registered voters or owners of one-half of the land area protest its formation. If the district is not protested, the jurisdiction may formally adopt a "resolution of formation" and authorize a vote by the electorate if there are 12 or more registered voters in the district. If there are fewer than 12 registered voters in the district, the vote only needs to be approved by these landowners (each acre of land counts as one vote). Both in the case of registered voters and landowners, the formation of the Mello-Roos district is approved in California only if a two-thirds super-majority vote is received.

"The Mello-Roos Act is designed to make it as easy as possible to gain passage of the special tax within the constraints of a two-thirds vote."[35] A Mello-Roos district is unique in that it may be created to build public facilities in already urbanized areas as well as areas under development. Given the rather formidable political hurdle of a two-thirds vote, this mechanism is not generally attempted unless local officials feel relatively confident that the district's residents will approve the measure. This underscores the great advantage of the Mello-Roos legislation that it allows for the boundaries of the special district to be gerrymandered so as to increase the likelihood of passing the measure. In urban areas, un-

derstanding the demographic profile of the typical library user and then targeting these groups by including them within the Mello-Roos district may well result in the successful passage of referenda.

The Mello-Roos district also works particularly well for undeveloped land when there are fewer than 12 registered voters within the district. In the case where one or more large landowners desires to create a Mello-Roos district with a local jurisdiction in order to develop property, obtaining the two-thirds vote by the landowner(s) is less of a problem than determining all of the necessary public improvements, services, and the resulting level of special tax levy necessary to support the development. Assuming an agreement between the developer(s) and the local jurisdiction can be reached on this, both parties have arrived at a feasible method of financing the public improvements necessary to serve the new residents of the development as well as the continuing cash flow neces-

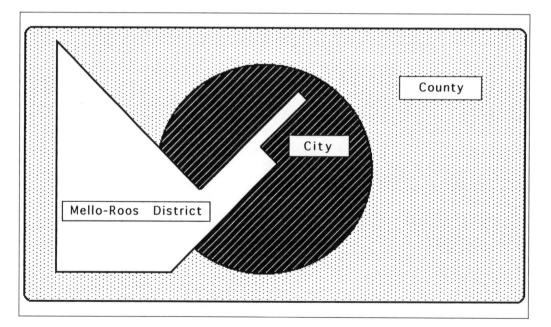

Fig. 6-6. Hypothetical Mello-Roos District

sary to operate the services. Further, both parties have arrived at a method of providing necessary public services for the community by allowing for the sale of tax-exempt special tax bonds to finance the necessary facilities. The principal and interest on the bonds will be paid back over a number of years from the collection of the special tax. Again, because of the potential risk involved since the bonds are backed only by the value of the land in the early stages of development, the interest rate demanded by bond purchasers is usually significantly higher than for general obligation bonds.

If the development grows rapidly, the availability of capital for the public facilities increases rapidly, but if the development slows or stops, the revenue from the development diminishes or ceases altogether. Herein lies one of the problems of relying on "dirt bonds"[36] to build public libraries or any other kind of public infrastructure. If a developer defaults, or if development in a special district stops before it is completed, the special tax may not be adequate to cover all of the public facilities planned. In some cases, public facilities that were to be built toward the end of the term of the development may not be constructed because of lack of funds, or may be delayed for years until enough money can be collected. The problem is that frequently police and fire stations, streets, or sewer lines are scheduled to be completed first and public libraries are often scheduled to be completed last. If the development is progressing as planned with no misfortune, this does not present a problem, but if economic difficulties are experienced, there is a risk that the library facility will be delayed or, worse, never built at all.

Regardless of the risks, in fast-growing markets such as California, the Mello-Roos Act has proven to be a potent new weapon in the hands of local officials trying to meet the infrastructure needs of newly developing communities. Although not a panacea, the Mello-Roos Act has proven an effective method for building new public library facilities. While those taxed should derive some benefit from the facility, there does not have to be a specific formula that directly relates the amount of the special tax to the proportion of benefit received.

> Mello-Roos financing is similar to assessment district financing in that the users of the financed facilities pay for them. In the case of assessment districts, the users pay through annual assessments; in the [Mello-Roos] community facility districts, they pay through a special tax. . . . Because under Mello-Roos the "benefit" to the taxpayer need not be tied directly to the property being taxed, facilities with broad community benefit, such as libraries or city halls, qualify for Mello-Roos financing.[37]

Because local jurisdictions can structure the special tax to meet the specific needs of each community or district, the potential for the tax to be responsive, fair, and politically palatable is increased.

Finally, the relationship between special district financing such as Mello-Roos and the use of the alternative method of levying development fees and exactions should be recognized. "It is important to understand that the driving force behind the proliferation of dependent special districts is the growing use of development or annexation agreements that establish the infrastructure responsibility of developers. The dependent special district is only a device that, by lower financing costs, makes exactions less painful for the developer."[38] As will be discussed later, the use of development fees can be an effective method of financing public libraries; however, it is in most cases a more expensive method than the use of the Mello-Roos district. While the two approaches are similar, one advantage of the Mello-Roos district is the tax-exempt nature of the special tax bonds. "A [jurisdiction], through its community facilities district, can borrow money at a lower interest rate, with tax-exempt bonds, than a developer can at the local bank."[39] Since the developer's costs are generally passed on to the prospective homeowner in the development in the form of higher housing costs, the homeowner will have to borrow even more money and must pay higher mortgage rates from commercial banks than the rates for the Mello-Roos bonds. Further, "unlike the use of developer's fees, Mello-Roos financing makes it possible to amortize the cost of infrastructure improvements over their useful life."[40] The special tax may be collected annually for 20 years or more to pay for the facility on a "pay as you use" basis instead of collecting it all up front in the form of a "pay as you go" development fee.

In many ways, the Mello-Roos special district financing approach benefits both local jurisdictions and developers. This symbiotic relationship is becoming more common as developers and local jurisdictions struggle to prosper and grow, and meet the demands for public improvements. While Mello-Roos districts are most commonly used with completely undeveloped land, there is another form of district financing that meets the needs of local jurisdictions and developers in areas that have already been developed but have fallen into disrepair. These districts are commonly known as redevelopment districts and they are created by redevelopment authorities or agencies.

Redevelopment Agencies

In many states, community redevelopment laws allow local jurisdictions to create redevelopment agencies and, subsequently, redevelopment districts. These districts encompass areas considered "blighted" or economically depressed. The intent is to stimulate private development by providing new public improvements that will help create an economic recovery. Clearly, this method is strongly rooted in the concept of public-private partnership which results in increased tax revenues for local jurisdictions as well as increased profitability for developers and other entrepreneurs. Local jurisdictions may assist private development through redevelopment districts in any number of ways, providing improved streets, lighting, water, and sewer services in addition to public buildings which may include cultural facilities like public libraries. The purpose of the public development is to attract private developers who will agree to build major private facilities such as hotels, banks, retail stores, and residential areas in the district.

While these districts can be established anywhere redevelopment is needed, they are usually located in centralized, downtown settings in need of and suitable for substantial projects. One of the most valuable commodities that a jurisdiction can provide the private sector in a redevelopment action is land. Often land within the redevelopment district is already owned by the local jurisdiction, but if not, redevelopment agencies in most states do have the power to acquire land by the use of eminent domain. Local jurisdictions can leverage the ownership of land in redevelopment districts by selling or leasing the land to developers, participating in the lease-purchase agreements for buildings, selling air rights, or other agreements made with private developers. In any case, the ultimate goal is to improve the local economy and increase tax revenues.

Although a redevelopment agency is a separate public entity, in many cases the governing board of the local jurisdiction also governs the agency, although sometimes the redevelopment agency has a separate board appointed by the governing board of the jurisdiction. In order to form a redevelopment district, a redevelopment agency must create a comprehensive plan for the property within the district boundaries. The boundaries of the district are frequently set not only to include the blighted areas, but also to maximize potential revenues, which means that the inclusion of commercial properties is generally preferred. In most states, the redevelopment plan includes showing how the plan dovetails with the general community plan as well as describing the impact of the district on surrounding areas. Usually, a public hearing is held to discuss the plan and obtain community input as well as debate the purpose of the redevelopment district and the financing methods to be used.

Tax Increment Financing (TIF)

The method most often used to finance the public improvements in a redevelopment district is called tax increment financing (TIF). While it varies from state to state, TIF can be used by most local jurisdictions including special districts. Under certain circumstances, sales tax increments can be used in California by redevelopment agencies; however, in most states (including California), property taxes form the basis of tax increment financing. When a redevelopment district is established, the tax revenues collected in the district are frozen in order to form a base level or base year. In most cases, the assessed property tax values are low in the base year since the area is economically disadvantaged. Once the public and private capital investments are built in the district, the economy is stimulated and increases in tax revenues are realized because of increased property values as well as enhanced commercial activity. In theory, the redevelopment project pays for itself. Any increase in revenues over the baseline is the tax increment, which is used to pay for the public improvements. This tax increment can be used in a number of ways to pay for the capital investments, depending upon statutory authority in any given state. The most common way is to use the tax increment to make the payments on

tax allocation bonds; however, the tax increment can be used to make payments against a lease agreement which is financed by the use of lease revenue bonds or certificates of participation.

Tax Allocation Bonds

While redevelopment statutes vary from state to state, a referendum is usually not required for a redevelopment agency to take on debt. Generally, this can be done with the approval of the governing board of the redevelopment agency and/or the local jurisdiction. Because it is uncertain that redevelopment projects will generate enough revenue to pay off indebtedness, and because the full taxing authority of the jurisdiction does not back the tax allocation bonds, the investment is somewhat more risky, and therefore the interest on bonds or certificates of participation issued by redevelopment agencies is usually higher than on general obligation bonds. However, redevelopment districts can be particularly helpful if a jurisdiction has reached its debt limit. "Because tax allocation bonds are a debt only of the redevelopment agency and not the surrounding city or county, local public officials can use tax allocation bonds to diversify their debt structure and relieve an excessive debt burden the general fund of the city or county may otherwise incur."[41]

Tax increment financing was first introduced in California in 1952, but it was not vigorously pursued until relatively recently. "Since the passage of Proposition 13 in California, tax increment financing has been widely used in California to support the issuance of revenue bonds to finance a wide variety of community improvements. Tax increment financing is also authorized and used in at least 25 states."[42] Financing public infrastructure through tax increment financing is somewhat like pulling oneself up by one's own bootstraps. The local jurisdiction invests substantial capital in a depressed area and hopes the increased economic activity will pay for the improvements. It follows that public improvements built as part of a redevelopment project should be as supportive of private development as possible. Public libraries work well since it is generally accepted that they attract people to wherever they are located, particularly if they are located near retail shopping outlets and business centers.

Sacramento Public Library

Over the years, public libraries have been included as part of redevelopment projects in many parts of the country. A 1986 study in California identified over 20 public library construction projects that had been built as part of a redevelopment district.[43] Further, the recently constructed main library in Sacramento is an example of participation in a redevelopment district with the use of TIF. A one-block area of downtown was converted from "blight" into an addition and renovation of the existing library building and construction of a parking garage as well as a multi-story office tower. Various developers bid for the project, and the successful developer signed a design development agreement with the redevelopment agency to design and built the entire development, including the library. The redevelopment agency retained approval rights over the design and supervised the construction. While this approach may not provide as much administrative control over a project as more traditional methods of project management, the citizens of Sacramento now have a greatly improved central library building. In this case, tax allocation bonds were sold and the tax increment is paying for the development as are parking fees generated by the parking garage.

Infrastructure Financing Districts

The use of tax increment financing for developing public infrastructure is not limited to redevelopment districts. California Government Code 53395 et seq. provides for the formation of infrastructure financing districts (IFDs) to develop land that is undeveloped, while redevelopment districts are used to redevelop previously developed land. One of the main problems with the use of TIF is that conflicts can occur between redevelopment agencies and other local jurisdictions regarding the loss of the tax increment once the redevelopment district has been formed. However,

> The IFD is not a new kind of redevelopment agency. For example, when redevelopment is involved, the tax increment can include those taxes that normally would have gone to other taxing entities such as school districts and the county. Conflicts often arise between the redevelopment agency and the affected taxing entities over the loss of taxes by those agencies. This cannot happen in a IFD. IFD law provides that each of the other taxing agencies must grant its approval before any of its portion of the increment can be collected by the IFD.[44]

Further, differences include the fact that IFDs do not have the power of eminent domain like redevelopment agencies, and an approval by either registered voters or landowners is required to establish the IFD.

IFDs may be used to purchase, construct, expand, or rehabilitate various types of public facilities including public libraries (California Government Code section 53395.3). These facilities must be able to provide benefits beyond the borders of the IFD, so public libraries, particularly regional branches and central buildings, are eligible since they generally provide community-wide benefit. Public libraries financed as part of an IFD must not replace existing facilities; however, it is interesting to note that a library financed by an IFD does not have to be located within the district. The method of establishing an IFD is similar to that of a Mello-Roos district, as are the voting procedures. Since the act is new, the author has not been able to identify any

Fig. 6-7. Sacramento Public Library, California (©Jeff Goldberg/Esto)

public library projects financed using an IFD. It is likely that this will change as local officials learn how to exploit this new financing method.

Rehabilitation Districts

While not so new, rehabilitation districts offer an alternative for public libraries that need some retrofit for a specific purpose. Some states have statutes that allow the establishment of rehabilitation districts to finance specific improvements for public buildings such as seismic improvements, geologic hazards, energy conservation, enhancement of electronic technologies, historic preservation, or for general improvement. Statutes for these kinds of programs vary widely from state to state and the availability of funds is often tied to the major public concern of the moment. Local jurisdictions should monitor their state legislature and bond ballot measures for possible appropriations of this kind.

One such statute with a fairly broad scope in terms of retrofit is California's Community Rehabilitation District Law of 1985 (California Government Code section 53370 et seq.). This statute provides a method for local jurisdictions to finance the rehabilitation, renovation, repair or restoration of specific types of public facilities, including public libraries. The law allows various financing methods including special assessments, special taxes, fees or charges, and senior obligation bonds. "Senior obligation bonds are very similar to tax allocation bonds because both are primarily secured by a portion of the property tax collected."[45] However, a major advantage of senior obligation bonds in California is that they require approval only by a simple majority of voters as opposed to the normal two-thirds supermajority. Because of the supermajority requirement, local jurisdictions in California have found it necessary to look at many alternate methods of financing capital improvement projects like public libraries. Further, methods that don't require a referendum, such as the implementation of development fees, have gained momentum in recent years.

Development Fees and Exactions

Because of the recent shift away from using general funds to finance infrastructure, many jurisdictions have implemented financing methods that require those directly benefiting from the needed public improvements to pay for them. This is done through special assessments, special taxes, user fees, or development fees and exactions. Development fees and exactions have become increasingly popular because they permit a jurisdiction to require those involved in the growth of an area to pay for the cost of developing the infrastructure needed to support the growth. This approach is usually used when a large tact of land is being planned for development by a large development firm or group of developers. Instead of the local jurisdiction paying for the necessary public improvements from the existing tax base, a fee is assessed on the new development to finance the public facilities needed to serve the development. This approach is most commonly used with very large developments such as planned cities or large subdivisions of tract housing, although it can also be used with commercial developments of office buildings, retail shopping centers, and even industrial developments.

Some local jurisdictions have no viable alternative to development fees except imposing a moratorium on development. This is certainly not of benefit to either developers or consumers who wish to locate in the area. Development fees are a unique way of addressing infrastructure needs caused by high growth. These fees are not to be confused with special assessments, although there are some similarities (particularly with the San Diego facility benefit assessments which require the payment of the assessment in lump sum at the time the developer obtains the building permit). Development fees are not special taxes or general taxes, since they are paid only once upon obtaining some form of development approval. In fact, they are not taxes at all since they are "voluntary" fees paid by a developer. It is argued that development is voluntary; that the developer is not *required* to develop property and therefore, must be willing to pay a fee for the privilege of developing their property. Establishing development fees does not require a referendum by the electorate nor does it require the approval of landowners (although there are frequently negotiations with the development community during the process). Development fees are established by ordinance or regulatory action of a local government and usually only imposed in high-growth areas.

Generally, the use of development fees and exactions is directly proportional to the rate of growth in a jurisdiction as well as the state. Development fees and exactions are allowed in the vast majority of states, but their use is particularly prominent in California, Florida, Texas, Oregon, Washington, Colorado, Arizona, Nevada, Virginia, Minnesota, New York, and some other states. Areas with the highest growth rate also tend to have the highest development fees. For example, in some areas of California, it is not uncommon for the development fee assessed on a single residential unit to run as high as $10,000 to $20,000 or more. Obviously, there must be a very strong demand for housing in order for a market to withstand such high fees. Where this kind of demand is not present, the use of development fees and exactions will be greatly diminished or nonexistent. Development fees are most common in areas that are having difficulty paying for infrastructure through more traditional methods and have had to look at new options to keep up with growth in their communities.

Because of increasing infrastructure financing pressures, many communities have been forced to use development exactions. Exactions can be land, a building, streets (including paving, lighting, curbs and gutters, signalization, etc.), water and sewer lines, or cash contributions to provide any other public improvements that will ultimately be transferred to the local jurisdiction and used for the good of the "users" of the new development. The method is most commonly identified with housing developments, where the local government imposes exactions or fees as a precondition for approval of the subdivision plan, although the approach is also used with commercial developments. Development exactions include development fees or impact fees since paying a fee is just another form of donation or contribution by the developer to obtain the local jurisdiction's approval of the planned development. However, for the sake of simplicity and because of common usage, the term *exaction* will be used to describe some form of in-kind contribution of real property by the developer and the term *fee* will be used for a cash payment required of the developer.

Development exactions in the form of land or facility contributions preceded the introduction of cash fees. The earliest and most common exactions are land and essential public improvements such as streets and sewer and water lines. One of the major problems with the use of exactions is that they are essentially in-kind contributions by the developer and difficult to quantify. It is hard to verify if they are being applied evenly and fairly to all developers. Since exactions are frequently negotiated on an individual basis, their application can create uncertainty for the developer as well as the potential for inequities. "Because the developer may not know in advance what exactions will be required for a specific project, requirements for exactions may make or break a project."[46] Since developers are always trying to reduce the risk of failure for projects, they are usually receptive to anything that decreases uncertainty. The use of development or impact fees is a way to increase certainty since their application is usually quantifiable and arrived at in some manner that can easily be calculated into the cost of the project. Instead of negotiating with the local jurisdiction over land and the construction of various facilities, the developer can apply the development impact fee formula that has been established by ordinance or regulation, and determine with a reasonable degree of confidence what the cash contribution will have to be in order to obtain approval of the project.

The idea of contributing cash in lieu of real property exactions is a relatively recent phenomenon. In essence, developers pay a fee for the infrastructure necessary to support the planned development and in exchange they receive approval of the development and greater certainty that the project will proceed in a reasonable and profitable manner. The local jurisdiction deposits this money into an account separate from the general fund and then constructs the public improvements specified in the fee assessment formula. Some communities integrate the use of development fees and exactions or leave some flexibility in the process if the developer prefers to donate land or construct some of the public improvements in lieu of fees. Whether fees, exactions, or both are used, the local jurisdiction must be able to demonstrate that the contributions do not exceed a reasonable cost of providing the specified improvements. "While the details of the standards may differ somewhat from state to state, many states have judicial or statutory criteria that set out the broad principles by which to assess the reasonableness of the connection between what is being exacted and what is needed in the way of public facilities to serve the new development."[47]

Direct Linkage: Reasonable, Equitable, and Proportional

In most states, local jurisdictions derive their power to implement development fees and exactions through their "police power" to regulate land use usually granted in the state constitution and/or statutes which provide authority to approve or disapprove new developments based on their impact on the public good. This authority varies to some extent but is present in some form in most states. "As a general rule, if the local government has the power to deny a project, then it also has the power to approve it subject to conditions that mitigate the reason for denial."[48] Herein lies the genesis of development fees and exactions. However, while local jurisdictions usually have the authority to impose fees and exactions, they cannot do so arbitrarily. The imposition of fees and exactions must be reasonable, equitable, proportional, and fair. There must be a direct relationship between the proposed development and the needed infrastructure. Further, there must be a reasonable and objective method of assessing the cost of providing the needed public improvements, and finally, jurisdictions may not assess fees that are higher than what is needed to provide the designated public improvements for the development.

It can be argued that the general concept of development fees is equitable because it requires those who are enjoying the benefits of new development to pay for the public services necessary to support it. But how does a jurisdiction equitably assess a fee to fairly cover the costs of the public improvements? In order to determine the amount of the fee, in most states, it is necessary to develop a specific plan for developing public facilities in the district. The plan will consist of a listing of all the public facilities needed, their size, and a cost estimate as well as a schedule for when each facility must be built. Based on this plan, the total amount of funding needed to build the public facilities over the duration of the development may be calculated.

Once this overall cost figure is known, a method for assessing the development fee must be created. Development fees may be based on any number of criteria, including the gross square footage of the project under development, the amount of acreage required, the amount of vehicular traffic the development will generate, or simply the number of land parcels under development. The actual amount of these fees will vary from several hundred to potentially thousands of dollars, depending on the cost of the public facilities needed as well as the number and type of units in the development.

For housing developments, the fee is frequently based on the number of parcels under development. For example, if the total public facilities capital cost to support a 5,000-unit tract housing development is $15 million, then the assessment per unit will be $3,000. Generally, the assessment is collected by the local governing agency when the building permit for each house is granted to the developer. As the development grows, the fees for public facilities are collected. The public facilities can be scheduled and built on a "pay as you go" basis. This allows for phasing of the public improvements, with streets, water, and sewer going in first and other facilities such as police and fire stations and public libraries built later. The problem is that these services may be provided much later than desirable because of the lag in the collection of fees. This can be avoided by the use of a debt instrument that is guaranteed by the revenue stream generated by the collection of development fees over a number of years. This allows for the public infrastructure to be built "up front" instead of waiting a number of years in some cases. However, the approach of borrowing against the anticipated collection of development fees is not widely accepted since the revenue stream is so unstable and vulnerable to changes in economic conditions.

Types of Facilities Financed

As discussed, in the early years of applying development fees and exactions, jurisdictions usually demanded assistance with only a relatively limited number of public improvements like streets, water and sewer lines, etc. However, it became obvious that these limited fees were not truly covering the cost of all of the public infrastructure needed to serve the new inhabitants of the development. "In the past, cities and counties have, to a certain extent, subsidized new development by installing infrastructure or by charging impact fees that did not pay for the entire cost of the infrastructure necessitated by the project."[49] Local jurisdictions began demanding more fees for any number of public service improvements needed to reasonably serve the new inhabitants. "The courts generally have placed no restrictions on the type of infrastructure that can be financed with development fees as long as that infrastructure is needed to serve the new development."[50] Further, as long as a reasonable link can be made between the public improvement and the development, the assessment of a fee is likely to be legally defensible. In many communities, development fees are collected in order to build parks, police and fire stations, schools, child care centers, public libraries, museums, and other cultural facilities. However, this "social infrastructure"[51] is more commonly financed in communities where the demand for new development is high.

Public libraries fall into a subset of "social infrastructure" called "intellectual infrastructure"[52] which includes public schools and cultural facilities. It is becoming obvious that a well-educated and informed workforce is necessary to support development of desirable high-tech industries in today's information-oriented economy. Public libraries help to provide this support as well as generally improve the quality of life in a community. Financing public library facilities through the use of development fees may well serve to further attract highly desirable private sector investment in both commercial developments and infrastructure in a progressive community.

Public Libraries Financed with Development Fees and Exactions

In several states where the demand for development has been high, such as California, Florida, and Colorado, the use of development fees and exactions for public libraries has started to take hold. Riverside County, California has financed public libraries in part with development fees in Moreno Valley and Temecula and is in the process of collecting fees for libraries in the community of Jurupa. The city of Chula Vista, California, is in the process of designing the South Chula Vista branch library, which will be financed by development fees combined with a state grant for public library construction. In Naples, Florida, the Collier County Public Library has been able to finance part of the new main library headquarters building along with several branches with development

Fig. 6-8. South Chula Vista Library, Chula Vista, CA

fees, and five more projects are currently in their capital improvement plan (CIP) to be funded entirely with impact fees. In Collier County's case, the county is able to borrow capital from local banks to build the library facilities, and the loan is guaranteed by the revenue stream from the development fees. The developers pay a fee of $180 per residential unit when the building permit is pulled. This fee is based upon a local 1988 impact fee ordinance that uses a formula of .33 square feet per capita for public library space requirements. There are many examples of the use of development impact fees around the country, but the fol-

lowing case study in Colorado provides an interesting perspective on the issue of equity participation which is a central issue in the use of these fees.

Loveland, Colorado: In the early eighties, the city of Loveland, Colorado, adopted a comprehensive development impact fee ordinance that resulted in the partial funding of a central public library facility. Loveland uses a capital expansion fee (CEF) approach to address the equity participation issue by allowing a developer to "buy into" infrastructure projects that will serve the residents of the new development.

These facilities may be either existing or planned for construction. The following description demonstrates how the application of the CEFs were to be used in concept to build a library in Loveland:

The 1983 cost of a new 30,000-square-foot library designed to serve 69,800 residents is $3,354,000. The new library replaces an obsolete one that has served the 32,700 existing residents. Thus, the city considers 43 percent of the cost, or $1,571,300, as replacement or betterment costs that primarily benefit existing residents. The cost of expanding the capital facility over and above what is needed to serve existing residents is $1,782,700. Since the community plan assumes that about 37,000 people will move into the community within the planning period, and since the library is designed to serve only the current residents and the 37,000 new residents, the city does not adjust capital expansion costs by the value of remaining excess capacity or under capacity at the end of the planning period. Furthermore, the project probably will not receive external funds, so the plan calls for no additional adjustment. The net growth-related costs of the library are therefore $1,782,700. Since only occupants of residences are expected to use the library, the plan allocates 100 percent of the cost to the residential sector. The CEF per dwelling unit is $121.

CEF Calculation Process: Library Example

Total capital costs from CIP	$3,354,000
Less: Replacement and betterment costs	
$\dfrac{32,700}{69,800} \times 3,354,000 =$	$1,571,300
Capital expansion costs	$1,782,700
plus/minus: value of excess/ under capacity	0
Expansion-related costs	$1,782,700
less: external funding sources	0
Net expansion-related costs	$1,782,700
times: portion of sector benefits (100% residential)	
Residential sector costs:	$1,782,700
divided by: capacity in units	14,700
CEF fee per unit	$ 121[53]

Unfortunately for Loveland, the anticipated growth did not occur as projected and only $180,000 in development impact fees was collected for the project. The building was ultimately built and financed from these fees plus funds obtained from the sale of the existing library building. The remaining funding came from the proceeds generated by the sale of general obligation bonds. Regardless, conceptually the Loveland approach provides a good example of a development fee that is based on careful planning and recognizes the importance of fairly distributing the fee according to a reasonable linkage to the impact created by each development without overcharging for existing deficiencies in infrastructure.

Rational Nexus and Fees for Off-Site Improvements

Along with showing linkage between the growth caused by new development and the infrastructure that the fee will pay for, the rational nexus test also requires the designers of the fee to demonstrate that the development is paying a proportional share of the costs of the needed infrastructure. The rational nexus test was established by the U.S. Supreme Court's *Nolland v. California Coastal Commission* 107 S.Ct. 3141 [1987]. It requires that the new development participate equitably in financing infrastructure needed to serve it, but pay no more than its require share. This is true whether or not the needed infrastructure is on-site (within the boundaries of the development) or off-site (elsewhere in the community.). In short,

. . . a development could be required to provide facilities needed by it and other developments as long as its participation was limited to a proportionate share. This is the rational nexus test which has gradually come to be embraced by virtually all state court systems as the standard of reasonableness for development exactions. The emphasis in the rational nexus test on the idea of proportional participation in shared-use facilities is the dimension that makes possible the increasing use of impact fees, since most of their applicability is to facilities needed to serve many developments.[54]

When considering the validity of development fees, courts also consider the quality of the plan developed to support the fee structure. The plan itself can forge the link between the fee, the development, and the needed infrastructure.

A number of factors determine the establishment of a valid impact fee.

The structure and design of an impact fee ordinance will continue to be of prime importance in the determination of its validity. Factors that are important in devising an ordinance include its relationship to a comprehensive plan and capital improvements program, techniques for discounting other forms of development contributions from impact fees, a method for defining development impacts and service standards, designation of service areas, and a system for collecting and administering revenues.[55]

Planning the needed infrastructure based on specific service areas and standards is extremely important for any type of needed public improvement including libraries if the development fee ordinance is to stand up in court. In order to ensure equity, the method of determining the development fee for each and every potential project should be standardized. The community must accurately determine the size of the building and the cost of a project which is to be financed with development fees. For libraries, this may be done on an appropriate service standard basis such as so many square feet per capita, readers' seats per capita, books per capita, etc., or on a more sophisticated planning basis using a needs assessment, facilities master plan, and even a building program to determine the size and service requirements of library facilities.

While many public libraries built with development fees are branch libraries that serve specific new developments, it is important to understand that such fees can help pay for larger regional and central library facilities as was the case in Loveland. Any development may have an impact on community's public facilities beyond the area of that development. For example, if it can be demonstrated that a development will have an impact on the community's main sewer system beyond what can be absorbed by facilities in the immediate area, it is possible to increase the development fee to help pay for the expansion of the main sewer treatment plant and a main trunk line which will serve several developing areas of a community. As another example, a developer may be assessed not only a fee for a local park within the confines of the proposed development but also a fee for a regional park which may be miles from the development but will be used to some extent by the development's inhabitants. As in the case of Loveland, this approach can be generalized to many public improvements, including public library facilities.

Conceptually, if regional and central sewer systems, water systems, major arterial streets, and other public improvements can be financed from development fees, there is no reason that regional and central library facilities cannot be funded with development fees as well. Just as a central water system distributes a necessary product through a hierarchical system, public library buildings can be seen as a system or network for the distribution of information. Regardless of the distribution medium—paper-based or electronic—it is not unreasonable to argue that new development should pay a fair share of the enhancement of these facilities at a regional and central level. The difficulty is not in the extension of the argument, but in the assessment method. In other words, how does one determine the costs in an equitable manner?

It is simply a matter of analyzing the costs of all of the facilities and equipment in a library system and developing a formula that can be demonstrated to provide the cost on a per-capita or per-residence basis. This formula can then be used for collecting development fees to construct, expand, or remodel regional or central library buildings in addition to the branch libraries serving specific local service areas under development. While it is unlikely that development fees could be used to completely finance all needed facilities of a library system, their collection could obviously be of tremendous assistance in paying for the facility needs caused by the new growth, particularly in high growth areas.

Because of rational nexus, the importance of developing a facilities master plan for public libraries is evident when development fees are to be used. The importance of good planning should be self-evident in any case, given the costs of public facilities and the difficulty in finding funds for infrastructure. However, the rigor which must be applied with the use of development fees may be avoided if a development agreement is used in lieu of a broad-based development fee ordinance. This is because development agreements do not require a precise linkage or proportionality between the development and the proposed public facility, as development fees do. In short, development agreements allow a great deal more flexibility for the local jurisdiction to "wheel and deal" with the private sector.

Development Agreements

Many jurisdictions have turned to the use of development agreements which provide a legal mechanism for negotiating development deals with the private sector. Development agreements have been used for some time as a negotiating tool between redevelopment agencies and developers. However, recently in states where there is a statutory basis, development agreements have become a viable,

even desirable, method of negotiating contracts between local jurisdictions and private developers for the purpose of providing new growth on previously undeveloped land. California was the first state to provide legislation that specifically authorized development agreements (California Government Code section 65864 et seq.), while Florida provided similar legislation in 1986 (Florida Government Code section 163.3220 et seq.). Because of their popularity in California and Florida, similar legislation may occur in other states in the future.

Development agreements allow local jurisdictions to negotiate with developers for a mutually beneficial agreement regarding the development of land within the jurisdiction's regulatory control. These agreements enable developers to reduce risk by establishing a specific set of ground rules for the proposed development. In a development agreement the local jurisdiction assures the developer that the development will be approved under the land-use rules, regulations, and ordinances existing at the time of the agreement, in some cases with assurance that the development can proceed (providing the developer with a vested right for the development) as agreed to in the development agreement. In return for this approval, the developer agrees to provide the jurisdiction with specific benefits in the form of exactions, dedications, contributions, or fees for public infrastructure. The developer has bought predictability, and to the extent possible in real estate development, probability that the project will go forward. The jurisdiction gains all kinds of potential benefits — from expanded water and sewer plants to golf courses and public libraries, for example.

The development agreement freezes land-use regulations so the developer is off the hook for any future changes as long as development is completed before the end of the term of the agreement. This is particularly important for large developments that have several phases and will take years to complete. By reducing the risk, and thereby insuring the project's profitability, the developer can provide sometimes very significant public improvements. In some cases, development agreements are subject to repeal by referendum; however, this process is difficult and unlikely unless there is considerable rancor over the agreement. If the political environment is stable regarding development, and the development agreement is well negotiated, the benefits obtained for the public sector can be quite amazing. This is particularly true in hot development markets where developers are particularly eager to strike a deal and get their project underway.

Because the development is assured, it is frequently possible to build the public improvements at the beginning of the project. They may then be enjoyed immediately instead of waiting for many years for enough development fees to accrue to finance construction. Further, because of the reduction in risk, the project may be more comprehensive and better planned because the local jurisdiction's planning staff will have input into the project in the early planning stages. This process of early review and planning means that needed infrastructure can be clearly defined and agreed upon in advance of any development. While still controversial in many communities, development agreements provide a basis for a cooperative, nonadversarial relationship between developers and local jurisdictions. They allow both sides to come together to plan, define responsibilities, and negotiate to provide desirable growth for a community while also finding a way to fund needed infrastructure to support that growth.

Development agreements require local jurisdictions and developers to sit down and bargain in good faith. Both sides must obtain some benefit and a sense of security from the agreement or it will never be executed. Development agreements can be used in large urban or suburban communities as well as smaller rural areas, but agreements in rural areas may become somewhat lopsided toward developers if the community is highly desirous of growth or its negotiation team is not skilled at the art of driving a hard bargain. "In most cases, local governments cannot match the resources and expertise brought to the bargaining process by sophisticated land developers, which may result in development agreements that are badly bargained and badly drafted from the point of view of local government, adjacent and neighboring landowners, and other interested parties."[56] While significant gains can be obtained through the use of development agreements, obviously care must be taken. Preparation is the key. It is usually true that " . . . localities with the most aggressive and knowledgeable staffs win the most favorable and profitable agreements."[57] If this expertise is not available locally, it may be helpful to employ consultants to assist with the negotiation process.

Regardless of the local jurisdiction's expertise, development agreements still may be beneficial because they allow flexibility and the ability to tailor the agreement to specific community problems. "Because development agreements are negotiated on a case-by-case basis, they enable developers and local governments to craft mutually satisfactory arrangements for public facilities and services outside of the local government's general ordinances and formulae for developer exactions."[58] Because development agreements are individualized and negotiations are entered into voluntarily by both parties, the exactions and fees obtained during bargaining do not have to conform to the existing local ordinances. As stated earlier, the rational nexus rule does not apply with development agreements. Local jurisdictions as well as developers are essentially free to bargain for whatever they can get, so the negotiating process can be beneficial to both sides. Both parties can get their most important and pressing needs out on the table, with the opportunity for these needs to be met. Using this process, it is possible for local jurisdictions to obtain exactions on a scale not otherwise possible.

In addition to the number and type of exactions, the method of construction can be negotiated as well. For example, it may be advantageous to the developer to provide in-kind land for a public improvement as well as to build the project for the local jurisdiction. The developer might see this as advantageous because the project could be built quickly and at a lower cost than by paying a fee. However, care must be taken to make certain that quality control safeguards are in place.

Many issues must be carefully examined when developing the contract for constructing a public facility. For example, who has control over the site selection? Will the developer be able to select a piece of property on the back side of the development which has poor access, is too small to allow for future expansion of the library, and has a configuration that makes it difficult to build a functional building? Who has control over the development of architectural plans? How is the building to be constructed? Will the developer construct the building in a design/build manner or will it be bid like any other public project? Local contractors are often unhappy when they don't get the opportunity to bid on public projects. Who has construction administration control over the project? In other words, how will quality control be maintained? How will cost overruns be paid and by whom? It is important to specify answers to these issues in the contract so the developer cannot turn over an unsatisfactory building to the public agency. To avoid many of these problems, the architect should usually be the owner's choice, not the developer's. While in some

instances a design/build approach can be effective, it is not generally recommended for public library projects. Further, there should be some form of construction supervision independent of the developer or the result is similar to having the goat guarding the cabbage patch. However, the developer can be the contractor as long as there is adequate monitoring of compliance with contract documents in which all details are spelled out.

Public Libraries Financed by Development Agreements

A number of recent public library buildings have resulted from development agreements. The Carmel Mountain Ranch public library project is a 10,000-square foot-turnkey library provided by a development agreement in the San Diego. Several public library construction projects have benefited from development agreements in Collier County, Florida. In 1981, the Collier North Branch was built on three acres of land obtained through a development agreement. The East Naples Branch, which was partially financed with development impact fees, also received a site of approximately one acre in a shopping center through a development agreement. Further, as part of a development agreement, where the county agreed to maintain roads in a new development, the Marco Island Branch was built upon a development exaction of one and half acres of land. The provision of land is a fairly common development exaction utilized in development agreements, particularly if the developer is "land rich" but "cash poor."

Oceanside, California: In 1985, the city of Oceanside, California, negotiated a development agreement with Rancho Del Oro Developments covering a 1,900-acre parcel.[59] Under the terms of the agreement, the developer provided the city with exactions relating to street improvements and a park as well as a library/community center. In return, the city promised that specific land-use regulations in place at the time of the agreement would apply to the development for the ten year term of the agreement.

> Pursuant to the Agreement, the Master Developer has contributed $20,000 for fund raising and other purposes related to development of a new City library. If the City decides to construct a library or community facility within the park site, the Master Developer will contribute up to $100,000 for site, planning, and preparation of construction documents.[60]

This development agreement appeared at the time to be a good way to get a new branch in the Rancho Del Oro area, however, because of a last-minute modification of the agreement, a park was built instead of the library. This unfortunate occurrence for the local library supporters points out how fluid and potentially difficult development agreements can be to negotiate. Even after many hours of time and effort, last-minute changes in the agreement can result in the loss of a project. This fact can be seen as well in the following example of a proposed library project in Tucson, Arizona.

Tucson, Arizona: When local jurisdictions are free to strike the best deal possible with local developers using development agreements, these deals may involve financing and constructing significant public library facilities in urban areas. One example of the process of negotiating a private-sector deal with developers is chronicled in the

Fig. 6-9. Tucson-Pima Public Library, Arizona.

1988 article entitled "Public and Private Funding Create a New Library for Tucson."[61] While this project was essentially a redevelopment project, it used many of the negotiation techniques of a development agreement. The citizens of Tucson passed a referendum that included general obligation bond funds for a library. No site had been picked since the city's intent was to use the construction of the new main library to leverage private development in a downtown area. Their goal was to revitalize the downtown area and demonstrate that a successful public-private partnership could be used to meet the needs of a growing Tucson.

The city issued an RFP for the development of a city block within a redevelopment district upon which a central library and parking garage were to be incorporated. The developers were free to propose the best possible development project which would be attractive to them as well as to the city. The city allowed developers to propose different concepts and encouraged innovation.

> Methods of developer participation that were discussed included leasing or selling air rights; a joint financial agreement for financing, construction, and ownership; and a shared use of a parking facility. . . . The city saw substantial benefits to the developer in participating in a joint development with the library. Not only would substantial pedestrian traffic be generated, but a primary and stable occupant for nearly 100,000 square feet within the development would be provided. In addition, the private tenants would have access to the resources of a major public library.[62]

The city's staff committee, which was chaired by the library director with a subcommittee of the library advisory board, established selection criteria and evaluated the proposals.

Three development proposals were submitted in response to the RFP. After considerable review and revisions, a proposal was accepted "in principle," and the city staff once again set about negotiating the final agreement. An extremely complex and innovative agreement created a package deal that met the needs of the city and the developer. Its utilized exotic financing mechanisms including the sale and leaseback of city-owned buildings to the Tucson Local Development Corporation (a quasi-public/nonprofit corporation). Since state law required the city of Tucson to maintain control over the design and construction of the library, the city proceeded with the construction of the library financed by $15 million in general obligation bonds. In this case, this was probably fortunate, since the development surrounding the library ultimately failed to proceed.

Although the deal fell apart, the main lesson to be learned here is that libraries can be a strong economic and political incentive for private development. This fact must, however, be tempered with the realization that a tremendous amount of staff time and effort can go into creating a development agreement for naught. Economic realities can change as the agreement is being negotiated. Regardless of this fact, it may be in the best interests of a community and the library to explore the many possibilities available in urban areas where the value of land is high and where developers can be enticed into a public-private partnership with the carrot of the development rights to the land.

Public-Private Partnerships

This country has a long history of private- and public- sector cooperation in the building of infrastructure.

> Creating and maintaining a community are two tasks requiring a joint effort of the public with the private development sector. In theory, the private sector builds communities, while the public sector regulates building and supports it with public

facilities and services. Like most theories, however, this one is overly simple. Often, developers and communities join forces to build public/private projects, just as private developers finance and construct an increasing number of sorely needed public facilities.[63]

While both the public and private sectors have their own traditional roles and perspectives, there are times when they have mutual interests that can be satisfied by working together. "A public-private partnership is any mutually beneficial activity undertaken by government and business to solve community problems that yield benefits to both the private interest and community at large."[64] The trick is to identify areas of mutual benefit through negotiation and then bargain to a "private-sector deal." The process of public- and private-sector bargaining not only identifies the potential opportunities, but it also establishes the limitations. Once a potential project has been identified as desirable and feasible, the process of negotiation tends to bind the two sectors together because it creates a strong vested interest in the project.

Public-private partnerships make many people nervous because of reasonable concerns over the potential conflict of interest between a public agency fulfilling its role as land-use regulator while in effect entering the land development marketplace and acting like a private developer. Further, some citizens feel that such deals are tantamount to dealing with the devil. While prudence is required, it is not impossible to overcome these concerns with careful planning and adequate oversight by the citizenry. Further, it must be recognized that in some communities entering into public-private partnerships may be the only way to provide the needed infrastructure because of fiscal limitations imposed through declining general revenues or debt-limit restrictions. Once the initial resistance to dealing with the private sector is overcome, public officials and citizens often come to realize that this method can be extremely profitable for all concerned.

It has been recognized for years that public agencies can become involved in private profit-making activities in numerous ways. Angus Snead MacDonald, in his pamphlet *Morrow's Library*, discussed the idea of a public jurisdiction constructing with public funds a library building that was larger than needed and then renting prime commercial space in the building to private concerns. The income stream could help support either the operation of the library or help retire the debt on the building. This approach was summarized in the following example:

> 20,000 square feet was leased to an international commercial organization. The rental paid, after deducting operating expenses with taxes on the rented area, will amortize the cost of the entire building within twenty years. Then the library will have the whole building free and clear for its own expansion or to increase its operating income. Meanwhile the ground floor . . . accommodates a busy regional branch on a valuable site that would have been inadequately improved with a one-story building.[65]

While relatively few local jurisdictions have taken this advice, some have allowed private developers to assume the risk. In essence, in exchange for a new or improved library building, the local jurisdiction barters the use of available land along with the resulting improvements constructed on it by the developer. The developer then obtains a revenue stream from the lease payments for the additional space from commercial outlets or offices. Assuming the economy remains sound, the developer makes a profit as well as paying back the principal plus interest to the investors.

Profit Sharing

Some communities have taken this approach one step further and started participating in the profits for the development. This can be done by the developer paying an agreed upon portion of the profits from the development to the local jurisdiction as part of the purchase price for the sale of land to the developer. In this manner, the public agency participates in the project's profit potential, but it may also to some extent be exposed to the risks. While the uncertainty, and resulting risk, in the revenue stream for any development project is a major concern for both the developer and the public agency involved, the risks can sometimes be minimized if the local jurisdiction is willing to allow its profits to be secondary to the developer's. In this manner, the public agency can insulate itself from any risk of loss but still participate in profits if the revenue stream generated by the development is substantial enough and surplus income is available after the developer takes the profits due.

In most of these private-sector deals, the public agency's ownership of land is the primary driver. Because land is a commodity developers can't get enough of, public agencies can use the sale or lease of land as leverage in negotiating a development agreement. In communities where undeveloped (or underdeveloped) land is the biggest asset, this approach can become a very significant method of developing public infrastructure. In addition to the outright sale of the land, many local jurisdictions negotiate long-term leases for its use by private developers. With "participating leases," the public agency can participate in the profitability of the development just as when the property is sold to the developer, but, with this approach when the lease expires the public agency still owns the land as well as the improvements on it. This form of equity participation is becoming an extremely beneficial revenue-generating mechanism used most frequently in relatively hot development markets where the income stream generated is substantial enough to provide an adequate return on investment. Along with these creative profit-sharing financing methods, local jurisdictions have used their regulatory powers over land development to leverage the building of public projects through the transfer of development rights.

Air Rights and the Transfer of Development Rights

In urban areas, where land-use regulations have become complex and restrictive, the sale and transfer of development rights can be used to finance a public library project by providing an incentive for private developers. The right to develop land is one of the rights of ownership; however, the manner in which land is developed is often limited by local zoning requirements. Along with determining how the surface of land will be developed, land-use regulations often extend to how the "layers" above and below the property can be developed. The right to develop the space over a parcel of land is an air right, and in urban areas where land is very expensive and development regulations are restrictive, the sale or lease of air rights for the construction of physical improvements can be very lucrative.

In addition to understanding that the right to develop space over (or under) a parcel of land can be sold or leased to a developer, it is also important to understand that the right to develop land can be transferred from one parcel of land to another in some jurisdictions. In other words, if a piece of property is underdeveloped compared to what it could be under existing zoning ordinances, and the owner has no plans to develop the land in the future, the owner can sell the development rights to another landowner whose property has already reached the allowable limits of development. Sometimes this transfer of development rights is limited to adjacent parcels of land, but not always. In any event, the transfer of development rights can include air rights or any other form of development right. In urban areas, these transfers of development rights (TDRs), along with the sale or lease of air rights, can become extremely complex particularly when public property is involved.

Here is an opportunity for public library construction projects which library planners often overlook. In many urban areas, public libraries were built years ago on downtown sites that are extremely valuable today, and are frequently underdeveloped based on current zoning ordinances. These buildings, or more precisely, the land under them and the associated development rights, can be used as a tremendous incentive for public-private partnerships that can result not only in expanded economic development for a community, but also the possibility for a new or greatly expanded public library facility. A prime example of this is the expansion of the Central Library of the Los Angeles Public Library.

Los Angeles

The recent improvement of the Los Angeles Public Library's Central Library includes renovating the existing central library (the Goodhue building) and constructing an eight-story wing called the East Wing. In addition, the central library project included restoration of a garden, acquisition and refurbishment of an off-site parking garage, and acquisition of library furnishings and equipment including the installation of an automated catalog system. The East Wing building was constructed immediately adjacent to the Goodhue building and the two buildings will provide 530,000 square feet of public library space.

The project was financed and administered under a complex series of agreements between the city, a public corporation, a redevelopment agency, and a developer. When the project was first envisioned, it was designed to be self-funded through a number of creative financing techniques.

While for various reasons the project was not ultimately self-funded, it did involve the transfer of development rights from the library site to the site of a private developer. The library project was not planned to be built up to the maximum floor-area ratio (FAR) allowed for the parcel, and therefore the site's development rights were underutilized and available for transfer to another site. A nearby developer was interested in acquiring the development rights in order to build a larger project which was in the planning stages and paid $50 million for that privilege. Further, in order to get approval for the developer's own project, the developer had to provide a 942-space parking structure. In addition to the $50 million, the agreement was that the developer would construct an underground parking structure for those spaces under the garden on the library site. Further, the developer constructed the landscape improvements above the parking garage using the city's plans and funds. The cost of maintenance will be shared by the city and the developer.

In addition to this sale of development rights, a substantial portion of the overall project was financed with tax allocation bond funds provided by the community redevelopment agency since the library was located in a redevelopment district. Further, the East Wing portion of the project was financed by leasehold revenue bonds sold by the Municipal Improvement Corporation of Los Angeles, a nonprofit public benefit corporation formed by the city. The corporation sold lease revenue bonds and the city subsequently leased the East Wing building from the corporation under a lease-purchase agreement. When the bonds have been retired, the city will be able to purchase the property under the terms of the agreement. The use of a public corporation in conjunction with a lease-purchase agreement was instrumental in financing this project. It is obvious from this example that the use of various forms

Fig. 6-10. Rendering of the Los Angeles Central Public Library Building

of leases is an approach that is growing in importance in financing infrastructure including public libraries.

Leasing

Rather than actually purchasing capital assets, leasing a library building and equipment is another alternative. Besides being more expensive than general obligation bonds, the main disadvantage to leasing facilities is that for the duration of the lease, the facility is not under direct control of the library jurisdiction. This may result in maintenance problems or difficulties with needed improvements since, in effect, the library is a tenant. For this reason, the negotiations of the lease agreement are particularly important in obtaining not only the best financial terms but also provisions regarding the level of utility costs, availability of parking, frequency of required maintenance, etc. For all these reasons, leasing space is usually looked upon as a temporary solution for library facilities until a more permanent arrangement can be made.

The authority for a public agency to use lease financing comes from state statutes that vary from state to state. However, in most cases the ability to use lease financing is based on the local jurisdiction's authority to acquire and dispose of real property rather than its authority to incur debt. In most states, a lease obligation is not considered debt, and the public entity is free from the restrictions inherent in the use of many debt financing instruments, but public agencies must use lease financing prudently. "Whether any lease arrangement is economical depends upon market conditions, the current tax laws, the structure of the lease, and the relative costs of other methods of financing."[66] As will be shown, leasing by public agencies can take a number of forms, but one of the most common is the traditional operating lease.

Operating-Lease Agreements

Leasing space or equipment for public purposes including public libraries, is a way of using the space or equipment without buying it. For years, public libraries have leased photocopy machines, vehicles, and even buildings. In operating-lease agreements, the lessor is responsible for maintaining the equipment and facility as well as any insurance and applicable taxes. With equipment leases, the term of an operating lease is usually relatively short since it may not exceed the useful life of the equipment. In these operating leases or "true leases," the local jurisdiction (the lessee) uses equipment for a period of time and pays rent for it by appropriations from the annual operating budget. At the end of the lease agreement, the equipment returns to the lessor (usually a third party leasing corporation) unless the lessee decides to buy the used equipment at its fair market value at that time. Since the local jurisdiction typically does not obtain ownership of the equipment, the lessor may obtain the tax benefits of ownership. In addition to the tax benefits for the lessor in an operating lease, there are other tax benefits in the use of another form of leasing—the lease-purchase agreement.

Lease-Purchase Agreements

While the IRS does not consider lease-purchase as a true lease, and thus the tax advantages of ownership are not extended, there is one very important tax benefit generated from lease-purchase agreements when public agencies are involved, if the lease payments are provided for bona fide public government functions. When the local jurisdiction obtains ownership of the real property at the end of the term of the agreement, the lease is considered a tax-exempt lease, which means that any interest earned by investors from the proceeds of the lease agreement are tax free. This tax-exempt status results in lower interest rates and a more economical form of financing for governments.

The lease-purchase agreement is the most commonly used form of tax-exempt lease, but it goes by many names including installment sale agreement, conditional sales agreement, and lease-to-own agree-

ment. In a lease-purchase agreement, a public agency leases real property while it is in the process of purchasing it. Ultimately, what happens in a lease-purchase agreement is that the lessor rents or leases real property to the lessee over an agreed-upon period of time, at the end of which the lessee may exercise its option to purchase the property for what is usually a nominal sum (e.g., one dollar). The lease payments are structured so that the amount the lessee pays covers the principal and interests costs for the acquisition or construction of the capital asset being financed. One of the advantages of lease-purchase agreements is that they may be used to acquire not only equipment (including computer equipment) but also land and buildings. Obviously the scale involved in acquiring a multimillion-dollar facility through a lease-purchase agreement is different from acquiring a single piece of equipment, but the concept is essentially the same.

With lease-purchase agreements, the lessor might be a wealthy individual investor or group of investors, a private leasing company, a bank, another public agency such as a redevelopment agency, a nonprofit corporation, a joint powers authority, or other special authority. In any case, with large projects, the lessor must be able to generate considerable capital. Because of the capital needed to finance large projects, lease revenue bonds or certificates of participation are usually the preferred financing methods. These are becoming more commonly used for public libraries and other public infrastructure projects and they will be discussed in more detail in Chapter 3. Regardless of the actual method of financing, public agencies generally utilize lease-purchase agreements because they want to avoid acquiring additional public debt.

Properly structured lease-purchase agreements are not considered public debt in most states, although they may be considered as such by debt-rating companies when the financing securities of the jurisdiction are rated. Lease-purchase agreements do not equal debt because the only obligation of the public entity is to make lease payments from its operating budget and this obligation is not backed by the full faith and credit of the jurisdiction or any other dedicated revenue source. In most states, a lease-purchase agreement will have a nonappropriation clause that terminates the lease-purchase agreement if the local jurisdiction does not allocate funds in its operating budget for the lease payment in any given year. Obviously, the result of a lease-purchase agreement is that a public agency has been able to "borrow" money for public purposes. The investors have taken more risk than with general obligation bonds, because the guarantee of repayment is only as good as the local jurisdiction's ability and willingness to pay.

In other words, if a public facility like a public library is built with a lease-purchase agreement and at some point during the lease period the local funding agency decides that it does not have adequate revenues to meet all its obligations, it may determine that it will no longer honor the terms of the lease agreement or make lease payments. Obviously, this possibility is potentially disastrous not only for the library jurisdiction involved, but also for the project's investors because they no longer have a revenue stream to repay their "loan." These investors may try to repossess the facility from the public agency and then lease the property to other prospective lessees, but this would be costly because legally the remedy would not be straightforward and the facility would undoubtedly have to be converted in some manner for use by a new lessee. Investors usually bank on the prospect that this will never occur because a default on a lease-purchase agreement is generally very undesirable for a public entity. No local jurisdiction wants to have its credit rating and

reputation damaged since it will undoubtedly wish to issue other debt securities in the future. There are obvious reasons for a local jurisdiction not to default on a lease-purchase agreement; however, those reasons are not as compelling as with most other debt instruments.

For this reason, the interest paid on lease revenue bonds and certificates of participation is higher than on general obligation bonds. Further, since lease-purchase agreements are not true public debt like general obligation bonds, in most states a local jurisdiction may enter into a lease-purchase agreement based upon its own ordinance and without holding a referendum. The ability to avoid public debt, and therefore voter approval, is a particularly attractive aspect of lease-purchasing in communities that are at their debt limit or simply cannot pass a referendum for a needed public facility. While this financing method is viewed by some as a circumvention of the public's right to approve public capital projects, it is well within the right of any public body to approve allocations from the operating budget each year without specific voter approval of each item in the budget. Further, there is no large allocation of cash, but access to a financing method that allows for the cost of the capital asset to be repaid over a number of years. There are, however, drawbacks to using lease-purchase financing methods that require a sizable amount of capital. In order to raise the capital necessary, local jurisdictions usually have to tap into the securities market in some manner which means the involvement and expense of bond counsels, underwriters, and trustees. A number of financial mechanisms can be used to raise the substantial funds necessary for large public projects. As one example, occasionally lease-purchase financing can be arranged with developers with an interest in public infrastructure projects.

Developer Financing: Sometimes private developers can become lessors and called upon to construct a public facility in a manner commonly referred to as "build to suit." Occasionally, developers will find it is to their advantage to finance public infrastructure projects such as public library buildings with lease-purchase agreements. A developer may feel, for example, that building a branch library facility along with a shopping center development is a way to attract more people to the shopping center and thus increase the generation of store revenues. This approach can often be to the advantage of libraries since the siting requirements are very similar to retail commercial outlets that frequently inhabit shopping centers. In this scenario, the developer builds a library facility to suit the library jurisdiction, which then leases the facility. It is paid for out of operating expenditures with no added debt to the local public funding agency. At the end of the term, the library facility may be purchased at the option of the library jurisdiction; however, this is an option, not a requirement of the agreement. Exercising the option and acquiring the property is usually cost-effective, but if the area has become an undesirable location for the library, the facility may be abandoned in lieu of a more desirable location. If the facility is abandoned, all use and equity in the building, land, and equipment will be lost to the developer.

In this kind of lease-purchase agreement, the fact that the developer's loan is often from a bank or a group of private investors and therefore provided at relatively high commercial interest rates makes this approach expensive unless the developer is providing additional incentives. The loan is guaranteed by the value of the land and the improvements built on the land as well as the pledged lease payments. It is the concern over the security of the lease payments that causes problems in some states. The legality of the lease-purchase approach

has been questioned over the years by some:

> The lease-to-own arrangement may be specifically illegal in some states. In many places it isn't legal nor is it specifically illegal, so both parties, the library board and the developer, may be willing to take the chance. Many legal authorities look with disfavor on local public bodies doing anything not specifically allowed by statute.[67]

Care must be taken to avoid legal as well as public relations problems by having a thorough legal and public policy review of the proposed lease-purchase agreement. While it seems that the lease-purchase approach has enjoyed some resurgence in recent years since California's Proposition 13 passed, it has been around for a number of years.

Over the years, a number of public libraries have been built utilizing the build-to-suit method. This approach can be used with small or large library buildings. Two branch libraries in the Charlotte and Mecklenburg County Public Library in North Carolina were built in this manner. The 127,000-square-foot Kern County Library headquarters building in Bakersfield, California, was built-to-suit. In addition, the 68,000-square-foot headquarters building for the County of Los Angeles Public Library was built and financed by a developer. In this case, the county owned the land and leased it to the developer, who built the building with private financing and in turn leased it back to the county for monthly payments. Sometimes buildings can be acquired through a lease-purchase agreement which were originally financed and built by developers on speculation for a very reasonable cost because recessionary downturns in the economy require the developer to offer more attractive packages than usual. This happened recently, when the headquarters building for the Orange County (California) Public Library was acquired on a 20-year lease-purchase. Because

Fig. 6-11. Kern County Library, Bakersfield, CA

of the economy, the developer was willing to finish the building to suit the library and add further incentives by agreeing to generous maintenance provisions which were negotiated into the contract. In this instance, the public library received very favorable terms for a developer-financed and developer-built facility. If a developer cannot be found to arrange the financing for a project, or the terms or interest rate are not to the local jurisdictions advantage, alternative financing methods may need to be explored.

Lease Revenue Bonds: Lease revenue bonds are sold to investors and then repaid from lease payments provided by a public funding agency such as a city, county, or special district. The authority to utilize lease revenue bonds, like lease-purchase agreements, is provided by state statute.

Government entities like redevelopment agencies, nonprofit corporations, joint powers authorities, and special bonding authorities may issue lease revenue bonds in many states. One of the most frequently used methods is to have a nonprofit corporation issue revenue bonds on behalf of a local jurisdiction. The nonprofit corporation is usually set up by the local jurisdiction for the express purpose of acting as a financing vehicle for the capital project. However, the distinction between the two entities is important since the creation of the nonprofit organization means that the local jurisdiction itself is not directly issuing the bonds.

Simply stated, what frequently happens is that, after creating a nonprofit corporation, the local jurisdiction will lease land to the corporation. The nonprofit corporation will in turn issue lease revenue bonds and construct the facility on the site based on a lease-purchase agreement with the local jurisdiction. The nonprofit corporation then pays the bondholders from the proceeds of the lease payments obtained from the annual operating budget of the local jurisdiction. The lease payments are set up to pay both the principal and interest and thus retire the debt over a given time period. At the end of the lease-purchase agreement, title to the land and building is turned over to the local jurisdiction when the purchase option is exercised, as in the Los Angeles Central Library project.

The creation of a nonprofit corporation or special bonding authority can be further illustrated with an example from Illinois. While the ability to establish these authorities varies from state to state, the establishment of a public building commission is authorized in Illinois state statute and creates a financing mechanism for building public library facilities. The community of Springfield, Illinois, for example, created a public building commission, issued lease revenue bonds, and built a 95,000-square-foot library project. The following is a description of the Illinois Public Building Commission Act:

> Under the Public Building Commission Act, the commission owns the building that will be constructed. It rents the building to the library until expenses associated with the construction project have been met. As a lessee, the library obligates itself to pay the cost of the construction project and other expenses, including site acquisition, construction costs, building maintenance and building operational costs, and principal and interest on the bonds, which are secured by the building commission. The lessee has the authority to levy a tax for the principal and interest on the bonds without a referendum. While the Public Building Commission Act allows bonds to be paid in a 30-year period, library law stipulates the obligation shall be paid in a 20-year period.

> The building commission has the power to acquire fee simple title to real property, and all land acquired or owned by the commission are to be deemed for a public use. Any public library doing construction under the public building commission must convey the site and deed over to the commission during the lifetime of the bonds. The building commission will convey the site, deed and building back to the public library when all obligations of the project incurred by the commission have been paid.[68]

Typically, the use of lease revenue bonds with nonprofit corporations, special bonding authorities, joint powers authorities and redevelopment agencies is usually free from the requirement of a referendum. However, in some instances, a referendum may have to be held if a sufficient number of registered voters petition and force an election. Citizens' concern over the avoidance of a referendum for the use of lease revenue bonds should not be underestimated. In the mid-eighties, the community of Rome, Georgia, held a referendum for a new library building. It passed in the city limits but failed county-wide. The local public officials were determined to build the project because of obvious need and the fact that it had received support in the city. City and county officials got together and came up with a financing plan that employed the use of lease revenue bonds. Essentially, the City sold lease revenue bonds and then leased the facility to the County which is repaying the bonds from its operating budget. While the deal worked well and a wonderful new public library facility was built which has subsequently become the source of much local pride, the county commissioners that supported the lease payments in the face of voter refusal of the referendum found themselves voted out of office at the next election.

Joint Powers Authority (JPA): Another financing mechanism that occasionally receives criticism if it is used to circumvent the referendum process is the use of

Fig. 6-12. Sara Hightower Regional Library, Rome, Georgia

a joint powers authority (JPA). In some states, the authority to form JPAs is provided in state statute. In a JPA, two or more local jurisdictions (such as a city, county, or special district) may contract to establish an authority for the provision of a service, (such as public library service), as long as each jurisdiction is authorized in state code to perform the service independently. A JPA is a separate legal entity that has the authority to issue lease revenue bonds in some states, including California. Similar to a nonprofit corporation, the JPA can support the repayment of the bonds through the use of lease-purchase agreements with the agencies that formed it. "The advantage of this type of operation over the nonprofit corporation lease-purchase arrangement is that the govern-

mental jurisdictions involved remain firmly in control of the joint powers agency and the question of tax exemption for the bonds is established. The disadvantage of this type of financing is that, like the nonprofit corporation revenue bond arrangement, the cost of financing is higher than general obligation bonds."[69] Other than for relatively short terms when equipment is being acquired, the use of a lease-purchase agreement is usually more expensive than general obligation bonds, and this includes the use of certificates of participation as well as lease revenue bonds.

Certificates of Participation (COP): The use of certificates of participation (COP) is very similar to that of lease revenue bonds. COPs provide a local jurisdiction a method of raising large amounts of capital for public facilities and equipment by allowing access through the securities market to a broad base of private investors. COPs are a viable alternative to lease revenue bonds because they frequently require less time, effort, and expense to issue. As with lease revenue bonds, COPs are an investment security that is backed by a lease-purchase agreement and the resulting revenue stream of lease payments. Individual investors participate in the lease payments by purchasing a certificate, which is a partial but direct interest in the lease. COPs are usually sold in increments of $5,000 so that they can be purchased by a wide range of individual investors. Like bonds, COP's, need to be carefully evaluated by investors since they are only as good as the ability and willingness of the lessee to make good on the lease payments. In addition to assessing the general fiscal health of the local jurisdiction making the lease payments, investors usually look at how essential the facility is to the community, as well as how easily it could be converted to other uses should a default occur. Because of the added risk, as with lease revenue bonds, COP investors demand a higher interest rate than that provided by general obligation bonds.

COPs are not generally considered to be debt and therefore usually do not require a referendum. However, COPs are usually issued based on lease-purchase agreements that are triple-net, which means the lessor must pay all maintenance, insurance, and applicable taxes for the property. This is one of the distinctions between true leases and lease-purchase agreements. COPs can usually be issued by the same lessors as lease revenue bonds and the process usually goes as follows:

A typical certificate of participation ("COP") financing for a construction project might be structured as follows. A public agency that wishes to undertake a construction project enters into a tax-exempt lease with a non-profit corporation, joint power authority, leasing company, bank or other lessor. The lessor acquires the applicable site, either by purchasing it from a third party or by leasing it from the public agency. The lessor, with the assistance of the public agency, undertakes the construction of the project to be located on the site and leases the improved site to the public agency pursuant to a financing lease. The lessor's rights to receive payments under the lease are assigned to a trustee, which executes and delivers to an underwriter certificates of participation in the lease payments. A portion of each lease payment is designated as tax-exempt interest. The proceeds of the sale of the certificates of participation are used to pay the costs of acquiring and constructing the improvements.[70]

Like lease revenue bonds, COPs can be used to finance the acquisition of land, buildings, and equipment. The ability to finance equipment, with COPs can be very helpful for public libraries that are trying to acquire automated bibliographic systems or other expensive electronic equipment, because in many states acquiring equipment with general obligation bonds is prohibited. An example of this was the 1988 acquisition of a $5.3 million automated circulation system (ACS) from Data Research Associates by the Los Angeles County Public Library through a five-year lease-purchase agreement with the Security Pacific Merchant Bank of Los Angeles which was financed with COPs.[71] Even for projects that are primarily financed (building and land) with a general obligation bond issue, the equipment could be financed with certificates of participation through a lease-purchase agreement if the library is unable to raise private or other public funds for that purpose. However, it should be remembered that with COPs the term of the lease cannot exceed the useful life of the equipment being financed.

Full-sized public library facilities can also be financed with COPs. In 1988 the

Provided Courtesy of Whisler-Patri, Architects; Paul Bielenberg, photograph copyright 1992

Fig. 6-13. Oxnard Central Library, Oxnard, CA

city of Oxnard, California, financed a 72,000-square-foot central library building with an $11 million sale of COPs through a public facilities corporation. The city is making payments on a sublease and option-to-purchase agreement from its annual budget. Other projects such as the Humboldt County library, Eureka, California, are planning library projects that may utilize the sale of COPs to raise the necessary capital. Further, the community of Batesville, Mississippi, was recently able to sell approximately $600,000 of COPs for a public library building because of new enabling legislation.

The state of Mississippi recently created legislation which allows local jurisdictions to acquire public facilities, including public libraries, through the use of lease-purchase agreements and COP financing. The 1990 passage of the Acquisition of Public Buildings, Facilities, and Equipment through Rental Contracts Act, (Mississippi Code, 1972, Annotated, Section 39-8-1–39-8-13) allows public buildings to be constructed by entities other than the local government. The local government can then lease the facility for public use, with the option of purchasing the facility when the lease expires or at an earlier agreed-upon date. This lease-purchase approach provides additional flexibility to local Mississippi governments in need of new or improved public library facilities in Mississippi because there is no referendum requirement unless there are adequate petitions to require one. This approach to financing public library facilities is becoming more and more common across the nation. COPs are a creative financing technique that is becoming more accepted.

Sale-Leaseback and Sale-Saleback: Another creative financing technique that also uses leasing as the basis of the transaction, but has not caught on as well as COPs, is sale-leaseback. With this financing mechanism, local jurisdictions transfer an asset they already own, such as a building by selling the property to private investors or a nonprofit corporation while simultaneously leasing it back to retain use of the facility. The proceeds of the sale can then be used for facility improvements in the jurisdiction. "In some ways, a sale-leaseback arrangement resembles the refinancing of a home. It allows a local agency to get money out of an existing facility or equipment and to pay the money back over time. . . . The local agency receives an infusion of cash which it may pay back in installments, while still being able to use the facility or equipment."[72] Along with the obvious advantage of raising capital for the public agency, the main advantage to this kind of financing is the inherent tax benefit for investors.

There are two distinct scenarios with this approach, one that results in a true lease, and one that results in a conditional sale or lease-purchase. Each has separate tax implications.

> If a sale-leaseback is structured as a true lease, the seller-lessee is able to transfer the tax benefits of ownership to the buyer-lessor in return for favorable or low lease payments. If a sale-leaseback is structured as a conditional sale and the lessee is a state or local government or another tax-exempt organization, the arrangement can qualify as a tax-exempt lease, enabling the buyer-lessor to obtain tax-free income equal to the interest portions of the lease payments. Such an arrangement may be called a sale-saleback rather than a sale-leaseback.[73]

Recent changes in federal laws have limited the use and desirability of this financing method.

> The new restrictions in the Deficit Reduction Act of 1984 on the investment tax credit and depreciation eliminate many of the tax benefits in a sale-leaseback of older public buildings in need of costly repairs. Under pri-

or law the buyer or lessor of a building used by a state and local government unit was entitled to accelerated depreciation and also an investment tax credit when a qualified rehabilitation occurred. The new rules generally eliminate these tax benefits if the state or local government or a related entity has used the building for more than three months prior to the sale-leaseback.[74]

Any jurisdiction considering a sale-leaseback or sale-saleback should first consult an attorney and tax accountant familiar with the transaction to determine the impact of the most recent tax laws.

In a conditional sale, the local jurisdiction eventually gets the property back at the end of the lease period for a nominal "purchase" price, however, at the end of a true lease, the lessor owns the property and may sell it at fair market value to the local jurisdiction at its option. The obvious disadvantage in this approach lies in transferring a public asset with no guarantee that the local jurisdiction will be able to reacquire the property in the future. "A public agency must determine as a policy matter whether such a use of existing assets is appropriate in meeting present and future capital requirements."[75] Obviously "giving away" already owned public facilities may be viewed negatively by the public unless there are substantial gains. Each local jurisdiction must evaluate this approach to see if it makes sense given existing public facilities as well as needed improvements or new buildings.

Pooled Leasing

Another slant on the world of facility leasing is the approach of pooled leasing of capital improvements. Local jurisdictions use pooled leasing when they have projects that are too small to make a separate offering of COPs financially feasible. To use pooled leasing, jurisdictions may combine several projects within their jurisdiction or they may form a JPA with several other small jurisdictions and finance numerous small projects together with one COP offering. Pooled leasing is attractive because of the cost savings gained by the economy of scale achieved by pulling together several projects and financing them in one issuance. In addition to leasing, pools for capital improvements can be used with other kinds of debt instruments as well as COPs.

Marks-Roos Bond Pooling Structure: In 1985, the state of California created the Marks-Roos Local Bond Pooling Act (Government Code Section 6584 et seq.) which expanded the role of JPAs in financing public infrastructure. "The Marks-Roos Bond Pooling Act provides for the formation of a JPA that will in effect pool a number of specific local capital issues (G.O. Bonds, COPs, revenue bonds, lease-purchase, etc.) and combine them into an issue of one or more bonds or other instruments."[76] While public libraries are a capital improvement which can be financed under the act, no public library buildings have to date been financed in California utilizing this method. It remains, however, a possibility. Further, similar forms of legislation in other states provide a mechanism for local jurisdictions to cooperate in financing capital improvements such as public libraries.

Short-Term Notes

In addition to the long-term debt financing methods described, on occasion local jurisdictions need short-term financing methods to obtain loans for limited periods. This is usually necessary to obtain cash for a library construction project that is needed immediately but can be paid off in a relatively short period of time (usually less than a year) by the revenue generated from some form of tax levy already in place. Short-term loans of this nature are known to as tax anticipation notes or tax anticipation warrants. This approach is possible in many states, including Illinois, which has specific legislation authorizing tax anticipation notes and warrants issued for capital outlay purposes for financing public infrastructure including public libraries. Short-term notes merely provide a stopgap to help with shortfalls in revenue collections in any given year and are not to be used to finance the debt required to support a capital project over a long period.

SUMMARY

It is obvious there are many local funding sources as well as various financing methods to choose from, and the decision by library planners and local finance officials as to which approach to take is not always easy. Careful analysis of all of the possibilities is the key to finding the best method for a given project. By reviewing the different mechanisms presented here, local library planners can narrow the possibilities and identify several options that might fit the local situation. These options can be discussed with local government officials as well as the public and their advantages and disadvantages examined. Generally, the best approach will provide the most flexibility for project development and cost the least in terms of principal and interest.

REFERENCES

1. Eric J. Strauss, and Martin L. Leitner, "Financing Public Facilities with Development Excise Taxes: An Alternative to Exactions and Impact Fees" *Zoning and Planning Law Report* 11 (March 1988) p. 21.
2. Antero Rivasplata, *A Planner's Guide to Financing Public Improvements* (rev. ed) (Sacramento: Governor's Office of Planning and Research, May 1991, p. 4.

3. Strauss and Leitner, p. 19.
4. John Thompson, "Vacaville's Excise Tax—Two Years Later" *Western City* 66 (November 1990), pp. 3-5.
5. Richard F. Nash, ed. "Illinois Library Laws, State and Federal Laws" *Illinois Libraries* V. 60 1 (January 1978), pp. 6-63.
6. Ibid.
7. Ibid.
8. Ibid.
9. Robert H. Rohlf, "Financing Public Library Construction" *Illinois Libraries* 69 (November 1987), p. 626.
10. Philip S. Howe and Elizabeth M. Vogt, eds. "Illinois Revised Statutes, Chapter 81—"Libraries"—An Overview" *Illinois Libraries* 72 (May 1990), p. 419.
11. Richard B. Hall, "85 Percent Approved: Public Library Referendum 1991" *Library Journal* 15 June, p. 42.
12. Simon E. Leland, "The Financing of Library Construction Through Bond Issues" *Library Journal* (15 January 1930), p. 50.
13. Guy Garrison, "Ten Years of Library Elections in Illinois" *Illinois Libraries* 45 (September 1963), pp. 404-11.
14. Guy Garrison, "Library Elections in Illinois, 1963 to 1968" *Illinois Libraries* 52 (May 1970), pp. 428-35.
15. Albert C. Lake, "Library Bond Issues" in *Library Building: Innovations for Changing Needs*, ed. Alphonse F. Trezza (Chicago: American Library Association, 1972), p. 180.
16. Guy Garrison, *Seattle Voters and Their Public Library* (Research Series No. 2) (Springfield: Illinois State Library, 1961); Guy Garrison, "Voting on a Library Bond Issue: Two Elections in Akron, Ohio, 1961 and 1962" *Library Quarterly* 33 (July 1963), pp. 229-41.
17. William S. Berner, *The Influence of Pre-Voting Activity on the Outcome of Selected Library Bond Referendums* (Ph.D. dissertation, University of Illinois, 1970).
18. Ruth G. Lindahl, William S. Berner, *Financing Public Library Expansion: Case Studies of Three Defeated Bond Issues*

(Research Series No. 13) (Springfield: Illinois State Library, 1968), p. 64.

19. Guy Garrison, "Library Elections: A Selected Bibliography" *Illinois Libraries* 45 (September 1963), p. 375.

20. William S. Berner, "Planning Library Referendum Campaigns—A Survey of Recent Literature" *Illinois Libraries* 51 (February 1969), p. 115.

21. Donald E. Oehlerts, *Books and Blueprints: Building America's Public Libraries* (Westport, Conn.: Greenwood Press, 1991).

22. Leland, p. 50.

23. Richard B. Hall, "Referenda for Public Library Buildings 1987" *Library Journal* 15 June 1988, p. 30.

24. Richard B. Hall, "Referenda for Public Library Buildings 1988" *Library Journal* 15 June 15 1989, p. 31.

25. Richard B. Hall, "The Votes Are In: Public Library Referenda 1989" *Library Journal* 15 June 1990, p. 42.

26. Richard B. Hall, "Still a Boom for Bonds?" *Library Journal* 15 June 1991, p. 48.

27. Richard B. Hall, "85 Percent Approved," p. 36.

28. Douglas Porter, Ben C. Lin, and Richard B. Peiser, *Special Districts: A Useful Technique for Financing Infrastructure* (Washington: Urban Land Institute 1987), pp. v–vi.

29. Douglas R. Porter, Douglas R. and Richard B. Peiser, *Financing Infrastructure to Support Community Growth* (Washington: Urban Land Institute, 1984), p. 8.

30. Virginia L. Horler, *Guide to Public Debt Financing in California* (rev. ed.) (San Francisco: Packard Press, 1987), p. 106.

31. *Payment of Facilities Benefit Assessments and Development Impact Fees* (San Diego: Engineering and Development Department, Facilities Financing Division).

32. Rivasplata, p. 15.

33. Debora Vrana, "Mello-Roos Bonds: Recession Drives Local Developer Bonds to the Brink" *California Journal* 23 (January 1992), pp. 37-38.

34. Kenneth Leventhal, "Infrastructure Financing Innovations from California" *Professional Builder* 53 (October 1988), p. 32.

35. Rivasplata, p. 11.

36. Vrana, pp. 37-38.

37. Jeanie Fay, "How California's Cities Are Using Mello-Roos" *Western City* 62 (November 1987), pp. 7-8.

38. Thomas P. Snyder, and Michael A. Stegman, *Paying for Growth: Using Development Fees to Finance Infrastructure* (Washington: Urban Land Institute, 1986), p. 66.

39. Lori Raineri, "Mello-Roos Bonds—California's Answer to Financing Public Infrastructure in Developing Areas" *Government Finance Review* 3 (August 1987), p. 15.

40. Fay, p. 52.

41. Horler, p. 129.

42. Donna Hanousek, *Project Infrastructure Development Handbook* (Washington: Urban Land Institute, 1989), p. 86.

43. Ralph Andersen, *The Use of Redevelopment and Tax Increment Financing by Cities and Counties* (Sacramento: California Debt Advisory Commission, 1986), pp. L-2–L-26.

44. Rivasplata, p. 6.

45. Horler, p. 103.

46. Hanousek, p. 125.

47. James E. Frank, and R.M. Rhodes, eds., *Development Exactions: Issues and Impacts* (Chicago: American Planning Association, 1987) p. 11.

48. Rivasplata, p. 28.

49. Ibid.

50. Snyder, and Stegman. p. 36.

51. Hanousek, p. 125.

52. Barbara Weiss, ed. *Public/Private Partnerships Financing a Common Wealth* (Washington: Government Finance Officers Association), pp. xvii–xix; 226–33.

53. Mark P. Barneby, et al., "Paying for Growth: Community Approaches to Development Impact Fees" in *Development Impact Fees: Policy Rationale, Practice, Theory, and Issues.* ed, Arthur C. Nelson (Chicago: Planners Press, American Planning Association, 1988), p. 46.

54. James E. Frank, and Paul B. Downing, "Patterns of Impact Fee Use" in *Development Impact Fees: Policy Rationale, Practice, Theory, and Issues,* ed. Arthur C. Nelson (Chicago: Planners Press, American Planning Association, 1988), p. 17.

55. Terry D. Morgan, "Shortcomings of Impact Fee Law and Future Trends" in *Development Impact Fees: Policy Rationale, Practice, Theory, and Issues,* ed. Arthur C. Nelson (Chicago: Planners Press, American Planning Association, 1988), p. 115.

56. Richard H. Cowart, "Experience, Motivations, and Issues" in *Development Agreements: Practice, Policy, and Prospects,* ed. Douglas R. Porter and Lindell L. Marsh, (Washington: Urban Land Institute, 1989), p. 35.

57. Ana Arana, "Doing Deals: How California Communities Mix and Match Financing Techniques to Pay for New Development" *Planning* 51 (February 1986), p. 31.

58. Richard H. Cowart, "Negotiating Exactions Through Development Agreements" in *Private Supply of Public Services: Evaluation of Real Estate Exactions, Linkage, and Alternative Land Policies,* ed. Rachelle Alterman (New York: New York University Press, 1988), p. 219.

59. "Summary of Rancho Del Oro Development Agreement, Oceanside, California," in *Development Agreements: Practice, Policy, and Prospects,* ed. Douglas R. Porter and Lindell L. Marsh (Washington: Urban Land Institute, 1989), p. 206.

60. Ibid, p. 207.

61. Marcia King, and Rita Hamilton, "Public and Private Funding Create a New Library for Tucson" *The Bottom Line* Vol. 2, No. 1 (1988), pp. 10-13.

62. Ibid, p. 12.

63. Douglas R. Porter, et al., *Working with the Community: A Developer's Guide,* (Washington: Urban Land Institute, 1985), p. 1.

64. Weiss, p. 3.

65. Angus Snead MacDonald, "Libraries Unchained" *Library Journal* 15 January 1953, p. 78.

66. Rivasplata, p. 41.

67. Julius R. Chitwood, "Lesser-Known Financial Methods" in *Library Buildings: Innovation for Changing Needs* (Chicago: American Library Association, 1972), p. 185.

68. Joe Natale, ed. "Special Construction Considerations, Financing Public Library Construction" *Illinois Libraries* 73 (December 1991), p. 630.

69. Bertha D. Hellum, et al. "Financing Library Construction" *California Librarian* 31 (January 1970), p. 57.

70. "Financing Leases and Certificates of Participation" in *California Debt Issuance Primer,* (Sacramento: California Debt Advisory Commission, July 1990), pp. 3-19.

71. Roy V. Hanson, "When to Consider Lease/Purchase" *The Bottom Line* Vol. 3, No. 3, (1989), p. 4.

72. Rivasplata, pp. 40-41.

73. John A. Vogt and Lisa A. Cole, eds., *A Guide to Municipal Leasing* (Chicago: Municipal Finance Officers Association, 1983), p. 4.

74. David M. Gelfand, Robert S. Amdursky, et al., eds., *State & Local Goverment Debt Financing,* Vol. 1 (Wilmette, Ill.: Callaghan, 1986), p. 55.

75. "Financing Leases and Certificates of Participation," pp. 3-27.

76. Cy Silver, *Financing California Public Library Buildings, 1992* (Sacramento: California State Library, 1991), p. 7.

Private
Funding Sources 7

OVERVIEW

Partnerships with the private sector to build public libraries in the U.S. have been around for a long time. Benjamin Franklin was an avid fundraiser and supporter of libraries, but it wasn't until the mid- to-late 1800's that real progress was made in constructing major public libraries. Among the early philanthropists who built public libraries were James Lenox, John Astor, Walter Newberry, Enoch Pratt, George Peabody, and Johns Hopkins to name but a few. "During the first four decades of public library construction in the United States, fewer than thirty large buildings were completed at a total cost of $7 million. Three-fourths of these building funds came from private sources."[1] In addition to these major buildings, many smaller library facilities were constructed in small towns across the nation due to the efforts and generosity of many "founding families."

Andrew Carnegie

Private philanthropy sponsored by wealthy donors (of whom Andrew Carnegie is the most famous) has always been the backbone of private-sector financing for public library buildings. Carnegie enhanced the concept of private support for public libraries by providing more than 1,400 public library buildings all over the country. Were it not for the momentum generated up by the gifts of Carnegie and others like him, the development of public libraries in this country might have been seriously retarded.

Over a 25-year period, Andrew Carnegie gave over $40 million to local jurisdictions to construct public library buildings. Figure 7-1 shows the amount expended for public library buildings from 1897 to 1923.[2] For a full listing of all communities receiving Carnegie grants for public library buildings and the amounts of the grant see Appendix B of George Bobinski's *Carnegie Libraries*.[3] Even during its heyday, the decline of private funding for public libraries was beginning. Not long after the turn of the century, the overall percentage of public library construction funding that came from private sources began to slip.

As the Carnegie program declined, so did the dominance of private fundraising for capital improvements. Oehlerts estimates that for large public libraries, the percentage of private funding dropped down to approximately 15 percent from 1919 to 1945. This downward trend continued from the end of World War II to the mid-1960's. Table 7-1 shows that in 1945, private funds accounted for 16.7 percent of the total and then steadily dropped for each year reported until 1965 when less than 2 percent of the funds came from private sources.

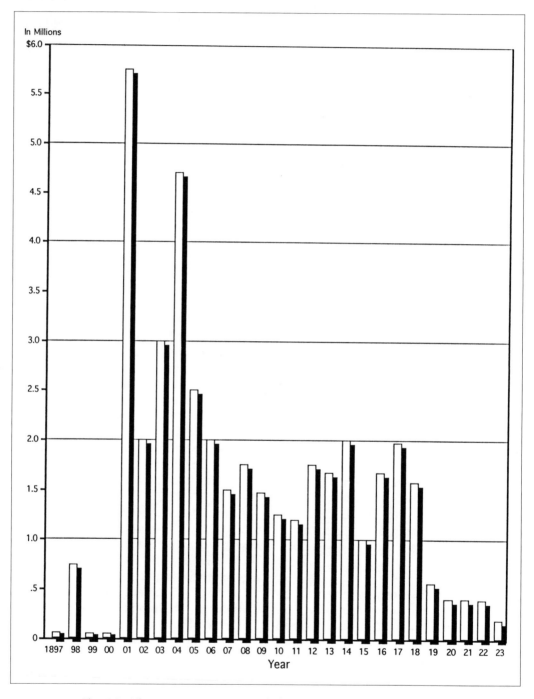

Fig. 7-1. Library Appropriations Made by Andrew Carnegie, 1897-1923

TABLE 7-1. Percentage of Private Funds for Public Library Construction (1946 to 1965)

1965	1.7%
1964	2.0%
1962	3.2%
1956	4.9%
1950	6.8%
1946	11.1%
1945	16.7%

In more recent years, there has been somewhat of a recovery from the all-time low reported in the early and mid-sixties. Figure 7-2 shows a graph of recent levels of private funding for public library construction. In the last twenty-four years since *Library Journal* began collecting statistics, funds from the private sector have averaged just under 9 percent (8.9%). While this percentage has varied during this time from a low of 3.6 percent in 1984 to a high of 14.6 percent in 1982, private funding does not any longer appear to be on the decline. As a matter of fact, private sources have remained remarkably stable during the last twenty-four years.

Major Campaigns for Public Library Buildings

While numerous single-benefactor gifts of sites and even entire buildings for public libraries have been made in many communities, overall there have not been many well-organized private fundraising campaigns for public library facilities in this nation. With the increased difficulty of raising substantial sums of money from public sources, library supporters may have to turn more frequently to private funds through capital campaigns in the future. However, a review of the *Library Journal* statistics shows that in only 40 instances has $1 million or more been raised from private sources for a public library building in the last 24 years. Table 7-2 lists these projects in descending order of the amount of private funds raised.

The total amount of private funds raised for these 40 projects was just under $89, million which is almost 30 percent of all private funds reported in *Library Journal*

Table 7-2. Major Private Capital Campaigns for Public Library Buildings

Location	Date*	Private Funds Raised** (in millions)
Dallas, TX	1982	$11.0
Richmond, TX	1986	8.0
Dearborn, MI	1970	4.2
Sioux City, IA	1990	4.1
Des Moines, IA	1988	4.0
Shreveport, LA	1981	2.8
Allentown, PA	1978	2.7
Charlotte, NC	1991	2.6
Gowrie, IA	1965	2.5
Houston, TX	1989	2.4
Las Vegas, NV	1990	2.3
Alsip, IL	1982	2.3
Chappaqua, NY	1979	2.3
Bakersfield, CA	1986	2.2
La Jolla, CA	1989	1.8
Corning, NY	1976	1.8
Frankfort, IN	1990	1.7
York, NE	1986	1.7
Bradford, PA	1991	1.6
Batesville, IN	1988	1.6
Canton, OH	1980	1.6
Bakersfield, CA	1988	1.5
Lansing, MI	1989	1.5
Martinsville, VA	1987	1.5
Carmel-by-the-Sea, CA	1989	1.4
Quincy, IL	1975	1.4
Las Vegas, NV	1971	1.4
Shawnee, OK	1989	1.3
Jai, NM	1979	1.3
Nashua, NH	1972	1.2
Wilmington, DE	1972	1.2
Old Town, ME	1991	1.2
Thomasville, NC	1991	1.1
Rutherford, NJ	1976	1.1
Longview, TX	1987	1.1
Monson, MA	1990	1.1
Stuart, VA	1991	1.1
Duluth, MN	1981	1.1
New York, NY	1972	1.0
Greenwich, CT	1970	1.0
Total		$88.7

*Date Reported in *Library Journal*
**Figures are rounded off to the nearest $100,000.
©Reed Publishing

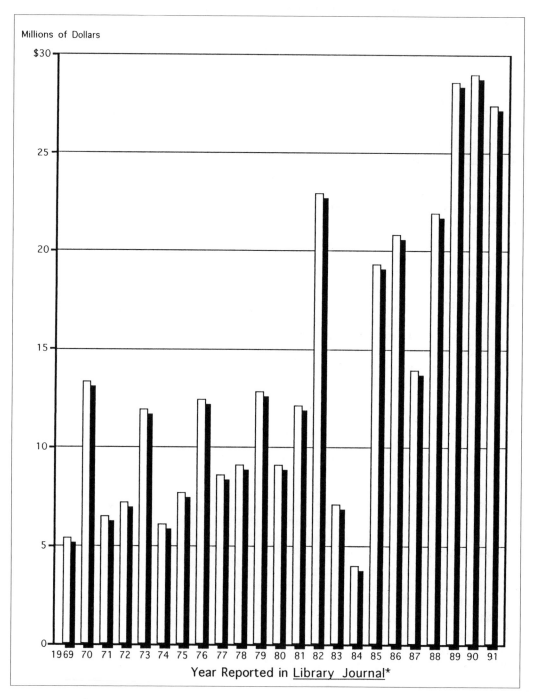

Fig. 7-2. Private Funds Expended for Public Library Construction by Year
* ©Reed Publishing

since 1968. Of this money, the top five projects (Dallas, Richmond, Dearborn, Sioux City, and Des Moines) account for over $30 million which is one-third of all private funds raised for these 40 projects. The Dallas campaign was a well-planned private fundraising drive that generated $11 million for the Dallas Central Library project, close to half of all funds reported raised in 1982 for public library construction from the private sector. The $11 million amounted to approximately one-quarter of the funds necessary to build the $42 million facility. To date, it appears that the Dallas campaign is the largest one-time private capital fundraising effort to finance a public library building, however, at present, the city of San Francisco is undertaken a private capital fundraising campaign with the goal of raising $30 million for the new San Francisco Main Library.

Still, even though private philanthropy and stewardship have been a cherished part of the development of public library buildings in this country, the trend has been away from the use of private funds since the turn-of-the-century. There are many reasons for this, not the least of which is acceptance of the argument that public libraries that are accessible to all citizens ought to be funded by the public through local, state, and federal taxes. However, this does not mean there is no longer a role for private funding for public library buildings, especially given the increasing costs of construction and sophisticated electronic equipment. Achieving a level of excellence is becoming more difficult for public libraries with these increased costs in addition to the difficulties of competing for public funds. This probably means that library supporters will need to become more effective at reaching out to donors and reclaiming some of the private funding lost in recent history. However, to be successful, it will be necessary to understand the basics of the private fundraising capital campaign.

THE PRIVATE FUNDRAISING CAPITAL CAMPAIGN

The following is an overview of the development and implementation of a private fundraising capital campaign for a public library facility. For more in-depth description of private capital campaigns in general which can be easily adapted for public library building projects, consult

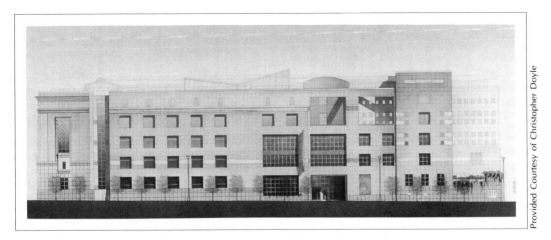

Provided Courtesy of Christopher Doyle

Fig. 7-3. Rendering of San Francisco Main Library

books by Kent E. Dove,[4] David J. Hauman,[5] Jeanine Builta,[6] H. Gerald Quigg,[7] and Joan Boisclair[8] among others. Since private philanthropy has been so important to the development of major public institutions, it is fortunate that such a well-developed body of literature is available. These publications represent many years of experience in private capital campaigns for different types of facilities across the country and provide a firm foundation for library supporters who wish to embark on a major fundraising effort.

A library that already has experience with an annual fundraising program and has begun to cultivate private donors will have a greatly enhanced chance for success in a capital campaign, but it is not impossible to launch a one-time capital campaign without previous experience; it is just more difficult. Those anticipating a large capital project sometime in the future may want to test the waters or simply prepare in advance for the major effort of a capital campaign by beginning an annual program or by attempting some private fundraising for a special project. In this way, the library management, friends group, and board of trustees can get a sense of what it will be like to launch a serious attempt at raising large sums of money. These initial efforts will not be easy, because of lack of experience as well as the difficulty of raising private funds for operating budgets or smaller projects than buildings. In many ways it is actually easier to raise substantial sums of money for large capital projects like buildings than for day-to-day routine projects and operating budgets. This is simply because the larger building projects stimulate the imagination of donors who want to be remembered for having contributed to something of major consequence and permanence.

Herein lies the attractiveness of the capital campaign and the challenge for library supporters. In order for a private capital campaign to be successful, library supporters must make sure the project is highly

visible and significant in the minds of the community and especially potential donors. Kathryn Stephanoff said it well in describing the private fundraising drive for the Allentown, Pennsylvania, public library: " . . . make your project attractive, vest it with prestige, dignify it with style, and surround it with an enthusiasm that is infectious and coruscating. Make it unthinkable for anyone who fancies himself as a mover not to be involved."[9]

People want to give to projects that will make a difference both to themselves and to the community. Because of the nature of the service as well as the broad base of the constituency, a public library is an ideal candidate for private fundraising. This is why library capital campaigns are often successful when they are effectively organized and run. "Successful campaigns seek and secure investments in a better society, a higher quality of life, an enriched culture, and they showcase humankind at its best, expressing love and hope and caring for others with greater needs."[10]

This principle of fundraising is true for large or small capital campaigns, as are many of the strategies, techniques, and methods that will be discussed. Capital campaigns can be used to raise money not only to construct new public library buildings, but also to expand and renovate existing ones and buy furnishings and equipment, opening-day book collections, artwork, landscaping, and other amenities that might not otherwise be available because of restrictions on the use of certain public funds. Capital campaigns can also be used to establish endowments for specific programs or activities such as building maintenance, or as a reserve fund that will grow through the magic of compound interest to where it can be used to improve the existing facility or to expand to new quarters. This approach was successfully used with the project in Carmel-by-the-Sea, California, as well as others.

In the broadest sense, a public library capital campaign is an organized effort to raise a substantial amount of money in a relatively short period of time for some form of capital expenditure related to the public library as an institution. These campaigns tend to be fairly intense because they don't last long, whereas annual giving programs go on in some form year after year. For smaller projects (less than $1 million), capital campaigns will tend to last for less than a year, but for larger projects they may last two to three years or more. Regardless of the duration of the campaign, one of the key factors in encouraging donations is the sense of urgency generated by the building project's timetable as well as the campaign leadership. One of the primary determinants of success will be the quality of the campaign's leadership. The campaign director's ability to recruit and inspire the volunteers who will actually solicit funds is paramount.

While most of the money for the capital campaign will be raised from a few major donors, it is important for the library to obtain smaller donations from many individuals. This is particularly true if the private fundraising drive is being held in conjunction with a request for public funds. Raising private funds from the average citizen demonstrates to local public funding officials that the project has broad-based community support. Officials can then assume that the community would support a decision to fund the project publicly or would pass a referendum to fund it if one were placed on the ballot. Private gift pledges can even be made contingent upon the successful passage of the referendum which was the case with the Dallas central library project. These kinds of combined public-private campaigns can be very effective. Not only does an early private fundraising effort raise awareness for the project, it also provides leverage at the polls if the gifts are contingent on the outcome of the referendum. In this way, the private funding (or the threat of the loss of it) can be used like a state or federal grant, which is contingent upon local matching funds, to stimulate

the approval of local public funds for the project.

Whether or not a private fundraising campaign is combined with a campaign for public funds, the effort involved in executing a well-run private fundraising drive is very significant. The campaign may be a roaring success and the funding goal met or exceeded, or it may fall short of the needed funding, creating embarrassment for the sponsors and even hampering or stalling the building project because of the shortfall. How do library supporters ensure that their capital campaign will succeed? The first steps are proper planning and deciding whether or not to employ a professional fundraising consultant.

Fundraising Consultants

If a professional fundraising consultant is to be hired, he or she should be brought on board as early in the campaign as possible—even before the preliminary planning has begun. Along with the obvious practical experience and expertise a consultant brings to a campaign, one of the main advantages of hiring a consultant is that this person can provide an objective perspective on the library as well as the community. This objectivity will be invaluable during the early stages of the campaign, particularly when it comes to evaluating different strategies. A professional fundraising consultant will help library supporters focus on the critical issues, and assess the chances of success, providing a "reality check" for campaign planners. Finally, a fundraising consultant can often lend the campaign an important degree of credibility it would not otherwise have.

Capital fundraising campaigns can be very taxing undertakings, and it is best to find a consultant with a good deal of experience and skill. There are numerous sources of information about consultants specializing in capital campaigns. One such document is the *Capital Campaign Resource Guide*,[11] which provides a listing of fundraising consultants with descriptions of the firms and their specialties. Information is also available from such national fundraising associations as the National Society of Fund Raising Executives (NSFRE). Local nonprofit organizations that have recently undertaken successful capital campaigns may also prove a source of good consultants since these consultants should already be familiar with the local community.

After a preliminary screening process, targeted consulting firms should be asked to submit a proposal including several references. After reviewing this information, it is usually best to interview several firms. Look for a firm that has solid, recent experience and is willing to be flexible. It may be that a full-time, on-site, consultant is not necessary for the campaign. The cost of fundraising consultants is directly proportional to the length of time they spend on campaign activities. If a reasonable degree of fundraising experience is available locally, it may be possible to have the consultant work on a retainer basis providing assistance only when necessary. Tasks for the professional might include conducting the feasibility study, reviewing a draft of the case statement, helping to write the campaign plan, or preliminary training of volunteer solicitors in lieu of managing the entire campaign.

Professional fundraising consultants typically charge between $500 and $1,000 per day. Depending on how much work they end up doing for the campaign, they can significantly increase the cost of raising money. However, as Harold Seymour stated many years ago, "You can't raise money without spending money, and within reasonable limits the return is likely to be commensurate with the investment."[12] However, beware of consultants who want to set their fee based on a percentage of the amount of money raised. This is not considered ethical by most professional fundraising associations and should not be accepted. The campaign leadership must feel comfortable working with the consultant. Beware, too of the consulting firm that sends one individual to interview, but assigns another (unknown, and usually less experienced) to the campaign. Finally, recognize that fundraising consultants are not miracle workers. They cannot raise money if it's not in the community to begin with. They will not be effective if campaign officials will not follow their advice or if local volunteers are not willing to do the job of soliciting funds. Fundraising consultants do not solicit donors themselves, but they can increase the chances of success by providing insight and knowledge gained from previous campaigns. This experience and expertise is likely to be very helpful during the strategic planning stages of the campaign.

Preliminary Planning

In order to be successful, any capital campaign must be based on proper planning. As discussed in the first two chapters, the amount of funds to be raised for the project must be determined by a needs assessment, facilities master plan, building program, preliminary architectural plans, and a good deal of study regarding the preliminary project cost estimate. This long-range planning sets out specific goals and objectives as well as a plan for how the library will achieve its goals. Along with defining the mission of the library, strategic planning describes the library services that the new facility will offer and what it will look like in terms of physical space and supporting furnishings and equipment. The result is a statement of the need for the project, which must be effectively communicated to the campaign leadership, volunteer solicitors, and ultimately to potential donors.

As with referendum campaigns, one of the best ways to foster a sense of commitment for the project is to involve the public, the fundraising leadership, and even potential donors in the planning process as early as possible. Gregory Lord says it well:

> What makes planning even more valuable is the opportunity it presents for involvement. If an institution's leaders are on the ball they will use the planning process to get people involved in mapping an organization's future—especially those people who have the power to bring about that future. Authentic involvement in a planning process promotes a sense of ownership among prospective donors and volunteers. People are simply motivated to work for and invest in the realization of plans they themselves have helped to develop.[13]

This approach makes sense because if donors are going to be asked to part with money, they should understand clearly what the library building project is trying to achieve and feel involved in defining the plan. As donors become more sophisticated (particularly large donors), they want to be involved to some extent in planning the project, to be sure their gifts will be well spent. Not all potential donors or campaign volunteers will want a hand in planning the project, but some may want to have an overview of the process as well as a description of the results. For donors or volunteers who were not involved early in the planning process, the best way to involve them and communicate the need for the project is the development of a case statement.

Case Statement

The case statement provides an overview of the project and succinctly states the campaign's goals and objectives, including a brief description of the building project and how it will meet the library's needs for the future. The library project's programmatic priorities should be brought out with a logo and various themes. The case statement should emphasize that the library is a stable cultural institution by demonstrating its historical roots and describing its accomplishments, particularly, any awards or honors the library has received. The leadership qualities of key staff and campaign volunteers should be noted, and it is frequently helpful to include brief testimonials from well-known and respected individuals. Basic financial information about the project should be presented in an abbreviated manner. The magnitude of gifts needed to support the project may be included with a list of "naming opportunities" for substantial gifts. The case statement should be designed to appeal to as many potential donors as possible and clearly present the case for why individuals should contribute to the project.

The document will present facts, but it is most effective when it appeals to potential donors' emotions, because the decision to give is often an emotional one. The case statement must strike a chord and thrill or even electrify potential donors. It is one of the main weapons in the arsenal of volunteer solicitors. By creating a sense of the project's urgency, the case statement can foster more immediate and extensive giving. It tells the donor why the library is a unique institution in the community and why it deserves the donor's special attention. Like all good fundraising campaign literature, the case statement should be written with the donor in mind, but it can also be an effective educational and recruitment tool for the campaign leadership and volunteers.

The case statement will undoubtedly go through numerous drafts. With each revision, input from staff, volunteers, and campaign leadership will contribute to a document that garners the support of a wide range of campaign participants. The statement will help recruit the campaign leadership by demonstrating that library planners have done their homework. Once the campaign chairperson is committed to the campaign, the case statement can be used to recruit the rest of the steering committee. Ultimately, however, the case statement and all other campaign literature that grows out of it, such as a prospectus (executive summary of the case statement), brochures, and factsheets, should be oriented toward potential donors.

The case statement, and all campaign materials, should be "written from the perspective of the donor, rather than that of the institution."[14] It must be attractively packaged and uncluttered. Further, it is important to remember that the type size and fonts should be clearly legible. The impact of the case statement will be lost if it is not read by the prospective donor. Photographs and other graphics should embellish the final product, as in the case statement for the new main San Francisco Public Library entitled "Building the House of the Book."

The case statement forms the basis of the capital campaign's public relations program. It will be mailed out to potential donors and brought along by volunteers during solicitations. In addition, it is used by fundraising consultants or the library's development staff during the feasibility study. An early draft can be shown to those being interviewed and their comments requested. Again, asking for advice produces a sense of involvement which can be used later to leverage support for the campaign.

Feasibility Study

The primary purpose of a feasibility study is to determine if the community will be able to support a successful fundraising drive for the library project. The feasibility study, or market study, allows library supporters to explore the possibility of a fundraising campaign without the risk of public embarrassment if the results point to a "no go" situation. The study can show library planners the community's perception of the library as well as the degree of support major fundraising effort would have. It will uncover any weaknesses in the proposed case statement and help

identify the potential campaign leadership and prospective donors. Further, it will point the way to what will be needed in terms of a campaign plan and organization.

Fundraising consultants are frequently used at this step because of their objectivity. Since they come from outside the community, they are frequently able to get more candid and accurate answers to the questions the study poses. While some firms use telephone interviews and direct-mail surveys, the most common and effective way to conduct a feasibility study is through personal interviews with the most influential community leaders. Depending on the size of the campaign and the community, somewhere between 25 and 75 interviews should be performed with individuals who are well respected and who could be major donors—bankers, realtors, attorneys, business owners, chief executive officers, and board members of local corporations, foundations, and the library, as well as affluent members of the library friends group. It is important to identify and interview potential donors and campaign volunteers as well as a few of the library's most loyal critics just to be sure to obtain a balanced and realistic picture.

The feasibility study provides an opportunity to gain information and assess the possibilities of major gifts in a nonsolicitational setting and also to cultivate potential donors and make a good first impression. Initial contacts with prospective donors are important. If they feel that a first-class feasibility study is being performed, they may be impressed by the library's efforts and more inclined to donate to the campaign when asked. Use the feasibility study as a way to educate prospective donors, but also ask them who they think the most important community leaders are and who they think would be willing to serve as part of the campaign leadership. Interviews should be conducted in a relaxed atmosphere which means that it is usually best to perform them away from offices and other distractions. The interviewer may learn a great deal about the relevance of the library's plan of service in the mind of the interviewee, the reasonableness of the campaign's financial goal, and the appropriateness of the proposed campaign's timing.

To get the desired information, it may be helpful to develop a questionnaire. While there is a good deal of information that would be desirable to gather during these interviews, certain facts are critical. David J. Hauman states this succinctly:

> The questionnaires used in these interviews can be quite extensive. The interviews themselves may be as brief as ten to fifteen minutes or extend well beyond an hour. Regardless of the format . . . each interview should extract three pieces of information from the interviewee:
>
> 1. Will you pledge to this campaign?
> 2. What amount is your pledge likely to be?
> 3. Will you work (volunteer) in the campaign?
>
> All the rest, important though it may be, is only information and cultivation. It is useful in positioning the institution or marketing services. It will not provide a "go/no-go" decision.[15]

Once the interviews are completed, the information obtained must be analyzed and recommendations made regarding the feasibility of the campaign. The results will need to be documented in a written report. There will likely be revisions in the case statement and possibly some rethinking of the campaign strategy at this point. If it appears that the community will support the proposed fundraising goal for the library project, the next step will be to take the information gained during the interview phase and use it to develop a campaign plan. As a first step, it may be helpful to invite all those who participated in the feasibility study to hear a presentation reviewing the study's findings. This provides those interviewed with a summary, and signals the beginning of the recruit-ment process for the campaign leadership.

Campaign Plan

A plan of action is required for a private fundraising campaign. Again, it is helpful to hire a consultant to write or assist in writing the plan, particularly the one who was involved with the feasibility study and is already familiar with the local situation. The plan must address a number of issues. First, it should provide an overview of the campaign's purpose, its financial goal, and any applicable gift policies. With respect to the latter, the plan should state whether gifts other than cash (real estate, stocks and bonds, personal property, etc.) will be accepted and indicate if the campaign will accept or even encourage multiyear gifts or challenge gifts. A policy regarding naming opportunities for donors should be stated, i.e., will the library or any of its elements be named for a donor who makes a singularly large gift?

Next, the logistics of the campaign's organization must be addressed. The plan should specify where the campaign headquarters will be located and how much office and meeting-room space is needed. A campaign organization chart should be developed showing the roles of the campaign leadership, volunteers, library development staff, and library director as well as the library friends. Detailed job descriptions should be included. The campaign plan should outline the process to be used for identifying donors and determining the level of gifts to come from individuals, foundations, corporations, and community groups. Further, it should define the process of soliciting prospective donors. This includes donor research, evaluation (determining how much money they should be asked for), and the proper assignment of a volunteer solicitor. The campaign plan should also indicate the procedures that will be used for donor record-keeping and the gift collection process. The plan should identify if these will be paper-based or computerized. Donor solicitation and record-keeping will be discussed in detail later in the chapter.

The Campaign Budget

Every private fundraising campaign of any consequence will need a budget, even if a substantial amount of goods and services are provided through in-kind donations. Costs for capital campaigns vary tremendously depending on the size of the campaign, its length, and the amount of assistance received from professional fundraising consultants. Capital campaign costs usually range from a low of two to three percent of the goal to as high as ten to 12 percent or even more. A range of between three and four percent is typical for many campaigns of moderate size with an allowance for some professional assistance. The shorter and more intensive the campaign, the less expensive it will tend to be, which is one of the reasons that capital campaigns have a definite beginning and end. Capital campaign budgets usually need to provide funds for personnel including consultants and library development staff; office expenses such as equipment, supplies, and postage; and campaign literature and materials such as production and printing of the case statement, brochures, and audiovisual aids.

Funds to finance the campaign can come from any number of sources, including the library's operating budget if the library's public funding agency agrees. Occasionally, it is possible to "borrow" from the operating fund, and then pay it back out of the funds raised. Sometimes funds from an endowment or a special contingency account can be used, or the funds can come from early donors within the library "family" who understand that some up-front money is required to raise money. It is great when volunteer solicitors can respond later in the campaign that all of a donation goes toward the intended purpose and not campaign costs!

Gift Table

Once the campaign s operational budget has been determined and provided for, a campaign gift table is established which allocates the number and the amount of each gift necessary to reach the campaign goal. The gift table, chart, or pyramid is used to establish the number of donors needed at various donation levels to meet the campaign's goal. Fundraising literature contains various formulas for how to set up gift tables and rules of thumb indicating how much money should come from the major donors. For example, the 80-20 rule indicates that 20 percent of the donors in a campaign will give approximately 80 percent of the money. However, more recent experience indicates that these figures may actually be closer to 90-10, meaning that 90 percent of the gifts may need to come from only 10 percent of the donors.

Another rule of thumb that has been used over the years is shifting somewhat:

> We used to believe in "the rule of thirds"— one gift equivalent to approximately 10 percent of the campaign goal added to the nine next highest gifts would equal approximately one-third of the campaign goal. The next 90 gifts would equal the second third of the campaign goal. All other gifts would equal the bottom third. If this were true, it would mean that the top 100 gifts account for between 65 and 70 percent of the entire campaign. Recent studies, however, indicate that the rule of thirds, while definitely true for larger campaign goals, does not apply to campaigns of less than $1 million. In smaller campaigns, the top 100 gifts make up only about 45 to 50 percent of the total.[16]

Others feel that the size of the top-end gifts should be increased (particularly in large campaigns) and that the first gift should be more than ten percent of the overall campaign goal:

> Regardless of the goal, the first gift should represent 10 percent to 20 percent of the overall goal. The closer to 20 percent, the higher the probability of success. The top three gifts ought to represent 30 to 50 percent of the

Table 7-3. Traditional Mathematically-Derived Gift Table ($1 Million Goal)

Gift Category	No. of Gifts	Percentage[18]	Amount of gift	Total	Cumulative Total
Lead	1	10	$100,000	$100K	$100K
Major	2	5	50,000	100K	200K
	4	2.5	25,000	100K	300K
	8	1.25	12,500	100K	400K
Special	16	.625	6,250	100K	500K
	32	.3125	3,125	100K	600K
	64	.15625	1,562.5	100K	700K
Community	128	.078125	781.25	100K	800K
	256	.0390625	390.63	100K	900K
	512	.01953125	190.53	100K	1,000K

overall goal. The top ten gifts ought to represent 40 to 60 percent of the goal. And finally, the 100 largest gifts ought to represent approximately 85 percent of the total goal.[17]

Consensus is difficult to come by in this area of fundraising, but it is clear that the vast majority of money must be raised from a relatively small number of donors.

Table 7-3 provides the traditional gift table which is created by doubling the number of donors as the amount of the gift is halved for each step down the table. The percentage listed is the percentage of the total amount of funds to be raised by each gift in a category. While the table is set up for a $1 million campaign goal, these percentages can be applied against any campaign goal to determine the amount of the gift for each of the levels.

In most campaigns, there are three or four gift categories such as lead (leadership) gifts, major gifts, special gifts and community or general gifts. Technically, the first gifts in any category are lead gifts, although that term is usually used to mean a campaign's first major gift. This gift is critical since it establishes a precedent for the campaign and sets the pace of the gifts that follow. The importance of the first two or three major gifts to the success of the campaign cannot be overemphasized, not only because they substantially reduce the amount of money remaining to be raised, but because all the remaining gifts will be

made relative to the first lead gifts. Most people give in relation to what others in their community have given. For this reason, it is extremely important to begin the solicitation process at the top of the gift table and work down the categories in stages. Always solicit the largest gift first, then the major gifts, the special gifts, and finally launch the community-wide general gifts campaign. In this way, the campaign calendar can be set up so that once all the major gift-giving is completed, the next (special) phase of the campaign can be started and completed before moving on to the broader-based public campaign.

Campaign Calendar

As part of the campaign plan, a campaign calendar should be established by the leadership in consultation with the fundraising consultant. In addition to the master calendar, each major division of the campaign may need its own calendar if the campaign is sizable. The calendar allows the campaign manager to break each task down into specific steps and enables the leadership to program activities and establish benchmarks for the campaign. It is particularly important to have an ending date so that campaign volunteers have a feeling of urgency and solicitations will move forward at a reasonable rate. Ending dates for each major activity provide this same sense of pressing need to accomplish the current phase in order to move on to the next stage. In many ways, the campaign calendar is a motivational tool as well as a planning tool.

One of the first things to consider when establishing the campaign calendar is the possibility of conflict with competing capital campaigns in the community. This should be avoided if possible, although in many communities some organization is running a fundraising campaign at any given time. But if conflict with already planned campaigns can be avoided, it is desirable. As mentioned, the length of capital campaigns varies widely depending on a number of factors, but library planners should probably count on anywhere between two to four years from the start of planning to finish. It usually takes a minimum of six months to a year of preparation just to get organized, and possibly longer if library supporters have never run a capital campaign and do not currently have an annual gift program.

The actual campaign will probably take one to three years or more once the leadership is in place and solicitation has begun. The major gift solicitation phase of the campaign won't go on for that long, but a multiyear campaign can help allow major donors to spread their gifts over several years and thus increase the size of the gifts. The first part of the campaign will be the nonpublic phase during which major donors will be quietly asked to provide assistance for the library project. Successful campaigns frequently do not go public until around 50 percent of the goal has been reached.

Campaign Publicity

While the major gift solicitation phase is not publicly announced in most capital campaigns, preliminary public relations efforts frequently precede the official launching of the campaign. It is useful to raise the visibility of the library in the months be-fore the campaign starts in order to prepare the public for the community-wide appeal for funds as well as arouse the interest of major donors. Stepping up adult and children's programming and obtaining additional media coverage for library events can be effective. Testimonials by influential people on how the library is simply indispensable to them can foster a positive public image of the library. The idea is to create a feel-good atmosphere around the library to enhance the public's receptivness to a major fundraising campaign. If successful, the preliminary public relations effort will prepare the ground for the announcement of the campaign.

It is usually best to announce the public phase of the capital campaign with a special kick-off event that will attract attention and promote the library project. Kick-off events can be used not only to honor major donors who have already given to the campaign, but to provide testimonials as to why others should contribute as well. This event, like other preliminary special events, is designed not to raise money but to make a splash and generate publicity for the campaign. During campaign planning, a distinction should be clearly made between special events that are fundraising activities and those that are "friend-raising" activities. The latter are not intended to make money (although breaking even is nice), but "to build goodwill, educate your audience about your library, and create an awareness of the library's role as an important community resource."[19] Special events raise the library's visibility at a critical time and should be planned as a form of donor cultivation. They "loosen the purse strings" to make potential donors more receptive to giving when campaign volunteers approach them for donations.

In addition to using special events to prime the gift-giving pump, many other ongoing public relations efforts will be helpful to the campaign when it goes public.

The campaign should ultimately be promoted through every channel available, including the library newsletter, neighborhood and corporate newsletters, local newspapers, radio, television, telethons, and direct mailings. One of the most important aspects of public relations for the capital campaign that should be written into the campaign plan is the development of campaign literature and presentation materials.

Campaign Literature and Presentation Materials

Almost all capital fundraising campaigns use some form of literature for direct mailings and distribution by volunteers during solicitation visits. In addition to the case statement and an abbreviated version thereof describing the library capital project, numerous other flyers and factsheets can be created to assist volunteers with donor interviews. Many campaigns put together volunteer and donor kits to help train volunteers and convince prospective donors of the worthiness of the cause. One of the most effective tools for volunteers is the question and answer (Q & A) sheet, which provides good responses to the most frequently asked questions and objections to giving. Reviewing this sheet can help volunteers respond quickly and effectively when they meet with donors. It is also useful to provide volunteers with documentation on how to go about setting up a solicitation and the ins and outs of actually asking for the gift. It may be helpful to print up the gift table for use with volunteers and donors, as well as a list of naming opportunities. This latter document should describe the various opportunities for donor recognition that are available and the level of gift required. Many campaigns also use booklets that describe the tax benefits of a donation.

Donor packets can be mailed out before visits, or they can be brought to the meeting and left for review until a follow-up visit can be scheduled. In addition to printed materials, audiovisual aids can help volunteer solicitors make the fundraising pitch. Flip-charts with graphics, pictures, models, and renderings of the new library building, as well as slide-tape or video presentations can all be effective. A slogan and a logo are very helpful and should be printed on campaign letterhead, envelopes, brochures, pledge cards, and mailing labels. These tools will be helpful particularly during the public phase of the campaign when the final appeal to the community at large is made through direct mailings.

Campaign literature used for personal solicitation or mailings should look good and project an image of quality; however, materials that look very expensive and even extravagant put off some donors and should be avoided. There is more to fundraising than fancy campaign literature, as Kathryn Stephanoff observes:

> . . . many persons I mentioned earlier who want to know how to do it (fundraise) expect the answer to be a brochure or, at most, a two-page letter. If that were the answer to fundraising, so much of it would be going on that we'd all be in danger of being killed in the cross fire of funds, flashing through space in response to tasteful and clever brochures or appeal letters, beguilingly addressed to "Dear rich person."[20]

The use of campaign literature and presentation aids must be kept in perspective. "Developing campaign materials which can inform and inspire is important; however, these materials will not win the campaign by themselves."[21] What will win the campaign? Commitment to the project and the capital campaign on the part of the campaign leadership and volunteer solicitors, and sincere, personal, face-to-face contact with prospective donors. However, in order for the personal commitment of the many campaign volunteers to be effective, the campaign efforts must be well organized.

Campaign Organization

Library Director

Behind every successful library capital fundraising campaign is a highly organized group of committed individuals who have the support and backing of the library staff and board. Although he or she will certainly be involved in any major fundraising drive, it is frequently best if the library's director operates behind the scenes. During the capital campaign, the campaign chairperson will be a prominent figure and act as the campaign's spokesperson. The library director will, however, be heavily involved in donor cultivation through a myriad of methods and will frequently be involved as part of a team during donor solicitation visits. The library director makes an excellent back-up person for the main volunteer solicitor because if questions of a technical nature arise concerning the library's plan of service or the proposed project, they can be answered on the spot by a knowledgeable professional. This is why, in part, the personal integrity and credibility of the library director are essential ingredients in any capital campaign.

Library Development Officer and Library Staff

In addition to the library director, a library development officer and staff will be extremely helpful during a major capital campaign. Not only will they be able to assist with donor identification, research, and cultivation, but they can be useful in coordinating volunteers, backing up the campaign chairperson, organizing meetings, and generally managing the campaign's correspondence and record-keeping. Good development officers can be particularly helpful with researching and initial contacts in the pursuit of foundation and corporate grants. Actually, the involvement of the entire library staff is important to the fundraising campaign. They will seldom be able to contribute substantial sums of money to the campaign, but if each one makes even a minimal pledge, campaign volunteers can use the staff's commitment as a talking point with other donors.

Library Board and Library Foundation Board

If one does not already exist, a library foundation is frequently established as the result of the planning for a capital campaign. One of the main advantages to library foundations is that with 501(c)(3) status they can accept tax-deductible gifts for a library's capital campaign or endowments. An excellent resource on establishing a foundation is John Edie's *First Steps in Starting a Foundation*.[22] Once legal assistance is obtained and the foundation has been established, campaign leadership by the foundation board members as well as the library's governing board members can be addressed. In some cases, there will be some overlap in the members, but in any event the relationship between the two boards must be defined early in the campaign to avoid counterproductive conflict in the later stages of the fundraising drive.

Both boards should be unanimously and strongly behind the capital campaign and show their support by contributing not only time but also some money to the campaign. One of the basics of fundraising is that along with starting at the top and working down the gift chart, donations should be solicited from the inside out. This means that donations should be solicited from individuals close to the library such as staff and board members first, and then work outward toward individuals in the community and foundations that are less involved with the library. As part of the "library family," library board members must donate as generously as they can if there is to be any hope of convincing others of the need for the project and their contribution. The board members' gifts will be viewed as pace-setting leadership gifts by the donors who are contacted subsequently.

For this reason, it is important to pick board members, in part, because of their ability to contribute financially to the library as well as their ability to represent the community through their social, business, and political contacts. Enthusiastic, hard-working supporters of the library who are well-respected community leaders and have previous fundraising experience make the best possible board members. The campaign's chances of success are immeasurably improved if the library's board members contribute generously in the beginning.

Who decides how much each board member should contribute and who solicits them? Usually they must do this themselves by rating, cultivating, and soliciting each other with the assistance of the library director and development staff. Board donations can be based on a recommended percentage of the individual's net worth or annual income, but most importantly they should give based upon their ability to give in relation to others. If the board members themselves can contribute 20 percent or more of the capital goal, the campaign will be off to an excellent start. Once board members have made their own donations, they will become extremely committed volunteer solicitors for the campaign and a valuable source of information about other potential donors.

Library Friends

Because of their contacts throughout the community, members of the library friends group are often very good at suggesting potential donors; and because of their enthusiasm for the library, they will often work hard as volunteer solicitors or in raising money themselves through special events and other activities. However, the fundraising activities of the friends group should be coordinated by the capital campaign leadership during the fundraising drive so that they are not in conflict with the overall campaign plan.

Library friends make excellent advocates for public libraries, particularly when they are involved in public relations activities. They can be very effective at donor cultivation by assisting with tours of the library and producing special events such as luncheons, dinners, and receptions. While members of the friends group generally don't contribute at a high level individually, they will occasionally surprise campaign officials with the amount of money they can raise as a group. They also can provide critically needed assistance stuffing envelopes for direct mailings or staffing the telephones in telethons during the public phase of the campaign.

Campaign Leadership

Campaign Chairperson

While the efforts of all volunteers are important, there is one individual whose contribution will be critical to the success of the capital campaign: the campaign chairperson. When recruiting the campaign leadership, it is best to start at the top and work down. Finding the right chairperson or cochairpersons is probably the most critical hurdle for any capital campaign. This position needs to be filled by a well-known and well-respected leader. Kent Dove describes the essential characteristics of the chairperson in the following passage:

The person chosen must be a person of proven capabilities who has influence and affluence and is willing to use them on behalf of the institution; one who is dedicated to seeing that the job is done on schedule; one who commands respect without demanding it; one to whom others will readily respond, because people give to and work for people, not causes; and one who has intimate knowledge of the institution and the full scope of its program. Additionally, the job requires one who has persistence that compels others to follow suit; is easily accessible; is willing to follow the campaign plan and procedures and accept direction; is willing to devote sufficient time to leadership, aware that early phases of planning and recruiting may require a considerable amount of the chair's time; has the determination to overcome obstacles and invalid excuses; and is willing and prepared at the start of the campaign to make a personal pledge that is generous, thoughtful, and proportionate.[23]

It is generally wise to recruit the campaign chairperson by having several influential board members visit the candidate and take along a summary of the feasibility study, a draft of the case statement, and a draft of the campaign plan if it is available. The committee should ask the candidate for input regarding the campaign documentation, and express their feeling that the candidate is the best person for the job. They should also thoroughly describe the duties of the position. The campaign chairperson's job description should include coordinating the campaign; recruiting the campaign committee chairpersons; overseeing the identification, evaluation, cultivation, and solicitation of major donors; managing volunteer recruitment and training; and monitoring the record-keeping procedures for pledges and payments.

Campaign Steering Committee

Once a campaign chairperson has been named, the next step is recruiting of the campaign committee chairpersons who will form, to a large extent, the campaign steering committee. The campaign chairperson should be in charge of choosing these individuals. Again, it is important to get the "movers and shakers" in the community involved in the campaign and on the steering committee. The committee should be balanced to include representatives of the business and corporate community, the "old money" in the community, and those who represent the "nouveau riche," in order to attract major donors from all sectors.

The selection of the division chairpersons for each gift-giving category (major, special, community, etc.) is critical to the campaign. These individuals, with the campaign chairperson, may feel that additional committees are needed for the campaign such as a public relations committee, a speaker's bureau, a special events committee, a prospect evaluation committee, an awards and recognition committee, or an internal audit committee. In most cases, the chairpersons of these committees should be on the overall campaign steering committee. Figure 7-4 shows the struc-

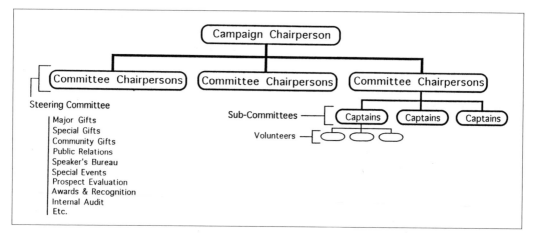

Fig. 7-4. Fund Raising Campaign Organization Chart

ture of a typical capital campaign.

The steering committee is the policy-making team for the campaign. It is usually best for these individuals to work to attain consensus and unanimity on as many decisions as possible, enhancing each member's commitment to the campaign. Loyalty, commitment, and accountability are all essential in a capital campaign effort. This is why each level of the campaign organization should be allowed to select the leadership for the next level down.

The hierarchy of the campaign, then, is composed of the general chairman, the divisional chairs he [she] recruits, the team captains that they recruit, and the volunteer solicitors they recruit. The organizational structure for a campaign really has only two functions. It divides an unwieldy number of prospects into manageable and workable groupings. And it provides a means of volunteer accountability. That's all.[24]

This organizational structure will carry the campaign through to the end because it is built on the firm foundation of personal friendships and individual reputations. When the steering committee or the various division committees hold their monthly meetings, each individual will be required to attend and report the progress made in recruiting volunteers and the success (or lack thereof) of the ongoing solicitations. No one wants to report to their friends and colleagues that they haven't made any progress recruiting volunteers or that they haven't been able to solicit many gifts for the campaign. Because of this, the monthly review meetings are a powerful motivational force in the campaign.

Volunteer Solicitors

"People give to people" is a revered fundamental of fundraising. Personal solicitation is by far the most effective method of raising money for large capital projects. Therefore, every capital campaign needs a substantial number of dedicated and well-

trained volunteers who will go into the community and ask for gifts for the library project. Capital campaigns work best with an adequate number of well-organized and influential volunteer solicitors who are deeply committed to the library project *and* have made their personal donations prior to any attempt to solicit others. "There should not be a single volunteer solicitor who has not first made a personal pledge to the campaign. . . . Non-donor volunteer solicitors simply don't have the same level of commitment to the campaign's success as those who have already put their names on the dotted line."[25] Enthusiasm and loyalty from volunteers is important, but financial commitment is essential in order to get the time and effort from them necessary to achieve success.

Experience has shown that personal contact with highly motivated campaign volunteers is the best way to obtain support for the library project. In the case of private fundraising drives, it is also extremely important that the right person does the asking, particularly with major donors. Volunteer solicitors must be matched with prospective donors so that all major donors are asked by a social and economic peer they know and trust. Similarity and familiarity usually produce the best results. For this reason, it is best to have businesspeople solicit other businesspeople, CEOs solicit CEOs, old money solicit old money, etc.

Another approach is to use teams when soliciting. It can work well to have two or three people see a prospective donor. One can be the library director as a resource person, and the other two can be friends or colleagues of the donor. However, with this approach each individual's role must be determined ahead of time.

It is usually best to limit the number of personal solicitations by any one person to between four and six. However, some volunteers will find that they really enjoy soliciting and are better at it than they thought. For these rare individuals, it is best to let the campaign benefit from their interest and talent.

In addition to asking for gifts, one of the main jobs of volunteer solicitors is to help build the donor list by asking prospective donors if they know of other potential donors. Since those who have already given to the campaign make the best volunteers, it is a good idea for volunteer solicitors to try to get individuals who have just contributed to the campaign to become volunteer solicitors themselves. Before volunteer solicitors can be sent out on their first calls, a lot of time and effort will need to go into identifying and evaluating prospective donors. In other words, who are the donors? Particularly, who are the major donors who will contribute to the capital campaign?

Donor Solicitation Process

The process of finding and soliciting donors for capital campaigns is essentially the same for all major donors whether they are individuals, community groups, corporations, or foundations. For capital campaigns to succeed, potential donors must be identified, researched, and evaluated as to the size of gift they are able to make. Next, an appropriate volunteer solicitor must be matched to the donor, a strategy for approaching the donor developed, and a cultivation process implemented to involve the donor with the library and the campaign. Finally, the donor must be asked for the gift and then thanked through various methods including some form of recognition if the solicitation is successful.

The solicitation process must always begin with effective donor identification and the subsequent creation of donor lists. The best prospective donors are individuals, community groups, foundations, corporations, and small businesses that are actively involved with and have previously given

to the library. This is all the more reason to start an annual fundraising campaign several years before attempting a large-scale capital campaign. Those who have made gifts to other nonprofit organizations in the community are also good prospects. Look on donor plaques in public buildings around town. Ask to trade or buy donor lists from other nonprofit organizations; amazingly enough, this practice usually does not hurt the fundraising efforts of either organization. Get membership lists from various community organizations and the chamber of commerce. If a member of the campaign leadership or the library board belongs to the local country club, have him or her obtain a list of members. Find out who sits on the boards of banks, colleges and universities, and other nonprofit organizations. Serving in the local United Way campaign or other charitable organizations is an excellent way to prospect for donors as well as make valuable contacts in the local fundraising world. Finally, concentrate most donor identification efforts on individuals, since 90 percent of private gifts to nonprofit organizations come from individuals and not foundations or corporations.

Major Individual Donors

To quote an old hunting adage, "You've got to hunt where the quarry lives." This applies equally well to soliciting gifts from major donors. The campaign leadership must identify and go after the "big money" in the community. Individuals who make major gifts are usually getting on in years. Generally, for every year after the age of 50, the amount of giving increases significantly for individuals with wealth. It is likely that the campaign's lead gifts will come from individuals who are seniors, somewhat conservative, and have an entrepreneurial family background. It is also usually necessary and worthwhile to spend a good deal of time cultivating these in-

dividuals before asking them for a donation. Further, it is frequently the case that
once they are won over they will remain
with the library and continue to donate on
an annual basis if asked. These individuals are frequently looking for stable organizations that provide an opportunity to
invest in the community in a way that
leaves a highly visible and lasting impression. The public library building project is
often a perfect fit.

Because major donors frequently look at
their donations more as investments than
gifts, they are often concerned about how
the money will be spent and whether they
will get a "good return" on their money.
"Andrew Carnegie did not think of his
library building program as philanthropy
but as a clever stroke of business, because
in return for construction funds he
demanded that the city invest its money
to furnish and maintain the library."[26]
This should be noted by those who are considering pursuing wealthy individuals for
a major capital gift to build a public library.
These individuals, like Andrew Carnegie,
may demand that the institution and the
funding agency that supports it provide an
adequate plan for the library's ongoing
operation and maintenance. It is not uncommon for major donors to attempt to
use the leverage of their gifts to assure that
the institution to which they are giving
will be well cared for. Obviously, this may
not be a bad thing for the future security
of the library.

Further, major donors may want to have
some say in the planning and design of the
facility. Unfortunately, this may not be so
good for the project. Many of the early
benefactors of public libraries "personally
influenced the selection of the architect
and the site of the building or guided the
project through the trustees they selected."[27] This issue of attaching strings to a
gift must be addressed in a policy statement early in the campaign, for it will certainly come up at some point during the

gift solicitation process. It is important to
be prepared with a clear and workable policy on the matter. Many library boards are
not willing to allow for any interference of
this type from donors. Others are willing
to receive their input as long as it is advisory and not binding.

This last viewpoint is well-described by
Richard Waters' account of the Dallas fundraising campaign:

> In the private sector, when our people went
> around soliciting funds, it was made perfect-
> ly clear to the donor at the beginning that
> they were buying into the library with their
> money, but that they were buying absolute-
> ly no say whatsoever about how that money
> was going to be spent. For example, they
> could not come back and say "I would like
> red carpet in my room and blue drapes." At
> the appropriate time, we gave them the op-
> portunity for input by showing them the
> plans, but if they expected to influence the
> design and furnishing of the building, then
> we said "Thank you no, we would rather not
> have your contribution." Fortunately, we
> didn't have to say no to anyone.[28]

However the matter is resolved, it is good
to keep in mind that the more the donor
can become involved in the project and the
library as an institution, the more likely
the library is to receive continuing donations from that individual.

Community Groups and Civic Organizations

Many local community groups, from the
friends of the library to civic organizations
such as Kiwanis, Lions, and Rotary, are
potential donors who can be approached as
a group for a donation. However, a word
of caution. It is important to wait to approach these groups until after the major
gift solicitations are completed and the
campaign has gone public, because many
of the donors capable of making a major donation may be members of these groups.
If the groups are approached too early in
the campaign, their members will feel that

they have already made their contribution and be less receptive to direct personal appeals. Further, the result is often that the amount of money received is considerably less than if these people had been solicited individually. Once these individuals have made their contributions to the campaign, then it is appropriate to approach them for additional support as an organization.

Corporations and Small Businesses

Corporations and small businesses often view their contributions as investments as well. Corporate gifts are usually made as part of a public-private partnership approach where there is some advantage for the company. Corporations and even small businesses are always looking for ways to improve their image and standing in the community. "Corporate gifts, it is well known, reflect a kind of enlightened self-interest on the part of a company. Rarely do companies give away money simply to be altruistic. Usually they are generous because there is something in it for them. To be successful in this arena, you must be prepared to think in terms of forming partnerships — of making mutually satisfying, yet ethical, business deals."[29] Training programs for employees or business research services are a natural area for partnerships between public libraries and private enterprise.

Most companies direct their private contributions toward communities and agencies that are located where the company does most of its business or in locations where there are major offices or plants supported by significant numbers of employees. For this reason, communities that have corporate headquarters or large physical installations located nearby are particularly well situated to ask for grants. In order to attract and keep high-quality employees, corporations are frequently interested in improving the quality of life in a community by supporting agencies like the public library.

Funds from corporations can come from various sources including corporate foundations, public relations and advertising budgets, and discretionary funds at the disposal of corporate executives. Whatever the source of funds, it is always helpful if the campaign leadership has a personal connection with an influential individual in the company, particularly if it is the CEO or a board member. Most successful solicitation efforts boil down to good relationships between people; and corporations, while sometimes appearing large and impersonal, are made up of individual people. Approaching corporations on a personal basis like any other donor is usually the best strategy.

Foundations

Approaching foundations through a personal contact is also the best way to obtain significant grants for capital campaigns. Again, start close to home with local and regional foundations that will be likely to have an interest in the project. Find out if board members or anyone in the campaign leadership has any contacts on the foundation board or administrative staff. If so, cultivate these individuals and find out what is necessary for a successful application. These personal contacts are the best way to open the door to foundation grants. If a connection is made at the level of the foundation's board, sometimes the proposal process is merely a formality and the grant a foregone conclusion. "Although the system of personal contacts may violate the concepts of equity and objectivity, it is unrealistic to disregard or dismiss it. While not all contacts produce results and not all funders can be influenced this way, the organizations with strong contacts generally will win more grants than the organization making a cold approach."[30] Foundations are more likely to make grants to agencies they know through personal contact, because the risk of making an ineffective grant is greatly reduced.

If campaign officials are unfamiliar with

foundation officials or, for that matter, with foundations that might make grants for capital projects, there are excellent resources that can be used to pinpoint potential sources of funding. Along with the *Directory of Building and Equipment Grants*,[31] there are several other reference tools that can help identify foundations that make grants for capital outlay purposes. The *Capital Campaign Resource Guide*[32] and the *Fund Raiser's Guide to Capital Grants*[33] both provide an index of corporations and foundations that make grants for buildings, renovations, endowments, equipment, and land purchases. When used with *The Foundation Directory*[34] and the *Corporate Giving Directory*,[35] these guides will provide the reader with valuable information about the geographic limitations, application timetables, and areas of emphasis for each prospective foundation or corporation. These tools used in conjunction with the *Grants for Libraries and Information Services*[36] index will help narrow down the field of prospective foundation donors.

Sending off proposals cold to just any foundation or corporation is a long shot at best. Finding foundations that have an interest in making capital grants for educational purposes such as public libraries is the first step. The next step is to research these foundations carefully through the directories and also use their tax returns (IRS 990 report) and annual reports. Call or visit their administrative staff. Again, once potentially sympathetic prospects have been identified, it is best to target those foundations and corporations for which a strong lobbying connection can be found, or else a lot of time and effort is likely to result in little or no money for the library building project. Remember, regardless of how well the grant proposal is written, the vast majority of proposals to foundations go unfunded each year. A little research and cultivation will go a long way with corporations and foundations as well as with individual donors.

Donor Prospect Research

Once donor prospects have been identified whether the potential donors are corporarions, foundations, or individuals, research must be done to find out more about their giving habits. This particular aspect fundraising is a natural for library staff, particularly those with a strong background in reference. Most prospect research will be coordinated by the library development staff in cooperation with the campaign leadership. "Simply stated, the job of the prospect researcher is to find out everything about prospective donors that might have a bearing on their potential gift, and then one more thing—to coach the volunteer on that knowledge."[37] Obviously, the goal of prospect research is to determine whatever can be known about the donor which will affect how the campaign leadership rates his or her ability to give, decides the strategy to use during cultivation, and assigns a solicitor, as well as determining the chances of actually getting a gift.

Once prospective donors are identified, the campaign should create and complete a donor profile. Profiles can be paper-based, but it is easier to keep them up-to-date on a word processing or database system. A good example of the format of a donor profile or donor research form can be found in the book *How to Solicit Big Gifts*.[38] This kind of record should be developed as early in the capital campaign as possible especially for donors who are likely to be lead and major donors. Donor profiles include personal and business information, financial information, philanthropic interests and priorities, previous and current involvement with the library, and personal and business contacts.

Personal information can be gathered from any number of sources, including the individual's resume, local newspapers, and the *Social Register*.[39] Information should be gathered regarding the prospect's family, including spouse, children, and parents.

Has the prospect been married before? Information about his or her education, age, political affiliation and even military service can be of assistance. Personal interests and commitments, favorite sports, and even hobbies can be of help as well.

One of the most important things to try to determine through research is the prospect's financial standing and ability to give. An effort should be made to document an estimate of the prospect's financial worth in terms of personal income and assets. The individual's profession, job title, salary, and amount of stock held are all important to this determination, as are stock proxy statements and 10-K reports. The kind and amount of personal property has a bearing on the wealth estimate. Is the person's house large and expensive and located in a prestigious neighborhood? The tax assessor's office can provide information on the property value. Ownership of automobiles, jewelry, and other real estate can be additional clues to wealth. Lifestyle choices like country club memberships and fancy vacations are also pertinent. Sometimes inherited wealth can be uncovered by examining wills in probate if a family member has recently died. Also, the amount of personal political contributions is a matter of public record.

Next, what are the prospect's philanthropic interests and priorities? Is he or she a member of community service organizations? What nonprofit organizations or charities has the person donated to in the past? This information can be obtained from the annual reports of other nonprofit organizations in the community. What is the prospect's past and current relationship with the library? Has he or she given to the library before, or never even been inside the building? What literary interests does the prospect have and how can these interests be exploited during planned cultivation visits? Finally, who are the prospect's friends, colleagues, and business associates? This is important because they can provide additional information if they are interviewed. These individuals could also become volunteer solicitors who may ultimately ask for the gift.

Along with facts gathered through personal interviews, much of this information is a matter of public record and available in various reference resources. Prospect research is a complex topic. Several books contain information on doing prospect research and sources of information. Kent Dove's book[40] has a chapter on "Identifying, Researching, and Rating Campaign Donors" which gives a good overview. Figures in H. Gerald Quigg's book[41] includes sources of information for prospects categorized by the information desired. And finally, an excellent resource on prospect research in library literature is Bobbie J. Strand's article "Finding and Researching Major Donor Prospects."[42] The appendix entitled "Sources for Information for Individual Research" is a particularly helpful guide. The network of Foundation Center libraries through out the country is also an obvious source of prospect information.

Admittedly, the process of prospect research may seem to some a little like spying on an individual, but it should be kept in mind that most of the information gathered is part of the public record. However, campaign officials should obviously respect the sensitive nature of the information in the donor profile and keep it confidential. This is particularly important in a small town where word gets around fast. Confidentiality is also important in the next step of the fundraising process: prospect evaluation.

Prospect Evaluation

Prospect evaluation, or prospect screening and rating, is the process of determining who the major donors in a capital campaign should be and how much each prospect's gift ought to be, based on the prospect research and any other information gathered from community leaders. The best way to get this information is to form a prospect evaluation committee. The campaign leadership should select a small, informal working group of people who are knowledgeable about the wealth of the prospective donors. "Prospect evaluation committees should include six to eight of the most knowledgeable people the campaign chair[person] or a designate can recruit. They should represent a broad spectrum of the community. Ideally, they should have served on a similar committee for a previous campaign. . . . the committee should consist of people who are in a position to know the income and assets, and hence the giving potential, of the major businesses and individuals of the community."[43]

Possible candidates for the committee are bankers (particularly trust officers), realtors, financial advisors and planners, stockbrokers, CEOs or board members of major corporations, attorneys, accountants, and other community leaders. Confidentiality will have to be provided for individuals who decide to serve in this capacity, since it would not be in their best interest were it widely known that they had done so. The committee's primary purpose is to review the donor prospect list and determine how much each individual, foundation, or corporation is capable of giving to the campaign. A secondary purpose is to suggest additional donor prospects as well as assist with additional donor research.

In determining how much each prospective donor should give, it is important to come up with a figure that matches what the prospect is capable of giving, not what individuals think the donor will give. Private fundraising campaigns are based on the concept of each donor giving their proportionate fair share. Committees usually settle on some form of unwritten formula that reflects a percentage of each prospect's

annual income or net worth, also taking into consideration any recent windfalls. Keep in mind that donors don't usually give more than five percent of their net worth to any one cause, although there are exceptions. In capital campaigns, it is important to set the gift level high enough so that the donor prospects have to "stretch" to make the gift, i.e., give at the upper limits of their own personal giving range.

During the meeting where the prospective donor list is being reviewed, each individual discusses what is known about each prospect's ability to give. A lot more time should be allocated to talking about the financial, philanthropic, and personal interests of a donor capable of making a $1 million gift than one who is likely to make only a $10,000 gift. Delve into the prospect's giving habits, personal interests, and relationship with the library. Is the person interested in genealogy and history? Is the library planning a separate historical special collection room? If so, a natural connection here can be used during future cultivation efforts and may form the basis for a naming opportunity as part of the donor recognition program. Finally, spend a lot of time on the prospect's family, friends, and colleagues. This information will be useful during the donor assignment process and will help make sure that the right person is sent to solicit the gift. Obviously, someone who knows the person well and is an economic and social peer will have a better chance of getting the gift commitment than someone who is not.

After the first run-through of the donor list, the prospect evaluation committee should meet again to match the prospective donors with the gift table. Generally, it is wise to have at least three to four prospects for each gift required at each of the gift levels. In other words, if one lead gift of $100,000 is necessary, the committee should identify three to four prospective donors who could make a gift of that size. If two major gifts of $50,000 are needed, the committee must find six to eight prospective donors who could make such a contribution, and so on down the list until the committee reaches the bottom 25 to 35 percent of the chart where the rest of the gifts will need to come from the community-wide fundraising effort. The donations will be primarily smaller contributions, but there should be a large number of them.

It is better to identify names on a four-to-one than a three-to-one ratio, since this gives the campaign a built in contingency. Remember, not all prospective donors will come through with a gift. A success rate of 25 to 50 percent is considered typical. It's better to have a few extra names and exceed the goal than not have enough and fall short. Finally, if the prospect evaluation committee is not able to assign an adequate number of names to the gift table categories, either the donor base is too small and more prospective donors will need to be identified, or the committee may have to raise its sights on the amount of donations each prospect is capable of making. If neither can be adequately accomplished, this is a clear sign that the capital campaign may not be feasible!

If the prospect evaluation committee is successful at assigning the necessary number of prospective donors to each of the gift categories, the committee will have accomplished its goal. Their work will be reviewed by the campaign leadership and adjusted somewhat (by including the names of the committee members on the list, for example) in order to obtain the final gift table. At this point, the campaign leadership should try to convince the committee members to become volunteer solicitors for the campaign. Since these individuals were responsible to a large extent for the creation of the gift request amounts, it is worthwhile to involve them in the solicitation process. They will exhibit a good deal of commitment to the numbers, and this feeling will usually rub off on other volunteer solicitors. Success in major gift solicitation is often directly related to the degree of confidence that the volunteer solicitors have about actually obtaining a gift in the desired amount. The campaign's performance will be measurably improved if members of the prospect evaluation committee who believe in the attainability of the gift figures are included in the solicitation process.

Donor Assignment

Along with providing confidence in the gift amounts, using prospect evaluation members as volunteer solicitors will be useful in donor assignment, which is the next step in the capital campaign. As they evaluated prospective donors, the committee members will have identified individuals who have good access to prospective donors because of their personal and business relationships. This information can help the campaign leadership determine whom to assign to prospective donors. Further, many of these committee members will be the best individuals to solicit some of the major donors. Getting them involved actively with the solicitation process will lead to the fullest use of their talents and connections.

When enough volunteer solicitors have been recruited, the donor list evaluated, and the gift table assignments made, the campaign leadership is ready to assign donors to specific volunteer solicitors. There are a number of ways to match donors and volunteers. "The important thing to remember, however, regardless of the method you choose to use, is that volunteers will be more effective when they have the opportunity to pick personally the prospective donors they will solicit. People generally want to do a good job and will pick people with whom they feel they can have a positive influence."[44] Generally, whatever the campaign leadership can do to foster a self-selection process, the better. There are numerous methods reported in the fundraising literature, but one easy method is simply to distribute donor lists to volunteer solicitors and have them indicate the individuals they would prefer to contact.

It is helpful if volunteers identify approximately twice as many prospective donors as they will need to contact since there will undoubtedly be overlapping and the campaign leadership will need some leeway in assigning donors. Volunteer solicitors may even be asked to prioritize the donors they select so the assignment process can be even more precise. Some donors will be requested by several volunteers and campaign officials will have to determine who will be the best solicitor by assessing information about the donors as well as the potential solicitors. A limited number of donors will not show up on any of the volunteer lists and will have to be assigned to a volunteer who may not know the donor, but may be a good match for other reasons (similar interests, economic standing, personality, etc.).

As discussed, the assignment of donors to volunteers should be made to a large extent on the basis of familiarity and similarity.

> The more compatible your donors and solicitors, the better your chances for success. There are many variables that will influence the donor/solicitor rapport, and the ten most essential are listed below. Keep them in mind when assigning your volunteers.
>
> Social status
> Philanthropic interest
> Hobbies/interests
> Economic status
> Expected level of giving
> Commitment to need
> Gender
> Age
> Ethnic background
> Personality[45]

There is a direct relationship between the success of the solicitation and the strength of the match between donor and solicitor based on these variables. In the case of major donors, the campaign leadership will have to assign the solicitor with particular care since so much is riding on those solicitations. Because the initial solicitation of the lead gifts is so critical to the success of the campaign, the campaign leadership will usually assign their best volunteers, appropriately matched, to these prospective major donors. Often those solicitors will be members of the steering committee.

Volunteer Training

Volunteer solicitors, including the members of the steering committee, will have to be adequately trained in the sometimes intimidating task of approaching a prospect and asking for money. To train volunteer solicitors, the campaign leadership should draw upon the experience of seasoned solicitors who have participated in previous community capital campaigns or else bring in a fundraising consultant. Volunteer solicitors should be educated about the campaign and the project while they are being trained in the process of gift solicitation. In addition to introducing volunteers to the strategic plan, the leadership should look at the orientation as a first step in a continuing process of informing the volunteers about the campaign's progress. This process should be continued throughout the campaign with monthly progress meetings and a campaign newsletter. The orientation session, progress meetings, and the newsletter can also be effective to generate the enthusiasm necessary for getting the campaign in gear and the job done on time. A sense of camaraderie and good-natured competition among volunteer solicitors can go a long way toward making sure the fundraising campaign attains its goal.

Volunteer solicitors should be instructed in all aspects of the solicitation process.

The goal is to increase their self-confidence and make them more comfortable at soliciting funds. After an initial presentation and overview of the process, volunteers should be teamed up during the training session to practice the various steps through role-playing. It is sometimes helpful to videotape the role-playing so the volunteers can scrutinize their performance. Exercises should be set up to practice making the initial appointment and presenting the opening for the meeting by explaining the purpose of the visit. Volunteers should also practice finding out what the prospective donor knows about the library, the campaign, and the project, as well as listening to the responses to these questions.

Volunteers should be well versed in presenting the project and making the case for it, utilizing support materials that have been prepared to assist in solicitation. Volunteer and donor kits may be used during the actual solicitation process as well as in the training sessions. Volunteers can practice discussing the various forms of donor recognition, (e.g., naming opportunities), and finally making "the ask," overcoming standard objections, and closing the solicitation process by getting the pledge card signed and thanking the donor appropriately. A good volunteer training program will make a lot of difference in the quality of the fundraising effort. It is an area of the campaign on which the leadership should concentrate.

Donor Cultivation

In addition to the specifics of asking for the gift, volunteers should also be trained in the various methods of donor cultivation that the campaign leadership will use. Donor cultivation is the process of informing prospective donors about the purpose of the capital project and the public library as an institution. This will increase their involvement with the library and ultimately create a strong financial commitment to the capital campaign. Donor cultivation is particularly important with major donors, and should begin well before the start of the capital campaign. This is a prime reason to have had an annual gift program in place before initiating a capital campaign. The longer involved and the more deeply involved prospective donors are with the library, the more likely they are to donate to the capital campaign and the larger their donations are likely to be.

There are many ways to cultivate and involve donors. Asking them to become members of the board or advisory committees is a good way to bring them insider status. Frequent mailings and newsletters from the library may help, but personal contact from board members, library friends, and the library director is usually the best. Luncheons and dinners with library supporters can be a good way of providing personal contact. Occasional telephone calls to ask for the donor's viewpoint on policy matters can also help with cultivation. Inviting prospective donors to tour the library or other recently constructed libraries in nearby communities can be extremely effective during the capital campaign. The objective is to make the prospective donor intimately aware of the library's service vision, its goals, and what it will take to achieve them. Providing the prospective donor with a sense of belonging to the library "family" and helping the donor to feel part of something important in the community are keys to cultivation. Remember that the donor's needs are important and that satisfying them in a mutually beneficial manner often results in a gift that will enhance the library's position in the community for many years. To this end, it is usually wise to cultivate the donor's spouse and children as well since they may often have a significant role in the gift decision. Once the donor has made a gift, he or she can become further involved in the library by being asked to become a volunteer solicitor for the capital campaign.

Asking for the Gift

"If you don't ask, you won't get the gift" is a fundraising principle that is almost always true. No matter how effectively a campaign is planned, how good the leadership is, or how many donors are available, if volunteer solicitors don't effectively make "the ask," the campaign won't succeed. Successfully asking for money involves expressing one's commitment and enthusiasm for the project in a contagious and compelling manner. If volunteer solicitors firmly believe in the cause for which they are soliciting, are proud of the library project, and are well prepared, the chances of success are markedly improved. Solicitors should take the attitude that they are giving prospective donors an opportunity to invest in a worthwhile project and not be embarrassed about asking for money. When a community service of this nature is performed by volunteers, there is absolutely no need to apologize for asking for financial support.

Each major donor should be visited in person by solicitors. One way to do this is to make an appointment by telephone and follow up in writing to confirm the meeting. This approach can work well, but sometimes a more informal solicitation is best especially if the volunteer knows the donor well. It is often preferable if the donor and solicitor meet in the course of their regular daily activities and in comfortable surroundings. Sometimes effective solicitations can take place on the golf course or during fishing trips with close personal friends. However, if volunteers are not this close to their prospective donors, the situation will be somewhat more formal.

Formal or informal, volunteers should have a strategy in mind before they approaching each donor. A planned approach is usually more successful than an off-the-cuff interaction. If the volunteer knows the donor well enough to predict what his or her concerns and objections will be, it is usually best to plan to deal with these up front. Solicitors should attempt to put the donor at ease and in a good mood at the beginning of the visit but also clearly indicate the purpose of the meeting. Establishing rapport with the donor is essential in order to get unguarded responses to questions, which helps the solicitor to know how much the donor understands about the library project as well as the campaign. The aim of this first part of the visit (or the first visit, if the solicitation will take place over two visits) is to understand the donor's position and find some basis for common ground.

To do this, the volunteer must elicit information before soliciting money.

> . . . Getting information entails asking, learning, and exploring. It involves understanding what you need to know about your prospect's current situation so that you can effectively tell your story. In other words, you want to find out why the prospect might be interested in giving to you. Through careful questioning, you can check on the validity of your assumptions about a person; elicit new information, uncover values, attitudes, and needs that are relevant to the potential gift; and locate the prospect's position in relation to the giving process.[46]

It is wise to let the prospect do most of the talking while the volunteer listens carefully for ways to tie the donor to the library project.

Once the donor's interests are understood, the next step is to emphasize what the library project can do for the donor by looking at the project from the donor's point of view. Present the case succinctly and emphasize the positive. Successful solicitors must be able to make the case for the project in a clear and convincing manner, referring to the case statement and using visual aids as well as other information provided in the volunteer and donor kits. They should demonstrate their conviction and commitment to the project and indicate that they have already contributed to the campaign themselves. Show the donor the gift table and indicate how much others have given. Tell the donor how much has already been raised and describe the plan to raise the remaining funds. If the solicitation is a lead gift, provide incentive by indicating how important this first gift is to getting the campaign off the ground and providing a way to stimulate additional gifts by others who will follow.

Discuss the donor's specific interests and demonstrate how they pertain to the library project. Reviewing the donor recognition possibilities can be an effective way to tie the donor's interests to the project. If a person is interested in children, indicate how much would have to be given to have the children's room or a story hour area named after him or her. Breaking the project down into separate parts often helps get the donor to focus on a specific amount of money. It is also helpful to discuss the alternative ways that the donor can give. Indicate that pledges may be spread over a two- or three-year period (this will usually increase the amount of the gift) or that the campaign is willing to accept stocks, bonds, real estate, or personal property in lieu of cash if the donor prefers. Discuss the possibility of making a challenge gift that is contingent upon others pledging an equal amount. This can be particularly helpful toward the end of the campaign to get the last remaining money committed.

Once the donor has been brought along to this point, it is time to ask for the gift. Always ask for a specific amount of money in a very direct manner. Don't beat around the bush. Also, don't tell donors what they "ought" to give, but do ask them if they "would consider giving" a specific amount of money. After the ask has been made, be quiet, sit still, and listen to the donor very carefully. Don't argue if the answer is no, but be flexible and try to find an alternative amount or a creative method that may help to get the gift. Patience and persistence usually pay off, but don't press the donor to the point of being obnoxious. If the donor raises objections and provides reasons why the gift will not be forthcoming, try to address those objections and find a way to remove the obstacles. If the donor indicates that a donation will be made, close the session with the signing of an individualized pledge card so that there is a clear record of what was agreed upon. Most fundraisers caution that a pledge card should never be left with a prospective donor so that they can "think it over." This will usually lead to a much smaller gift than anticipated or no gift at all. It is better to make another appointment with the donor and return with the pledge card to discuss the gift again at that time.

All donor visits should be documented by a report form so the campaign leadership can monitor the progress of solicitations. When the solicitation is successful, the donor must to be formally thanked by the campaign leadership as well as by the volunteer solicitor, and the expression of appreciation should come as soon after the pledge as possible (within a day or two). This lets the donor know that the gift really is important to the library campaign; it also serves to confirm and cement the donation.

This is also an opportunity to continue with the cultivation of major donors. Major donors are likely to provide annual donations if properly cultivated because they now have a significant interest in the library. Along with involving the donor with the library, one of the main aspects of cultivation is donor recognition.

Donor Recognition

Always view the library project and the capital campaign from donor's perspective. What are the donor's needs? What will make him or her feel important? What stimulates donors to give in the first place, and how do they want to be thanked? Some donors wish to remain anonymous. Recently, the Oshkosh Public Library in Oshkosh, Wisconsin, received an anonymous $5.5 million donation for expansion and renovation of the main library. Donors have various reasons for wishing to remain anonymous, but most appreciate and expect some form of recognition for their gift. In many cases, donors give in order to meet a need, to belong, or to gain the admiration of their community. Frankly, some donors want to provide gifts to campaigns that can do the most for them given the amount of money they can give. Others give because they want their family name to be preserved for many generations. For these individuals, naming opportunities are the most important form of donor recognition.

Occasionally, donations are substantial enough to have the entire library named after an individual or family; however, with the increasing cost of public library construction, this is becoming somewhat less common of an occurrence. In order to provide naming/recognition opportunities, the campaign leadership can break the library project down into segments that can be "purchased" for specific "prices." The price of rooms should be based on frequency of use, visibility, and prestige, not necessarily the actual cost of the space. With board approval, a list of naming opportunities could be drawn up and used with donors during the solicitation process. Donors could be shown the areas of the library that could be "acquired" based on the size of their donation. Public libraries can be easily divided into numerous spaces to provide naming opportunities. For example, donors could purchase a meeting room or conference room, the children's room or story hour area, special collection rooms, audiovisual rooms, literacy tutoring rooms, reading alcoves and bays, and many others.

Frequently, it is a good tactic to propose to a donor a room or space that will be of particular personal interest. For example,

a major corporation might be targeted to donate the business reference area or all of the new CD-ROM equipment needed to support the expanded reference service in the new building. Having donors acquire pieces of furniture and equipment is a common practice, especially with smaller projects and projects that need to raise money only for the library's furnishings and equipment. Figure 7-4 show's an example of this approach used by the Huntington Beach Public Library, Huntington Beach, California. There are naming opportunities on the outside of the library as well. Donors can give atriums, exterior courts, fountains, artwork, and even landscaping for the project. Some libraries have found success in "selling" bricks or brick pavers for the library. The Benicia Public Library in Benicia, California, sold brick pavers for $100 each and had donors' names engraved on the pavers, which were subsequently laid in a patio outside of the library. This provides a highly visible reminder of the support and generosity of those individuals whose names are carved in stone on the library site.

There are other methods of visually displaying the generosity of donors inside the library. Most libraries use plaques and donor walls. There is much that can be done creatively and attractively to honor donors in this manner. Scale models of donor walls can be designed and the full-scale mock-ups can be built and used during the campaign at kick-off ceremonies and ground breakings to provide incentive to prospective donors. This approach was successfully used with the Newport Beach Public Library project in Newport Beach, California. Donor walls and plaques usually identify different levels of giving; the larger the gift, the larger and more prominent the name of the individual, corporation, or foundation. This information is often published in the campaign literature, as this example from the Newport Beach Public Library campaign:

CENTRAL LIBRARY EXPANSION
PROGRAM AND DONOR OPPORTUNITIES

PROGRAM	DONOR OPPORTUNITIES
CHILDREN'S WING	$1,000,000
UPPER PLAZA AREA	100,000
SPIRAL RAMP	10,000
Spiral Walkway Sections (7)	1,000 ea.
Spiral Walkway Seating (7)	5,000 ea.
Pedestal Fountains (4)	1,000 ea.
ENTRANCE CIRCLE	
Pavers	2,000 ea.
Sculpture	100,000
BOOKS	
Individual	50 ea.
Shelf of Books	250 ea.
Shelving Units	500 ea.
Subject Collection	1,000 ea.
CHILDREN'S	SOLD
Storytime Theater	250,000
Contributors	500 ea.
Individual Seats (150)	150 ea.
Stage	5,000
Video Projection Unit	3,000
Video Monitor	1,000
High Resolution TV	3,000
Movie Projector	1,000
Sound System	3,000
Puppet Stage	1,000
Costumes and Props (50)	100 ea.
Large Lobby Aquarium	15,000 ea.
Tropical Aquariums	5,000 ea.
Visual Education Area, art display area	5,000

PROGRAM	DONOR OPPORTUNITIES
Toddler Discovery Sailing Yacht	5,000
Open-faced bins to store toys (50)	150 ea.
Parenting Alcove	5,000
Grandparenting Alcove	5,000
Visual Learning Center	5,000
Wide Screen Monitor	3,000
Beginning Reader Area	10,000
Furnishings (Tables) (3)	500 ea.
Pre-School Reading Area	10,000
Furnishings (Tables) (4)	500 ea.
Intermediate Reading Area	10,000
Furnishings (Tables & Carrels) (18)	500 ea.
Tutorial Center	10,000
Computer Work Station	3,000
Video Cassette Player with Monitors	2,000
Furnishings (Table & Chair Set)	2,000
Individual Learning Discovery Rooms (4)	5,000 ea.
Computer Work Station (4)	3,000 ea.
Video Cassette Player with Monitor (4)	2,000 ea.
Furnishings (Table & Chair Set) (4)	500 ea.
Special Non-Book Collections	
Individual Titles	50 ea.
Books on Cassette Section	1,000
Children's Periodical Section	1,000
TECHNOLOGY EXPLORATION LAB	50,000
Computer Learning Center	25,000
Technology Library	5,000
Equipment/Computer Work Stations (15)	4,000 ea.

Place Stamp Here

HUNTINGTON BEACH PUBLIC LIBRARY
7111 Talbert Avenue
Huntington Beach, CA 92648

Provided Courtesy of Ronald L. Hayden

Fig. 7-5. Huntington Beach Public Library Donor Opportunities

Gutenberg Collectors	$100,000 and above
Rare Book Collectors	$50,000 to $99,999
Masterpiece Collectors	$25,000 to $49,999
Limited Edition Collectors	$10,000 to $24,999
First Edition Collectors	$ 5,000 to $ 9,999
Classic Collectors	$ 2,500 to $ 4,999
Ad Libris	$ 1,000 to $ 2,499

Along with the possibility of naming the library after a donor, commissioning an oil portrait of the individual may be appropriate, if a singularly large gift is provided for the library project. While expensive, this is a particularly touching form of donor recognition, especially when combined with an unveiling ceremony. Major gifts can be recognized with a luncheon, dinner, or reception to honor the donor. Once the campaign enters its public phase, any form of ceremony that highlights significant gifts is useful not only for donor recognition but also for campaign publicity. Using the kick-off event to honor major donors is an excellent way to accomplish

Fig. 7-6. Newport Beach Donor Wall Mock-Up

Provided Courtesy of Elizabeth Stahr

this. Media coverage for major donations helps spread the word about the campaign. One way to focus community attention on the campaign is to have a picture published in the newspaper or shown on local television showing a major donor giving an oversized check to library supporters.

Going Public with the Campaign

Once all the major donors have been solicited and approximately 50 percent (typically between 40 and 60 percent) of the goal reached, the campaign will go public with a kick-off event. This is when the public relations program should go into high gear at this point. Up until now publicity has been fairly low-key, but from this point until the campaign goal is reached, every effort should be made to draw attention to the capital campaign and encourage donors to give. The object is to reach as many people as possible in the closing months of the campaign. The significance of the public phase of the campaign is expressed well by Kathryn Stephanoff:

> . . . we realized that the involvement of small donors helped to raise the temperature of the community. This involvement was always recognized and treated for what it was, not a fund raising activity, but a fever producing activity, a sentiment producing program that, in fact, did pay off.[47]

All kinds of hoopla can be generated to raise the library campaign's visibility in the community. This is limited only by the campaign leadership's creativity and time. One effective way to keep the campaign in the public eye is to erect a campaign thermometer on the library lawn. Pictures of this thermometer can occasionally be published in the paper to show the campaign's progress. Involving children in collecting money for the campaign in ways similar to the very effective March of Dimes campaigns is an excellent public relations strategy. It may not raise much money in

itself, but it may sway parents to ante up a little more in their donations. In addition to the general public relations programs, the public phase of the campaign will implement commonly used fundraising techniques such as direct mail, telephone solicitation, and special events.

Direct Mail

Many campaigns use direct mail in the public stage of the campaign because it reaches large numbers of people. It is best used in the midst of the major publicity efforts and is most effectively done in two steps. First, a mailer with a cover letter and campaign brochure is sent out with a pledge card and return envelope. The pledge card, or the contribution envelope shown in Figure 7-6, will usually provide the prospective donor with an opportunity to give to the campaign at various levels. Although it makes the mailing more expensive, including return postage on the envelope will usually double the return rate and thus the amount of donations generated. About a month or two after the original mailing, it is wise to send another follow-up mailing with a reminder letter and another pledge card and envelope. This mailing will inform prospective donors "that they may have overlooked the pledge card sent to them earlier, or forgotten to send it in," and the campaign leadership is sure that they don't went to miss this opportunity to support the library project. If time permits and enough volunteers are available, it may be helpful to follow-up specific donors with a telephone call instead of a second mailing. This further reinforces the importance of their donation and provides for some limited personal contact.

With each mailing it is best to target the intended audience and personalize the appeal letters as much as possible. This can be time-consuming, but it produces the best results. Who should be targeted? Send

Yes, I would like to make a charitable gift to the new library

_____ $50.00   _____ $100.00   _____ $250.00

_____ $500.00   _____ $1,000.00   _____ Other $_____

All gifts of $1,000 or more will be permanently recognized on a donor wall of honor.

...a *NEW LIBRARY* for Newport Beach...

Name _____

Address _____

_____

Thank You!
Make Check Payable To
NEWPORT BEACH PUBLIC LIBRARY FOUNDATION

Provided Courtesy of Elizabeth Stahr

Fig. 7-7. Pledge Card/Contribution Envelope

mailings to those on the donor list who have not been visited and to all previous donors of the annual gift program. Send the mailing to library patrons, vendors and suppliers. With respect to patrons, target the neighborhoods whose residents will use the library most and who have the means to make reasonable contributions—middle- to higher-economic-range homeowners who are well educated. Also, consider using the mailing lists of other nonprofit organizations that have recently held a capital campaign.

There are numerous tricks that get the recipient of the fundraising mailing to open the envelope and read the letter. Teasers on the front and back of the envelope usually work well, and there are many ways to make the letter more effective. First of all, it should be short and to the point (one page is usually best). It should use an emotional appeal to make the pitch for a gift and create a sense of urgency to get the potential donor to respond by a specific date. The letter should be signed by either the campaign chairperson or some other respected individual, and a postscript with important information should always be added. People invariably will read a postscript if nothing else in a letter. Personalizing the letter with hand-written notes is a good way to increase the response rate, but it is time-consuming. Numerous guides are available on how to write a good fundraising letter.

Telephone Solicitation

Telephone solicitation is more personal than direct mailing, but it has the draw-back of being a two-step process. A pledge card or confirmation letter must be mailed to the donor afterwards. Telephone banks are used much more often (and more effec-tively) for referendum campaigns than for private fundraising campaigns. A telethon can sometimes be an effective last-minute way to raise enthusiasm and the final do-nations for a fundraising campaign if a local network or cable station is willing to work with the campaign leadership. How-ever, for private capital campaigns the tel-ephone is limited in its effectiveness and usually used sparingly.

Door-to-Door Solicitation

While personal visits based on an in-troductory call are one of the most effec-tive ways of soliciting for capital campaigns, volunteers can also collect door-to-door in targeted neighborhoods. However, this approach does not work par-ticularly well for capital campaigns with the possible exception of those in small towns where people know one another well. Now-a-days people are relatively hesi-tant to give money to strangers at their door, particularly significant amounts of money.

Special Events

Most successful capital campaigns tend to bring people together through special events. There are several purposes for spe-cial events in capital campaigns, and the fact is that most special events don't raise much money, if any. Some events are held for visibility, and others to cultivate or recognize donors. Some are held to actual-ly raise money, but this is harder to do than it seems. Special events take a lot of time, energy and money to produce. They should not be attempted unless a good deal of the event's cost can be defrayed by in-kind con-tributions. The problem with special events is that frequently the enormous time and energy spent to organize them would be better directed toward major donor research and cultivation. In other words, one major donation of $50,000 might take one-tenth the time to obtain and provide five times more money than a special event would raise. Another draw-back to special events is that often major donors who would have given a significant amount of money if properly cultivated and asked end up giving a relatively small amount by purchasing a ticket, but feel that by having done so "they have done their part" to support the campaign.

If special events are to be used for fund-raising, they should be made as interesting and amusing as possible in order to attract people. Again, look at the event from the prospective donor's point of view: will it be an evening of fun and entertainment or will it be another $1,000-dollar plate of rub-ber chicken and hours of boring speakers? One of the best ways to attract people of wealth to a special event is to make it "the" social event of the season. This can be difficult to accomplish, but one of the best ways is to bring in a celebrity speaker. Many people will pay to have access to a humorous or glamorous celebrity. Some-times they will pay significant fees to sit next to or close to the celebrity at dinner or be afforded additional contact with the individual prior to or after the main event. Even if celebrities can not be obtained, this approach can be used with prominent peo-ple in the local community or region. Suc-cessful events can often be designed around giving a prominent individual an award for service to the library.

It is wise to try to hold special events like black-tie galas or dinners in the library itself because this helps to make the connection between the event and the library campaign. This was the case with two dinners that raised $150,000 each for the remodeling of the library in Pasadena, California. Often this will be the first time prospective donors have entered the library and they will have the opportunity to browse through the building before and after the main event. Be sure to build in plenty of conversational time for people to mix and make contacts. This is desirable from their standpoint as well as the library's, because the campaign leadership and volunteers can use this time to make contacts and cultivate donors. During the event, it is important to thank all who participated to make the event possible, from the friends group to the local merchants who provided in-kind services. A few impassioned presentations about the library project and the capital campaign fundraising effort can be made. It is usually best to have testimonials from the campaign leadership and other major donors who have already committed to the effort, but keep them brief, straightforward, and enthusiastic.

Recent books by Schmader,[48] Liebold,[49] and Freedman[50] provide ideas for special events or are instructive in planning a special event. Don't forget to use special events to celebrate milestones with the campaign's volunteers, and by all means plan a victory party at the end of the campaign to honor campaign leadership, volunteers, and major donors. This kind of recognition will make volunteers willing to do it all again if another capital campaign is needed sometime in the future. It will also mean that some will be willing to continue working for the library as part of an annual gift program. In order to be sure there is a next time, every campaign needs an efficient and fiscally responsible method of record-keeping to avoid any concern over the propriety of the use of the funds received.

Monitoring and Record Keeping

A successful campaign must have a good quality record-keeping system. There is a plethora of campaign monitoring and record-keeping systems available; however, the tried and true systems that keep things simple are usually the best. Whether the system is paper-based or electronic, record-keeping is important because it fosters an information management approach to running the campaign and monitoring it's progress. This approach will make the campaign leadership, staff and volunteers more effective and productive.

Donor lists will need to be created and, later, donor profiles. A solicitation report form and individual pledge cards must be devised and used. Master and division records must be created to track donors' solicitations as well as their payments once gifts are received. Gift acknowledgment procedures must be built into any fundraising system to make certain that donors are thanked in a timely manner. A reporting system to track the progress of solicitations must be developed so that the campaign chairperson knows if the campaign is on track or falling behind. Further, there needs to be a method of keeping volunteers informed about the progress of the campaign. Campaign staff must set up a system to record pledges when they are received and to send out timely reminders when they are not. Finally, a system of recording the campaign's expenses must be devised to accurately report the costs associated with running the campaign.

The Final Campaign Report

At the end of the capital campaign, campaign officials should close it out by writing a final report. This report should provide documentation about all aspects of the campaign and include a copy of the feasibility study, all campaign literature including the case statement, the campaign plan, and all other associated documents.

The report should include a summary of all volunteer solicitors including the campaign leadership as well as all donors (and those prospects who didn't contribute). This information can be used for future for the next capital campaigns, and also for annual fund programs or any special fundraising projects that come along. Many of the names of the donors, even the small donors, will be useful in the years to come when the library is looking for funds to operate the new or improved facility. This is true not only when the library is trying to raise private funds, but also when it is pursuing public tax appropriations with local public funding officials.

Other Benefits of the Capital Campaign

While it is true that the general community-wide phase of the capital campaign does not raise the most money, it does provide a broad base of support for the library which will be invaluable in the future. Small donors often expect a lot for their gifts, but their involvement with the library may be one of the greatest assets of a public library director and board at annual budget hearings or whenever there is budget-cutting pressure.

> The small givers hold the librarian inthrall forever. This permanent bond, though personally taxing, is, in the long run, I think, one of the major benefits of a private fund drive. This is created by a strong vested interest, and vested interest, in my book, is as secure a base of operation as one can hope for.[51]

Clearly, there is a role for private fundraising for public library facilities. It is not only compatible but complementary with public funding for the institution.

REFERENCES

1. Donald E. Oehlerts, *Books and Blueprints: Building America's Public Libraries* (Westport, Conn: Greenwood Press, 1991), p. 15.
2. Joseph L. Wheeler, and Alfred Morton Githens, *The American Public Library Building: Its Planning and Design with Special Reference to Its Administration and Service* (New York: Charles Scribner's & Sons, 1941), p. 484.
3. George S. Bobinski, *Carnegie Libraries, Their History and Impact on American Public Library Development* (Chicago: American Library Association, 1969), pp. 207-42.
4. Kent E. Dove, *Conducting a Successful Capital Campaign: A Comprehensive Fundraising Guide for Nonprofit Organizations* (San Francisco: Jossey-Bass, 1990).
5. David J. Hauman, *The Capital Campaign Handbook: How to Maximize Your Fund Raising Campaign* (Washington: Taft Group, 1987).
6. Jeanine Builita, *The Campaign Manuals (Volumes I & II)* (Cleveland: Third Sector Press, 1984).
7. Gerald H. Quigg, ed. *The Successful Capital Campaign: From Planning to Victory Celebration* (Washington: Council for Advancement and Support of Education (CASE), 1986).
8. Joan Boisclair, ed. *Capital Campaign Resource Guide* (San Francisco: Public Management Institute, 1984).
9. Kathryn Stephanoff, "Private Sources" in *Facilities Funding Finesse: Financing and Promotion of Public Library Facilities*, ed. Richard B. Hall, (Chicago: American Library Association, 1982), p. 14.
10. Dove, p. 2.
11. Boisclair.
12. Harold J. Seymour *Designs for Fund-raising* (New York: McGraw-Hill, 1966), p. 87.
13. James Gregory Lord *The Raising of Money* 3rd ed. (Cleveland: Third Sector Press, 1985), p. 32.
14. Del Martin, "Marketing: Tools of the Trade" *FRI Bulletin* (April 1991).
15. Hauman, p. 12.
16. Quigg, p. 20.
17. Hauman, p. 56.
18. Boisclair, p. 74.
19. April L. Harris, "Special Events and Their

Role in Fund Raising" *Journal of Library Administration* Vol. 12, No. 4 (1990), p. 40.

20. Stephanoff, p. 16.

21. David Heetland, "The Six Essential Steps of a Capital Campaign" *Fund Raising Management* 21 (September 1990), p. 34.

22. John A. Edie *First Steps in Starting a Foundation.* (Washington: Council on Foundations, 1987).

23. Dove, p. 31.

24. Hauman, p. 64

25. Ibid., p. 103.

26. "Mr. Carnegie's Investments" *Library Journal* 27 (June 1920), p. 329.

27. Oehlerts, p. 17.

28. Richard L. Waters, "Panel Discussion" in *Facilities Funding Finesse: Financing and Promotion of Public Library Facilities,* ed. Richard B. Hall (Chicago: American Library Association, 1982), p. 39.

29. Victoria Steele, and Stephen D. Elder. *Becoming a Fundraiser: The Principles and Practice of Library Development* (Chicago: American Library Association, 1992), p. 107.

30. Andrew J. Grant "The Realist's Guide to Foundation and Corporate Grants" in *Directory of Building and Equipment Grants,* 2nd ed. Richard M. Eckstein (Loxahatchee, FL: Research Grant Guides, 1992) p. 14.

31. Richard M. Eckstein, *Directory of Building and Equipment Grants,* 2nd ed. (Loxahatchee, FL: Research Grant Guides, 1992).

32. Boisclair.

33. Yvette Henry, ed. *Fund Raiser's Guide to Capital Grants* (Washington: The Taft Group, 1988).

34. Stan Olson, ed. *The Foundation Directory* (New York: Foundation Center), Annual.

35. David S. Hicks, ed. *Corporate Giving Directory.* (Rockville, MD: Taft Group), Annual.

36. *Grants for Libraries and Information Services* (New York: Foundation Center), Annual.

37. Hauman, p. 16.

38. Daniel Lynn Conrad, *How to Solicit Big Gifts* (San Francisco: Public Management Institute, 1985), pp. 48-51.

39. *Social Register* (New York: Social Register Association), Semiannual.

40. Dove, pp.90-103.

41. Jan L. Grief, "Prospect Research" in *The Successful Capital Campaign: From Planning to Victory Celebration,* ed. H. Gerald Quigg (Washington: Council for Advancement and Support of Education (CASE), 1986), pp. 45–49.

42. Bobbie J. Strand, "Finding and Researching Major Donor Prospects" *Journal of Library Administration* 12, No. 4, (1990), pp. 53-71.

43. Hauman, p. 16.

44. Ibid, p. 84.

45. Boisclair, p. 123.

46. Steele and Elder, p. 67.

47. Stephanoff, p. 15.

48. Steven Wood Schmader and Robert Jackson, *Special Events: Inside and Out* (Champaign, IL: Sagamore Publishing, 1990).

49. Louise Condak Liebold, *Fireworks, Brass Bands, and Elephants: Promotional Events with Flair for Libraries and Other Nonprofit Organizations* (Phoenix: Oryx Press, 1986).

50. Harry A. Freedman, *Black Tie Optional: The Ultimate Guide to Planning and Producing Successful Special Events* (Rockville, MD: Taft Group, 1991).

51. Stephanoff, p. 17.

Summary, Conclusions & Trends in Financing Public Library Buildings 8

Good planning is a critical first step for any project, but this is particularly true for public library building projects. Library supporters must create a clear vision of their library of the future by planning strategically and performing a needs assessment, developing a facilities master plan, building programs and architectural plans for each proposed library building. It is essential to involve the community, and particularly its leadership, during these strategic planning phases in order gain the solid support and political approval needed for the financing of the project. If this is not accomplished, the risk of project failure increases dramatically. Only by involving the community in the preliminary planning for the project can a true sense of ownership be attained and the financing ultimately assured.

Estimating the cost for the library building is an on-going process, a continuum starting with the initial estimate, proceeding through a preliminary estimate and ultimately ending with a final audit for the project. The budget is constantly changing and being refined as the project proceeds through architectural plans development to construction. Project costs for public libraries have increased significantly in recent years. Rising construction costs, furnishings and equipment costs as well as land costs have all contributed to this trend. Since projects cost so much more, library supporters must plan even more carefully than in the past. This has gener-

ally increased the use of additional professional services for planning such as library consultants, professional cost estimators, interior designers, financial consultants, construction management and value engineering firms. The overall life cycle costs for the facility are as important today as the initial capital outlay since the costs of operating facilities have also increased dramatically in recent years. Today, more than at any time in the past, the importance of careful and accurate project cost estimating cannot be overemphasized.

After a solid estimate is obtained, the next step is assessing the potential funding sources and financing mechanisms. There are many sources and methods available, and each approach has advantages and disadvantages. The challenge is to find the sources and methods which best fit the given project. While there are many different financing vehicles available, there are only four main sources of funding for public library construction: federal, state, and local public monies; and private sources. In many cases, it may be advantageous to mix the various funding sources, although this approach takes special care and planning since time schedules and funding requirements may conflict. Over the years, the various funding sources have become interrelated. For example, federal funds have been known to stimulate state funds for public library construction, as state and federal grants have often stimulated local and private funds. Similarly, private funds

279

frequently stimulate local public funds and vice versa. The public library is a marvelously flexible institution which has been able to adapt itself and obtain funds from many sources. In fact, this may be one of its strongest suits since the strategy of obtaining funding from a diversified number of sources is usually a good one.

Fortunately, the amount of funding available for public library construction purposes has increased dramatically in recent years. Over 80 percent of all funds obtained for public library construction in the United States have been expended in the last two decades. Further, almost 40 percent of all funds reported in *Library Journal* in the last 24 years have been expended in the last 5 years (1987-1991)! In the last 3 years alone, the total expenditure for public library construction in this country has averaged over $300 million per year. While this recent growth is encouraging, when the dollars are adjusted for inflation, the growth in actual dollars is not nearly as impressive. Figure 8-1 shows in graphic form the total amount of funds reported for public library construction from 1968 through 1991 compared to those amounts adjusted for inflation. Even though total funds have been increasing recently, the adjusted figures have been decreasing, except in recent years, when they have been holding their own.

What the remaining years of the century will bring for public library capital outlay is difficult to predict, particularly given the difficult recessionary times the nation is currently experiencing combined with the increasing national debt burden. It is obvious, however, that the federal role in funding public library construction has generally been on the decline. Federal funds have dropped from an average of 21 percent of the total funds expended for public library construction in the early years of *Library Journal* data collection (1968-1979), to an all time low of 5 percent for the last 5 years. During these recent years, federal funds have accounted, on average, for less than $15 million per year! This is a far cry from the all time high year of 1979 when over $80 million of federal funds for public library construction were reported due to a large extent to the EDA public works and federal general revenue sharing funds appropriated in the late 1970's. While the LSCA Title II program has been the mainstay of federal public library construction funds with close to $350 million of appropriations, the program has been erratic and declining in recent years. Undoubtedly, it will take a significant change in policies at the federal level regarding the financing of infrastructure like public libraries to reverse this general downward trend.

While federal funds have been declining, state funds for public library construction have been on the increase. In the early years, state funds accounted, on average, for only 4 percent of all funds expended, but in the last 5 years this figure has doubled to 8 percent. In the last 5 years, on average, state sources have provided over $22 million per year. This totals to over $110 million which is over 50 percent of all state funds appropriated for public library construction during the 24 year data collection in *Library Journal!* Further, major programs such as those in California ($75 million), Massachusetts ($35 million) and Georgia ($13 million) will continue to provide an increased stream of state revenues for public library construction at least in those states. While state funds have been generally on the increase, they unfortunately have not increased enough to make up for the loss of federal funds. During the early years, the two sources combined accounted for approximately 25 percent of all funds, but in the last 5 years this combined figure is down to only 13 percent.

Because of this, private and local public funds which used to account for 75 percent of all funds, now account for closer to 87

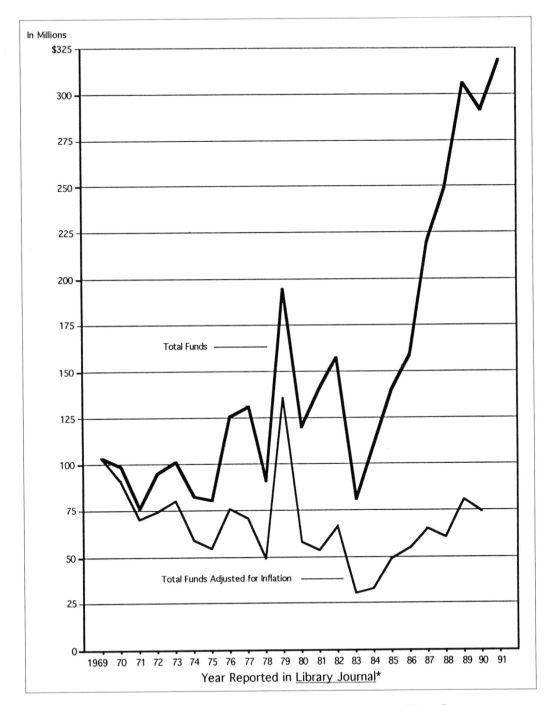

Fig. 8.1. Total Funds for Public Library Construction Adjusted for inflation

©Reed Publishing

percent of all funds for public library construction. Local public funds have always been the mainstay of capital outlay for public libraries, providing 67 percent of all funds in the early years and increasing to almost 78 percent in the last 5 years. While general obligation bonds have been the preferred method of financing public libraries at the local level, there has been an increasing interest in the use of various "creative financing" techniques especially since the advent of California's Proposition 13 in 1979. Many communities across the nation have been forced to look at alternative funding sources such as development fees, excise taxes, special benefit assessments, special "parcel" taxes, as well as alternative financing mechanisms such as tax allocation bonds, lease revenue bonds, certificates of participation (COPs) etc. In the future, public libraries will need to become more aggressive in pursuing these alternative financing methods because of the increasing reliance on local public funds for public library construction together with the increasing competition for and scarcity of local dollars. This will include public/private partnerships in many communities where the development of the public library project can be shown to be of mutual benefit to both the public and private sector.

Public libraries have strong historical roots in private sector financing thanks to the generosity of Andrew Carnegie and other "founding families." Unfortunately, this approach to financing public libraries has been on the decline throughout most of this century. Around the turn of the century, private funds accounted for approximately 75 percent of all funds expended for public library construction. This figure decreased to a low in the mid-1960's of less than 2 percent before increasing and leveling off at around 9 percent for the last 24 years. In recent years, private donors have been a very stable source of funds, but they have generally accounted for less than 10

percent of all capital outlays. Overall, private funding has not been heavily used for public library construction in modern times with a few notable exceptions (Dallas, San Francisco, and others), but, there is increasing interest in this source.

The process involved in private fund raising capital campaigns is fairly well documented in the literature. Private fund raising drives involve conducting a feasibility study, developing a campaign plan, providing leadership and organization, as well as drafting a case statement. They also require the proper identification, research, evaluation, cultivation and solicitation of donors capable of making major gifts substantial enough to raise approximately 50 percent of the campaign goal prior to entering the public phase of the fund raising drive. In capital campaigns, the majority of funds will actually be donated by a relatively small minority of people. However, with commitment and hard work, the private fund raising capital campaign for public library buildings is feasible in many communities as long as the goal is within the financial realm of possibility. Because of the broad base of the constituency and the nature of the service, public libraries make an ideal institution for donors to give to in order to "make a difference" through an investment in their community. The key is strategic planning, a committed campaign leadership, and an effective volunteer campaign organization as well as personal contact with donors since most often "people give to people" not to causes.

This is true not only for private fundraising drives, but also for referenda campaigns for public libraries. Personal contact with committed campaign volunteers appears to be the most potent force in convincing the electorate to support a public library issue at the polls. In referenda campaigns, this can be accomplished in a number of ways including door-to-door canvassing, speakers' bureaus, special events, endorsements and to some extent the use of telephone banks. The presentation of rational facts is important, but the library issue is best sold to voters based upon a number of emotional themes. The distribution of the campaign's message through literature and paraphernalia is effective when direct mail, leafleting and the media are utilized to reinforce the emotional issues. Successful campaigns concentrate on the voters who are most likely to vote "Yes" and ignore the "No" voters. It is essential to target individuals who are favorably inclined toward the library and work hard to make sure they go to the polls through numerous GOTV activities. The last few weeks is the critical time when most campaign efforts need to be concentrated for maximum impact.

Fortunately, the majority of library referenda campaigns which are attempted, succeed. However, in order to be successful, library supporters must be willing to enter into the political fray and become strong advocates for the new or improved facility.

Campaigning for public libraries, whether through a private capital campaign or a referendum campaign, can be fun and exhilarating, but it is also hard work. If successful, not only will the campaign itself raise the status of the library in the eyes of the community, it also frequently enhances the reputations of those involved in the support effort. There are many "fringe benefits" to be gained by the use of a grassroots effort to improve the public library, not the least of which is the creation of a vested interest in the library by many individuals in the community.

One of the truly difficult challenges in the future may not be the raising of capital for building public libraries, but finding the on-going funds to operate them. When a sense of ownership through participation in a capital campaign is instilled in a large group of community volunteers, the public library's operational budget will be as secure as it can possibly be. To this end, public library administrators and trustees know they have been successful in their efforts when local governmental officials suggest cutting the library's operational budget, and there is a ground swell of supporters who come forward and say "Oh no, you don't! You're not going to cut that budget, that's *our* public library, we worked for it!

Postscript

Since the completion of the manuscript, the *Library Journal* construction statistics for 1992 have been published. Because of the significant developments reflected in this data, a postscript for this chapter is warranted to highlight the resulting trends. The most significant aspect of this data, is that 1992 was obviously a boom year for funding public library construction because a total of $473 million was reported expended which is up almost 50 percent ($155 million) from the previous year's level of $317 million. This increase raises the average for the last 5 years to over $325 million per year which is a substantial increase over the previous 5 years average of $275 million.

The increase in 1992 funds was supported by significant increases in local, state and private funds. However, the federal funds in 1992 increased only slightly from the year before. In 1992 federal funding dropped to 3.6 percent of all funding for public library construction which is an all-time low for this category! It is increasingly evident that public library planners will need to continue to rely on funding sources other than the federal level.

In summary, the 1992 data reinforces a continued positive growth curve for public library construction funding, however, this optimism must be tempered with the consideration that there will likely be a "correction" in this most recent surge of funding in the upcoming years when the impact of the recession catches up with the statistical reporting mechanism. Because of the lag in data reporting, the likely down turn in public library construction projects caused by the recession of the early 90's will probably begin to show up in the next few years of reports. How long this slippage will last is directly related to how long the effects of the recession continue to be felt at the state and local levels. Once the recession ends, there will undoubtedly be a back log of projects which will subsequently begin construction and be reported, thereby once again raising the levels of public library construction expenditure to even greater heights. Public library construction has been and will continue to be cyclical in nature just as the national economy and various sectors of private enterprise.

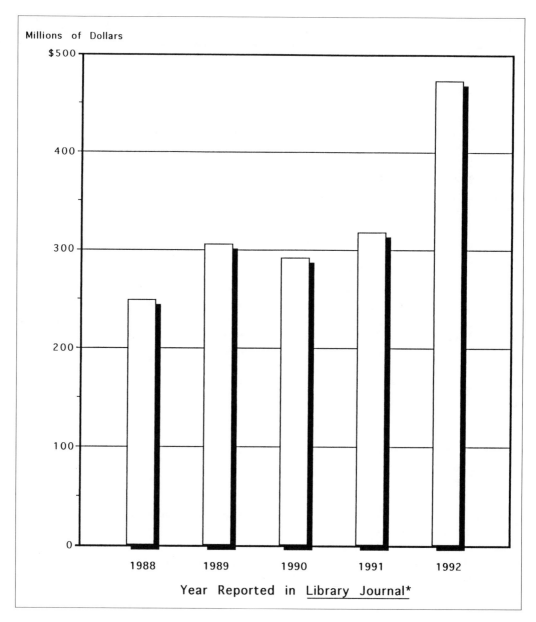

Fig. 9-1. Total Public Library Construction Funds for Last 5 Years

Index

Richard B. Hall is currently the Library Bond Act Manager for the California State Library where he is administering a $75 million state bond act for public library construction. As manager for two state library construction grant programs in Georgia (1978 - 1989) and California (1990 - present), the author has been involved with over 200 library building projects in the last 15 years. Mr. Hall has published extensively and also consults privately on the planning, financing and design of public library buildings.